OLYMPIC PENINSULA

JEFF BURLINGAME

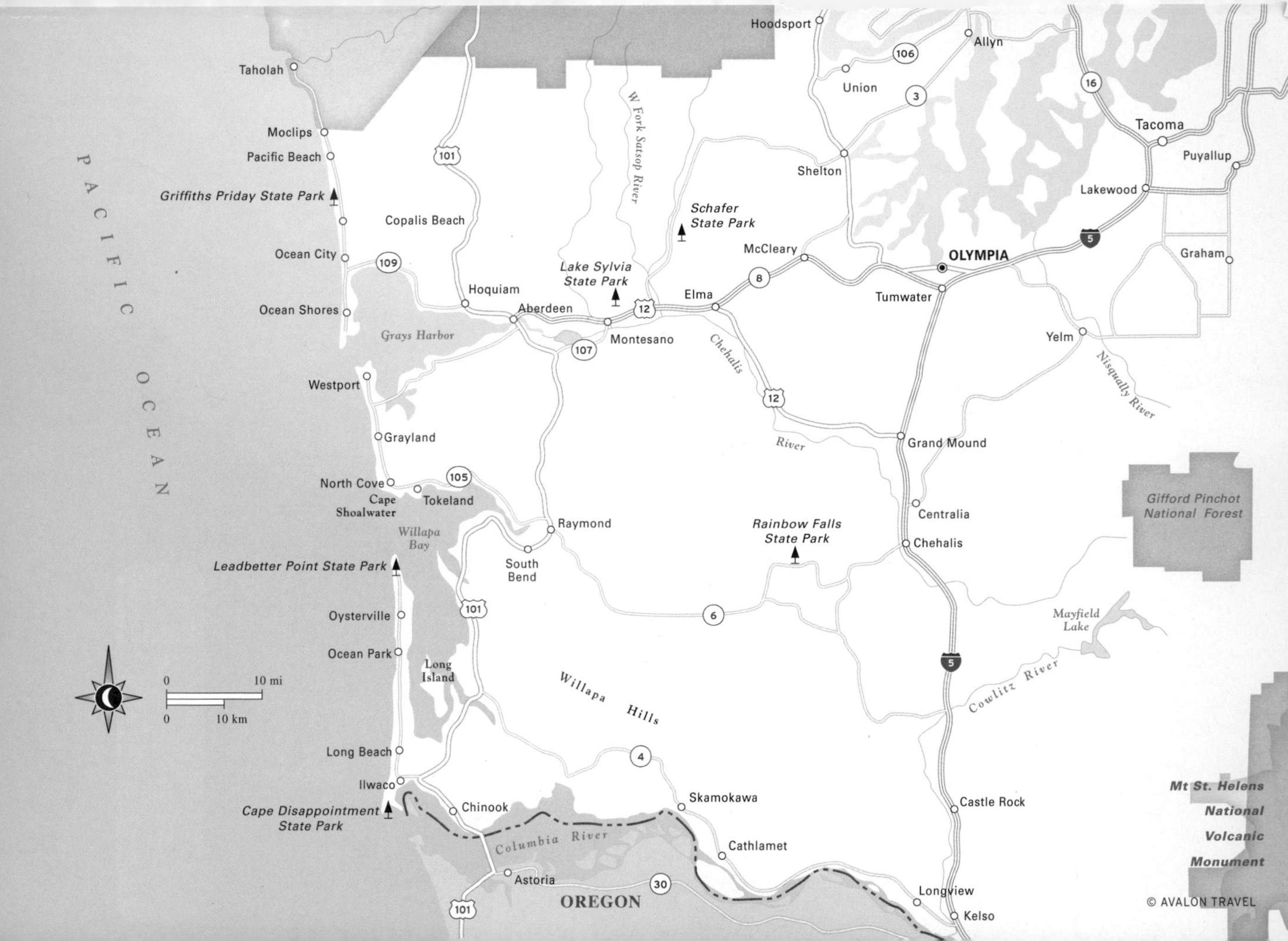

PACIFIC OCEAN
Taholah
Moclips
Pacific Beach
Griffiths Priday State Park
Copalis Beach
Ocean City
Ocean Shores
Hoquiam
Aberdeen
Grays Harbor
Westport
Grayland
North Cove
Cape Shoalwater
Tokeland
Willapa Bay
Leadbetter Point State Park
Oysterville
Ocean Park
Long Island
Long Beach
Ilwaco
Cape Disappointment State Park
Chinook
Columbia River
Astoria
OREGON
Raymond
South Bend
Willapa Hills
Skamokawa
Cathlamet
Montesano
Lake Sylvia State Park
W Fork Satsop River
Schafer State Park
Elma
McCleary
Chehalis River
Rainbow Falls State Park
Hoodsport
Union
Allyn
Shelton
Tacoma
Puyallup
Lakewood
OLYMPIA
Tumwater
Graham
Yelm
Nisqually River
Grand Mound
Centralia
Chehalis
Gifford Pinchot National Forest
Mayfield Lake
Cowlitz River
Castle Rock
Longview
Kelso
Mt St. Helens National Volcanic Monument
101
109
105
107
12
8
6
4
30
3
106
16
5
0
10 mi
0
10 km
© AVALON TRAVEL

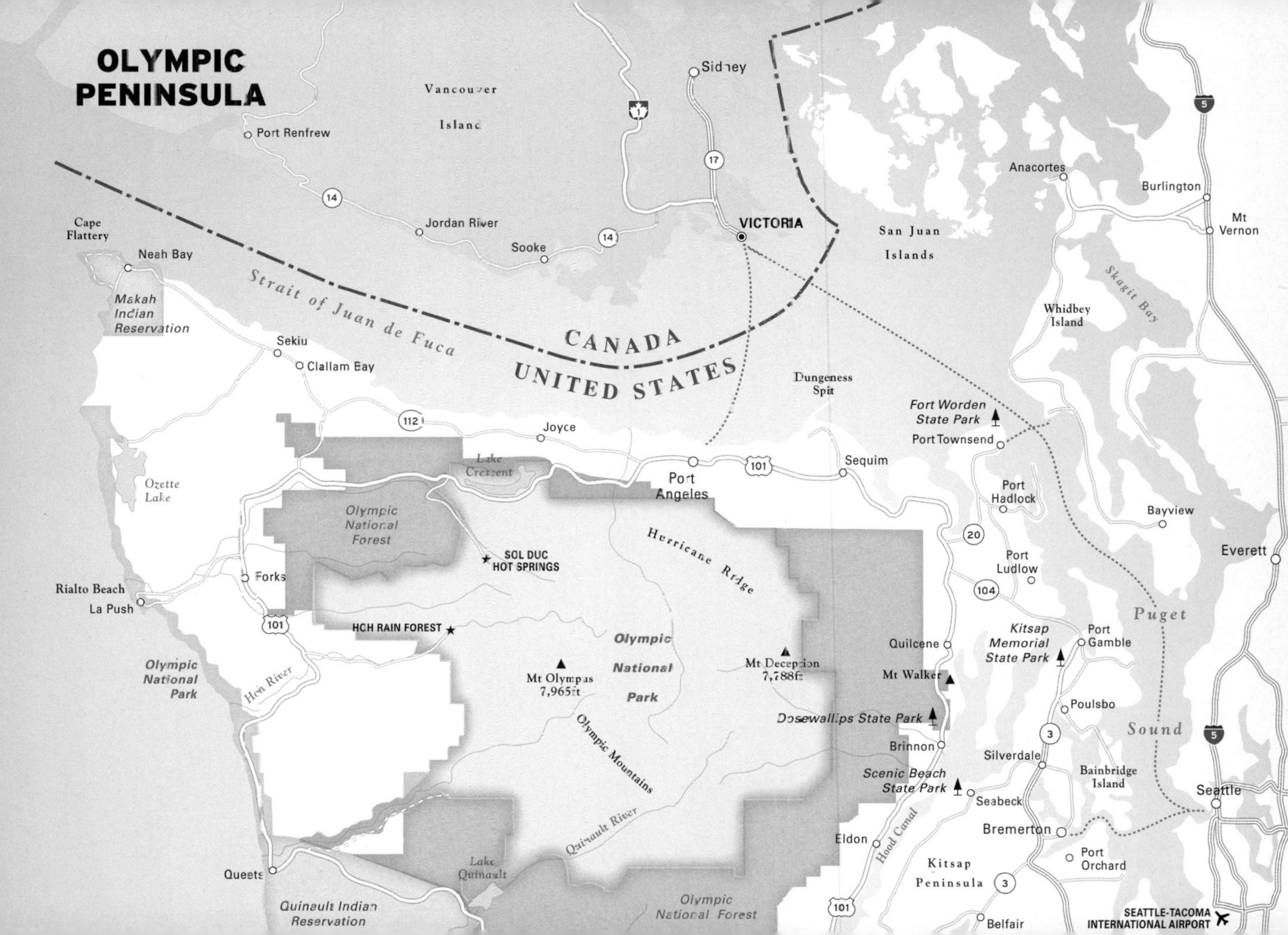
OLYMPIC PENINSULA
Vancouver
Island
Port Renfrew
Sidney
1
17
14
Jordan River
Sooke
VICTORIA
San Juan
Islands
Cape Flattery
Neah Bay
Makah Indian Reservation
Strait of Juan de Fuca
CANADA
UNITED STATES
Sekiu
Clallam Bay
112
Joyce
Dungeness Spit
Fort Worden State Park
Port Townsend
Anacortes
Burlington
Mt Vernon
Skagit Bay
Whidbey Island
Ozette Lake
Lake Crescent
Port Angeles
101
Sequim
Port Hadlock
Bayview
Olympic National Forest
SOL DUC HOT SPRINGS
Hurricane Ridge
20
Port Ludlow
Everett
104
Forks
Rialto Beach
La Push
HOH RAIN FOREST
Olympic National Park
Mt Deception 7,788ft
Quilcene
Port Gamble
Kitsap Memorial State Park
Puget
Mt Walker
Mt Olympus 7,965ft
Hoh River
Poulsbo
Dosewallips State Park
Olympic Mountains
3
Sound
Brinnon
Silverdale
Bainbridge Island
5
Scenic Beach State Park
Seabeck
Seattle
Quinault River
Bremerton
Eldon
Hood Canal
Port Orchard
Lake Quinault
Queets
Kitsap Peninsula
Quinault Indian Reservation
Olympic National Forest
Belfair
SEATTLE-TACOMA INTERNATIONAL AIRPORT

OLYMPIC NATIONAL PARK
Strait
Pysht
Ozette
Indian Reservation
OZETTE
112
LYRE
RIVER
113
Dickey
Lake
Olympic
National
Park
Ozette
Lake
Lake
Pleasant
Sappho
BEAR
CREEK
KLAHOWYA
101
FAIRHOLME
Lake
Crescent
Beaver
STORM KING
RANGER
STATION
Olympic National Forest
SOL DUC
Forks
MORA
La Push
Quileute
Indian
Reservation
Bogachiel
State Park
MINNIE
PETERSON
HOH
OXBOW
COTTONWOOD
PACIFIC OCEAN
UPPER
CLEARWATER
YAHOO
LAKE
101
COPPER MINE
BOTTOM
KALALOCH
QUEETS
Olympic
National Forest
Queets
QUINAULT
RAIN FOREST
RANGER STATION
Lake
Quinault
GATTON
CREEK
Amanda Park
WILLABY
Quinault
Reservation
0
10 mi
0
10 km
101

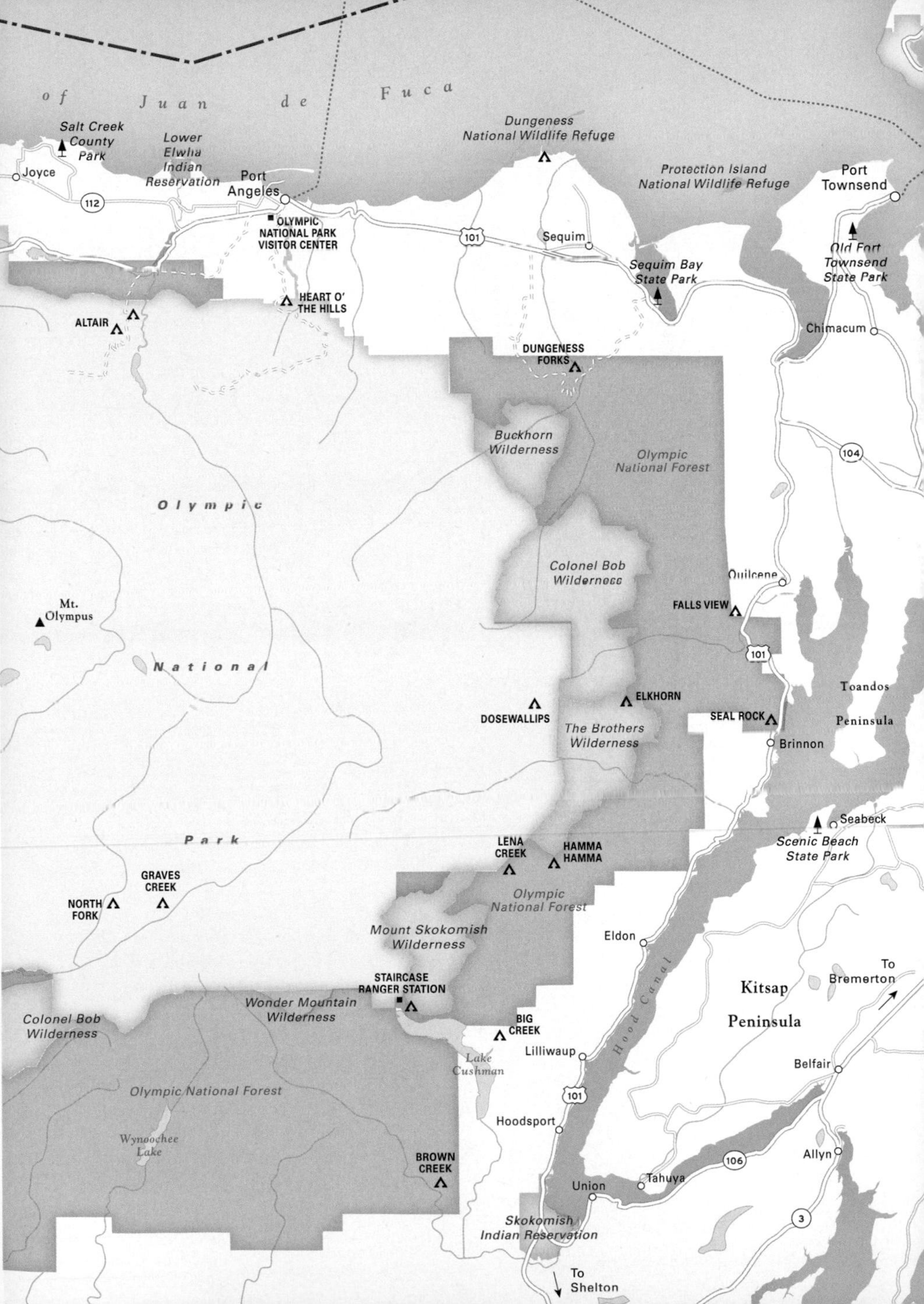

of Juan de Fuca
Salt Creek County Park
Lower Elwha Indian Reservation
Joyce
112
Port Angeles
OLYMPIC NATIONAL PARK VISITOR CENTER
Dungeness National Wildlife Refuge
Protection Island National Wildlife Refuge
Port Townsend
101
Sequim
Sequim Bay State Park
Old Fort Townsend State Park
ALTAIR
HEART O' THE HILLS
Chimacum
DUNGENESS FORKS
Buckhorn Wilderness
Olympic National Forest
104
Olympic National Park
Colonel Bob Wilderness
Quilcene
FALLS VIEW
Mt. Olympus
101
Toandos Peninsula
ELKHORN
DOSEWALLIPS
SEAL ROCK
The Brothers Wilderness
Brinnon
Seabeck
Scenic Beach State Park
LENA CREEK
HAMMA HAMMA
GRAVES CREEK
NORTH FORK
Olympic National Forest
Mount Skokomish Wilderness
Eldon
Hood Canal
To Bremerton
Kitsap Peninsula
STAIRCASE RANGER STATION
Wonder Mountain Wilderness
Colonel Bob Wilderness
BIG CREEK
Lake Cushman
Lilliwaup
Belfair
Olympic National Forest
101
Wynoochee Lake
Hoodsport
Allyn
BROWN CREEK
106
Tahuya
Union
3
Skokomish Indian Reservation
To Shelton

Contents

DISCOVER

the Olympic Peninsula

From rainforests to snowcapped mountains to rivers, beaches, and lakes, the Olympic Peninsula offers seemingly endless terrain.

In the west, you can hike through elk habitat to the top of Colonel Bob Mountain, dig clams in the wet coastal sand from Mocrocks to Long Beach, and explore the far reaches of the Hoh River Valley. Spend long days hiking Olympic National Park trails and short nights sleeping under the stars, or drive to the end of a two-lane highway to view the infinite Pacific Ocean at La Push.

Up north, traverse the Strait of San Juan de Fuca Highway to reach Cape Flattery, the northwesternmost point in the contiguous United States. Bike the scenic Olympic Discovery Trail through Sequim's rain shadow. Trek to the end of Dungeness Spit, or soak tired muscles in the remote Olympic Hot Springs.

In the eastern part of the peninsula, you can kayak in the sun beneath the snow-topped peaks at Lake Cushman, fish abundant rivers, and indulge in local delicacies including Dungeness crab in cities such as Poulsbo and Gig Harbor.

This is a place where the calendar might say summer has already begun, but the weather is overcast and drizzly. Rain is part of the region's charm—as well as the reason it's so beautiful in the first place. Locals hardly seem affected by

Clockwise from top left: a log truck and its load; Hoh Rainforest; Ruby Beach; Sequim-Dungeness Valley; goat at Grays Harbor County Fair; Cape Flattery.

it, beginning their days with layers of clothes and peeling them off (and adding them back again) as the weather calls for. Smart visitors will do the same.

The Olympic Peninsula is also constantly evolving. It's a blue-collar area with first-class natural amenities, including fish and timber, that provide jobs of all sorts. Today, it's just as common for the peninsula's residents to promote these same resources in the name of tourism. The city of Forks, once known as the "Logging Capital of the World," became the *Twilight* capital of the world after Stephenie Meyer set her best-selling books there. As the *Twilight* fad fades, Forks again searches for a new identity. Just as the rains and rivers have carved the land, the area's peoples are carving its history. I consider both the people and the land testaments to how special this place is, and one visit (hopefully with good weather) is all the evidence you'll need to agree.

Clockwise from top left: former site of the Elwha Dam; Hurricane Ridge in Olympic National Park; Lake Crescent; houseboat on the way to Point No Point Lighthouse in Hansville.

Planning Your Trip

Where to Go

The Kitsap Peninsula and Hood Canal

There are more cities and people here than in any other part of the Olympic Peninsula, mostly due to the proximity to Seattle, Tacoma, and the rest of busy Puget Sound. Get away from the bustle with a visit to **Lake Cushman** or **Dosewallips State Park,** or venture into Olympic National Park to hike the **Staircase Rapids Loop.** The sixty-five-mile-long **Hood Canal** provides opportunities to scuba dive, fish, kayak, and, when the weather's nice, relax on a scenic beach. The **Kitsap Peninsula** is separated from the western portion of the Olympic Peninsula by the Hood Canal, but it shares much of the natural beauty of its larger sister. The eastern part of the Olympic Peninsula is known for its quaint small towns including nautical **Gig Harbor** and picturesque **Poulsbo,** known for its Scandinavian-themed shops and restaurants.

Port Angeles and the Northern Peninsula

Scenic Highway 112 intersects with Highway 101 near the bustling hub of **Port Angeles,** then carves a path through small towns along the Strait of Juan de Fuca before ending at **Neah Bay,** home to the Makah Indian Reservation. Just west of Neah Bay is **Cape Flattery,** the northwestern-most point in the contiguous United States. The northern peninsula is a hotbed for recreation—it's home to popular Olympic National Park destinations such as the **Sol Duc Hot Springs** and **Lake Crescent,** surrounded by miles of hiking trails. **Hurricane Ridge** is a breathtaking vista. Westward lies the coastal portion of Olympic

Hurricane Ridge in Olympic National Park

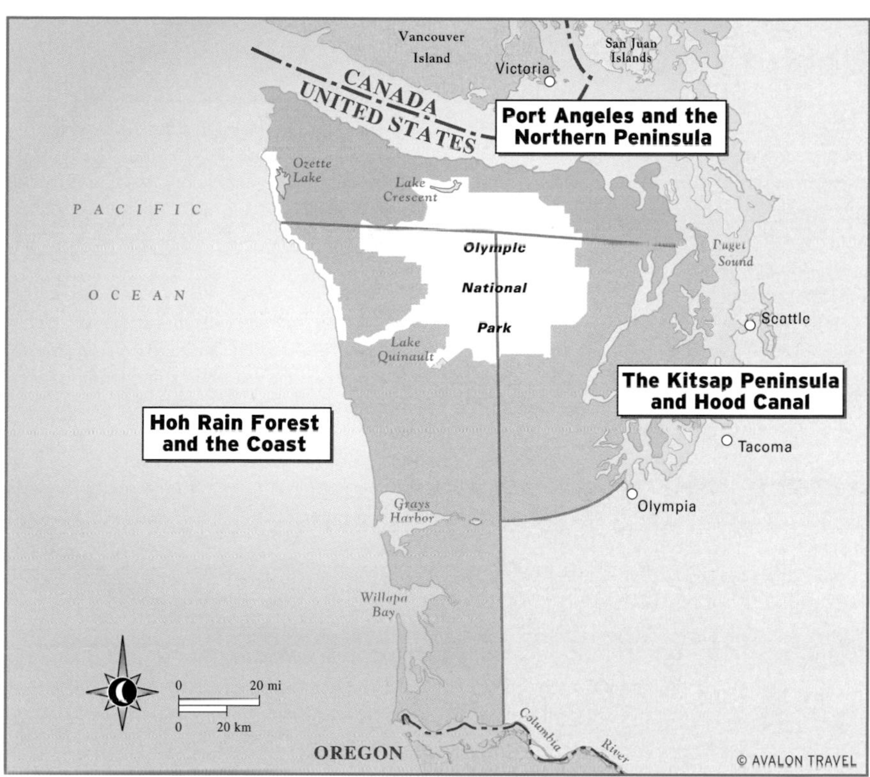

National Park and **Lake Ozette,** Washington's third-largest natural lake.

Hoh Rain Forest and the Coast

Miles of driftwood-covered beaches, clear lakes and rivers, lush rain forests, and towering, water-carved sea stacks are among the many **natural wonders** of the western Olympic Peninsula. Massive amounts of rainfall keep the area green and foster the lushness of the **Hoh Rain Forest,** while nearby glacier-covered **Mount Olympus** towers above everything. **Lake Quinault,** in the southwestern part of Olympic National Park, is surrounded by the Quinault Rain Forest and offers recreation for hikers, anglers, and wildlife-watchers. Cities such as **Aberdeen, Hoquiam,** and **Forks** offer a taste of slow-paced small-town life. On the coast, the pebbles of **Ruby Beach** are actually fragmented garnets, and **Cape Disappointment State Park** is the terminus of Lewis and Clark's historic expedition.

When to Go

The typical Pacific Northwest tourist season is **summer,** running from Memorial Day through Labor Day. That's the only time of year when the rain holds off long enough for you to get out of the car to explore. Of course, the most popular spots are crowded when the sun does come out.

Many mountain trails are covered with snow the majority of the year, and many tourist sights are closed during **winter.** But there are still things to do: Sequim and the Dungeness Valley are almost always dry; storm-watching specials are offered at many hotels in coastal communities; and museums are often open year-round. Winter is also the best time to sled, snowshoe, and ski.

To beat the crowds, visit in late **spring** or early **fall.** Sure, there's often rain during those times, but rain is what makes the region beautiful. Besides, what did you expect from an area full of rain forests?

Before You Go

If you want to hit all the highlights of **Olympic National Park,** allow a minimum of three days, because those highlights are spread out over such a wide area.

Visitors who plan on hopping a ferry at Port Angeles to visit Canada need a **passport.** (A regular driver's license no longer cuts it with the authorities of either Canada or the United States.)

Passes

Entering Olympic National Park requires a **park pass,** which you can either purchase online prior to visiting or at any park entrance. As of 2012, entry to all Washington state parks requires a **Washington State Discover Pass,** which also can be purchased online, at any staffed state park, or from a recreational license vendor.

Transportation

Several **bus** systems run throughout the peninsula, but they are best for traveling within the county they are based in, not for a means of trekking across the entire region. Thus, a **car** is pretty much a necessity. All the major rental companies have stations at Seattle-Tacoma International Airport. For travel by **train,** Amtrak has several stops in Western Washington, including ones in Olympia, Tacoma, and Seattle. **Ferries** connect the Olympic Peninsula to Puget Sound to the east, and Canada to the west.

The Best of the Olympic Peninsula

One of the best parts about the Olympic Peninsula is that you don't need to stray far from its main thoroughfare, Highway 101, to experience a good number of area highlights. **Highway 101** travels around the perimeter of the peninsula and Olympic National Park, making it possible to see the best the area has to offer in a limited amount of time. This itinerary imagines that you're arriving from Seattle or Tacoma, and takes you around the peninsula starting on the eastern side, going to the northern portion, and finishing on the coast.

Day 1

Begin in the eastern portion of the peninsula, heading north from **Shelton** along Hood Canal. At Hoodsport, head west on Highway 119 for a trip along **Lake Cushman** to **Staircase** for a short day hike. Return to Hoodsport for a quick stop at **Hoodsport Winery,** then head to **The Tides Restaurant** for some of the region's famous oysters or continue north to grab an excellent Eagle Burger at **Eagle Creek Saloon** north of Lilliwaup.

After lunch, take a hike at **Mount Walker** or **Dosewallips State Park** before heading on to Port Townsend to check out the town. Have dinner in town and spend the night at the **Ann Starrett Mansion** with its grand spiral staircase.

Day 2

Put on your walking shoes and hit the road toward **Fort Worden State Park,** which used to be an active military fort. Once you've traversed some of the park's 434 acres, get back on Highway 101. Drive to **Sequim,** and bask in the area's rain shadow and visit its many lavender farms.

Bike riders should hop on the **Olympic Discovery Trail** at some point, and nature lovers definitely need to venture north to the **Dungeness Spit** for a bird-watching hike.

Fort Worden State Park in Port Townsend

Head toward Port Angeles early enough to enjoy lunch at **Chestnut Cottage,** then stroll the **Waterfront Trail.** Meander through the **Museum at the Carnegie** or play a round of golf at **Peninsula Golf Club.** Have a glass of wine with dinner at **Bella Italia,** then tuck in for the night at the **Port Angeles Inn.**

Day 3

You won't be driving too far today, as you head south of Port Angeles to explore two of the most popular sections of **Olympic National Park.** First up is **Hurricane Ridge** and its outstanding visitors center, from which point you can take one of several scenic hikes or have a picnic lunch among the blooming wildflowers, subalpine meadows, and snowcapped mountains. When you're finished, return to Highway 101 and head west to **Lake Crescent** to take a quick walk on the **Marymere Falls Nature Trail,** and admire 90-foot-high Marymere Falls or fish for some trout. Stop at **Lake Crescent Lodge** for a bite, then circle around to the lake's north side and stay at **Log Cabin Resort** for the night.

Day 4

The sulfuric waters at **Sol Duc Hot Springs** will be sure to help you relax. Whether you hike **Sol Duc Falls Trail** prior to or after soaking is up to you. Have a quick lunch at the Sol Duc Hot Springs Resort's **Poolside Deli** before once again hitting the road.

For a worthy detour, take the Highway 113 junction north to connect with scenic Highway 112, then head west to **Neah Bay** and **Cape Flattery,** if for no other reason than to say you've been to the northwesternmost point in the contiguous United States. Visit the Makah Indian Reservation and the tribe's fascinating museum, the **Makah Cultural and Research Center.**

Retrace your path and return to Highway 101 to continue the loop south into the *Twilight*- and logging-centric town of **Forks.** Visit the **Forks Timber Museum** to shop for logging- and *Twilight*-related memorabilia. To end the day, jump on Highway 110 to **La Push** and hit **Rialto Beach** for a sunset stroll. **Mora Campground,** about two miles from Rialto Beach, is a great place to spend the night.

La Push

Wine Time

With all the rain that falls on the Olympic Peninsula, you might be surprised to hear exactly how many wineries are located here. Well, that's because the grapes used here are grown in the drier eastern part of the state. Still, plenty of the wineries on the peninsula offer opportunities to sip and swirl. Here are some of the best and brightest. Cheers!

THE KITSAP PENINSULA AND HOOD CANAL

- **Walter Dacon Wines:** Located near Shelton, this winery focuses on Rhone- and Mediterranean-style wines, and ages its grapes in French and American oak barrels. Try the Skookum Red (page 54).

- **Hoodsport Winery:** This winery has been around for almost four decades. All its wines are top-notch, but its fruit wines truly stand out. Chocolate truffles and specialty coffee are also sold here (page 60).

PORT ANGELES AND THE NORTHERN PENINSULA

- **Camaraderie Cellars:** This small craft winery is located two miles west of Port Angeles, and gets its grapes from Eastern Washington. The winery produces only 3,000 cases per year but has managed to place its product in several regional restaurants (page 98).

- **Harbinger Winery:** Housed in a former logging truck shop three miles west of Port Angeles, Harbinger selects its grapes from several different Eastern Washington vineyards, and crushes them within hours of harvest. The result? Try the cabernet sauvignon and you'll find out. Here's a hint: It's good. They also brew beer here. A double bonus (page 98)!

Westport Winery

HOH RAIN FOREST AND THE COAST

- **Westport Winery:** This family-owned business grows grapes, has an interesting outdoor art museum, and serves food at its coastal location between Aberdeen and Westport. The fruity wines here don't lack for taste; the Duckleberry Grunt is one of the best. A portion of the proceeds from each bottle sold here goes to local charities (page 156).

Day 5

Return to Highway 101 and head south. Make a left at Upper Hoh Road, and travel along the Hoh River to the entrance to Olympic National Park. Spend some time exploring one, or several, of the trails in the **Hoh Rain Forest,** then visit the **Hoh Rain Forest Visitor Center** to learn about the natural forces that make the Hoh Rain Forest unique.

Stop at the **Hard Rain Café** for a half-pound Mount Olympus burger, then continue south to where Highway 101 will take you out to the Pacific Ocean. Stroll uniquely colored **Ruby Beach** to look at the sea stacks just offshore. Dine at the

Kalaloch Lodge before heading south to **Lake Quinault,** home to the Quinault Rain Forest. Be sure to get there in time to catch a sunset over the water at **Rain Forest Resort Village,** where you'll be spending the night.

Day 6

Begin the day with a 31-mile drive around Lake Quinault. Stop to take photos at one of the many waterfalls here or the open meadows where Roosevelt elk graze. Trek down kid-friendly **Quinault Big Cedar Trail** to see one of the world's largest western red cedar trees, then hop back on Highway 101 and drive south to the Moclips Highway, where a right turn will take you to Highway 109 and back out to the coast. Head to **North Beach,** where you'll be able to explore a handful of small towns.

Swing by the **Museum of the North Beach** to learn about local history, then head a few minutes farther south for lunch and to sample some award-winning wines at **Ocean Crest Resort.** Head down 101 again to Pacific Beach and visit the picturesque, planned-development town of **Seabrook.** Grab some ice cream and take a stroll through town, which looks like a Hollywood movie set, and across the highway, down to an often-empty beach for a before-dinner walk. Eat dinner and grab a beer at Seabrook's only place to eat, **Mill 109 Restaurant & Pub,** then spend the evening in one of the many cottages for rent here.

Day 7

Drive south to **Ocean Shores.** Once there, visit **Damon Point State Park** for spectacular views of Grays Harbor and the Olympic Mountains, then stop at the **Coastal Interpretive Center** to learn the history of the relatively new city you're in.

Grab lunch at one of the many local restaurants here, then rent mopeds for an hour and cruise through town and along the beach. Next, head east on Highway 109 out of town and stop at the **Quinault Beach Resort & Casino** for a little action at the blackjack tables. Head east to **Grays Harbor National Wildlife Refuge** in **Hoquiam** to walk the boardwalk and take photos of the many shorebirds that call the area home.

Drive to **Aberdeen** and tour the tall ships ***Lady Washington*** and the ***Hawaiian***

Hoh Rain Forest in Olympic National Park

cascading waterfall at Willaby Creek near where it flows into Lake Quinault

Chieftain. Exit town via Highway 12, and swing into **Montesano** for a quick walk at **Lake Sylvia State Park.**

For your last dinner on the peninsula, you should make your way back to the coast, to **Westport.** Take in the view of the marina and linger over drinks at **Half Moon Bay Bar & Grill,** then bid adieu to the Olympic Peninsula before tucking in for the night at the **Chateau Westport.**

Three-Day Weekend with the Kids

Full of wonder, mystique, history, and educational opportunities, the Olympic Peninsula is the perfect place to take kids of all ages. The three-day weekend below assumes a starting point of Port Townsend and an ending point of Ocean Shores.

Friday

Take a step back in time at **Fort Worden State Park,** where kids (armed with flashlights) can explore old bunkers built in the early 1900s and active in both world wars. It's great for history buffs as well as movie lovers—this is where Richard Gere's *An Officer and a Gentleman* was filmed.

Next, head to the **Port Townsend Marine Science Center,** located in the park, to get up close and personal with starfish and sea anemones. Then take a walk along the beach and see what creatures can be found in the wild. Take a family photo with the **Point Wilson Light,** built in 1913, in the background. This is just one of many old lighthouses you'll find on the Olympic Peninsula.

Head into **Port Townsend** to savor some out-of-this-world ice cream or Italian ice at **Elevated Ice Cream.** There's a candy shop here, too. In the evening, settle down in your already-booked hotel in Port Townsend.

sunlight through the steam at Sol Duc Hot Springs

Saturday

Kids will enjoy a trip to **Hurricane Ridge** in Olympic National Park in any season. In winter, the road to the ridge is open every day, weather permitting; kids can make snowballs, sled, snowshoe, and cross-country ski. The area has two rope tows and a ski lift, too.

When the weather warms up in late spring, the area is dotted with wildflowers. Take a scenic nature walk. Stop first at the **Hurricane Ridge Visitor Center** for maps, information about guided tours, and to see exhibits. You can see everything from the ridge, including Canada!

After a few hours at Hurricane Ridge, grab a bite in **Port Angeles** and then head to the Sol Duc River Valley. Take a one-mile hike on the **Sol Duc Falls Trail,** where kids will enjoy walking among the forest's tall trees. The big payoff is beautiful Sol Duc Falls. Relax sore muscles in the pools at the **Sol Duc Hot Springs Resort,** and then make your way to **Forks** for dinner at **Pacific Pizza** or **Sully's Drive-In.** If you are traveling with *Twilight*-loving children, check out Forks High School and the other spots Bella, Edward, and Jacob frequented. Don't worry about finding your way here: There are plenty of signs and maps in nearly every establishment to point you in the right direction. Spend the night in Lake Quinault.

Sunday

Hit the beach! Even during the summer that might mean wearing warm layers at least for part of the day, because it can get chilly here on the coast. First, head to Ocean Shores to buy a kite from **Ocean Shores Kites.** It's almost always windy here, so you're practically guaranteed a successful flight.

Ocean Shores is home to the **Pacific Paradise Family Fun Center,** where kids can hang out for hours playing arcade games and winning tickets for prizes. They can also play mini-golf here or ride bumper boats during the warmer months. Stop by one of numerous local shops to browse for beach-related trinkets, and pick up giant bags of soft and chewy saltwater taffy at **Murphy's Candy & Ice Cream.**

Horseback riding on the beach is often available, and you can rent bikes from **Apollo Activities** to further explore this coastal town. For a more educational option, look no further than the **Coastal Interpretive Center** and its aquariums and exhibits about the region's sea life and mammals.

Best Hikes

Whether you are an athlete or someone who prefers short and easy trails, pulling on some sturdy shoes and getting out into nature is a must. You won't regret it—the Olympic Peninsula is one of the most beautiful natural settings in the world. You can purchase day passes at many trailheads, or pick up multiday passes if you plan to tackle several hikes. A Northwest Forest Pass works for national parks, while you need a Discovery Pass for lands managed by the state. Remember to check trail conditions beforehand and follow Leave No Trace principles.

THE KITSAP PENINSULA AND HOOD CANAL

- **Staircase Rapids Loop:** This scenic four-mile loop with a negligible elevation gain includes several water views and a new cable suspension bridge (page 59).
- **Falls View Canyon Trail:** This easy 1.5-mile hike has a good payoff at the end: a 120-foot waterfall off the Big Quilcene River (page 65).

PORT ANGELES AND THE NORTHERN PENINSULA

- **Hurricane Ridge:** Towering over Port Angeles, Hurricane Ridge is one of the most popular destinations in Olympic National Park. Several trails that leave from the visitors center provide panoramic views of the Strait of Juan de Fuca and Olympic National Park (page 106).
- **Marymere Falls Nature Trail:** A popular trail due to its location and its limited elevation gain, this is one of the few trails on the Olympic Peninsula that has stairs running on the side, allowing hikers access to the upper portion of the 90-foot falls (page 107).

Hurricane Ridge in Olympic National Park

- **Sol Duc Falls Trail:** Hike straight to the falls and back (an easy two miles round-trip), or complete the 5.3-mile loop through old-growth forest (page 108).

HOH RAIN FOREST AND THE COAST

- **Bogachiel River Trail:** This 12-mile round-trip trail gains only 400 feet of elevation in total, and provides a trip surrounded by moss-covered old-growth trees and views of the Bogachiel River (page 124).
- **Hall of Mosses Trail:** Less than a mile long, this easy-to-access trail smack in the middle of the Hoh Rain Forest may be the most popular trail on the Olympic Peninsula (page 130).

The Great Outdoors

While there are plenty of great museums, restaurants, and shops to make the Olympic Peninsula interesting year-round, it's definitely the great outdoors that most visitors come here to experience. This five-day tour highlights some of the best recreational opportunities available.

Day 1

Begin on the eastern side of the peninsula, stopping at **Mikes Beach Resort** north of Eldon to rent dive gear and explore the waters of **Hood Canal** for squid, rockfish, eels, and possibly a Pacific octopus or two. Through the resort's property you can gain access to some of the best reefs and underwater canyons on the canal. Those without diving experience can instead grab a kayak from the resort and explore the southern canal from above.

Afterward, picnic at **Dosewallips State Park** before heading north to **Fort Flagler State Park** on Marrowstone Island for a short hike. Settle in for the night in **Port Townsend.**

Day 2

Bicycling is very popular in the northern peninsula, thanks to the awesome **Olympic Discovery Trail,** which you can jump on north of Olympic Cellars in **Sequim** and ride to the city pier in Port Angeles for lunch before returning to your car. Those desiring more of an off-road cycling experience should head south of Sequim to get muddy on the **Lower Dungeness Trail.**

Next, travel south of Port Angeles to **Hurricane Ridge.** Once there, hike the **Cirque Rim Trail** and look down on Port Angeles. Beginning at the visitors center, hike as many of the other trails as you're able: Each one has something different to offer. Return to the highway and head west to **Lake Crescent Lodge** for the evening.

Day 3

Head out to **Marymere Falls Nature Trail,** which is less than a mile long, for a wake-up hike, then head back to Lake Crescent Lodge.

kayaking on Lake Crescent

Best Campgrounds

The only time span that's suitable for camping on the Olympic Peninsula is between Memorial Day and Labor Day—at least for those who want to stay dry. During this limited window, it's important to scout out campgrounds far in advance to make sure you can secure a spot.

THE KITSAP PENINSULA AND HOOD CANAL

- **Hamma Hamma Campground:** This shady site is situated on the shores of the Hamma Hamma River, about 20 miles from Hoodsport. It is near the Living Legacy Trail, an interpretive loop that is wheelchair-friendly for the first quarter mile (page 61).
- **Staircase Campground:** Just one hour north of Olympia, this campsite is surrounded by the ancient old-growth Douglas firs that dominate this side of the peninsula. It is made up of 47 sites and provides access to a variety of nearby hiking trails (page 61).

PORT ANGELES AND THE NORTHERN PENINSULA

- **Fort Worden State Park:** Reserve one of the 80 campsites here far in advance; this destination is super popular. That's because this former military fort is conveniently located and full of activities, including tours of the remaining buildings from the original fort (page 83).
- **Dungeness Recreation Area:** Located just outside both Sequim and the Dungeness National Wildlife Refuge, this 64-site campground is located on a bluff above the Strait of Juan de Fuca and offers a 1.1-mile trail along the bluff that overlooks the strait (page 92).

HOH RAIN FOREST AND THE COAST

- **Mora Campground:** Close to the Quileute Indian Reservation at La Push, Mora Campground is just two miles from Rialto Beach on the Pacific Ocean. It has running water all year long and is a perfect home base for exploring this part of the peninsula (page 127).
- **Hoh Rain Forest Campground:** With 88 campsites situated in the middle of old-growth forest and alongside the Hoh River, the Hoh Rain Forest Campground might be the campground that best epitomizes the Olympic Peninsula. From the campground you have access to several trails that lead around that river and through that forest (page 131).
- **Twin Harbors State Park:** Once a military training ground, this 172-acre beachfront location near Westport now is home to more than 260 campsites of all varieties with access to trails, bird watching, and other activities associated with beach exploration (page 165).

Grab a kayak there, and take in the glacier-carved beauty of **Lake Crescent** from the water. Next, head to the north side of the lake to connect to Highway 112. Travel the scenic highway west along the Strait of Juan de Fuca to **Neah Bay.** Hike the short **Cape Flattery Trail** to glance out at Tatoosh Island and the decommissioned Cape Flattery Lighthouse. You are now standing at the northwesternmost point in the contiguous United States.

Hop back on the highway, then venture down Hoko-Ozette Road to eight-mile-long **Lake Ozette.** Hike three miles down the **Cape Alava Trail** for a moment of reflection. When you hit the beach here, you will be standing at the westernmost point of the contiguous United States. Walk along the beach, then retrace your steps back to Highway 101. Head south to **Forks,** where you'll spend the night.

Day 4

Rise early to take advantage of the area's prime salmon- and trout-fishing opportunities at **Bogachiel State Park,** just south of Forks,

Neah Bay

where the Bogachiel River lies. Or, if you'd prefer to be in the water with the fish rather than to catch them, pick up a wetsuit and a board at **Wilderness Creative** in Forks, then head west to La Push to catch some Pacific Ocean waves.

Once you've caught your share of fish or waves, head south to **Lake Quinault** for a waterfall- and big tree-filled series of short hikes along the North Shore and South Shore Roads on either side of the lake. Hit the **Quinault Rain Forest Nature Trail** and the **Trail of the Giants** before catching a beautiful sunset from the **Rain Forest Resort Village** or while sipping a drink from inside the **Salmon House Restaurant.**

Day 5

Head south for an hour to **Ocean Shores,** then rent mopeds from **Affordable Mopeds** and cruise back north on the beach to visit the small beach towns nearby. Some of the moped-rental shops also rent bikes, which can be pedaled along the usually quiet streets from the center of the town to the North Jetty and everywhere between. Check out the equine options at **Chenois Creek Horse Rentals,** and go for a horseback ride on the beach.

Next, sate your inner birder with a visit to the **Grays Harbor National Wildlife Refuge** in **Bowerman Basin** in the town of Hoquiam. Bring your binoculars to catch a glimpse of some of the 200 species of birds that have been spotted here. Head into **Aberdeen,** and play a set of tennis at 14-acre Sam Benn Memorial Park, then go south to Westport to surf at Westhaven State Park's **Half Moon Bay.**

End your night at a bed-and-breakfast in any of the beach towns you've visited.

The Kitsap Peninsula and Hood Canal

Look for ★ to find recommended sights, activities, dining, and lodging.

Highlights

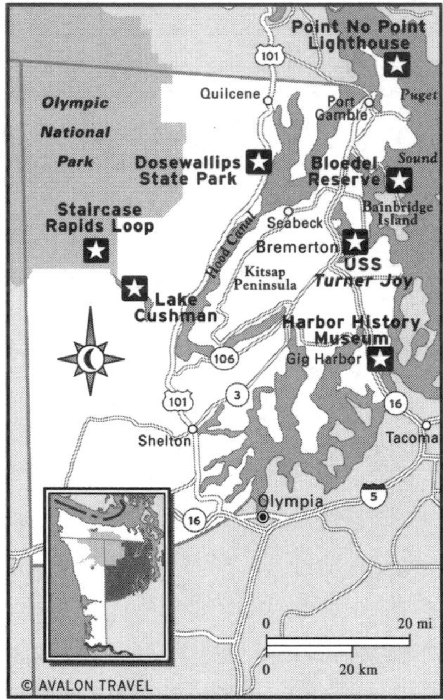

★ **USS *Turner Joy*:** The U.S. Navy destroyer that once played a vital role in the 1964 Gulf of Tonkin incident is on display and available for tours, and even overnight stays, in Bremerton (page 31).

★ **Harbor History Museum:** This museum, housed in a new 7,000-square-foot waterfront building on the edge of town, preserves the region's history (page 37).

★ **Bloedel Reserve:** This 150-acre public garden sits on grounds once owned by a former timber baron. Now, a visitors center welcomes those searching for a moment of serenity among the area's natural beauty (page 44).

★ **Point No Point Lighthouse:** Built in 1879, the oldest lighthouse on Puget Sound is still operational, and available for tours much of the year (page 51).

★ **Lake Cushman:** This 10-mile-long reservoir offers an abundance of recreational opportunities in the summer. The outlying areas of the lake, located in Olympic National Forest, are a great spot for wildlife-watchers and hikers alike (page 58).

★ **Staircase Rapids Loop:** A newly built wooden suspension bridge that crosses the Skykomish River turns what had become an out-and-back hike into a spectacular loop trail (page 59).

★ **Dosewallips State Park:** One of the prettiest of the state parks, Dosewallips is a trail-filled paradise located in the foothills of the Olympic Mountains, bordered by the Dosewallips River on one side and Hood Canal on the other (page 64).

The eastern Olympic Peninsula offers road-weary visitors an opportunity to enjoy some semblance of city life. This portion of the peninsula is by far the busiest, thanks to its close proximity to the large population base of the Seattle-Tacoma area, as well as the existence of a ferry system that shuttles people and their cars here from the Puget Sound area and those who travel here through the northern Olympic Peninsula from British Columbia, Canada. It should surprise no one that those places with ferry terminals—including Bainbridge Island and Bremerton—are among the busiest, with pretty parks and restaurants set up around the terminals to greet travelers. Gig Harbor is another happening spot, not because it's accessed by the state ferry system, however, but because a major state highway connects it to busy Tacoma, located across a strait of Puget Sound known as the Tacoma Narrows via a pair of twin suspension bridges. Still, the area is a big one, and there are lots of opportunities to get away from the crowds and city life. Fantastic areas such as Lake Cushman, the Theler Wetlands, and Dosewallips State Park all provide opportunities to get lost, literally and figuratively, in nature. Jump into any of the surrounding wilderness areas such as Brothers, Buckhorn, or Mount Skokomish and getting lost becomes a lot easier. Head into Olympic National Park to visit the alpine meadows and lakes around the park's 6,000- and 7,000-foot peaks and it gets better: From vantage points here you often can see the metropolitan areas in the far distance, yet their sights, sounds, and smells seem a world away.

The eastern portion of the Olympic Peninsula is dissected by water in many spots, most notably by Hood Canal, a 65-mile-long and 1.5-mile-wide saltwater fjord separating the Olympic Peninsula from Kitsap Peninsula. Highway 101 runs north-south along the canal's entire western side, while a series of highways and rural roads intermingle on its eastern side. To its east, the Kitsap Peninsula is bordered by Puget Sound, and several inlets slice into its body creating

Previous: Gig Harbor; Hood Canal. **Above:** Hood Canal Bridge.

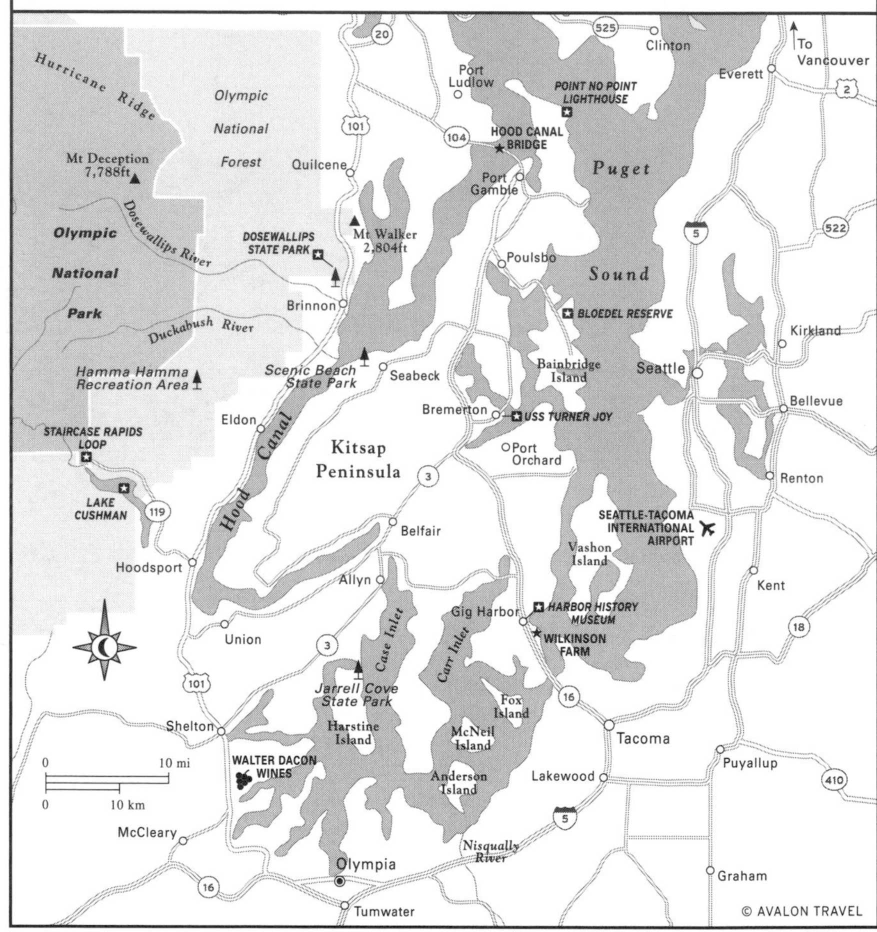

inlets, bays, and harbors—natural, calm-water paradises for boaters, kayakers, anglers, and wildlife.

The proximity and easy access to the more populated areas along the I-5 corridor along eastern Puget Sound create an interesting dichotomy here. To the east lie the city dwellers. To the west, those who prefer solitude. The eastern Olympic Peninsula is where the two factions meet, finding common ground in the natural beauty and wonder that surrounds them.

HISTORY

No matter where one travels, it's the names that best tell the history of an area. Here, as they are throughout the rest of the Olympic Peninsula, they're mostly Native American names—Lilliwaup, Dosewallips, Hamma Hamma, Kitsap—with some European and early American names—Hood, Bremerton, Bainbridge, Shelton—sprinkled in. The Indians' story dates back thousands of years, and today each of the hard-to-pronounce names tells a portion of it. Tribal and local museums tell the rest: how they lived off the generous land, battled with diseases and the "White Man," and were pushed by treaties to reservations where their history was passed down orally from generation to generation. The "White Man's" history in the area is written and a lot more clear-cut. Hood Canal, for example, was named by George Vancouver, a captain in the British Royal Navy, who named it Hood Channel (later mistakenly changed to "Canal") after British Navy Admiral Samuel Hood "discovered" it in 1792.

Soon after, fur traders came to the area and riches were made by harvesting the area's trees and the promise of a transcontinental railroad that would make marketing that lumber much easier. Railroads were built, but none of that magnitude. Like almost all areas on the Olympic Peninsula, the eastern section has seen many periods of boom and many periods of bust, mostly based on the availability of natural resources. As the entire Olympic Peninsula shifts from solely depending on those natural resources for sustenance toward relying on economies built on diversity, including tourism, the ways of the past don't disappear entirely. They're still here, just a little more hidden than they used to be.

PLANNING YOUR TIME

As with all areas on the Olympic Peninsula, the best time to visit for those who want to guarantee the many seasonal sights and businesses will be open is the period from Memorial Day to Labor Day. The weather is best then, too, and many of the recreational opportunities require good weather to be completed, at least safely and without too much mud being involved. Some of the best aspects of the area, however, stay open year-round, such as the museums, small-town shops, and restaurants. Public transportation is available in many of the cities and towns, but car travel remains the best way to see the area. It allows you the flexibility to hop from sight to sight, not having to skip the ones on your "maybe" list because you ran out of time.

Every part of Olympic National Park is amazing, but if there were a section of Olympic National Park one had to deem *least* spectacular, it most likely would be the park's eastern section, which is the region of the park that's covered in this chapter. That's because more of the big-name attractions are located in the northern and western sections, and there is only one car-friendly access road into the park's east side. That doesn't mean, of course, that there isn't plenty to be found here, because there is, including the often-overlooked Staircase, the closest major access point in Olympic National Park to Seattle and Tacoma, in the southeastern section. **Olympic National Park passes** ($25 per car, $12 per pedestrian or bicyclist) are good for seven days.

Visits to the many state parks here require a **Discover Pass** (www.parks.wa.gov, $10 per visit or $30 per year).

ORIENTATION

Whereas the rest of the Olympic Peninsula is easy to navigate due to its simple network of highways (there's only one major highway you'll need to use), the eastern section of the peninsula is a bit more complicated, thanks to the prominence of the state's ferry system and also to the many major highways that crisscross the Kitsap Peninsula. Highway 101 still is here, running north-south on the western side of Hood Canal from north of Quilcene through Shelton and beyond. But now, on the Kitsap Peninsula, you have to add in Highway 3 (essentially running north-south from Port Gamble to Shelton); Highway 16 (north-south from Gorst to Gig Harbor), and several other smaller highways and roads.

Kitsap Peninsula

Even among longtime locals, Kitsap Peninsula sometimes suffers from an identity crisis: Is it part of the Olympic Peninsula, or isn't it? Were it not for the glacier-carved fjord of Hood Canal separating Kitsap Peninsula from the western portion of the Olympic Peninsula, there would be little question. Today, the two sections of the peninsula are connected by the Hood Canal Bridge in the north and a small section of land in the south where Highway 3 and Highway 106 meet. The area also is accessible by ferry directly from Seattle and by bridge from Tacoma. The area's personality also is a bit split. Much of the same natural beauty that can be found on the rest of the Olympic Peninsula is here. There are plenty of waterways, trails, and open areas to explore. But there are strip malls, high-class boutiques, fancy hotels, historical sights, and areas of congested traffic, too. While it's most often disingenuous to say an area has it all, at least as far as the Olympic Peninsula is concerned, Kitsap pretty much does.

GETTING THERE AND AROUND

Kitsap Transit (360/377-2877 or 800/501-7433, www.kitsaptransit.org) travels through all of Kitsap County, including Poulsbo and Bainbridge Island, several times a day. Driving from Sea-Tac Airport to the Kitsap Peninsula will take you a little more than an hour if you head south on I-5 and cut over through Tacoma and Gig Harbor.

SEABECK

The only real dot on the map anywhere for miles around, the small town of Seabeck is located on the western side of Kitsap Peninsula, on Seabeck Bay. The town's marina makes it a popular spot for anglers and boaters. The area's one true jewel, at least the one true human-made jewel, is the ★ **Willcox House** (2390 Tekiu Rd. NW, 360/830-4492 or 800/725-9477, www.willcoxhouse.com, $189-279 d). The site was once home to a private resort owned by Joe Emel, whose home still stands and is used as a community center. A replica of a cabin built by Emel's son also is here, as are a picnic area, 1,500 feet of saltwater shoreline, and showers with restrooms. To reach Seabeck from the Kitsap Peninsula town of Silverdale, head west for eight miles on Seabeck Highway NW.

BREMERTON

The Port Washington Narrows splits Bremerton in two parts, east and west, and the sections are connected by two bridges, the Manette and the Warren Avenue. The waterfront areas of both sections are the only parts of town that could be considered touristy, as most of Bremerton is filled with working-class neighborhoods and scattered businesses, many which have seen better days. The waterfront areas, however, have a lot to offer, including boardwalks, restaurants, shops, museums, and a happening ferry terminal, from which point Seattle is just a 55-minute boat ride away.

Sights

Puget Sound Navy Museum

For a town its size, Bremerton is loaded with museums. The **Puget Sound Navy Museum** (251 1st St., 360/479-7447, www.pugetsoundnavymuseum.org, 10am-4pm Wed.-Mon. Oct.-Apr., free but donations accepted), formerly known as the Bremerton Naval Museum, is the best of the bunch. It is one of just 12 museums still funded by the U.S. Navy, and it's easy to see why this one remains open. There are more than 18,000 items in the museum's collection, including permanent exhibits on submarines and on what life is like onboard a naval aircraft carrier. This isn't a

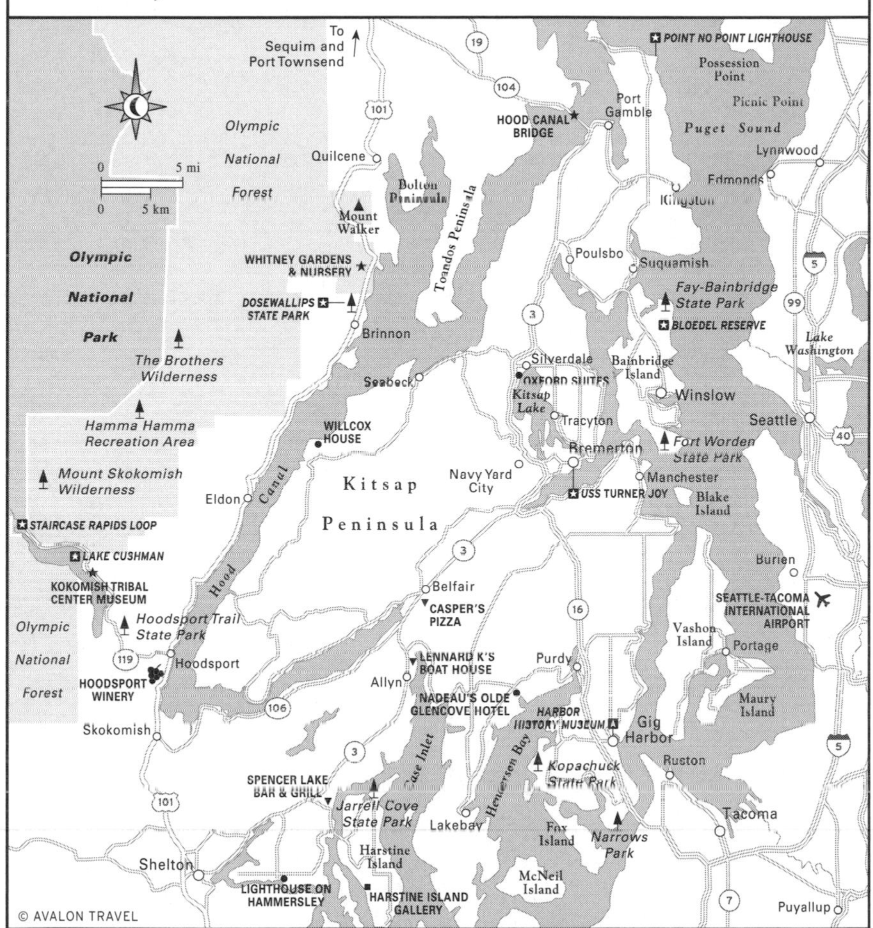

stuffy museum only for old folks. There's something here for every age, and even for landlubbers, to see. Check out the Japanese sword collection.

★ USS *Turner Joy*

Decommissioned in 1982, the **USS *Turner Joy*** (300 Washington Beach Ave., 360/792-2457, www.ussturnerjoy.org, 10am-5pm daily Mar.-Oct., 10am-4pm Wed.-Sun. Nov.-Feb., $12 adults, $10 seniors, $7 ages 5-12, under 5 free) launched in 1958 as a destroyer and took part in several tours in the Pacific. The ship is most famous for the role it played in the Gulf of Tonkin incident in August 1964, which escalated the United States' involvement in the Vietnam War. Since 1981, the ship has been on display here as a floating museum open for tours year-round, serving as a "haunted" Halloween vessel during the last week of October, and even offering overnighter programs where groups get to stay the evening aboard the 418-foot ship.

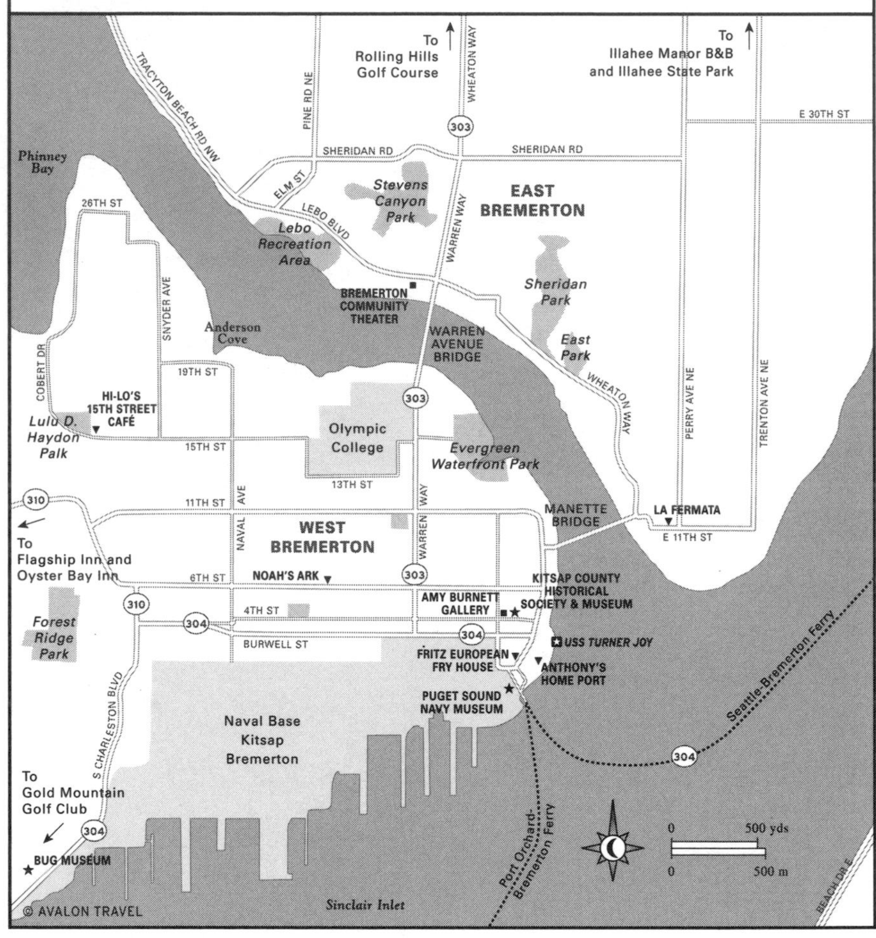

Kitsap County Historical Society & Museum

The **Kitsap County Historical Society & Museum** (280 4th St., 360/479-6226, www.kitsaphistory.org, 10am-4pm Tues.-Sat., noon-4pm Sun., $4 adults, $3 ages 6-17, kids under 6 free) includes some water-related history, and being focused on a peninsula, how could it not? But the majority of the exhibits focus on land-based trades and history, including that of Native Americans, farmers, and loggers that helped shape the area.

Bug Museum

This one's for the kids, but nonsqueamish adults also will enjoy the **Bug Museum** (1118 Charleston Beach Rd. W., 800/870-4284, www.bugmuseum.com 10am-5pm daily, free), located across from the Puget Sound Naval Shipyard. This attraction features several species of bugs, and there's also an eight-foot-long ant farm on display. The unique museum also hosts birthday parties and tours.

Other Sights

As home to the Seattle-Bremerton ferry terminal, **Bremerton Harborside** is one of the most happening spots in the city. Not only are there plenty of chain and local businesses here as well as the Kitsap Conference Center, but there also is a public park with five pretty copper fountains, neat landscaping, and a boardwalk with access to art galleries and museums. A few blocks north of the ferry terminal along the Port Washington Narrows, there's **Evergreen Waterfront Park,** a 10-acre mostly open space with boat launches, basketball and volleyball courts, and numerous picnic tables and barbecues.

Illahee State Park (3540 NE Bahia Vista Dr., 360/478-6460, www.parks.wa.gov) is three miles north of East Bremerton and home to 75 acres where you can crab, picnic, fish, hike, scuba dive, and camp at one of several sites ($22 tents, $33 RVs) complete with showers. A bluff separates the park into two sections: the beach and a wooded area. There are two former naval guns located near the beach located along Port Orchard Bay.

The second-highest peak on the Kitsap Peninsula can be found seven miles northwest of Bremerton off Gold Creek Road at **Green Mountain.** The peak is only 1,600 feet, but because it's on a peninsula the views here on clear days are excellent and wide. You can see nearby sights such as **Lake Tahuya,** and you can see faraway sights such as the Seattle skyline, Hood Canal, and Puget Sound. There are several well-maintained trails here, including **Gold Creek Trail, Wildcat Trail,** and **Beaver Pond Trail,** but they often get muddy and wet and also are open to motorcyclists, so be warned on both counts.

Sports and Recreation

Golf

Golf lovers will absolutely fall for **Gold Mountain Golf Club** (7263 W. Belfair Valley Rd., 360/415-5432, www.goldmountaingolf.com, $30-52 greens fees), which is considered by many to be the best on the Kitsap Peninsula. There actually are two courses here: the flatter Cascade course and the hillier Olympic course. Though both are good, the Olympic course is best. It has hosted many professional events, and is consistently ranked as one of the best courses in the Pacific Northwest. **Rolling Hills Golf Course** (2485 NE McWilliams Rd., 360/479-1212, www.rollinghills-golfcourse.com, $20-33.50 greens fees) is another local golfing option and has two putting greens and a driving range, and is a par-70 course.

Entertainment and Events

Like most community playhouses, the **Bremerton Community Theatre** (599 Lebo Blvd., 360/373-5152, www.bremerton-communitytheatre.org) acts as a showcase for the best local actors, and stages other touring events through the year. The **Bremerton Symphony Association** (535 5th St., Ste. 16, 360/373-1722, www.bremertonsymphony.org) also stages events year-round from the Bremerton Symphony Orchestra, Bremerton Symphony Concert Chorale, Bremerton Symphony League, and the Bremerton Symphony Youth Orchestra.

What is believed to be the oldest outdoor theater in the area, the **Kitsap Forest Theater** (3000 Seabeck Hwy., 206/542-7815, www.foresttheater.com) is located seven miles west of Bremerton on the way to Seabeck. The Mountaineers Players host regular shows here, many of which work well set on a tree-lined stage.

For more than 60 years, the **Armed Forces Festival and Parade** has been held during the third week of May, and it has built up quite a reputation during that time. Today, festival organizers say it's the largest parade of its type in the nation. So big, in fact, that slots in the parade need to be applied for because there are not enough spots for everyone who wants to participate to do so. A golf tournament, motorcycle rally, fun run, cooking competition, and a scholarship program are held in conjunction with the event.

The **Kitsap County Fair and Stampede** (1200 Fairgrounds Rd. NW, 360/337-5376) is an annual stop on the Professional Rodeo Cowboys Association's ProRodeo tour, which means there are plenty of bulls, horses, and clowns here during the latter part of August. Of course, there are also rides, entertainment, food, and more at this 100-plus-year-old community get-together.

Labor Day Weekend's **Blackberry Festival** (360/377-3041, www.blackberryfestival.org) may be set in a relatively small town, but that doesn't mean it is a small-town festival. Held on the city's popular boardwalk, the festival draws tens of thousands of people each year in celebration of the blackberry. The fruit is everywhere here. Expect jams, pies, wine, and cider, the Berry Fun Run, and much more. Vendors sell non-blackberry-related items, too, and there is music and other forms of entertainment held throughout the three days of the festival. And it's all free.

Bremerton's waterfront is a happening place all summer long, but it is particularly so Friday nights in July, when the free **Concerts on the Boardwalk** (360/377-3041) series takes place.

Shopping

Bremerton is a good place for a lot of things, but shopping isn't necessarily one of them. The can't-miss stores here are few and far between, but there are some neat places if you look hard enough. One of them is the **Amy Burnett Gallery** (402 Pacific Ave., 360/373-3187, www.amyburnettgallery.com, 11am-6pm Thurs.-Sat.) in Bremerton's Arts District. The works here aren't cheap, but they're gorgeous.

Not many tourists are into buying large plants or garden items simply due to the difficulty of getting such purchases home. Even if you're not looking to buy, **Elandan Gardens** (3050 W. Hwy. 16, 360/373-8260, www.elandangardens.com, 10am-5pm Tues.-Sun. Apr.-Oct., 10am-5pm Fri.-Sat. Nov.-Mar.) is a place you want to visit, if only to look. The bonsai garden here is gorgeous, and the landscaping and locally made sculptures are neat to look at, too.

Accommodations

Designed for the business traveler, the **Flagship Inn** (4320 Kitsap Way, 360/479-6566, www.flagshipinn.com, $75 d) includes a computer and printer for guests' use in the lobby, continental breakfast, and coffee, tea, and fresh fruit available 24 hours a day.

Located close to the Bremerton Naval Shipyard and the Naval Museum, the **Oyster Bay Inn** (4412 Kitsap Way, 360/377-5510, www.oysterbayinnbremerton.com, $79 d) has in-room CD players, a free fitness center, valet parking, and complimentary breakfast at the on-site restaurant and lounge.

Three guest rooms with private balconies highlight the **Bird's Eye View B&B** (8226 Kaster Dr. NE, 360/698-2448, www.bremertonbb.com, $135-150), but a modern touch is added with wireless Internet access in each. Breakfast is made with local ingredients, including edible flowers.

A larger hotel catering to frequent travelers, the **Oxford Suites** (9550 Silverdale Way NW, Silverdale, 888/698-7848, www.oxfordsuitessilverdale.com, $129-189 d) makes you feel at home with a complimentary hot breakfast buffet, as well as complimentary evening receptions featuring appetizers and your choice of wine, beer, or soft drinks. It's also pet-friendly and has room service.

Food

The best bang for your buck in Bremerton can be found at ★ **Hi-Lo's 15th Street Café** (2720 15th St., 360/373-7833, 7am-3pm daily, $6-12), but only if you're looking for breakfast or lunch. They don't serve dinner here, but they don't need to; the reputation they've built over the years for the first two meals of the day is strong. The place is quirky, and the breakfasts big and hearty. Try The Standard, if only for the yummy house potatoes.

Anthony's Home Port (20 Washington Ave., 360/377-5004, www.anthonys.com, 11am-10pm daily, $12-35) may be a chain, albeit a small, regional one, but that doesn't mean it's not worthy of mention as a place to visit. Located next to the Kitsap Conference

Center, the restaurant has excellent views, and an even more-excellent alder-planked salmon dinner.

Noah's Ark (1516 6th St., 360/377-8100, www.noahsark-restaurant.com, 10am-8pm Mon.-Sat., $5-10) is kind of a greasy spoon and isn't very fancy, but it has been in the community since 1974 for a reason: It's good, and no burger costs more than $5.99.

If you've never been to a place that specializes in french fries and beer, well, you should go. That's exactly what ★ **Fritz European Fry House** (94 Washington Ave., 360/479-1088, 7:30am-9:30pm Mon.-Fri., 10am-10pm Sat., 11am-8pm Sun., $3-12) has to offer, along with deep-fried baskets of chicken, sausage, and more. But the Belgian-style fries are the real treat, served in a paper cone with your choice of more than a dozen dipping sauces, including curry ketchup and Thai peanut.

La Fermata (2204 E. 11th St., 360/373-5827, 5pm-10pm Tues.-Sat., $12-37) in East Bremerton, near the water and the Manette Bridge, is a welcome slice of Italy in blue-collarville.

Silver City Restaurant & Brewery (2799 NW Myhre Road, Silverdale, 360/698-5879, 11am-10pm Mon.-Thurs., 11am-11pm Fri.-Sat., 11am-9pm Sun., www.silvercity-brewery.com, $19-31) is best known for its award-winning beers, but the food here is fantastic and artistically presented as well. This place is also kid-friendly.

Information and Services

Information in Bremerton is easy to come by. There's an information booth and the city's ferry terminal, and there's also the **Bremerton Area Chamber of Commerce** (286 4th St. 360/479-3579, www.bremerton-chamber.org, 9am-5pm Mon.-Fri.).

Getting There and Around

Kitsap Transit (206/373-2877 or 800/501-7433, www.kitsaptransit.org) provides bus service across the entire Kitsap Peninsula, and also offers a **foot ferry** (www.kitsaptransit.org, $2) that runs several times a day from Bremerton across Sinclair Inlet to ferry docks in Port Orchard and Annapolis. The foot ferry is a busy one, shuffling roughly 500,000 passengers across the inlet each year.

Washington State Ferries (800/843-3779 or 888/808-7977, www.wsdot.wa.gov) also makes the 55-minute trip from Bremerton to Seattle several times a day. One-way costs for the 35-minute trip are $8 for walkers; $7.65

Silver City Restaurant & Brewery in Silverdale is known for its award-winning beer.

for motorcyclists and their bikes; and $17.30 for drivers and their cars.

HIGHWAY 3

Highway 3 serves as the main connecting route between Shelton, on what is considered the main portion of the Olympic Peninsula, and Bremerton, in the central part of Kitsap Peninsula. Highway 3 slices through many small towns and communities on its way north into Kitsap Peninsula.

Sights

Located at Case Inlet in Southern Puget Sound, the **Allyn Waterfront Dock & Park** (18560 Hwy. 3) features a boat launch, a dock, a playground with gazebo, and plenty of room for picnicking at one of the prettiest and less-frequented water-access points in the area. The dock is historic, built in 1922, and was used for mail delivery and as a stop for the local ferry. Each July, the free **Allyn Days Festival,** with its oyster-shucking competitions, beer garden, and excellent salmon dinner, is held here.

Bordered by Case Inlet on the east, **Harstine Island** is a large island mostly filled with forests and just a smattering of residents, businesses, and parks. Pickering Road, about seven miles northeast of Shelton off Highway 3, is the only road leading to the island.

At Harstine's northern tip is **Jarrell Cove State Park** (391 E. Wingert Rd., www.parks.wa.gov), a tent-only campground that's a popular pit stop for boaters and kayakers. There are campsites here ($22-36) open year-round, as well as some trails and an opportunity to view wildlife.

Despite its lack of many permanent residents, the island isn't devoid of culture. The **Harstine Island Farmers Market** is held Saturdays during the summer at the Harstine Island Community Club (3371 E. Harstine Island Rd. N.), and the **Harstine Island Gallery** (970 E. Maples Rd., 360/426.8840, www.harstinegallery.com, noon-5pm Sat.-Sun.) features beautiful and unique pottery created on-site by John Dunlap.

Sports and Recreation

The four miles of **Theler Wetland Trails** (off Hwy. 3 across from Belfair Elementary School, Belfair, www.thelertrails.org) are a must-see for nature lovers. Their setting among the 75 or so acres of wildlife preserve at the point where the freshwater of the Union River meets up with Hood Canal's saltwater is full of fish, birds, beaver, otters, foxes, and much more. The interpretive-sign-filled trails themselves are accessed through an artistic steel gate and are easy to navigate. All are wheelchair-accessible, flat, and short, the longest being the 1.5-mile Union Estuary trek. The wetlands were donated by the Theler family, and today serve not only as a recreational site but also as an educational one for area students. The **Mary E. Theler Community Center** (360/275-4898) is located on-site, and also is used for educational purposes, hosting community events throughout the year. The **Native Plant Demonstration Gardens** are located behind the community center. There's also an exhibit center here, though it's open only sporadically. During certain seasons, including migratory season, guided bird walks are held.

The 27-hole **Lakeland Village Golf Course** (200 E. Old Ranch Rd., Allyn, 360/275-6100, www.lakelandvillagegolf.com, $36 greens fees) is in the middle of a residential community near Anderson Lake and is open to the public year-round.

Shopping

The **Belfair Farmers Market** (www.belfairfarmersmarket.org, 10am-4pm Sat., May-Sept.) is held in Theler Center's south parking lot off Hwy. 3 across from Belfair Elementary School and uses a portion of its proceeds to fund scholarships for local high school students.

Accommodations

The best lodging bets for those traveling Highway 3 are located in and around Shelton and Bremerton, but the **Belfair Motel** (23322

NE Hwy. 3, Belfair, 360/275-4485, www.belfairmotel.net, $57-75 d) isn't a bad option for those wishing to stay in this area. The rooms are basic, but they are clean and, for a $10 fee, pets are welcome, too.

Food

Spencer Lake Bar & Grill (1180 E. Pickering, Shelton, 360/426-2505, www.spencerlake.com, 7am-midnight Sun.-Thurs., 7am-2am Fri.-Sat.) is kid- and adult-friendly, with its mostly American menu of hamburgers, seafood baskets, and chicken. The food here is good and so is the setting on this quiet and lesser-known lake.

If a good view in a relaxing setting is what you're after, **Lennard K's Boat House Restaurant & Bar** (18340 Hwy. 3, Allyn, 360/275-6060, www.lennardks.com, 11am-midnight Mon.-Fri., 8am-1am Sat.-Sun.) has what you're looking for. The restaurant has a large outdoor deck that overlooks the North Bay of beautiful Case Inlet, and a lawn so you can enjoy a burger and a microbrew outside when the weather is nice. The food here may be average American fare, but the location is second to none.

Casper's Pizza & Barbecue (23730 NE Hwy. 3, Belfair, 360/275-7427, 11:30am-8pm Mon.-Fri., noon-8pm Sat., noon-7pm Sun.) has gluten-free pizza that doesn't taste much different from the real stuff, a bulldog for a logo, a real-life bulldog for a shop mascot, and a deep-dish bacon, pepperoni, sausage, and salami pizza named the Bulldog. Why the obsession with bulldogs? Well, it is the local high school's mascot. Since this is the place locals go for pie, it's also a perfect fit.

GIG HARBOR

Gig Harbor (pop. 7,200) looks exactly like one would expect the harbor in a Hollywood movie to look like. It's small, there are plenty of water and boats here, and the city's pedestrian-friendly waterfront is loaded with businesses selling everything from ice cream and clam chowder to books and contemporary clothing. The city is located in south Puget Sound directly across the water from the metropolitan city of Tacoma, which means there's often a steady stream of urbanites crossing the Tacoma Narrows bridge to explore here (and then paying a $5.50 toll on the other Narrows bridge to return home). That the toll doesn't deter them from coming speaks well to what Gig Harbor has to offer. In addition to its excellent waterfront and renowned maritime-related historical museum, Gig Harbor has plenty of parks and water-access points perfect for kayakers and boaters looking to take a lazy run through the sound or even across it to Tacoma's beautiful Point Defiance Park.

Sights

★ Harbor History Museum

The **Harbor History Museum** (4121 Harborview Dr., 253/858-6722, www.harborhistorymuseum.org, 10am-5pm. Tues.-Sun., $7 adults, $6 seniors and military, $5 ages 7-17, children under 6 free) recently relocated to a new, larger facility on the waterfront and has become the gem of Gig Harbor. About 7,000 square feet of permanent exhibits include a restored one-room schoolhouse, artifacts that tell the rich history of the area—such as information about the three Narrows bridges, including the one that collapsed during a major storm in 1940—a 65-foot fishing vessel and a sailboat, information about the area's first Native American settlers, and more. The museum has new exhibits, too. Check out the calendar to learn about special events occurring during your visit.

Wilkinson Farm

Just outside downtown Gig Harbor it is as if time stood still at **Wilkinson Farm** (4118 Rosedale St. NW, 253/851-8136). The farm dates back to the early 20th century when it was developed by the Wilkinson family and was run as a dairy and a farm. The big barn was built in 1915. In 2001, the city bought the property to preserve it, and there still is a holly orchard, outhouses, and more to see. In 2008, the property that once belonged to

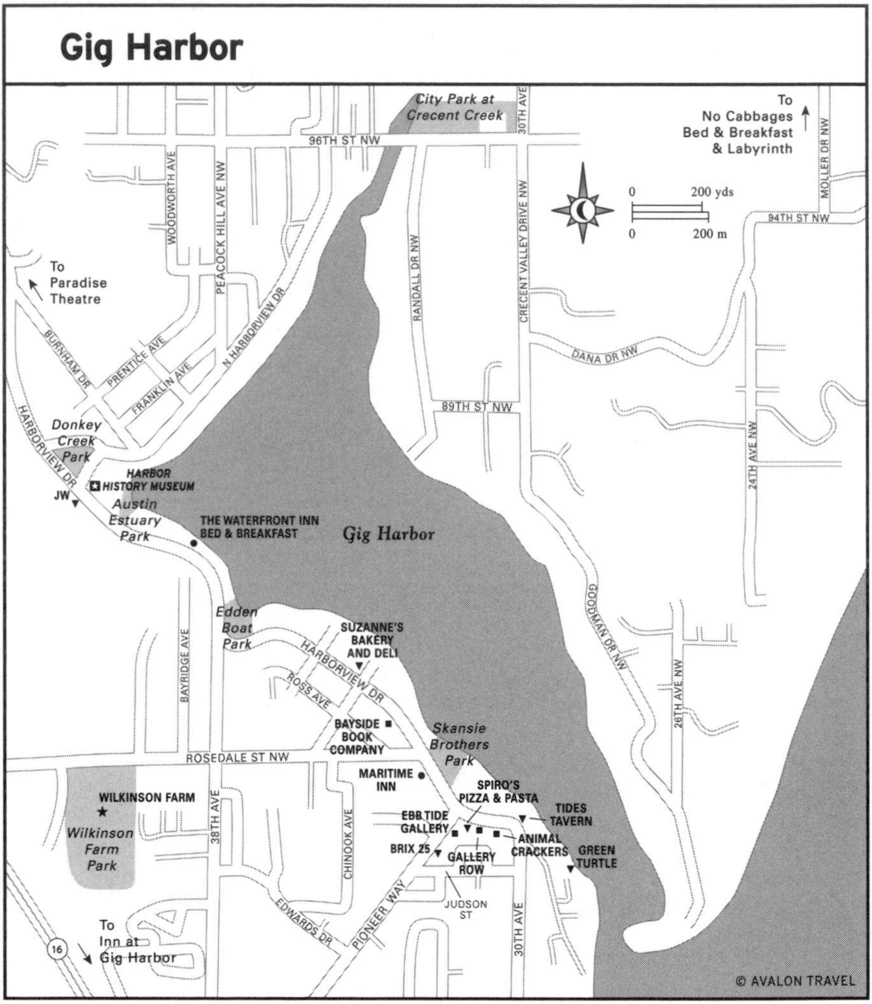

Gig Harbor

early pioneers was added to the state's list of historic barns.

Narrows Park

Narrows Park (1502 Lucille Pkwy., www.penmetparks.org, 7am-dusk daily) offers stunning views of the twin Narrows suspension bridges, which connect Gig Harbor to Tacoma. The 34-acre park on the shores of the Puget Sound has paved paths, a sandy, rocky beach, a gazebo, and telescopes to help get an even closer look at both bridges.

Kopachuck State Park

Kopachuck State Park (11712 56th St. NW, 253/265-3606, www.parks.wa.gov, $21-25 tent) is about five miles west of Gig Harbor and is a 109-acre marine and camping park that offers swimming, fishing, hiking, and picnic areas. There is a lot to see here, too, including wildlife such as starfish, hawks, and raccoons, and the snowcapped tops of the Olympics in the distance. The park used to be a seasonal fishing spot for the Puyallup and Nisqually tribes. Unique to this wooded park getaway is **Cutts**

Island, reachable only by boat about 0.5 mile from shore. The park is open year-round 8am-dusk for day use. The campgrounds are usually open late April to early October. There are 41 tent spaces, and most can accommodate large RVs, although there aren't any hookups. Tent camping is first-come, first-served. Be warned, however: The campgrounds are occasionally closed due to tree-health concerns. Always call ahead to check on campground status.

Sports and Recreation

The only public golf course in Gig Harbor is **Madrona Links Golf Course** (3604 22nd Ave. NW, 253/851-5193, www.madronalinks.com, $25-27 greens fees). It's an 18-hole, par-71 course with decent greens and an even more decent price tag.

Gig Harbor is a favorite spot for water enthusiasts who like to boat, kayak, and sail in adjacent Puget Sound during the warmer months. **Gig Harbor Rent-A-Boat** (8829 N. Harborview Dr., 253/858-7341, www.gigharborrentaboat.com) is the best place to get powerboats, paddleboards, kayaks, and more, and to sign up for tours, including the neat self-guided kayak tour where your personal smartphone becomes your tour guide.

Entertainment and Events

Paradise Theatre (9911 Burnham Dr. NW, 253/851-7529, www.paradisetheatre.org) hosts shows in its new performance venue.

The Galaxy Theatre Uptown (4649 Point Fosdick Dr. NW, 253/857-7469, www.galaxytheatres.com) is a luxury movie theater that offers family fun as well as a 21-and-over VIP room that includes beer, wine, luxury seats, and servers. At $11 for an adult ticket, the reserved-seating place is a little more expensive than most movie theaters in the area, but the extra cost is worth it for the quality.

The Gig Harbor Art Walk (www.gigharborguide.com) is held 5pm-8pm the second Thursday of every month in downtown Gig Harbor. It recently was recognized by *Sunset* magazine as one of the best art walks in the Northwest. There's a reason for that: There is plenty to see and do here.

Find fresh food and buy arts and crafts at the **Gig Harbor Farmers Market** (www.gigharborfarmersmarket.com, 9am-3pm Sat. Apr.-Dec.) in downtown Gig Harbor.

The first full weekend of June is the time for **Maritime Gig** (www.maritimegig.com), which includes a grand parade, historic boat displays, food, and entertainment. The **Gig Harbor Garden Tour** (www.gigharborgardentour.com) is an annual event that takes place in early summer.

Enjoy outdoor music in the park during **Summer Sounds at Skansie** on Tuesdays from June through August at Skansie Brothers Park (3207 Harborview Dr., 253/853-3554). Outdoor movies are held at Skansie Brothers Park and Donkey Creek Park (8714 Harborview Dr., 253/857-4842) on alternating weekends.

The **Gig Harbor Summer Arts Festival** (www.peninsulaartleague.com) is usually a two-day event held in July and showcases art from more than 100 artists, and there are food vendors, too.

A newer, but popular event is the **Gig Harbor Food and Wine Festival** (www.harborwineandfoodfest.com). It's usually held in August.

The Cruise the Narrows Classic Car Show (www.gigharborcruisers.com) is usually held at Uptown Gig Harbor in August and features a variety of makes and models of cars including classics.

The **Greater Gig Harbor Open Studio Tour** (www.gigharboropenstudiotour.org) is usually held in September, and it's a time when local artists open their studios for public tours.

See local, regional, and international films during the **Gig Harbor Film Festival** (253/851-3456, www.gigharborfilmfestival.org) held each October. The **Gig Harbor Tree Lighting** is the first Saturday in December at Skansie Brothers Park (3211 Harborview Dr.), and it's followed the next week by the

Gig Harbor Annual Lighted Boat Parade (253/851-1807).

Shopping

It's fun to shop in Gig Harbor because whether you're downtown or in the new Uptown Gig Harbor area, there is something for everyone, from boutiques to arts and crafts stores, gifts, and more. Downtown's shops line the picturesque waterfront area.

It will be easy to add to your art collection here, thanks to the sheer number of art shops in the area, such as **Gallery Row** (3102 Harborview Dr., 253/851-6020, www.gigharborgalleryrow.com, 10am-5pm Mon.-Sat., noon-5pm Sun.). It features several local artists and a variety of works from jewelry to acrylics. Or head to the **Ebb Tide Gallery** (7809 Pioneer Way, 253/851-5293, www.ebbtidegalleryofgifts.com, 10am-5pm daily).

Animal Crackers (3026 Harborview Dr., 253/858-1795, www.anicrackers.com, 9am-7pm Mon.-Sat., 10am-7pm Sun.) has new and gently used baby and kids' clothing and toys. There are a lot of premium brand names here.

For fashion for mom, head to **Emilie Gallery & Boutique** (3133 Harborview Dr., 253/858-7736, noon-5pm Sun.-Mon., 11am-5pm Tues.-Sat.) where there are not only clothes, but also jewelry and gift items. For more gifts or some local wines, head to **The Keeping Room** (7811 Pioneer Way, 253/858-9170, www.gigharborwinegiftshop.com, open daily, 12:30pm-5pm daily).

Find all sorts of treasures from games to clocks to model planes and boats at **The Harbor Mercantile** (7807 Pioneer Way, 253/851-8510, 11am-5:30pm Mon.-Sat.).

Book lovers will be happy in downtown Gig Harbor, as there are three bookstores within walking distance of each other. The newest is **Gig Harbor Book Company** (inside Harbor Landing Mall, 3226 Harborview Dr., 253/970-9899, 11am-5:30pm Tues.-Sun.), which has books of all types, but is strongest on children's books, classics, history, and fantasy.

Shop and dine at **Uptown Gig Harbor** (4701 Point Fosdick Dr., www.uptowngigharbor.com, 10am-8pm Mon.-Sat., 11am-6pm Sun.). The newer shopping destination features several men's, women's, and children's clothing shops such as Ann Taylor LOFT, Chico's, Justice for Girls, and Indigo Plum to name a few. There are also places to dine and get a mani/pedi, catch a movie, or enjoy an ice cream cone from Ben & Jerry's.

Accommodations

If you want to stay mere steps away from the water in Gig Harbor, ★ **The Maritime Inn** (3212 Harborview Dr., 253/858-1818, www.maritimeinn.com, $129-198 s or d) is the place. The rooms in this award-winning boutique hotel are welcoming, luxurious, and romantic. Many have jetted tubs, fireplaces, and super-nice sheets. The location and the free continental breakfast make this place special.

The Best Western Wesley Inn (6575 Kimball Dr., 253/858-9690 or 888/462-0002, www.wesleyinn.com, $170-220 d), just a short drive from downtown Gig Harbor, is a clean, nice place to stay and has a pool and a complimentary breakfast. It's a great choice for traveling families, as the most expensive rates apply only to the suites with balconies and whirlpool tubs.

Located on Gig Harbor Bay on the edge of town, **The Waterfront Inn Bed & Breakfast** (9017 N. Harborview Dr., 253/857-0770, www.waterfront-inn.com, $99-219 s or d) offers a variety of cozy rooms with stunning views.

Just minutes from downtown Gig Harbor is a stunning country estate called **Bear's Lair Bed & Breakfast** (13706 92nd Ave. Ct. NW, 253/857-8877 or 877/855-9768, www.bearslairbb.com, $125-225 s or d). The more expensive rate is for the Carriage House that is private and separate from the main house and features more than 1,000 square feet of space.

No Cabbages Bed & Breakfast & Labyrinth (10319 Sunrise Beach Dr. NW, 253/858-7797, www.nocabbages.com, $80-135 d) is all about creating a serene and peaceful environment to rejuvenate and recharge the soul in a rustic, naturally Northwest environment. Located about five minutes from downtown, the B&B allows "good dogs and good kids" to stay. The views are of the forest that surrounds the grounds.

The Inn at Gig Harbor (3211 56th St. NW, 253/858-1111, www.innatgigharbor.com, $161-215 s or d) has everything you want from a well-appointed hotel: nice rooms and plenty of them, a conference center, restaurant, and fitness center and day spa to mention a few of the amenities.

On beautiful Wollochet Bay, about five minutes from Gig Harbor, is the **Westbay Guest Cottage** (2515 48th Ave. NW, 253/265-3033 or 800/420-3033, www.westbaycottage.com, $145-250 d). The home features a full kitchen and it's not a B&B. There's a two-night minimum, and up to four people can fit in the larger room.

Bring Fido to the **Westwynd Motel** (6703 144th St. NW, Purdy, 253/857-4047 or 800/468-9963, www.westwyndmotel.com, $62-105 d), located outside Gig Harbor in the small town of Purdy. This quaint place features one- and two-bedroom rooms with kitchenettes. It's one of the best bargains around.

Also just outside Gig Harbor is the ★ **Nadeau's Olde Glencove Hotel** (9418 Glencove Rd., 253/884-2835, www.glencovehotel.com, $75-85 s or d). Originally built in 1897 as a resort hotel, this Victorian stunner was the private home of the current owners for many years until they decided to again open it to tourists. Often sought out for weddings, the historical home is tucked among towering trees off the beaten path, about 12 miles from Gig Harbor. The rooms are cozy and comfortable and surprisingly affordable.

Food

★ **Tides Tavern** (2925 Harborview Dr., 253/858-3982, www.tidestavern.com, 11am-10pm Mon.-Thurs., 11am-11pm Fri., 9am-11pm Sat., 9am-10pm Sun., $10-24) is a place where you can arrive by car or boat, and it's been an institution on the Harbor since 1973. Not only are there juicy burgers, thick clam chowder, and the freshest fish-and-chips here, but there's also a large beer and wine selection. Sit on the deck or enjoy the view from inside. This place isn't fancy by any means, but a visit to the Harbor isn't complete without stopping. The only caveat? You have to be 21 or older. It is a tavern, after all.

If you are looking for something a little more upscale with a water view, **The Green Turtle** (2905 Harborview Dr., 253/851-3167,

The Maritime Inn is just steps away from the Gig Harbor waterfront.

www.thegreenturtle.com, 11am-2pm and 4:30pm-9pm Mon.-Sat., $22-34) is next door to the Tides Tavern. It serves a variety of classic fresh seafood dishes—some with a bit of an Asian flair. Lunch and dinner are served here, and if you are planning on the latter, reservations are recommended.

If Asian food is what you're craving, head to the **Thai Hut** (4116 Harborview Dr., 253/858-8523, www.thaihut.net, 11am-3pm daily, $8-11). The decor leaves much to be desired, but this quaint place serves up some good food that's loved by locals. If ambience is also on your wish list, head to ★ **Le-Le** in Uptown Gig Harbor (Point Fosdick Dr. NW, 253/514-6382, www.lelerestaurant.com, 11am-9pm Mon.-Thurs., 11am-11pm Fri.-Sat., 11am-9pm Sun., $14-29). Expect classic Thai and Vietnamese dishes and, on weekends, live pianists playing as you dine. Try the *banh xeo* (Saigon crepe) or the Vietnamese macaroni.

Another beautiful place to eat is the award-winning ★ **Brix 25** (7707 Pioneer Way, 253/858-6626, www.harborbrix.com, 4:30pm-9:30pm Mon.-Sat., $26-36). There's an extensive wine list, handcrafted cocktails, and fine Northwest dishes that will make your mouth water, such as sausage and squash ravioli ($24) and Brix Signature Beef Bourguignon: braised beef short ribs and tender veggies swimming in a thick and rich burgundy sauce paired with creamy Yukon Gold mashers ($28). If you are planning to eat dinner here, reservations are recommended.

New to the Gig Harbor scene but also quickly making a name for itself is **JW** (4107 Harborview Dr., 253/858-3529, www.jw-gigharbor.com, 4pm-10pm Fri.-Sat., 4pm-9pm Sun.-Thurs., closed Mon., $19-27). Try the honey walnut prawns on the appetizer menu for $10.

A popular new, casual place to grab a burger is the **Blazing Onion Burger Company** in Uptown (4701 Point Fosdick Dr. NW, 253/514-6703, www.blazingonion.com, 11am-10pm Sun.-Thurs., 11am-11pm Fri.-Sat., $9-13). It's also a great place to watch the game.

Grab a craft beer, in a can, at **7 Seas Brewing** (3006 Judson St #110, 253/514-8129, www.7seasbrewing.com, 11am-8pm Sun.-Tues., 11am-9pm Wed.-Sat.). This award-winning company has a taproom that's open Wednesday through Sunday and offers not only beer, but cool merchandise.

For pizza and the works, go to **Spiro's Pizza & Pasta** (3108 Harborview Dr., 253/851-9200, www.spirosgh.com, 11am-9pm Sun.-Thurs., 11am-10pm Fri.-Sat., $10-25) or **Pizzeria Fondi** (4621 Point Fosdick Dr., 253/851-6666, www.fondi.com, 11am-9pm Sun.-Thurs., 11am-10pm Fri.-Sat., $7-14), where it's all about panini, pasta, pizza, and of course, dolci (dessert).

Get a big fat cinnamon roll for breakfast or a big fat sandwich for lunch at **Susanne's Bakery and Deli** (3411 Harborview Dr., 253/853-6220, 7am-5pm Tues.-Sun., closed Mon., $6-10).

Information and Services

The **Gig Harbor Chamber of Commerce** (3125 Judson St., 253/851-6865, www.gigharborchamber.com, 10am-5pm Mon.-Fri.) is conveniently located near the city's popular waterfront and has a friendly staff.

Getting There and Around

Being located so close to a major city has its advantages. Gig Harbor is served by a major bus system, **Pierce Transit** (253/581-8000 or 800/562-8109, www.piercetransit.org), which connects the small town with metropolitan areas in Puget Sound and beyond.

Recently, a second bridge over the Tacoma Narrows to Gig Harbor has been built, and crossing it requires paying a toll. There is no toll to cross over from Tacoma into Gig Harbor, but it costs $5.50 per car to cross the Narrows in the opposite direction.

BAINBRIDGE ISLAND

Bainbridge Island (pop. 21,000) is sort of a middle ground for travelers. It rests in the middle of Puget Sound directly west of and just a 35-minute ferry ride away from Seattle.

City dwellers and suburbanites alike often use the island as a local getaway, a water-surrounded playground filled with artistic shops, museums, and second homes. A bridge over the Agate Passage connects the northern portion of the island to the Kitsap Peninsula at Suquamish. From there, the entire Kitsap and Olympic Peninsulas are accessible by car.

History

The story of the history of Bainbridge Island reads similar to that of most other regions in Western Washington. For thousands of years, Native Americans, including those from the Suquamish tribe, lived on the island, fishing its coastal waters and bays, hunting its wildlife, and harvesting its timber for personal use.

British Royal Navy Captain George Vancouver, as he did at several places in this section of the world, left his mark here, too. In 1792, Vancouver spent several days at what now is known as Blakely Harbor in the southern part of the island. Vancouver named several of the island's sites, as did U.S. Navy Lieutenant Charles Wilkes, who visited the area in 1841. Wilkes named the island after William Bainbridge, who had been a naval hero during the War of 1812. In 1855, Suquamish leader Chief Kitsap signed a treaty with the U.S. government stating his tribe would vacate the island and move north.

Americans, as well as Asian immigrants looking to work in the area's logging and shipbuilding industries, began moving to the island. Until recently, the largest sawmill in the world was located here, at Port Blakely. Fort Ward was built on the southern portion of the island in the early 1900s to help protect the U.S. Naval Station at Bremerton. The fort was decommissioned in the 1950s and today serves as a popular state park. Many of the island's current residents commute by ferry to Seattle and beyond for work. In 1991, the city of Winslow, located near the mouth of Eagle Harbor in the west, annexed the rest of the 10-mile-long and 5-mile-wide island. Today, the entire island is known as the City of Bainbridge Island, and Winslow is the name for its artsy, waterfront center.

Sights

Bainbridge Island Historical Museum

History, of course, is what can be found at the **Bainbridge Island Historical Museum** (215 Ericksen Ave. NE, 206/842-2773, www.bainbridgehistory.org, 10am-4pm daily, $4 adults, $3 students and seniors, $10 family) The museum doesn't attempt to do anything

During summer, the Pierce Transit trolley runs throughout Gig Harbor.

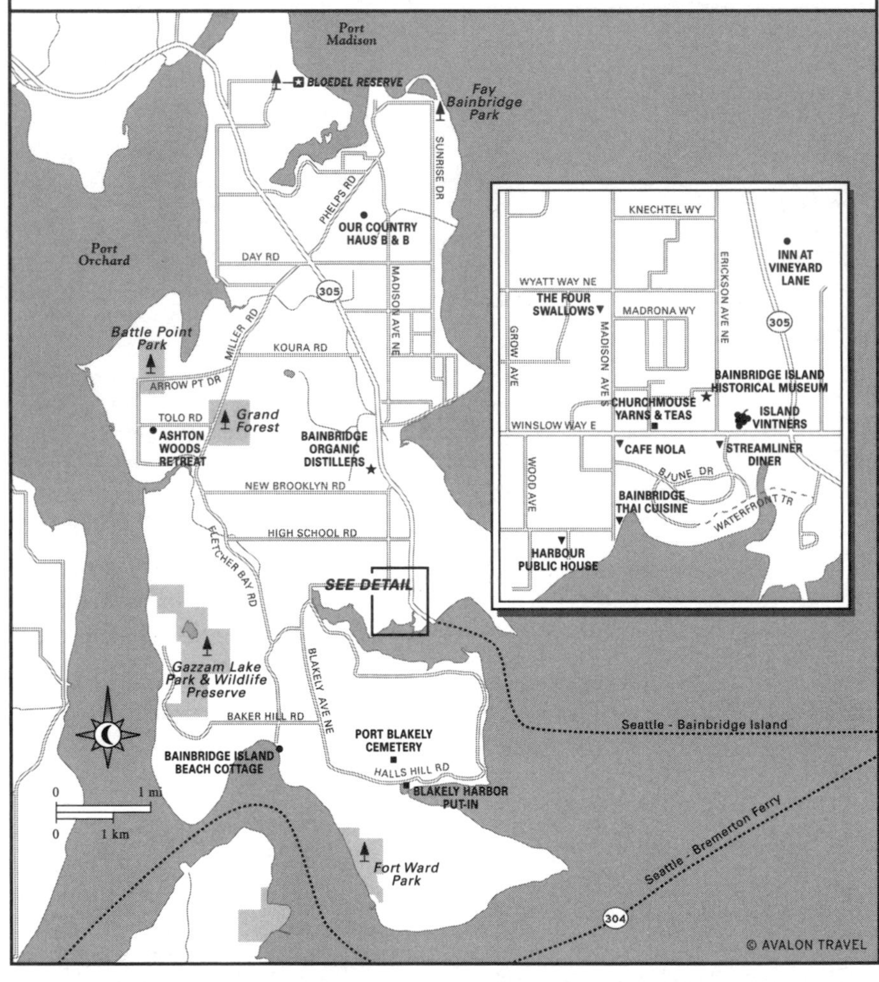

but tell the story of the island, as its new permanent exhibit, *An Island Story: A Voyage Through Bainbridge History,* would indicate. Such focus is a good thing, as there isn't much space in this one-room building, a former schoolhouse built in 1908 and located at Strawberry Hill Park, just three blocks from a busy ferry terminal. But focus doesn't mean lack of depth. There's a wealth of history here, including photographs, art, books, a friendly and knowledgeable staff, and much more. The history of Japanese American internment during World War II paints a fascinating story of how much society has changed in a relatively short period of time.

★ Bloedel Reserve

By name alone, it's difficult to tell what **Bloedel Reserve** (7571 NE Dolphin Dr., 206/842-7631, www.bloedelreserve.org, 10am-4pm Tues.-Sun., $15 adults, $10 seniors, $8 ages 5-12, children under 4 free) actually is.

After you've set foot on this quiet, 150-acre public garden located on the northern tip of Bainbridge Island, it still may be difficult to describe exactly where you are, if only because words aren't easy to come by here. There's a Japanese garden, towering trees, trails, views of Port Madison Bay from a bluff, a reflection garden with pool, and much more. Also on the grounds is the former home of timber baron Prentice Bloedel and his wife, Virginia. The mansion now is a visitors center. The reserve used to be limited to just 20 people at a time to maintain the serenity. That isn't the case anymore, but the reserve's end-of-the-road location six miles east of Highway 305 helps keep most traffic away.

Fort Ward Park

It's not quite as big as the Bloedel Reserve, but **Fort Ward Park** (www.biparks.org) is a great place to visit in its own right, with 137 acres of recreational opportunities, including 2.5 miles of hiking trails, and nearly a mile of saltwater shoreline. The military history here is another reason to visit. The fort once was part of a vast coastal defense system and specifically designed to protect the Bremerton Naval Shipyard. The fort was decommissioned in 1958 and it became a state park two years later. Today, it is owned by the Bainbridge Island Parks & Recreation District. A paved road that runs along the beach portion of the park is closed to vehicles, which makes it a great place to walk or ride bikes. There are more than a dozen picnic tables and a boat launch area ($7) on-site, and the park is a great place to scuba dive.

Fay Bainbridge Park

Located at northeast tip of the island, **Fay Bainbridge Park** (www.biparks.org) is at the opposite end of the island from Fort Ward, and what it has to offer is opposite in many ways, as well. While Fort Ward, for example, only has primitive campsites, camping is Fay Bainbridge's main draw. There are 26 standard sites ($23), 15 tent sites ($15), and 26 sites with water for RVs ($23). The park's proximity to bustling Puget Sound makes it a popular one during summer months, especially at the beach area. Location isn't the only thing that makes it popular, though. There are showers here, horseshoe and fire pits on the beach, kitchen shelters, boating facilities, a playground, and more. Another, now permanent, attraction is the historic bell at the park's entrance. It came from San Francisco in 1883 to be used as a school bell, and eventually ended up here.

Gazzam Lake Park and Wildlife Preserve

Despite some development, Bainbridge Island still is heavily forested. As such, there are plenty of opportunities to get out, away from it all, and explore. The **Gazzam Lake Park and Wildlife Preserve** (www.biparks.org) area in the island's southwestern section is a good place to start. The 445-acre park is full of forests, wetlands, and trails, many of which are unspoiled by man or development of any sort. This means the wildlife here, including deer, owls, and coyotes, is indeed wild. Access the area from Deerpath Road in the south or Marshall Road in the north.

Sports and Recreation

The most popular inland trail system on the island can be found off Miller Road in the west and Mandus Olson Road in the east at **Grand Forest.** There are only three miles of trails here, but they are heavily forested. Manzanita Park to the north off Day Road West has two miles of trails that are frequently used by horses.

Hikers who want to stay nearer to the water should visit the former mill site at **Blakely Harbor Park** (off Blakely Ave. NE). One trail here leads north to the **Port Blakely Cemetery,** the first cemetery in the area and created in 1880. **Battle Point Park** (11299 Arrow Point Dr. NE) is one of the more-developed parks on the island. Located at the site of a former naval radio station, the park's soccer fields, basketball courts, and play areas get plenty of use year-round, as does its jogging trail. The navy's former transmitter station has been renovated and now is used as a gym.

Entertainment and Events

Wineries

There are several wineries sprouting up on Bainbridge Island. At **Island Vintners** (450 Winslow Way E., 206/451-4344, www.islandvintners.com, 2pm-6pm Mon.-Wed., 2pm-7pm Thurs., 1pm-7pm Fri.-Sat., noon-6pm Sun.) you can sample three of the local wines in this tasting room. About seven small boutique wineries belong to the **Winery Alliance of Bainbridge Island** (www.bainbridgewineries.com). Four of them have their own tasting rooms and are a short walk from the ferry terminal. There are more wineries in addition to the ones that belong to the alliance. Perhaps that's why in 2010 *Sunset* magazine named Bainbridge Island the new Northwest wine destination.

Bainbridge Organic Distillers (9727 Coppertop Loop NE, Ste. 101, 206/842-3184, www.bainbridgedistillers.com, 11am-5pm daily) features an ultra-sleek tasting room. Spirits are crafted in small batches here. It's one of the first and few distillers in the state.

Festivals and Events

Fridays generally are universally loved, as far as days of the week go, but they are even more so here, especially the first ones of each month. That's when the **First Friday Art Walks** are held in Winslow and galleries, salons, bakeries, and wine shops participate. During the last few months of the year, the first-Friday love spreads north, where **First Friday Concerts** (Island Center Hall, 8395 Fletcher Bay Rd.) are held on a corner stage in 90-year-old Island Center Hall.

Saturdays also are pretty popular on the island, particularly so from April through mid-November, thanks to the **Bainbridge Island Farmers Market** (Town Square at City Hall Park, Madison Ave. and Winslow Way, www.bainbridgefarmersmarket.com, 9am-1pm Apr.-Nov.).

The **Chilly Hilly** bike ride is 33 miles long, hilly, and held in February, which is how it gets its name. It also attracts thousands of riders. In March, the unique **Celluloid Bainbridge Film Festival** is held at the Historic Lynwood Theater (4560 Lynwood Center Rd.) to celebrate and watch films with local connections, meaning the film either could have been shot on the island or featured a past or present resident as part of its cast or crew. Surprisingly, for such a small town, there are many big-screen connections. Past films shown include *It Came from Outer Space,* Woody Allen's *What's Up, Tiger Lily?,* and *The Last Detail,* featuring Jack Nicholson.

In June, the **No More Schoolapalooza** means concerts in Waterfront Park, and July in Winslow is popular for its **Grand Old Fourth** celebration, including a parade and street fair, sans fireworks. Summer at Waterfront Park is synonymous with music. In July the Concerts in the Park series begins here, and in August, there's an outdoor music festival.

Shopping

If you are into yarns, stop by **Churchmouse Yarns & Tea** (118 Madrone Ln. N., 206/780-2686, www.churchmouseyarns.com, 10am-6pm Sun.-Wed., 10am-8pm Thurs.-Fri.). There is a variety of yarns, patterns, and more here.

The Eagle Harbor Book Co. (157 Winslow Way E., 206/842-5332, www.eagleharborbooks.com, 9am-7pm Mon.-Fri., 9am-6pm Sat., 10am-6pm Sun.) is a small, local bookstore that has a lot of book selections, both new and used.

Bainbridge Arts & Crafts (151 Winslow Way E., 206/842-3132, www.bacart.org, 10am-6pm Mon.-Sat., 11am-5pm Sun.) features more than 300 artists' works. It was founded in 1948. The exhibitions here are constantly changing.

Accommodations

Actually two cottages—a studio and a two-bedroom—the ★ **Bainbridge Island Beach Cottage** (4323 Pleasant Beach Dr.

NE, 206/999-9655, $150-250) sits on Pleasant Beach at the southern end of Bainbridge Island, and is just a block away from a movie theater, restaurants, and shopping. Doing the math makes it easy to see: You probably want to book ahead since there's a very limited number of availabilities here. The view is spectacular, the yard is large, and the interior homey.

Designed like a French country-style carriage house, **Our Country Haus B&B** (13718 Ellingson Rd. NE, 206/842-8425, www.ourcountryhaus.com, $150 d) is available year-round as a nightly, weekly, or monthly rental.

On the site of the former Bainbridge Island Vineyard and Winery, the **Inn at Vineyard Lane** (978 NE Vineyard Ln., 206/842-9300, www.innatvineyardlane.com, $169-179 d) features amenities ranging from waterfront activities to wine tastings. Meeting space for corporate retreats also is available.

Food

★ **Café Nola** (101 Winslow Way E., 206/842-3822, www.cafenola.com, lunch 11am-3pm Mon.-Fri., dinner 5pm-9pm Thurs.-Mon., brunch 9:30am-3pm Sat.-Sun., $16-31) is going to be crowded, that's almost a given. Its location near the busy ferry terminal is one reason, but the main reason is that the food served here is unique and good. Yes, this technically is a café, but the menu isn't a soup-and-sandwiches type place. The items here are spendy. The French toast, made with challah bread, has been featured on the Food Network.

Located directly on the water, the **Harbour Public House** (231 Parfitt Way SW, 206/842-0969, www.harbourpub.com, 11am-midnight daily, $13-19) is a fish-and-chips joint with a history. The building it's located in used to be a family's home and was built in 1881.

The Four Swallows (481 Madison Ave. N, 206/842-3397, www.fourswallows.com, 5:30pm-close Tues.-Sat., $15-39) is a sparkly clean restaurant with an extensive wine bar, featuring Italian and Pacific Northwest cuisine.

★ **The Streamliner Diner** (397 Winslow Way, 206/842-8595, www.streamlinerdiner.com, 7am-2:30pm Mon.-Sat., 7:30am-2:30pm Sun., dinner 5pm-9pm Tues.-Thurs., 5pm-9:30pm Fri.-Sat., $15-25) has a rhyming name that makes this place hard to forget and a tasty breakfast and lunch menu that makes it even harder.

Fancy is one word used to describe **Bainbridge Thai Cuisine** (330 Madison Ave. S., 206/780-2403, www.bainbridgethai.com, 11:30am-9:30pm daily, $9-15), thanks to its location at the Bremerton Waterfront and its food presentation, for which every attention to detail is covered. The added bonus: The quality of the food here matches the presentation.

Information and Services

The **Bainbridge Island Chamber of Commerce Visitor Center** (590 Winslow Way E., 206/842-3700, www.bainbridgechamber.com, 9am 5pm Mon. Fri., 10am 3pm Sat.) is across the street from the police department and just up from the parking lot from the ferry terminal at Eagle Harbor. There's visitor information at the terminal, too.

Getting There and Around

The busy **Seattle-Bainbridge Island Ferry** itself is part of the Washington State Ferries system, and is often very crowded although it makes several trips between the two cities each day. One-way costs for the 35-minute trip are $8 for walkers; $7.65 for motorcyclists and their bikes; and $17.30 for drivers and their cars.

Once you're on the island, **Kitsap Transit** (206/373-2877 or 800/501-7433, www.kitsap-transit.org) picks up at the ferry terminal and offers several routes around the island and across the Agate Pass Bridge to the Kitsap Peninsula and beyond.

POULSBO

One step into downtown Poulsbo (pop. 9,300) and it's easy to see why the city is known as Little Norway. That Scandinavian culture will be the focus of your experience here is rammed home early and often. The town's entrance sign reads Velkommen til Poulsbo, and Norwegian flags fly alongside American ones from shops and homes. Front Street, the town's thoroughfare, runs north-south along Liberty Bay, and is filled with Scandinavian-themed shops, restaurants, and cafés. Many of those businesses have Norwegian-themed murals painted on the outside, and there's a Sons of Norway chapter here that's nearly 100 years old. The marinas here are busy ones, and Liberty Bay is filled with boats and floatplanes.

Exactly why Poulsbo is so obsessed with Scandinavia isn't much of a mystery. As far as modern times go, the town was founded in the 1880s by Norwegian immigrant Jorgen Eliason, who had arrived in the United States just a few years prior. Other Norwegians followed, and the town was named Paulsbo, after a city in Norway with the same name. When the city applied for a post office, the spelling of the town's name was misinterpreted and spelled Poulsbo, which stuck when the city was incorporated in 1907. For a while, Norwegian was the only language spoken in town. It was decades before English became the city's predominant language. Logging and fishing were for years, and to some extent still are, the predominant trades practiced here. During World War II, hundreds of U.S. military personnel were housed here. Today, Poulsbo's old waterfront downtown is in full support of the Little Norway theme, though there also are more industrialized areas of town located off Highways 305 and 307 that do strip away a bit of Poulsbo's charm.

Sights

Set on the northern end of Discovery Bay, the **Port of Poulsbo** is beautiful and historic in itself, with gorgeous mountain views and a location in the heart of Poulsbo. Visitors come here to relax and walk the docks and lengthy boardwalk to **American Legion Park** or **Liberty Bay Park,** and to watch the boats cruise around and in and out of the bay. Many visitors don't drive to the area; instead, they bring their boats and dock them at the marina. The **Marine Science Center** (18743 Front St. NE, 360/598-4460, www.poulsbomsc.org, 11am-4pm Thurs.-Sun., donations accepted) here is fun for the entire family, full of tidepool touch tanks, animal displays, an octopus named Mr. Bob, and programs designed to educate young and old alike on the area's sea life and issues affecting its survival.

Sawdust Hill Alpaca Farm (25448 Port

the Marine Science Center in Poulsbo

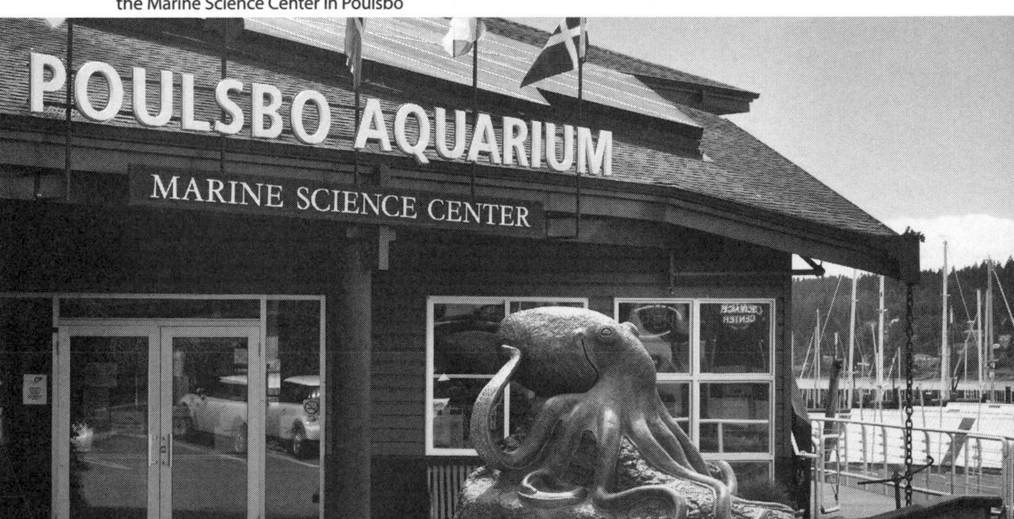

Gamble Rd. NE, 360/286-9999, www.sawdusthillalpacas.com, 11am-4pm daily, tours by reservation only, $10, $5 under age 12) is a 15-acre working farm a few miles north of Poulsbo. Though there are other animals here, the cute alpacas are the draw, and children are encouraged to hug the cuddly critters. There is a small gift shop that features alpaca clothing, yarn, and other goods.

Sports and Recreation

Being located on a protected bay makes Poulsbo a great spot to launch canoes and kayaks, and **Olympic Outdoor Center** (18743 Front St., 360/697-6095, www.olympicoutdoorcenter.com) is a good place to rent them from. They also have paddleboards and other gear. Most important, the staff is knowledgeable and can point you in the right, and safest, direction for your adventure. Classes and tours also are offered.

Entertainment and Events

That Poulsbo residents like to celebrate its Scandinavian heritage is evident by the annual festivals it hosts. Those festivals begin in earnest in mid-May, when the **Viking Fest** (www.vikingfest.org) takes over the town in honor of Norway's Constitution Day of May 17. There's a carnival, a parade, food vendors, entertainment, a scholarship competition, and one lucky local woman who gets to wear the crown of Miss Viking Fest throughout the three-day event . . . and possibly beyond.

The heritage celebrations pick up again (if they ever really ended) in June when the **Skandia Midsommarfest** celebrates the solstice with pole dancing (the midsommar pole, that is) and music. Games for the kids, a tug-of-war, burlap sack races, and lots of food are capped by a bonfire and solstice proclamation by the Sons of Norway Vikings.

Jule Fest is a traditional daylong Scandinavian Christmas celebration (www.poulsbochamber.com) with a holiday bazaar, music around the Christmas tree on the waterfront, and, to end the day, the arrival of the Lucia Bride accompanied by Vikings. Father Christmas and the Lucia Bride then light the Christmas tree. There's also a large bonfire to warm your hands.

Every Saturday from April through mid-December, the **Poulsbo Farmers Market** (www.poulsbofarmersmarket.org) is held at the Poulsbo Village Medical-Dental Center at the corner of 7th and Iverson Streets. The market is one of the only ones on the peninsula that runs an extended season, and the benefits are obvious. Instead of entirely neglecting fall and winter, as most do, this market offers pumpkins and Christmas-related goods.

Shopping

There are several boutiques, art galleries, and specialty shops here, mostly on or around Front Street in the downtown area, that you'll want to make time to look at. Don't miss **The Verksted Gallery** (18937 Front St., 360/697-4470, www.verkstedgallery.com, 10am-5:30pm daily). It's one of the oldest art co-ops in the state, and there are a lot of great things to discover.

Boehm's Chocolate (18864 Front St., 360/697-3318, www.boehmspoulsbo.com) is a Northwest favorite. Stop by and grab yourself a sea salt caramel. Hours vary by season, but the shop is open seven days a week.

Accommodations

A fully modern and very clean hotel, the **Poulsbo Inn & Suites** (18680 Hwy. 305, 360/779-3921, www.poulsboinn.com, $99-115 d) features amenities such as a fitness center, hot tub, business center, and ecofriendly "green" water and electrical usage. All rooms include a large-screen TV and are especially tidy.

Built as a farmhouse on the shore of Liberty Bay, the **Brauer Cove Guest House** (16709 Brauer Rd. NE, 360/779-4153, $125 d) has two rooms, waterfront access, and a secluded location. Weekly and monthly rates also are available.

★ **The Manor Farm Inn** (26069 Big Valley Rd. NE, 360/779-4628, www.manorfarminn.com, $140-170 d) may be showing its age a bit, but the guest rooms are well-maintained, and the grounds here are as relaxing as the four-course breakfast is good. The spaciousness and the deck of the Carriage Room can't be beat for those who want to get away from it all.

If acres of gardens, beautiful rooms, quiet, and seclusion are your thing, **The Green Cat Guest House and B&B** (25819 Tytler Rd., 360/779-7569, www.greencatbb.com, $115-139 d) is the place to stay when you're in the area. Part of the quiet comes from the owners' policies: infants and small children are not allowed to stay here.

With just two guest rooms in a Colonial-style house, the **Foxbridge** (30680 Hwy. 3 NE, 360/697-4875, www.foxbridge.com, $125 d) promises individualized guest service, and even offers meals for travelers with special dietary needs such as vegetarian, vegan, and gluten-free. The owners recently upgraded their entire grounds.

Food

★ **Casa Luna of Poulsbo** (18830 Front St. NE, 360/779-7676, 11am-9pm daily, $11-30) is a little hole in the wall down an alley off the main road in the center of town. It's sandwiched tightly between two buildings and if you aren't looking for it, you'll miss it. If you like Mexican food, that will be a sad thing. It's charming with its "hidden" location and exposed brick walls, and the food tastes fresh and better than a lot of the chain restaurants you're more likely to find throughout the area.

At **Tizleys Europub** (18928 Front St. NE, 360/394-0080, www.tizleys.com, 8am-midnight Tues.-Sat., 8am-10pm Sun.-Mon., $9-23) you can get a variety of schnitzels, a Scandinavian-style platter of fish, boiled eggs, and havarti, and a great selection of European beers and handcrafted cane sodas.

Burrata is a creamy cheese that inspired the creation of **Burrata Bistro** (19006 Front St. NE, 360/930-8446, www.burratabistro.com 4:30pm-9:30pm daily, $10-25). Here, all the pasta dishes are handmade. Try the manicotti stuffed to capacity with cheeses and baked in marina and béchamel for $13. The focaccia is fresh, too, and perfect for dipping in olive oil, balsamic vinegar, or some of that divine pasta sauce you'll find on your main dish.

Information and Services

The **Greater Poulsbo Chamber of Commerce** (19735 10th Ave. NE, 360/779-4848, www.poulsbochamber.com, 9am-5pm Mon.-Fri.) is the main visitors center in town, and its location off Northeast Lincoln Road is a good one that makes for an easy and quick stop for those heading to the old downtown area. Several stores downtown have area-related literature available, as well.

Getting There and Around

To reach Poulsbo from Tacoma, drive 50 miles (1 hour) north across the Tacoma Narrows on Highways 16 and 3. An alternate route from Seattle is to take a car ferry west across Puget Sound to Bainbridge Island and then head northwest on Highway 305, for a total commute time of about 2.5 hours, depending on the time of day and the ferry schedule.

PORT GAMBLE

Just off the eastern edge of the Hood Canal Bridge, and at the edge of the northwestern section of Kitsap Peninsula, lies the unincorporated community of Port Gamble, a former mill town currently seeking to revitalize its Victorian district, which is a National Historic Landmark. The town's Buena Vista Cemetery is home to the first U.S. Navy sailor killed in action in the Northwest, which happened in 1856. Before it closed in 1995, Port Gamble's mill was the longest continually operating sawmill in North America. Many tourists come here in the summer and take part in a popular, self-guided walking tour of the city, a map of which can be found on the city's website, www.portgamble.com.

Sights

Of Sea and Shore

Also known as the Port Gamble Historic Museum, **Of Sea and Shore** (32400 Rainier

Ave. NE, 360/297-8078, www.portgamble.com/visitin/museum, 9:30am-5pm daily, adults $4, students, seniors, military $3, children under 6 free) is located upstairs in the general store building, which also houses a full-service café and a spa. The museum isn't necessarily orderly, but it is completely full of glass cases and cabinets many might consider strange—such as a hammerhead shark preserved in a jar of alcohol and a dried shark that hangs from overhead. The stories told here aren't written.

★ Point No Point Lighthouse

Around Port Gamble Bay and up to the northern tip of the Kitsap Peninsula in Hansville lies **Point No Point Lighthouse** (9009 Point No Point Rd., www.pnplighthouse.com, free). Completed in 1879, this is the oldest lighthouse on Puget Sound. The lighthouse still operates and is listed on the National Register of Historic Places. The United States Lighthouse Society is headquartered here in the former lighthouse keeper's quarters. Point No Point Light is available to tour noon-4pm on weekends April-September. The lighthouse grounds are fun, too, and there's even a store where you can get your ice cream fix.

Festivals and Events

Port Gamble's record-setting mill may be gone, but its milling history still is celebrated each year during the **Old Mill Days** (www.oldmilldays.com) held at the end of September or early October. Logging competitions are held during the three-day event, and there also is a car show, live entertainment, ice carvings, a carnival, a skateboard competition, food, a beer garden, and much more.

Halloween time brings a different sort of visitor to Port Gamble, one who's interested in the paranormal, for the **Port Gamble Ghost Conference** (360/297-7251, www.portgamble.com). For a $55 registration fee, conference attendees get two days of lectures, demonstrations, and ghost tours.

Accommodations and Food

Port Gamble's former service station now is home to ★ **Mike's Four Star BBQ** (4719 NE Hwy. 104, 360/297-4227, www.mikesfourstarbbq.com, 11am-8pm Thurs.-Sat., 11am-5pm Sun., $10-15), home to some uniquely named sandwiches and good all-around barbecued meat including pulled pork and beef ribs. Try the Carolina Piggy sandwich made from handmade sausage and pulled pork.

Point No Point Lighthouse

The **Port Gamble Guest Houses** (address provided upon booking, 360/447-8473, www.portgambleguesthouses.com, $225-475) are two guesthouses, numbered 1 and 2, that hold anywhere from 6 to 12 people, depending on the house. Guest House 1 includes the **Jamieson Suite,** a one-bedroom, one-bath section of the house with a fireplace and kitchen.

The **Farm Kitchen Guest House** (24309 Port Gamble Rd. NE, 360/297-6615, www.farmkitchenguesthouse.com, $350-450) is a fully furnished home that sleeps up to 10 located on 18 acres and next to a massage studio. There's a large master suite and a full laundry, and the yard is so large that the home can be rented for both weddings and as a place to hold a reception.

Getting There and Around

Getting to Port Gamble from Tacoma involves a 50-mile drive north on Highways 16 and 3, and takes a little more than an hour. From Seattle, you can either head south on I-5 for 30 miles to Tacoma and follow the above directions from there, or take a car ferry to Bainbridge Island and drive northwest on Highway 305 from there, for a total time of 2-3 hours, depending on ferry schedule, traffic, and time of day.

Shelton

The largest city in the area (but still with only 9,200 residents), Shelton's claim to fame, like many small towns on the Peninsula, is its link to the once-booming, now holding-on logging industry. The Simpson Lumber Company still is a powerful player in the forest products industry, however. The blue-collar town is the only incorporated town in all of Mason County, and it sits on the western edge of Puget Sound at the head of Oakland Bay. The town originally was known as Sheltonville. Big employers in Shelton include Walmart, Taylor Shellfish Farms, and a maximum-security state prison.

SIGHTS

Yes, there are two **Mason County Historical Society Museums** (427 W. Railroad Ave., 360/426-1020, 11am-5pm Tues.-Fri., 11am-4pm Sat., donation; Port of Shelton Fairgrounds), one in downtown Shelton and one at the Port of Shelton Fairgrounds (formerly known as the Mason County Fairgrounds). The main one downtown is housed in the city's historic library building, which was donated to the city in 1914 by the wives of two local timber barons and now is listed on the National Register of Historic Places. For those interested in learning about the area they're visiting, or even the area they're just passing through, this is a good place to stop. Logging and farming displays and old photos dominate here, and those with local connections can trace their genealogy. The fairgrounds museum, which houses larger exhibits including a neat model railroad display, is only open during special events and by appointment.

There's a locomotive—a real one—housed at 3rd Street and Railroad Avenue downtown. It's nickname is **Tollie,** and it's a long-retired steam locomotive that was donated to the city in 1959 by the Simpson Logging Company once diesel engines replaced steam-powered trains. Tollie is towing a railcar with a small load of logs and the red Caboose No. 700, which serves as Shelton's **Visitor Information Center.** Both Tollie and its caboose are on the National Register of Historic Places. Downtown also is home to the timber baron neighborhood, a series of homes where industry leaders once lived with their families.

A visit to the **Skyline Drive-In** (182 SE Brewer Rd., 360/426-4707, www.skylinedrive-in.com, opens at dusk, Apr.-Sept., $7 adults, $1 ages 6-11, children under 5 free) feels as

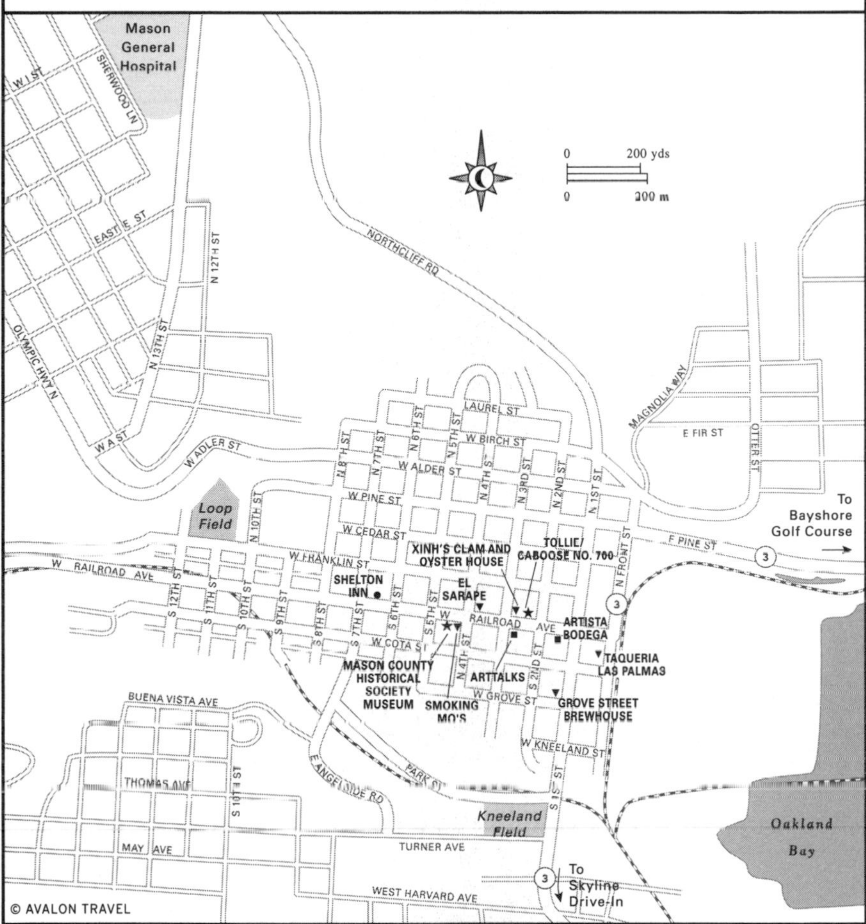

if you're jumping in a time machine, setting the dial on 1958, and pressing the button. There are fewer than 400 drive-ins left in the United States and one of them is here, operating seasonally since 1964. There's a snack bar here and pets are welcome. Just don't forget to bring an FM radio if you'd like to sit outside and watch the double feature or in case your '57 Chevy only has AM.

For a chance to see spawning salmon, stop by **Goldsborough Creek,** which runs through downtown Shelton.

SPORTS AND RECREATION

Hiking

The perfectly named **Huff 'n' Puff Trail** (across from Shelton High School on Shelton Springs Rd.) has miles of tree-lined trails and is a peaceful hike through the woods.

Kennedy Creek Salmon Trail

Distance: 0.5 mile round-trip
Duration: 15 minutes-1 hour
Elevation gain: None

Effort: Easy
Trailhead: south of Shelton off Old Olympic Highway
Directions: From Highway 101 south of Shelton, turn onto Old Olympic Highway. Take the road for 0.75 mile and turn onto a gravel road marked with the Kennedy Creek Salmon Trail sign. About 0.5 mile down the road is the parking area.

Kennedy Creek Salmon Trail (360/427-9436, www.spsseg.org) turns into a fascinating outdoor learning center each fall, when the area is inundated with tens of thousands of salmon rushing out of Oyster Bay and up Kennedy Creek to spawn. There are several lookout platforms on the trail, and interpretive signs explain exactly what is happening here. In a word, it's nature. The best time to visit is in November, though the spawning can occur anytime from late October through December.

Biking

Bicyclists will enjoy the area's open roads and low traffic levels. The 24-mile-long **Mason Lake Loop** northeast of Shelton is one of the best and prettiest rides around.

Golf

Salish Cliffs Golf Club (behind Little Creek Casino at the junction of Hwy. 101 and Hwy. 8, 360/462-3673, www.salish-cliffs.com, $89 greens fees) opened in late 2011 and is an 18-hole, par-72 championship course that appears to be the only place in sight when you're on it. The course is on a hill and there are no homes built on it as there are on many courses throughout the state. The clubhouse has a large mezzanine that overlooks two of the holes, and there's a full restaurant inside. Carts are required here, which should be considered a bonus to most, due to their standard GPS systems. This is an upper-end golf course, so proper golf attire is required to play.

Lake Limerick Country Club (790 E. Saint Andrews Dr., 360/426-6290, www.lakelimerick.com, $17 for 9 holes) is a private nine-hole, par-36 course also lined with trees. There is a second set of tees for those wishing to play a full 18 holes. There's also a restaurant, pro shop, and monthly specials.

Water Sports

Oyster Bay and **Oakland Bay** are good places to kayak, and both lead to **Hope Island,** an unforgettable trip but one that is for advanced paddlers only.

ENTERTAINMENT AND EVENTS

Nightlife

Though it's the first-ever microbrewery in Mason County, **Grove Street Brewhouse** (233 S. 1st St., 360/462-2739, 3pm-8pm Mon.-Wed., 3pm-9pm Thurs.-Sat., noon-5pm Sun.) didn't take long to find its niche. Housed in a former Pontiac dealership building, Grove Street has a full kitchen and is kid-friendly, though the brewed beers are the real treat here. Try the Albino Pale Ale or, for lighter beer lovers, the German-inspired Cota Kotsch. A "guest tap" highlights beers from local breweries.

Casinos

The ever-expanding **Little Creek Casino Resort** (91 W. Hwy. 108, 360/427-7711 or 800/667-7711, www.little-creek.com) used to be just another smallish Indian casino located in the middle of what, to most people, basically was "nowhere." Today, Little Creek is a full-fledged resort with a deluxe hotel, restaurant, hundreds of slot machines, table games, an entertainment lineup that tops that of most venues in Western Washington, and an 18-hole golf course built by an award-winning architect. Though most people's trips to the Olympic Peninsula center on nature and getting out and discovering it, those who would rather spend their time in one location can do so here. Because basically, Little Creek has it all.

Wineries

A trip to Shelton wouldn't be complete without a stop at **Walter Dacon Wines** (50 SE Skookum Inlet Rd., 360/426-5913 or

866/939-4637, www.walterdaconwines.com, noon-6pm Wed.-Sun.). This winery is dedicated to making Rhone- and Mediterranean-style wines with grapes it sources from Washington State.

Art Galleries

For a small town, Shelton is full of all kinds of art, and it can be found both outdoors and indoors. Downtown on Railroad Avenue, the work of Tim Crane dominates, and a logging memorial at 2nd Street, though not Crane's work, is fascinating. Many outdoor murals also are scattered throughout the town. Inside, colorful **ArtTalks** (122 S. 3rd St., 360/432-1101, www.arttalks.net) does custom framing and features many pieces from local artists.

Festivals and Events

Every Saturday from May through September, the **Shelton Farmers Market** (www.sheltonfarmersmarket.com) sets up shop downtown on 3rd Street, opening its doors (OK, there are no real doors) to people searching for deals on crafts, food, jewelry, and more. There's musical entertainment here each week, too.

The **Mason County Forest Festival** (www.masoncountyforestfestival.org) has been going strong since the 1940s as the area's top event celebrating the forest-related heritage of Shelton, the rest of the county, and, for that matter, the entire Olympic Peninsula. Logging competitions and a four-day-long carnival are the highlights here, although watching the Paul Bunyan Parade, and its gigantic Paul Bunyan replica, loop through downtown Shelton can be a fun way to spend a Saturday morning for those who want to mingle with the locals.

Formerly known as the Mason County Fair, the **Mason Area Fair & Rodeo** (www.masoncountyfair.org) is held the last weekend in July at the Port of Shelton Fairgrounds, formerly known as the Mason County Fairgrounds. That may be a lot of "formerly," but fortunately the more than 100-year-old event still is current. The fair features three days of entertainment, animals, food, music, and a carnival. One unique aspect of this small-town fair is that kids under age 16 are admitted free of charge. Adults have to pay $5. The popular rodeo ($12 adults, $5 children 6-16, children under 5 free) is held each year on Friday night.

OysterFest (www.oysterfest.org) takes place the first full weekend of October at the Port of Shelton Fairgrounds and is a big deal in these parts, where Hood Canal to the north produces some of the best oysters around. This is a cornucopia of delights for lovers of the slimy bivalves. Don't be misled by the festival's name, however. The event does host the West Coast Oyster Shucking Championship and there is plenty of oyster-eating going around, but there's also entertainment for kids and adults, art and photography competitions, and vendors galore. The best thing about these vendors? None are allowed to copy another's food, therefore variety is excellent.

SHOPPING

As the largest city for miles, it may come as no surprise that Shelton is the hub, such as it is, of shopping activity in the area. Railroad Avenue is the center of that hub. There is a healthy selection of antiques stores here for the treasure hunters at heart, including **The Daisy Pot Antiques & Apparel** (327 W. Railroad Ave., 360/432-3688, 10am-5pm Mon.-Fri., 10am-2pm Sat.). There's also ladies apparel and things to make your home beautiful here. **The Owl in the Attic Antiques** (415 W. Railroad Ave., 360/426-6137, 11am-5pm Wed.-Fri. and most Sat.) buys and sells antiques and carries a decent selection of historical wood furniture pieces, glass, pottery, and dolls. Find a pretty clock, art, linens, and other items for your home at **Very Ltd. Antiques** (413 W. Railroad Ave., 360/426-2268, 11am-5pm Wed.-Sat.).

If it's a thrift store adventure you seek, scour household goods, clothes, and even some new merchandise at **Treasures** (305 W. Railroad Ave., 360/427-3858, 9:30am-5:30pm Mon.-Sat., 11am-5pm Sun.).

Independent bookstores seem to be a dying breed, so it's refreshing to explore the aisles of books at **Sage Book Store** (116 Railroad Ave., Ste. 102, 360/426-6011, www.sagebookstore.com, 7am-6pm Mon.-Fri., 9am-5pm Sat., 9am-3pm Sun.). Stop in for the delicious locally roasted Raven's Brew Coffee and for wireless Internet access.

From gifts to home decor items, look no further than charming **Simply Home** (502 W. Franklin St., 360/426-1905, 10am-5:30pm Tues.-Fri., 10am-4pm Sat.).

Be sure not to miss **Artista Bottega** (129 W. Railroad Ave., 360/490-7565, 10am-6pm Mon.-Fri., 10am-4pm Sat.), a marketplace for local artists that features a variety of works from crochet to baby items, photography, and glass. Everything sold here is handcrafted.

ACCOMMODATIONS

With themed rooms including the Zen Room, ★ **A Lighthouse on Hammersley** (292 E. Libby Rd., 360/427-1107, www.lighthouseonham.com, $145-165 d) brings a lighthearted "resort" feel to the shores of Hammersley Inlet. The facility includes nearly 10,000 square feet of common areas, and all guest rooms face the water. There's also a stone fireplace, beautiful kitchen, and a deck you can lounge on while looking at the water. This place is a hidden gem.

Centrally located in downtown Shelton, the **Shelton Inn** (628 W. Railroad Ave., 360/426-4468, www.sheltoninn.com, $68-88 d) is a convenient base for budget travelers wanting easy access to the entire Olympic Peninsula. The on-site restaurant, Blondie's, is known for hearty breakfasts.

FOOD

Xinh Dwelley is originally from Vietnam, but her cooking style can't be classified as Vietnamese; nor is it really American. At ★ **Xinh's Clam and Oyster House** (221 Railroad Ave., 360/427-8709, www.xinhsrestaurant.com, 5pm-9pm Thurs.-Sat., $14-22) she creates award-winning food that is all her own, and that's why she has received so many rave reviews from regional and national media. When available, she serves fresh geoducks. Another specialty is pan-fried oysters and her cioppino, full of fresh Northwest seafood.

Grove Street Brewhouse (233 S. 1st St., 360/462-2739, 11am-9pm Mon.-Thurs., 11am-11pm Fri.-Sat., 11am-8pm Sun., $7-10) is a full-service brewhouse that serves great beer and food for people of all ages. There are some good bar goodies here, such as warm, soft pretzels, oyster shooters, and blueberry jalapeño jelly over cream cheese. For more substantial bites, there's a large selection of subs, hot dogs, pizzas, and more. And there's a kids' menu, too. Get a homemade beer, while they get a homemade soda pop.

Somewhat similar to Grove Street is **Smoking Mo's** (203 W. Railroad Ave., 360/462-0163, www.smokingmos.com, 11am-8pm Tues.-Thurs., 11am-9pm Fri.-Sat., 11am-8pm Sun., closed Mon., $9-29), a burgers and barbecue joint that's relatively new to the scene but quickly earning a good reputation both with locals and with visitors that happen to stumble upon the business. Long waits are sometimes common, especially on weekends, but the food is delicious once you receive it. Whether it's worth the wait is in the eye of the beholder.

Sometimes you just have to have some chips and salsa, or a big plate of nachos, or beans and rice with something gooey and cheesy. If that sounds good, **El Sarape** (318 W. Railroad Ave., 360/426-4294, www.elsarape.net, 11am-10pm Sun.-Thurs., 11am-11pm Fri.-Sat., $8-16) is a great place to get your Mexican food fix. Portions are generous, prices reasonable. **Taqueria Las Palmas** (116 E. Cota St., 360/432-3220, 11am-close) is another great option in this category that locals really love.

INFORMATION AND SERVICES

The **Shelton-Mason County Chamber of Commerce** (housed in the red caboose behind locomotive Tollie on Railroad Ave.

downtown, 360/426-2021 or 800/576-2021, www.sheltonchamber.org, 9am-6pm Mon.-Fri., 9am-3pm Sat.-Sun.) is an important stop for those interested in the city itself and the areas in the rest of Mason County and beyond.

Those needing medical assistance can contact **Mason General Hospital** (901 Mountain View Dr., 360/426-1611). There's an emergency room here, the only one around for miles.

GETTING THERE AND AROUND

Getting to Shelton from Tacoma is fairly straightforward and involves just one turn. Head south on I-5 to Olympia, then head north on Highway 101 to Shelton. The total trip is 52 miles at highway speeds, but a major traffic-jam hot spot near Joint Base Lewis-McChord will snarl your commute most daylight hours. Plan for at least an hour. Getting to Shelton from Seattle just involves an extra 30 miles on I-5.

Mason County Transit (360/426-9434 or 800/281-9434, www.masontransit.org) has routes throughout the city and county, runs north to Brinnon, and east to Olympia. From Olympia, buses connect to Grays Harbor County, Tacoma, Centralia, and more. The bus system here isn't intricate, but it does serve the region fairly well.

South Hood Canal

South Hood Canal is a somewhat lesser-known portion of the Olympic Peninsula. Like most of Western Washington, however, this section of the peninsula provides recreational opportunities galore and offers diverse geography including large lakes like Lake Cushman, a popular island, and, of course, the unique warm-water channel that is Hood Canal itself.

SIGHTS

Hamma Hamma Recreation Area

The **Hamma Hamma Recreation Area** (two miles northwest of Eldon, off Hamma Hamma Rd.) is, well, a place to recreate. Located south of The Brothers Wilderness, the area's main lodging highlight is the **Hamma Hamma Cabin** (360/765-2200, www.recreation.gov, $40-60), a rustic two-bedroom structure built in 1937 by the Civilian Conservation Corps and located in the Hamma Hamma River Drainage. The trailhead for the **Living Legacy Interpretive Trail** (1.5-mile loop) is in the Hamma Hamma Campground and accesses the Hamma Hamma River. The interpretive trail runs through an area where the Civilian Conservation Corps did a bunch of firefighting work in the 1930s.

Two miles west of the park on Forest Service Road 25 is the **Lena Lakes trailhead,** which leads to lower **Lena Lake** and its free campground. Those who wish to continue on can visit **Upper Lena Lake** at the base of 5,995-foot-high **Mount Lena.**

Mount Skokomish Wilderness

West of Hamma Hamma Recreation Area on Forest Service Road 25 lies Mount Skokomish Wilderness, 13,291 acres of rugged, river-filled terrain just north of Lake Cushman and managed by the National Forest Service. Three 6,000-plus-foot peaks are here, **Mount Pershing, Mount Washington,** and **Mount Skokomish,** as are a couple of quality hiking trails. Primitive **Mildred Lakes Trail** is a tough, 9-mile round-trip hike that requires getting wet and dirty, but the reward is a series of three lakes where there's great fishing, no people, and several campsites. **Putvin Trail** is a much easier hike in terms of terrain, if not in terms of elevation gain, as it rises 3,700 feet in approximately four miles from the Hamma Hamma River to beautiful

Lake of the Angels, which is frozen for a good portion of the year.

★ Lake Cushman

Lake Cushman is a 10-mile-long blue-watered reservoir chiefly created in the mid-1920s by the damming of the Skokomish River—locals and visitors alike have spent many summer days there fishing, boating, swimming, or waterskiing. The lake's outlying areas, located in the Olympic National Forest, offer wildlife viewing and hiking trails with beautiful views. The lake was undeveloped until two lakeside resorts popped up in the late 1800s; it was named after Orrington Cushman, who acted as an interpreter for Washington Governor Isaac Stevens during negotiations with local Native American tribes in the 1850s. Amazingly, the lake still seems remote, despite much recent development in the area. Popular activities here include swimming, fishing, picnicking, boating, scuba diving, hiking, camping, and kayaking.

Skokomish Park at Lake Cushman (7211 N. Lake Cushman Rd., 360/877-5760, www.skokomishpark.com), which used to be Lake Cushman State Park, has historically been popular with boaters, anglers, swimmers, and campers. However, a recent land dispute between the Skokomish tribe and the property owners shuttered most of the park for a period of time, except for the boat launch and RV waste station. But the park has now reopened and is worth checking out.

Skokomish Tribal Center and Museum

The entire southwest Hood Canal area near the mouth of the Skokomish River is home to the Skokomish Indian Reservation and a tribe that has for years fought to maintain land in the area it has called home for centuries. Nothing is stronger evidence of the tribe's long relationship with the area than its name, which means "Big River People" in the Twana language. A more detailed explanation of that history can be found at the **Skokomish Tribal Center and Museum** (80 N. Tribal Center Rd., Skokomish, 360/426-4232, www.skokomish.org, 8am-5pm Mon.-Fri.). There are numerous displays inside, including a large carving of an orca whale, totem poles, historic tribal artifacts and documents, masks, and woven baskets, an art form at which the Skokomish are well known for being proficient.

Staircase

Staircase is in **Olympic National Park,** northwest of Lake Cushman at the headwaters of the Skokomish River. It's an off-the-beaten-path paradise that almost always cracks the Top 10 list of anyone who visits here. There is no staircase here, but there once was. It was made of cedar, called the Devil's Staircase, and created in 1890 when U.S. Army surveyors came upon a rock bluff they found impossible to pass. Today, Staircase is at the end of a dusty gravel road and home to fishing and hiking opportunities galore.

The **Staircase Ranger Station** (360/877-5569, www.nps.gov/olym, open in summer, no set hours) offers information and exhibits about the area, as well as wilderness permits and bear canisters. There is also a wheelchair available for rental.

Staircase is the closest major access point in Olympic National Park to Seattle and Tacoma. To get there from Sea-Tac Airport, head south on I-5 through Tacoma. There, you can either cut across through the Kitsap Peninsula and over, or head farther south to Shelton and up Highway 101. Either route will take about two hours, though the former will also cost you a toll fee over the Narrows Bridge at Gig Harbor.

Hoodsport Trail State Park

Hoodsport Trail State Park (two miles northwest of Hoodsport off Hwy. 119) is best known for its hiking, which there isn't much of. But what is in the 80 wooded acres here is high-quality and secluded, much of it bordered by Dow Creek, which flows year-round. There are two main trails here, a lower loop (0.5 mile) and an upper loop (1.5 miles). Both trails venture into a canopy of second-growth fir trees.

SPORTS AND RECREATION

Hiking at Staircase

The hiking at Staircase can be as long or as short as the hiker wants it to be. The 0.9-mile hike along Shady Lane to Lake Cushman is popular, as is the extremely strenuous, yet fairly rewarding, 2.9-mile hike to **Wagonwheel Lake,** the trailhead sign to which says, Very Steep!

Those looking for longer hikes here have the rest of Olympic National Park at their disposal. The 15-mile **North Fork Skokomish Trail** heads north past primitive **Nine Stream, Two Bear,** and **Home Sweet Home Campgrounds** up through a river valley, forest, and a subalpine meadow all the way to the Duckabush River. Call 360/565-3131 to check the status of Staircase Road in winter.

To reach the three trailheads listed below from Shelton, travel north on Highway 101 and then turn west onto State Route 119. Head 9.3 miles and make a sharp left on Forest Road 24. In 1.7 miles it becomes a gravel road. Continue for another 3.7 miles and make a right turn at a junction and drive 1.2 miles to the ranger station and campground.

★ Staircase Rapids Loop

Distance: 4 miles round-trip
Duration: 1.5-3 hours
Elevation gain: 150 feet
Effort: Easy
Trailhead: Staircase Ranger Station

This trail is mostly for day hikers, but that doesn't mean hard-core hikers also won't enjoy the loop trip through old-growth trees past the Skokomish River's fast-flowing Staircase Rapids. While this often-overlooked area of Olympic National Park has plenty of natural treasures to behold, there's also a new man-made one to gawk at. In 2013, a new suspension bridge modeled after Tacoma's iconic Narrows bridges was built to replace an old bridge that washed away in flooding and turned the hike into an out-and-back one rather than a loop. This family-friendly hike can be accessed year-round.

Flapjack Lakes

Distance: 15 miles round-trip
Duration: 5-7 hours
Elevation gain: 3,200 feet
Effort: Moderate
Trailhead: Staircase Ranger Station

This hike might be lengthy (though you can always just go partway then turn around and head back), but it still only takes a moderate effort to complete, mostly because the elevation gain is spread out over such a long distance. There's also enjoyable scenery (such as a waterfall on Donahue Creek) along that way. Once you reach the smallish, subalpine lakes, you'll want to spend some time resting and enjoying the scenery before you return to the trail's start. Included in that scenery are the Sawtooth mountains, a range of the Olympics, and regular mountain goat sightings. Many people even choose to make this a multiday trip, camping out at the lakes among the wildflowers.

Shady Lane Trail

Distance: 1.7 miles round-trip
Duration: 1 hour
Elevation gain: 50 feet
Effort: Easy
Trailhead: Staircase Ranger Station

Shady Lane is an apt name for this short and popular trail, which begins to the west of the ranger station with a 0.1-mile wheelchair-friendly section and continues through a forest filled with moss-covered trees and lichen-covered rocks and along the North Fork Skokomish River (which you will eventually cross via small bridge), past the remnants of an old mine, to near Lake Cushman. This path is wet and sometime soggy year-round, and yes, it is indeed very shady.

Golf

There may only be nine holes at the **Lake**

Cushman Golf Course (210 NW Fairway Dr., 360/877-5505, $16 weekday, $18 weekends for nine holes), but they are scenic, surrounded by Douglas fir trees and with mountain views. The course is seasonal, so it's best to call in advance.

Water Sports

Those who like to frolic in the water have several opportunities to do so here, but Lake Cushman, with its 23 miles of shoreline, is by far the best, and easiest, place in which to do so. At Lake Cushman you can water-ski, boat, swim, kayak, fish, and more. Those who need to rent canoes, kayaks, rowboats, pedal boats, or small powerboats can do so at **Lake Cushman Resort** (4621 N. Lake Cushman Rd., 360/877-9630, www.lakecushman.com). Those looking to instead explore the waters of Hood Canal should contact **Mikes Beach Resort** (38740 N. Hwy. 101, Lilliwaup, 360/877-5324, www.mikesbeachresort.com), which has a knowledgeable staff, and rents diving gear, rowboats, and kayaks year-round. In Hoodsport, **Hood Sport 'N Dive** (24080 N. Hwy. 101, 360/877-6818, www.hoodsportndive.com) is a good place for divers to check out and get outfitted for underwater exploration.

ENTERTAINMENT AND EVENTS

Casinos

Owned and operated by the Skokomish Indian Nation, the **Lucky Dog Casino** (19330 N. Hwy. 101, 360/877-5656, www.myluckydogcasino.com, 8am-1am Sun.-Thurs., 8am-2am Fri.-Sat.) is small as far as casinos go, but it's still the best place to go in the area to find any real semblance of big-city nightlife. There are hundreds of slot machines and the **North Fork Bar & Grill,** which serves all three meals, late-night snacks, and specials such as Sunday night steak dinners for $7.99. The **Drift Lounge & Bar** serves drinks and has a tiny food menu.

Wineries

Hoodsport Winery (23501 Hwy. 101, 360/877-9894 or 800/580-9894, www.hoodsport.com, 10am-6pm daily) may not be the biggest winery on the Olympic Peninsula, but its series of award-winning wines always rank among the best. The winery has several fruit wines, including apple, blackberry, cranberry, and pear, along with the typical cabernets, chardonnays, merlots, and an interesting blend called Island Belle. Its tasting room is small but charming, and the winery's walls are filled with medals and ribbons from awards it has won since the family-run business first opened shop in 1978. The winery's location can't be beat, with views of the Olympic Mountains and Hood Canal. The winery takes part in several special events each year, including a Red Wine & Chocolate tour in which some of the winery's chocolates, which are on sale in the tasting room, are paired with its wines.

Festivals and Events

Celebrate Hoodsport Days has been the area's premier Independence Day celebration for more than a quarter century. A pancake breakfast kicks off the weekend-long event, and a street fair with dozens of vendors, a live auction, and a festival-ending fireworks show are among the highlights. Typically, the event is held the first full weekend of July.

The **Hood Canal Salmon Derby** (www.northwestsalmonderbyseries.com) held each August on Hood Canal in Hoodsport is part of the **Northwest Salmon Derby Series** fishing competition, but don't let that fool you into thinking the event is only for anglers competing for cash prizes. There's also a barbecue and a free kids' fishing competition.

SHOPPING

As it's easy to deduce, shopping isn't the reason most people visit these parts. There is at least one neat shop here, however, and it's the **Cameo Boutique and Wine Shop** (6871 E. Hwy. 106, Union, 360/898-3200, 10am-5pm daily), which offers a lot of Washington wines and more you won't find anywhere else. It also has gourmet treats, gifts, and home decor

Hoodsport Winery

items. Some locals call it "Bin 106" because of its location on Highway 106.

ACCOMMODATIONS

Glen-Ayr Canal Resort (25381 N. Hwy. 101, Hoodsport, 360/877-9522, www.glenayr.com, $80-200 d) sits on the shore of Hood Canal and has hotel rooms, a rental townhouse, and more than 30 RV spaces as well as 700 feet of private beach.

Also on the shores of Hood Canal, ★ **Alderbrook Resort** (7101 E. Hwy. 106, Union, 360/898-2200, www.alderbrookresort.com, $236-446 d) is a high-end luxury resort and spa, where guests can be treated to a hot-oil scalp massage, herbal-infused steam room, and more, before retiring to enjoy the chocolate truffles that are delivered to each room. The restaurant here is top-notch, but expensive, and guests enjoy a private beach.

A full-service facility, ★ **Lake Cushman Resort** (4621 N. Lake Cushman Rd., Hoodsport, 800/588-9630, www.lakecushman.com, $70-140 d) offers a plethora of waterborne activities, from fishing to boating to scuba diving. In addition to the popular cabins, tent sites ($20-72) and RV sites ($25-37) are available.

With an assortment of cottages sleeping anywhere from two to six people, the **Robin Hood Village** (6780 E. Hwy. 106, Union, 360/898-2163, www.robinhoodvillage.com, $140-340) also features RV spaces ($38). Some of the historic cottages were built in 1934 by Donald Beckman, a Hollywood set designer who worked on the original Robin Hood film.

Camping

The ★ **Hamma Hamma Campground** (877/444-6777, www.recreation.gov, $10) is a good lodging option for both tents and trailers. There are 15 total sites, all surrounded by trees.

Located just north of the Skokomish Indian Reservation off Highway 101, **Potlatch State Park** (21660 Hwy. 101, Potlatch, www.parks.wa.gov, $15-21) is a 57-acre park on the shores of Hood Canal that has camping, boating, shellfish harvesting, and Junior Ranger activities for the kids. The park sits on a site once used for gift-giving ceremonies by the Skokomish tribe.

East of Union on Hood Canal is **Twanoh State Park** (12190 E. Hwy. 106, www.parks.wa.gov), a 182-acre marine park with roughly 50 campsites for both tents ($22) and RVs ($31-36). The water here is some of the warmest on the peninsula, and it is a popular spot for swimming and picnicking.

Near the Staircase Ranger Station there is a 47-site campground, ★ **Staircase Campground,** with accessible restrooms ($12-25, year-round). The campground is located adjacent to the Skokomish River, and some of the sites here are on the river. There are flush toilets and potable water available here, but only during the summer months.

FOOD

The **Eagle Creek Saloon** (31281 Hwy. 101, Lilliwaup, 360/877-6729, noon-9pm

Mon.-Sat., 8am-9pm Sun., $10-20) has a large cheeseburger on top of its building, and definitely is worth stopping at for a bite to eat, especially for its towering Eagle Burger. It's almost the only place to go in Lilliwaup (pronounced lilly-wop), a town of fewer than 500 residents bisected by Hwy. 101 and bordered by Lilliwaup Creek at the junction where the creek runs into Lilliwaup Bay on Hood Canal. A half mile upstream from the creek's mouth lies beautiful Lilliwaup Falls, though they are located on private land and not open to the public. The town is one of the oldest communities on Hood Canal and once had hopes of becoming a large city. Those hopes were dashed when plans for a railroad fell through.

The Tides Restaurant (27061 N. Hwy. 101, Hoodsport, 360/877-8921, 7am-3pm Mon.-Thurs., 7am-8pm Fri.-Sun., $10-15) is a bit north of Hoodsport on Highway 101 and features typical diner foods—deep-fried seafood, hamburgers, salads—but oysters are what's done best here.

The **Model T Pub & Eatery** (24821 N. Hwy. 101, Hoodsport, 360/877-9883, 11am-11pm Mon.-Sat., 11am-10pm Sun., $8-14) has deep-fried seafood, burgers, salads, and sandwiches. For those on the way to Lake Cushman, the **Girls Café** (2440 N. Lake Cushman Rd., Hoodsport, 360/877-9000) is a decent dining option.

INFORMATION AND SERVICES

The **Hoodsport Visitors Center** (150 N. Lake Cushman Rd., 360/877-2021) is a good resource for area information. The center is operated by the Mason County Chamber of Commerce, and thus has access to the wealth of maps and other information the much-larger chamber has to offer.

The closest hospital is **Mason General Hospital** (901 Mountain View Dr., Shelton, 360/426-1840).

The waterwheel across the highway from Alderbrook Resort still works.

North Hood Canal

Many of the most fascinating aspects of Hood Canal lie deep below its warm waters, in the form of an underwater ecosystem that's unique in its diversity. For that reason, scuba diving is a popular pastime here, and several launch points and shops are available for those who participate, or would like to learn to participate, in the activity. For above water travelers, the area surrounding the northern part of the canal offers miles of scenic nature trails with their abundant wildlife-viewing opportunities. For towns, there isn't much here. The Emerald Towns of **Quilcene** and **Brinnon,** along with the equally small burg of **Eldon,** are the largest.

SIGHTS

Hood Canal Bridge

Being the world's longest floating saltwater bridge doesn't make for an easy life. Opened in 1961 as a link between the Kitsap and Olympic Peninsulas, the bridge, at least the western half of it, sank during a severe storm in February 1979. During the storm, sustained winds of 80 mph, and gusts up to 120 mph, pounded the 8,000-foot-long bridge, blowing open the hatches in its supporting pontoons, allowing them to fill with water and sink. The section was rebuilt, and the bridge reopened 3.5 years after the closure. The older eastern section of the bridge was replaced in May and June of 2009. Today, the bridge is ordered closed when sustained winds of 40 mph hit the area. The bridge was controversial when it opened, because many Olympic Peninsula residents did not want their quiet area to be so easily accessed from the busier Kitsap Peninsula and beyond. Today, there's even a group of citizens called the Hood Canal Bridge Alliance who are concerned about the noise, congestion, and safety issues caused by the bridge.

Quilcene Historical Museum

Quilcene's mining and logging history is kept alive at the **Quilcene Historical Museum** (151 Columbia St., Quilcene, 360/765-4848, www.quilcenemuseum.org, 1pm-5pm Fri.-Mon., late Apr.-late Sept., by appointment rest of year). Housed in a recently remodeled, blue-roofed building, the museum also hosts the popular **Wine Tasting Gala** fundraiser each year in early August. One of the museum's goals is to purchase the historic Worthington Mansion and the 10 acres it sits on with hopes of restoring the home and preserving it for future generations.

Mount Walker

Tucked just inside the Olympic National Forest border near Quilcene, Mount Walker is a 2,805-foot-tall peak that has the distinction of being the easternmost mountain in the park's Olympic range. Its location in an area where everything else is at sea level makes this a popular peak. From the top you can see for miles. Literally. You can see the Seattle skyline (a 60-mile drive from Mount Walker) and many regional peaks, including Mount Rainier in the Cascades. The best part? Mount Walker can be accessed either by a semi-difficult, five-mile round-trip hike on the **Mount Walker Trail** through century-old Douglas fir, hemlock, and cedar, and rhododendrons, or you can drive to parking lots at either of the mountain's two lookouts.

Whitney Gardens & Nursery

If plants are your thing, the 6.8 acres of them at **Whitney Gardens & Nursery** (306264 Hwy. 101, Brinnon, 360/796-4411 or 800/952-2404, www.whitneygardens.com, 9am-6pm daily) should make you very happy. Rhododendrons and azaleas are the garden's specialties, and more than 15,000 people visit the garden each year. A majority of them come in summer, when the beautiful flowers are blooming, but the nursery is open year-round.

★ Dosewallips State Park

One of the best-maintained state parks around, 425-acre **Dosewallips State Park** (one mile north of Brinnon on Hwy. 101, 360/796-4415) seems to have it all. Much of the park's northern section is bordered by the Dosewallips River, its entire eastern side by Hood Canal, and its western portion is in the foothills of the Olympic Mountains. As one might guess, recreational activities abound. Wildlife viewing, oyster harvesting, clamming, fishing, river swimming, boating, and beachcombing are just some of what's available here, and a neat viewing platform just to the north of the Dosewallips River bridge occasionally offers views of wild elk trekking through the grassy field below. Several miles of trails also wind through the park, and beautiful, widespread **Rocky Brook Falls** are just to the north of the park. There are 70 tent sites ($20-31), 55 utility sites ($32-42), three unique platform tents, and three cabins ($60).

The Brothers Wilderness

The Brothers is a 6,866-foot-high mountain with a unique double peak that makes it one of the most popular in the Olympic Mountains. The Brothers Wilderness is the more than 16,000 acres surrounding the peak bisected by the Duckabush River and the **Duckabush River Trail.** The trail begins at the Collins Campground just outside the wilderness area and climbs 22 miles through a glacier-carved valley surrounded by cedar, fir, and hemlock trees. Along its way into the national park, the trail is bisected by a number of other trails leading in almost every possible direction and to many sites, including **Mount Steel, Mount Duckabush,** and **Marmot Lake.** There are many backcountry campsites along the way, and a backcountry permit (available on trails at the park's entrance) is necessary for each one. Other Brothers Wilderness highlights include **Mount Jupiter** (elev. 5,701) and its corresponding trail.

SPORTS AND RECREATION

Beaches

One of the best aspects of Hood Canal is the ability to harvest clams and oysters from many public beaches along the waterway. Some spots are only accessible by boat, but many simply require a walk to the shoreline, the proper gear, a license, and a knowledge of the local regulations. The license and regulations can be taken care of at the Washington Department of Fish & Wildlife's website (www.wdfw.wa.gov). Good places to harvest in the area include **Dosewallips State Park, Duckabush, Pleasant Harbor, Quilcene Bay,** and **Triton Cove.** Manila clams, mussels, and oysters all are harvestable when seasons are open to do so. For up-to-date information on seasons, visit www.wdfw.wa.gov/fishing/regulations.

On a clear day at **Indian George Creek Beach** (1.25 miles south on Linger Longer Rd. off Hwy. 101, Quilcene) you can see across Quilcene Bay to East Quilcene or picnic on the sometimes-sandy, sometimes-rocky beaches. This is an undeveloped beach, but there is a restroom and a public parking lot. After years of industrial use threatened its natural beauty, the area is now a protected restoration site. For a good boat launch, continue down the road to the **Quilcene Marina** (1731 Linger Longer Rd., 360/765-3131) on Dabob Bay.

Point Whitney Beach and Shellfish Lab (1000 Point Whitney Rd., Brinnon, 360/796-4601) isn't exactly a place where people go to lounge in the sun or to dip their toes in the water (and there really isn't a lot of that on the Olympic Peninsula anyway), but it is a beautiful and serene spot on Hood Canal at which you can visit an informational kiosk and learn about the area's tidelands and its marine life. Restrooms also are available here.

Hiking

Mount Townsend Trail

Distance: 8.2 miles round-trip
Duration: 4-6 hours
Elevation gain: 2,900 feet

Effort: Difficult
Trailhead: Northwest of Quilcene, off Forest Road 2760
Directions: From Highway 101, turn West onto Penny Creek Road. Follow this for 1.5 miles and then turn left on Big Quilcene River Road/Forest Road 2760. Drive for 13.5 miles (don't be confused when you see at sign at 12.5 miles for the Mount Townsend Trail; that actually goes to a lower trailhead to another hike) and make another left on FR 27-19. The trailhead will be another 0.75 mile down this road.

Mount Townsend Trail (www.fs.usda.gov) is one of the most popular trails in the area, if not all of the Olympic Peninsula, because of the fantastic views at the summit of 6,280-foot Mount Townsend. The popular upper trailhead begins at 4,000 feet. The trail quickly enters the Buckhorn Wilderness and travels through thick fir and hemlock trees past tiny Windy Lake and eventually to an open mountaintop, where you can see perfect views of Mount Baker, Mount Rainier, and, on the nicest days, the southern coast of Vancouver Island. Depending on which routes you take, the round-trip can be 6-10 miles. The views make the hike well worth it regardless of the distance necessary to get there.

Falls View Canyon Trail

Distance: 1.5 miles round-trip
Duration: 45 minutes-2 hours
Elevation gain: 300 feet
Effort: Easy
Trailhead: 3.5 miles south of Quilcene at Falls View Campground
Directions: From Highway 101, turn into Falls View Campground 3.5 miles south of Quilcene. Park to the left in the day-use picnic area, or park at the gate if the campground is closed.

Falls View Canyon Trail is an easy trek down a canyon to the Big Quilcene River and a 120-foot waterfall that appears to come roaring out of nowhere due to the large cliff-side trees surrounding its waters. Water flow can become light in summer but heavy in spring and fall. Also at Falls View Campground is a trailhead for the much easier **Falls View Loop Trail** (0.1 mile), which leads to an overlook of both the falls and the river.

Rainbow Canyon Nature Trail

Distance: 1 mile round-trip
Duration: 30 minutes-1 hour
Elevation gain: None
Effort: Easy
Trailhead: Rainbow Day Use Area, five miles south of Quilcene near Walker Pass
Directions: Five miles south of Quilcene on Highway 101, turn left onto Mount Walker Road. Follow this road for 0.25 mile to the Mount Walker parking lot. Across the street is a driveway to a campground. Head into the campground; the trail will be clearly marked.

As its name suggests, this hike leads to a canyon via a path filled with switchbacks, Douglas fir, fern, and several overlooks. See Elbow Creek drop over a cliff in the form of a small waterfall into a pool below.

Big Quilcene Trail

Distance: 11.5 miles round-trip
Duration: 5.5-8 hours
Elevation gain: 3,489 feet
Effort: Moderate-difficult
Trailhead: 16 miles outside Quilcene, first off Forest Service Road 27, then off Spur 2750
Directions: From Highway 101, turn west onto Penny Creek Road. Follow this for 1.5 miles and then turn left on Big Quilcene River Road/Forest Road 27. Follow this for 9.25 miles and turn left onto Forest Road 2750. Continue 4.75 miles to trailhead.

The Big Quilcene Trail actually is broken into two parts: upper and lower. The upper trail almost immediately enters the Buckhorn Wilderness, a 44,258-acre section of the Olympic National Forest filled with valleys and peaks. Buckhorn Mountain (elev. 6,956) is the highest here. The trail follows the Big Quilcene River past mile-high Camp Mystery to Marmot Pass at 6,000 feet. Spectacular panoramic views await on clear days, and, yes, there are plenty of marmots scattering through the undergrowth here. The best views are just north of the pass. From the pass, you can travel south into the Olympic National Park via the **Constance Pass Trail.**

Murhut Falls Trail

Distance: 1.6 miles round-trip
Duration: 1.5-3 hours
Elevation gain: 250 feet
Effort: Easy
Trailhead: Off Duckabush Road, south of Brinnon
Directions: From Highway 101, turn west onto Duckabush Road at milepost 310 between Shelton and Quilcene. Drive 6.3 miles and turn right at the junction with the sign to Murhut Falls Trail. Travel the remaining 1.3 miles to the trailhead.

Murhut Falls Trail is in the middle of the Duckabush Recreation Area and is an excellent hike for families. This former logging road is full of wildflowers in the summer and leads to a 130-foot, double-tiered waterfall. Watch for mud during the rainy season—and oftentimes after it.

Ranger Hole Trail

Distance: 2.1 miles round-trip
Duration: 1.5-4 hours
Elevation gain: 200 feet
Effort: Easy
Trailhead: 15 miles south of Quilcene, four miles down Duckabush Road
Directions: Approximately 37 miles north of Shelton, turn west at milepost 310 off of Highway 101 and onto Duckabush Road. Drive 3.6 miles to Interrorem Cabin, where you can park to access the trailhead.

Ranger Hole Trail is surrounded by fern and second-growth forest. The hike begins at the 500-square-foot, moss-covered **Interrorem Cabin,** built in 1907 and now the oldest Forest Service building on the Olympic Peninsula. Today, you can rent the cabin (877/444-6777, www.recreation.gov, $50). From the cabin, the trail leads down to the Duckabush River and the favorite fishing hole of park ranger Emery Finch, who was the first person to call the Interrorem Cabin home.

Water Sports

Tarboo Lake is a 24-acre active fishing hole in late spring and early summer, thanks to the hatchery-reared rainbow trout planted there each year. To get there, travel north of Quilcene on Center Road for 5.5 miles, then take a left on Tarboo Lake Road for three miles. Nearby **Crocker Lake** and **Leland Lake** also are two spots locals frequent that are seeded with rainbow trout each year.

Pleasant Harbor State Park (two miles south of Brinnon, east of Hwy. 101) doesn't have any services to offer visitors, but it does offer fishing, boating, canoeing, and scuba diving opportunities on Hood Canal, and private **Pleasant Harbor Marina** (308193 Hwy. 101, 360/796-4611 or 800/547-3479, www.pleasantharbormarina.com) is on-site and offers overnight moorage.

Wildlife Viewing

There's no shortage of spots to view wildlife on the Olympic Peninsula. Nearly every nature hike has some kind of wildlife lining its path, as does nearly every pullout off Highway 101 overlooking Hood Canal. But for those specifically looking for that one spot where they can see it all, head to the area around Tarboo Bay and Dabob Bay. The bays feed into one another and are fed by Tarboo Creek. At the mouth of the creek, the forested **Tarboo Wildlife Preserve** (4.5 miles northeast of Quilcene), as the Washington Department of Fish & Wildlife calls it, is home to bald eagles, spotted owls, shorebirds, bear, deer, and many more animals. To get there, head north of Quilcene on Center Road, and take a right onto Dabob Road. Go 1.5 miles and make another right on Dabob Post Office Road, then travel south until you reach the area. Expect primitive. There is no established parking area or facilities here, but you can park in spots alongside the road.

FESTIVALS AND EVENTS

Each Memorial Day Weekend, the two-day **Brinnon ShrimpFest** (360/796-4456, www.emeraldtowns.com) sets up shop on a grassy field at Dosewallips State Park east of Highway 101 and welcomes thousands of people to celebrate (and eat!) Hood Canal shrimp and other types of area seafood. Most years,

Olympic Music Festival

It may be held on an 1890s farm in what amounts to the middle of nowhere, but that doesn't stop people from across the country from coming to Quilcene each summer to listen to music at the Olympic Music Festival. The festival runs weekends from June through the first weekend of September and features some of the best chamber musicians in the United States. The concerts are held inside a barn, while people picnic and recreate in the 55 garden- and forest-filled acres surrounding it. The festival was founded in 1984, by former Philadelphia String Quartet member Alan Iglitzin, who lives with his pianist wife on the former dairy farm. For more information, visit www.olympicmusicfestival.org.

there are roughly 100 vendors selling their goods. But most important, there's shrimp being cooked several different ways and sold frozen for $12 a container. The frozen stuff sells out fast, and proceeds from the event go to local programs.

The area's most-acclaimed celebration by far is the **Olympic Music Festival** (7630 Center Rd., 360/732-4800, www.olympicmusicfestival.org), held every weekend day from the end of June through early September inside a barn in the middle of a 55-acre Quilcene farm. It's a strange setting—one where patrons sit on church pews and hay bales to watch the performers—in which to hear the chamber music the festival features, but it's also one that somehow works. Outside the barn, there's plenty of space to relax and picnic tables galore. The festival was created in 1984 by a former violinist of the Philadelphia Orchestra named Alan Iglitzin, who still is the festival director. Mozart, Beethoven, and Brahms in a century-old barn? Yes, and it's an award-winning event.

A relative newcomer to the area's entertainment scene is the **Full Moon Festival** (322 Munn Rd, Quilcene) held each August at the Munn Ranch in Quilcene. The musical event is a benefit for the American Cancer Society, and past performers have included Jimi Hendrix's brother Leon, and members of The Kingsmen.

If there was one event where those who love local art could gather and check it out, it would be at the **Olympic Art Festival** (40 Washington St., www.olympicartfestival.com) held three times a year at the Olympic Art Gallery in Quilcene. Dozens of area artists who work in all sorts of mediums attend each festival, and there also is entertainment.

SHOPPING

Shopping certainly isn't high on the list of reasons people choose to visit any parts of the Olympic Peninsula, especially the eastern portion where small towns dominate. Still, there are many local shops worth checking out if you're in the area. There are many bargains to be found thanks in part to low overhead and also to the anxiousness of local artisans to share and sell their unique creations.

Wildwood Antiques (293211 Hwy. 101, Quilcene, 360/765-0425) has a large number of consigners and an even larger number of antiques. It's certainly not the fanciest place on earth, but there are special treasures to be found here for the curious and patient.

The yard at the **Olympic Art Gallery** (40 Washington St., Quilcene, 360/765-0200, www.olympicartgallery.com, 11am-5pm Mon., Fri., Sat., 12:30pm-5pm Sun.) is a small gallery unto itself, with several pieces on display, including two tall trees guarding the building's entrance. Inside, there are Northwest-inspired works by several local and regional artists for sale, including the book *Fast Moving Water*, by photographer Keith Lazelle.

The Picket Fence (21 Dutch Ln., Quilcene, 360/774-0444, www.the-picket-fence.net, 10am-4pm the first weekend of every month) specializes in handcrafted goods for the home and garden, but there's much more than that here. Shoppers looking for unique crafts may be surprised to find such talent in Quilcene, but that's exactly what's here in this cute and tiny shop.

The Plaid Pepper (294963 Hwy. 101, Quilcene, 360/301-3244, www.theplaidpepper.com, 9am-4pm Tues.-Sat.) is another unexpected gem located in tiny Quilcene. The shop features local gifts, lavender-based goods, teas, and coffees, including the Dabob Bay Blend, made exclusively for the store.

ACCOMMODATIONS

A family-owned and -operated establishment for three generations, the **Hadlock Motel** (181 Chimacum Rd., Port Hadlock, 360/385-3111, www.hadlockmotel.com, $79-179 d) is quaint and convenient to the waterfront for crabbing, beachcombing, Jet Skiing, and other water-based recreation.

Hikers will definitely enjoy the **Mount Walker Inn** (61 Maple Grove Rd., Quilcene, 360/765-3410, www.mountwalkerinn.com, $65-105 d). There's a forest in the backyard and each room is an individual cabin with free wireless Internet, which comes in handy for looking up the locations of the nearby trailheads, of which there are many.

Overlooking peaceful Pleasant Harbor Marina and Hood Canal, ★ **The Harbor House** (308913 Hwy. 101, Brinnon, 360/796-4064, www.pleasantharbormarina.com/pleasantharborhouse, $100-150) is a bed-and-breakfast that has two large suites complete with wet bars, fireplaces, and fully stocked refrigerators. Each suite is 750 square feet and has a queen-sized bed.

Located on a still-operating farm, the **Elk Meadows B&B** (3485 Dosewallips Rd., Brinnon, 360/796-4886, www.elkmeadowswa.com, $65-140 d) offers a variety of lodging options, from classic B&B-style rooms to riverside tent cabins. It also offers a beautiful and quiet setting for those who value relaxation first and foremost.

A vacation cottage that sleeps up to four guests, the **Dabob Bay Cottage** (Piper Rd., Quilcene, 360/765-3947, www.dabobbaycottage.com, $100-125 d) has an entire mile of private beach for guests to fish, kayak, or simply enjoy a picnic. But you'll have to do it all without any furry friends. Pets aren't allowed here.

The literally named **Cabin on the Canal** (111 Pleasant Harbor Rd., Brinnon, 206/782-3868, www.cabinonthecanal.com, $140) is just that, an updated vacation cabin with accommodations for up to four guests on the banks of Hood Canal. The cabin has a complete kitchen, and a large deck with a view of the canal.

Camping

Newly renovated and inexpensive, the **Quilcene Community Campground** (294964 Hwy. 101, Quilcene, 360/385-9129, www.countyrec.com, $12) is the perfect choice for family campers on a budget, and it's next to the town's community center, too.

Operated by the U.S. Forest Service, the **Seal Rock Campground** (two miles north of Brinnon on Hwy. 101, 360/765-2200, www.fs.usda.gov, $18) is one of the few National Forest campgrounds located on saltwater, with harvestable oysters in season and available for public use. There are more than 40 campsites here, and you often can see and hear seals splashing in Hood Canal, which is just steps away from most campsites.

With a restaurant on-site and excellent homemade pies, **Halfway House RV Park** (41 Brinnon Ln., Brinnon, 360/796-4715, $25) makes a handy home base for RV adventures on the Olympic Peninsula. The 22 RV sites are a bit crammed together, though, so be warned.

FOOD

Known for seafood and especially clam chowder, the ★ **Olympic Timber House** (295534 Hwy. 101, Quilcene, 360/765-3500, www.olympictimberhouse.com, 11am-8pm daily, $12-36) has Northwest-themed decor and is a hidden gem on the Olympic Peninsula. Weekend evenings, Black Angus prime rib is on the menu, and the Main Street Meatloaf is available every day. Consider that a good thing, as this is one of the best restaurants around.

A family-run business, the **Twana Roadhouse** (294793 Hwy. 101, Quilcene, 360/765-6485, www.101brewery.com, 7am-8pm Mon.-Sat., 8am-8pm Sun., $7-21) has everything on the menu from homemade cookies to pizza to full breakfasts.

Located in the heart of Brinnon alongside Highway 101, the **Halfway House** (41 Brinnon Ln., Brinnon, 360/796-4715, 7am-7pm Mon.-Fri., 8am-7pm Sat.-Sun., $10-15) is a bright little diner with a living room-like ambience. Eating steak soup here, especially when the wind is whipping across from Hood Canal, is a great way to warm up your body as you continue on your journey.

Named by *Esquire* magazine as one of the best bars in the country, the ★ **Geoduck Tavern** (307103 Hwy. 101, Brinnon, 360/796-4430, $6-13) has great food and its owners have a sense of humor: one of the wall-mounted deer heads here has a speaker built into it, and patrons sometimes surprise each other by making the deer head talk. *Esquire* cited the bar's burger dip (two hamburger patties, swiss cheese, grilled onions on a homemade sourdough roll with a dipping sauce made from roast-beef drippings) as best, but the oyster sandwich is where it's at.

Located at the Pleasant Harbor Marina, the **Galley Deli** (308913 Hwy. 101, Brinnon, 360/796-4611, 8am-7pm Mon.-Thurs., 8am-8pm Fri.-Sun., $8-14) serves pizza, sandwiches, espresso, hamburgers, and soup, and has a barbecue every Friday and Saturday night.

INFORMATION AND SERVICES

The North Hood Canal Chamber of Commerce operates two visitors centers, one in Quilcene (295142 Hwy. 101, 360/765-4999) and one in Brinnon (306144 Hwy 101, 360/796-4350), the latter of which is located in the Brinnon Community Center Building and has a large yard with a covered area good for picnicking.

GETTING THERE AND AROUND

The quickest route to Quilcene from Tacoma is across the Tacoma Narrows bridges to Gig Harbor, then north on Highways 16 and 3, west on Highway 104, then south on Highway 101 to Quilcene. That trip is 75 miles and takes 1.5-2 hours, depending on traffic and season. There's also the option of taking a ferry from Seattle, but doing so will add another couple of hours to your trip.

Jefferson Transit (360/345-4777 or 800/833-6388, www.jeffersontransit.com) provides service from northern Olympic Peninsula cities to Brinnon, while **Mason County Transit** (360/426-9434 or 800/281-9434, www.masontransit.org) picks up from Brinnon and runs through Quilcene, Duckabush, and Eldon to Shelton.

Port Angeles and the Northern Peninsula

The northern Olympic Peninsula is home to the two largest lakes on the peninsula, Lake Crescent and Lake Ozette; both are easily accessible by car and offer numerous recreational opportunities. Due to its location alongside the peninsula's main thoroughfare, Highway 101, Lake Crescent is the easier to access and certainly the more visited of the two. Today, the lake has 5,100 square feet of surface area, but it actually used to be much larger. Some 7,000 years ago, a landslide split the deep, glacially carved body of water in two, creating a second small lake to the east that is now known as Lake Sutherland. A bit farther off-the-beaten path, massive Lake Ozette is near the northern border of the coastal section of Olympic National Park and features two three-mile-long boardwalks that link it to a low-use section of the Pacific Ocean.

The Olympic Peninsula's entire northern coast is bordered by the Strait of Juan de Fuca, a roughly 100-mile-long and 12-mile-wide waterway separating the United States and Canada's Vancouver Island. Named after a Greek mariner who visited the area in the 1500s, the strait is a vital water passage that links the commercial areas of the Puget Sound to the Pacific Ocean and points beyond. A ferry connection here between Port Angeles and Victoria, British Columbia, links the United States and Canada.

It may sound virtually impossible, but those looking to escape the water—at least the form of it that falls from the sky by the bucketful throughout most of the peninsula—even have a place to go here. Situated in a rain shadow created by the Olympic Mountains, the northeastern city of Sequim receives only 17 inches of rain a year. That's less than the city of Los Angeles and several other sunny spots across the world receive. There are even sections of Sequim where you can find a wild cactus or two.

The northwesternmost point in the contiguous United States is here, too, at Cape Flattery on the Makah Indian Reservation. Those looking for culture in the form of city life can find it in both art-filled Port Angeles and Port Townsend—a Victorian-themed city,

Previous: New Dungeness Lighthouse at Dungeness Spit near Sequim; lavender farm in Sequim. **Above:** Historic Joyce Depot Museum.

Look for ★ to find recommended sights, activities, dining, and lodging.

Highlights

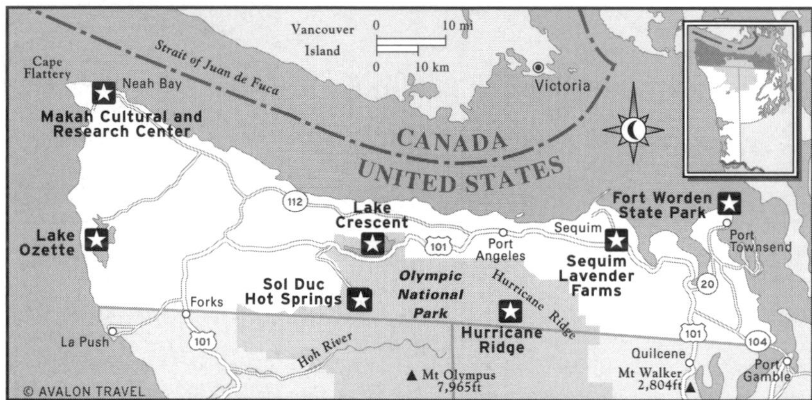

★ **Fort Worden State Park:** This state park, which was an operating military fort up until 1953, is home to an artillery museum, marine center, a lighthouse, and various interpretive trails (page 76).

★ **Sequim Lavender Farms:** Visit one of the many lavender farms in Sequim to learn about the (not always) purple plant and its many uses (page 86).

★ **Hurricane Ridge:** This ridge, high above the Elwha River Valley, offers breathtaking views, an abundance of hiking trails, and one of only three ski lifts in all of the U.S. National Parks (page 105).

★ **Lake Crescent:** Once two separate bodies of water, Lake Crescent is cold, clear, and some 600 feet deep. It's also the natural habitat of two species of trout that don't exist anywhere else in the world (page 105).

★ **Sol Duc Hot Springs:** The natural spring waters found here offer warmth in a resort-like setting. Those looking for something more will also find freshwater and chlorinated swimming pools (page 106).

★ **Lake Ozette:** The largest lake on the Olympic Peninsula is a jumping-off point for several coastal trails, as well as a popular recreation point on its own. Walk along the Cape Alava boardwalk to reach the westernmost point of the contiguous United States (page 113).

★ **Makah Cultural and Research Center:** This museum's permanent exhibit has hundreds of ancient Makah artifacts from an excavated Lake Ozette village on display (page 114).

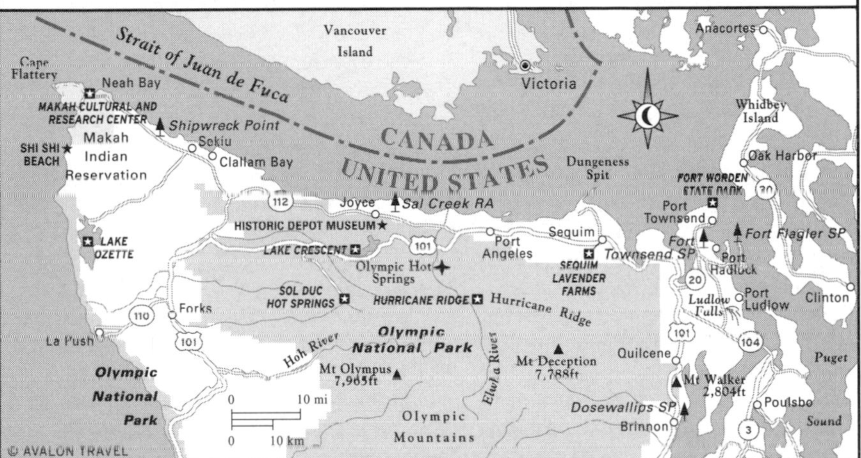

like its neighbor to the north, Victoria, British Columbia—with plenty of history and artsy residents.

HISTORY

As is the case with most of the Olympic Peninsula, the members of several scattered Native American tribes were the only residents here for thousands of years. Evidence of their existence has been found at several of the area's landmarks, most of which had been given names by the Native Americans long before those names were either changed outright or altered when the first European explorers visited in the 16th century. Later explorations led to colonization and settlements that capitalized and expanded thanks to the area's abundant natural resources. Sometimes, those explorers brought with them disease, which killed many Native Americans. Other times, they brought hostility, which led to wars in which more Native Americans lost their lives as their tribes signed treaties that pushed them onto reservations.

As had the Native Americans, whites began to settle along the coastal regions, where they too could benefit from access to the many vital water sources and tree-lined forests. Port Townsend was the first town on the peninsula, settled in 1851 by a New Englander drawn to the area by the personal and financial opportunities he felt it offered. Lumber mills quickly sprouted, and the area's economic identity as a logging mecca was born. It's an identity that still exists, at least in part, today, although most of the old-growth trees are gone and tourism now plays a large financial role in every corner of the Olympic Peninsula. The establishment of Olympic National Park in 1938 has only helped solidify tourism as an economic necessity.

PLANNING YOUR TIME

Most people will say the best time to visit is July and August, when the rain that saturates the area is at a minimum and temperatures are at their yearly highs. While this is indeed the time of year the weather is nicest, and also when businesses and sights are open longest (and the only time some are open at all), there's also a certain charm to be found here the rest of the year, when crowds are sparse and nature is doing its best to dampen and maintain the waters and forests that make the place so special during those summer months. Though there are shuttles and bus tours that will take you through the area originating at several local cities, the best way to see the area is by car. Parking is difficult to come by during peak hours at some of the more popular attractions, including Hurricane Ridge and Sol Duc Hot Springs.

Some of the region's biggest attractions, including Hurricane Ridge, Lake Crescent, and Sol Duc Hot Springs, fall within Olympic National Park. The northern region of the park (covered in this chapter) is likely its most popular portion, due to these popular attractions as well as the fact that this region is the quickest to get to from the densely populated Puget Sound region to the east. Hurricane Ridge, Lake Crescent, and Sol Duc Hot Springs are all easily accessible to vehicle traffic, making them crazy busy during the tourist months. Locals may do so during summer months, but tourists never avoid these places for good reason. They are brilliant and unique park highlights. All Olympic National Park sights listed in this chapter require an **Olympic National Park pass** ($25 per vehicle, $12 per pedestrian or bicyclist, good for seven days, available at all park entrances where a pass is required).

ORIENTATION

To navigate the area successfully, it's really only necessary to know two highways, Highway 101 and Highway 112. Everything you need to see begins and ends on these state routes, with Highway 20 shooting off Highway 101 to Port Townsend in the east, and Highway 113 relinking Highway 101 with Highway 112 in the west near Lake Pleasant, north of Forks.

Port Townsend

Port Townsend (pop. 9,100) is located at the northern tip of small Quimper Peninsula and was the first established town on the Olympic Peninsula. The town was originally named Port Townshend after a friend of English explorer Captain George Vancouver. Early settlers predicted the town would be one of the most prosperous seaports on the West Coast. This speculation earned the town the nickname "City of Dreams." The port did do quite well in the mid- to late 1800s, and many of the large Victorian-style mansions still present today were built during that time. Much of those prosperous predictions were based on the hope that a transcontinental railroad would be built and end in Port Townsend. When that never transpired, the city was dealt an economic blow. Then, as it did in most places across the United States, the Great Depression sank the city. Some of the mansions fell into disrepair and were demolished. Others barely held on, waiting for the day when their beauty and sturdy architecture would be appreciated by someone wishing to restore them.

Port Townsend saw a resurgence of sorts in the 1970s, and many people began realizing the town's natural beauty and came to retire in the area. In recent years, Port Townsend has developed a reputation as a safe haven for artistic souls. Today, the city's main draws are its Victorian heritage, homes, and shops, as well as adjacent Fort Worden State Park.

SIGHTS

Fort Flagler State Park

Located on unheralded and quiet Marrowstone Island, 794-acre Fort Flagler State Park operates in the shadow of nearby Fort Worden State Park, though its history is similar and its 19,100 feet of adjacent shoreline even more beautiful than what can be found at Fort Worden.

Like Fort Worden, Fort Flagler has a rich military-based history. Flagler was one of three U.S. Army forts built near the turn of the 20th century to guard the entrance to

Port Townsend

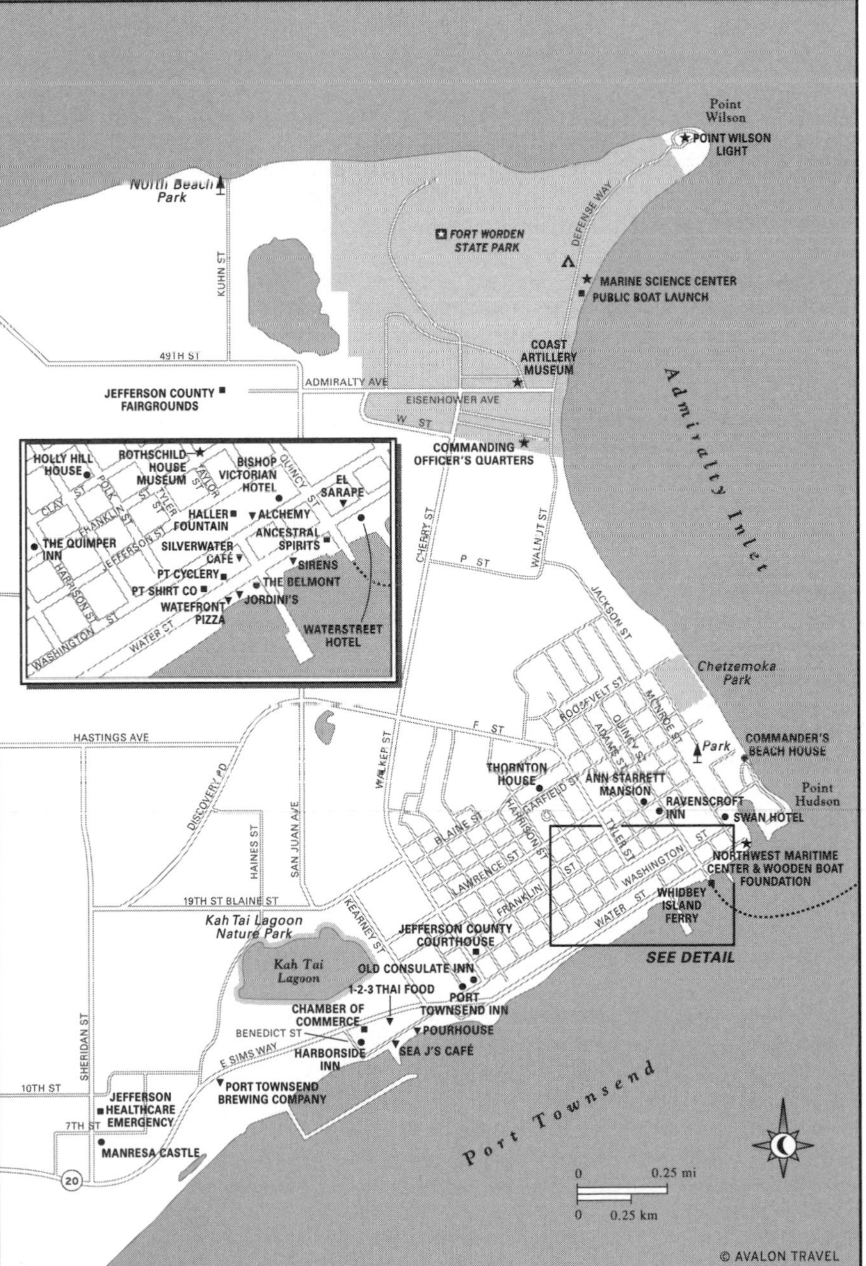

Puget Sound. Fort Flagler originally was the headquarters of the Harbor Defense of Puget Sound triumvirate, known as the "Triangle of Fire," but its location soon proved too remote, and the headquarters were moved to Fort Worden. During World War I, Flagler was a training center for army troops, a purpose it also served during World War II. The fort closed in 1953, and it became a state park two years later. Today, its former barracks—including the Hospital Steward's House and two Non-Commissioned Officers' Quarters buildings—can be rented by the public, as can numerous campsites. Miles of trails cross through and travel around the park, and the tiny **Marrowstone Point Lighthouse,** while closed to the public, has a unique history of its own. The adjacent keeper's building now houses the **Marrowstone Marine Field Station.** There's also a military museum located across from the park's office. The only store on the island is the **Nordland General Store** (7180 Flagler Rd., 360/385-0777, www.nordlandgeneralstore.com), where you can pick up some locally made goods, rent a boat, or grab some bait for your fishing adventures.

★ Fort Worden State Park

It's often easy access and proximity to Port Townsend that brings visitors to Fort Worden State Park. What keeps them here, and brings them back time and time again, is the park's history, scenery, and plethora of available activities.

As were Fort Flagler and Fort Casey, Fort Worden was built to help protect Puget Sound, and to help it do so it was equipped with the most modern defense weaponry available. That weaponry was upgraded with the times until the U.S. Army abandoned the fort in 1953. For several years after, Fort Worden was home to a state juvenile detention facility. It became a state park in 1973. In 1981, the film *An Officer and a Gentleman*, starring Richard Gere, Debra Winger, and Louis Gossett Jr., was filmed at Fort Worden and at various sites in Port Townsend.

The weapons and Hollywood film crew may be long gone, but Fort Worden's appeal remains strong. Located at the tip of Point Wilson, many of the former fort's buildings remain and are either available to tour or used for other purposes. That is the case with the **Coast Artillery Museum** (360/385-0373, www.coastartillery.org, 10am-5pm Fri.-Sat., 11am-4pm Sun.-Thurs., May-Aug., 11am-4pm daily, rest of the year, $4 adults, $2 children 6-12, under 6 free), which is housed in some former barracks. The museum's highlights include two disappearing guns and a 3-D model of the gun Battery Kinzie. The 6,000-square-foot **Commanding Officer's Quarters** (noon-5pm daily, May-Sept., $4 adults, $1 children 3-12) is another building that remains from the old days and is available to tour. The **Port Townsend Marine Science Center** (360/385-5582 or 800/566-3932, www.ptmsc.org, hours vary greatly by season, $5 adults, $3 kids 6-17, children under 6 free) is a can't-miss, especially for children, who will be able to get up close and personal with various sea creatures via touch tanks and glassed-in exhibits. The center also offers tours, lectures, slide shows, and more.

Those who want to spend some time outside can do so by exploring the park's 434 acres, which are filled with campgrounds and interpretive trails. The **Point Wilson Light,** built in 1913 and automated in 1976, isn't open for tours but still marks the entry into Admiralty Inlet from the Strait of Juan de Fuca.

Northwest Maritime Center & Wooden Boat Foundation

Anyone who is into boats, even if that means just looking at them, definitely needs to visit the **Northwest Maritime Center & Wooden Boat Foundation** (431 Water St., 360/385-3628, www.nwmaritime.org, 10am-5pm daily, free). The center's goal is to preserve the area's maritime heritage and it certainly accomplishes such. The 26,000-square-foot center offers many educational programs including sailing classes and camps; boat charters and tours; historic vessels; a boat shop; library; meeting space; boat house; and more. Following a lengthy fundraising campaign, the center moved to a new facility in 2009 and is now located in the middle of Port Townsend's downtown waterfront. One highlight is the center's compass rose, a beautiful outdoor work of art displaying the main directions of the compass and made up of the names of community members who donated to the new center. The center's second floor features a library and rotating exhibits.

Rothschild House Museum

The **Rothschild House Museum** (404 Taylor St., 360/385-1003, www.jchsmuseum.org, 11am-4pm daily, $4 adults, $1 ages 3-12, under 3 free) once was home to the family of German immigrant D. C. H. Rothschild, and now is owned by the state park system and listed on the National Register of Historic Places. The most unique aspect of the home may be that it was only ever owned by the Rothschild family, and minimal changes have been made since it was built in 1868. Much of the original furniture and decor are still intact, and one exhibit features several floral gowns from the Rothschild family. The house isn't very large nor is its outside ornately decorated, as are many of the older homes in town, because it was built prior to all of the area's Victorian-inspired homes. This fact only adds to the home's charm, particularly when you step through the front door. Outside, the grounds are filled with beautiful flower gardens and you'll get a neat view of Port Townsend Bay.

Ludlow Falls

Ludlow Falls (off Breaker Ln. between Paradise Bay Rd. and Oak Bay Rd., Port Ludlow) is an active salmon stream that flows almost year-round. In season, you can watch salmon head upstream to spawn. **The Ludlow Falls Interpretive Trail** (www.olympicpeninsulawaterfalltrail.com) is located on private lands, but the public is allowed access to the one-mile-long, easy-to-hike trail. Interpretive signs dot the trail, and there are several viewing points along the way. The trailhead is located in the Village Center parking lot. The falls are pretty, though not large or spectacular, and descend through lush greenery to Ludlow Creek.

Kah Tai Lagoon Nature Park

The 85-acre Kah Tai Lagoon Nature Park seems out of place in its location surrounded by businesses in the center of Port Townsend. But the lagoon—and the wildlife that call it home—was there first. The lagoon's name comes from the Indian name for the area around modern-day Port Townsend. Supporters of the lagoon, which now is a city park, have for decades fought against development for its survival. Today, many species of birds use the lagoon to rest and feed, and there are 2.5 miles of trails in and around the park. You won't quite be able to escape the city noises here, especially during the work week, but in some areas you can come close.

Chetzemoka Park

With more than five acres and expansive mountain views, **Chetzemoka Park** (900 Jackson St., Port Townsend, 360/385-7212) includes ADA-accessible facilities, a tropical water garden, flower gardens, and a beach with tidelands. The park, as are many other sites and things in and around Port Townsend, is named after S'Klallam Indian chief Chetzemoka.

Fort Townsend State Park

A 367-acre park with nearly 2,000 feet of marine frontage on Port Townsend Bay, **Fort Townsend State Park** (Old Fort Townsend Rd., 360/385-3595, www.parks.wa.gov, $10 one-day Discover Pass required) offers woods with hiking trails, facilities for boaters and crabbers, and various athletic fields. This former U.S. Army fort was built in 1856, abandoned a couple years later, then used as a hospital during the Civil War. The fort was reopened in 1874 and remained in use until 1895, when a fire destroyed the barracks.

Today, there's nothing of significance left to see, but there are several markers reminding visitors what once was here. The park still is an interesting place, particularly due to its series of interconnecting trails. The longest is the 1.5-mile **Pump House Trail,** which winds through the middle of the park. The **Bluff Trail, Cemetery Trail, Big Trees Trail,** and **Fern Garden Trail** are all shorter and lead hikers to exactly what their names would indicate. Dogs are welcome here but must be on a leash. Some of the trails are open to bikes, too.

SPORTS AND RECREATION

Hiking and Biking

Gibbs Lake is a Jefferson County park (West Valley Rd., Chimacum) that includes seven miles of mountain biking trails, some with built-in jumps and elevated logs for balancing and doing tricks, all around a 45-acre, tree-lined lake. A majority of the trails here are best-suited for mountain bikers and horses, but they also can be hiked. The best for that purpose is the **Walter Hoffman Trail** (1.75 miles), which begins at the parking lot and loops around most of the lake. If you connect with **Jack's Track Trail** (0.75 mile) you can loop around the whole lake, ending back at the parking lot from which you departed. There's also camping, fishing, and a ropes course.

P.T. Cyclery (252 Tyler St., 360/385-6470, www.ptcyclery.com, 9am-6pm Mon.-Sat. summer, noon-6pm Tues.-Sat. winter) has mountain bikes, road bikes, kid trailers, and more for rent, and also has everything those looking to repair their own bike—or buy a new one—might need. The staff also has a great knowledge of where exactly you can use your bikes locally.

Water Sports

As one might expect in an area surrounded by water, there are plenty of places to fish in Port Townsend. The **Union Wharf** (end of Taylor St. on Port Townsend Bay) is one such place, where anglers can fish from a newly constructed dock built after the original collapsed. There are several other public docks in downtown open to crabbing and fishing. You can do the same at the **Marine Science Center** (Fort Worden State Park, 532 Battery Way, Port Townsend, 360/385-5582, www.ptmsc.org) and at the **Point Hudson Jetty** (end of Water St.). South of town, **Anderson Lake State Park** (Hwy. 20 and Anderson Lake Rd.) is a good place to fish for trout. Fishing licenses are required at all of the locations listed above and are available at the website of the Washington Department of Fish & Wildlife (www.wdfw.wa.gov).

Or you can leave it all up to the pros and consult with them to help plan your fishing trip. The best people to talk to are at the **Peninsula Sportsman Guide and Outfitting Service** (360/379-0906, www.peninsulasportsman.com). They offer expert guides that take families or singles fishing for halibut, cod, trout, crab, shrimp, and more. A variety of trips are available.

PT Outdoors (1017-B Water St., 360/397-3608, www.ptoutdoors.com) is an outfitter that offers gear for kayaks for rental and stand up paddlers (SUPs), both of which are great ways to get out into the waters of Port Townsend Bay and catch a different view of the city behind you. They also run special kayak tours of Fort Worden and Bird Island.

A full-service marina and RV park that includes such amenities as free wireless Internet access for guests, the **Port Townsend Boat Haven** (2601 Washington St., 800/228-2803, www.portofpt.com/marine-services/marinas) has everything for travelers, including showers, laundry, a boat launch ramp, dump station, upland storage, covered storage, and travel lifts of up to 300 tons capacity.

Golf

Those wishing to golf in the area have two solid choices. The oldest public golf course in the state, **Discovery Bay Golf Club** (7401 Cape George Rd., 360/385-0704, www.discoverybaygolfcourse.com, $28 weekdays, $35 weekends) has a full 18 holes with spectacular views of both the Olympics and Cascades, as well as walking trails and other amenities for the nongolfers in the family. Billing itself as the "driest golf course on the Olympic Peninsula," the **Port Townsend Golf Club** (1948 Blaine St., Port Townsend, 360/385-4547, $25 summer, $18 winter) has low greens fees as well as discounts for seniors and youngsters.

ENTERTAINMENT AND EVENTS

Nightlife

A community fixture since 1997, the **Port Townsend Brewing Company** (330 10th St., 360/385-9967, www.porttownsend-brewing.com, noon-7pm Sat.-Tues., Thurs., noon-8pm Wed., noon-9pm Fri.) features 10 varieties of beers and ales brewed right on the premises, a year-round tasting room, and a summertime Friday night concert series with Northwest jazz and blues artists.

With an extensive selection of microbrews, live music every Friday and Saturday, and fresh seafood on the menu, **Sirens** (823 Water St., 360/379-1100, www.sirenspub.com, noon-close daily, $8-20) is a favorite of locals, but tourists are welcome, too. The food menu is full of burgers and seafood appetizers, and the view from the outdoor deck is one of the best in the area.

Fans of live music and those who like to dance will enjoy the offerings of the **Upstage** (various locations, 360/385-2216, www.new-upstage.com). Once located in the historic Terry Building, the business is now looking for a new home and using various interim venues to host its wide variety of live music almost every night of the week, including gigs by some popular Northwest-based performers, and open mike nights on Mondays. With the venues rotating, it's necessary to call to figure out where the goods are being laid down on your particular evening of interest.

If local beers are your thing (and why wouldn't they be when you're on vacation?), the **Pourhouse** (2231 Washington St., 360/379-5586, www.ptpourhouse.com, noon-close daily), should be on your agenda. With 200 types of beer available in bottles, and more than a dozen on tap, and live music outdoors during the summer, the Pourhouse is a nice place to grab a beer and a bite.

Art Galleries

If Native American arts and crafts are your thing, **Ancestral Spirits** (701 Water St., 360/385-0078, www.ancestralspirits.com, 10:30am-6pm daily) is a great place. It's one-stop shopping for everything from baskets to carvings, textiles, and jewelry, with a special emphasis on the tribes of the coastal Pacific Northwest. The store features native drums, paddles, masks, blankets, totem poles, and more.

With more of a fine arts emphasis, **Earthenworks** (702 Water St., 360/385-0328, www.earthenworksgallery.com, 10am-5:30pm Sun.-Thurs., 10am-7pm Fri.-Sat.) carries the metalwork of Tom Torrens, and also carries the glass, ceramics, textiles, and woodworks of several other artists. The gallery has been around since 1977, when it was created by Donald and Cynthia Hoskins.

A nonprofit gallery and organization dedicated to promoting local arts, **Northwind Arts Center** (2409 Jefferson St., 360/379-1086, www.northwindarts.org, noon-5pm Thurs.-Mon.) sponsors educational programs, workshops, and venues for both visual and literary arts. The center has a large showcase gallery for artists, a workshop space, and a large main exhibit gallery that features paintings and sculptures.

A private gallery displaying works from both the Northwest and around the world, **William's Gallery** (914 Water St., 360/385-3630, www.williams-gallery.com, 10am-6pm Mon.-Sat., noon-5pm Sun.) also has a monthly featured-artist program and regular gallery shows featuring ceramics and pottery, woodworks, photography, textiles, jewelry, glass, and more.

Owned in a co-op arrangement by local artists since 1997, the **Port Townsend Gallery** (715 Water St., 360/379-8110, www.porttownsendgallery.com, 10am-6pm daily) highlights the work of Olympic Peninsula artists in a wide variety of media, from paintings to pottery to more esoteric works such as silver gelatin photo prints.

Festivals and Events

The highlight of the **Rhododendron Festival** (various Port Townsend locations, www.rhodyfestival.org), held the third week of May, are the beautiful pink flowers, of course, which you'll see everywhere you look in the town during festival time and beyond. The grand parade, however, comes in a close second, and the associated activities—including the abundant food, carnival, and art shows—are pretty neat, too.

The summer concert season in Port Townsend is a good one, featuring a wide variety of music. **Festival of American Fiddle Tunes** (early July, 360/385-3102, ext. 110, www.centrum.org/fiddle), **Jazz Port Townsend** (last week of July, 360/385-3102, ext. 110, www.centrum.org/jazz), and the **Port Townsend Acoustic Blues Festival** (first week of August, 360/385-3102, ext. 110, www.centrum.org/blues) all take place at Fort Worden State Park, though the events also spill over into local bars. The events are hosted by the nonprofit **Centrum Foundation** (360/385-3102, ext. 110, www.centrum.org), which also sponsors several other events throughout the year.

Held every year in late September, the **Port Townsend Film Festival** (211 Taylor St. #33, 360/379-1333, www.ptfilmfest.com) has featured past appearances from Turner Classic Movies' Robert Osborne and famed actor Tony Curtis. A variety of national and regional feature and short films and a street fair with food highlight this event. This festival is a huge event in the city, so it's best to book lodging early if you plan to attend, or even if you just plan to stay in Port Townsend or the general area during the film festival weekend.

The **Wooden Boat Festival** (431 Water St., www.woodenboat.org, $15 for a day, $30 for weekend), held in early September, bills itself as the largest wooden boat festival in the world. It has been held every year since the 1970s and is a can't-miss event that draws tens of thousands of people. Hundreds of boats are on display during the event, including Native American canoes, tall ships, speedboats, and more. Opportunities to get on some of the boats exist, and there are public tours available. Demonstrations, food, art, tours, music, and more are also on the three-day agenda.

Held during the second week of August, the **Jefferson County Fair** (4907 Landes St., Port Townsend, www.jeffcofairgrounds.com, $6 adults, $5 seniors and students, $2 children 6-12, children 5 and under free) features all the goodness one would expect to find in a typical small-town fair in the West, including animal exhibits hosted by the local 4-H and FFA groups, fried food, fair rides, contests, entertainment, and games.

Port Townsend Gallery Walks are held 5:30pm-8:30pm the first Saturday of the month in downtown, while the **Port Townsend Farmers Market** (at Tyler St., between Lawrence and Clay, www.jeffersoncountyfarmersmarket.org) is open 9am-2pm Saturdays and 2pm-6pm Wednesdays during the summer months. The market has more than 70 vendors each week, including products from some 40 farms.

SHOPPING

Port Townsend is quite possibly the Olympic Peninsula's best shopping city and also its most walkable town. A majority of the shops are located downtown along and just off Water Street. You can find just about everything you're looking for here, from food and drink to art, books, clothes, trinkets, and local souvenirs.

PT Shirt Company (940 Water St., 360/385-1911, www.ptshirtcompany.com, 10:30am-5:30pm Mon.-Fri., 10am-6pm Sat.-Sun.) has several unique T-shirts, sweatshirts, hats, and more, many with catchy slogans or works of art related to Port Townsend.

Sunrise Coffee Company (315-B 10th St., 360/385-4117, www.sunrisecoffee.net) is a good spot to drink and/or purchase some specialty coffees roasted on-site. If you look for them, you'll see many of the Sunrise's blends in stores and restaurants across the Olympic Peninsula, too. Crack O'Dawn and Blue Moose Blend are two of the best.

New Age fans, or those just looking for some incense, spiritual goods, or a related book or two, should visit **Phoenix Rising** (696 Water St., 360/385-4464, www.phoenixrising-pt.com, 10am-6pm daily).

Chefs in any group must spend at least a few minutes at **The Green Eyeshade** (720 Water St., 360/385-3838 or 888/785-3838, 9:30am-6pm Mon.-Thurs., Sat.-Sun., 9:30am-8pm Fri.). The small appliances, gadgets, dinnerware, cookbooks, linens, and more often are unique, and many items are imported from around the world. If you're lucky, you'll be in town when a cooking demonstration is scheduled.

Wandering Angus (914 Water St., 360/301 0913, www.wanderingangus.com, 10am-6pm daily) takes its name from a W. B. Yeats poem and is a Celtic-themed business selling music, jewelry, crystals, kilts, and more.

The Twisted Ewe (919 Washington St., 360/379 9273, www.thetwistedewe.com, 11am-5pm Mon.-Sat., noon-5pm Sun.) is a yarn and needlework shop with many custom patterns.

ACCOMMODATIONS

$100-150

Located on the second and third floors of the historic N. D. Hill building, the ★ **Waterstreet Hotel** (635 Water St., 800/735-9810, www.waterstreethotelporttownsend.com, $50-140 d) is entered through the Pacific Traditions Gallery, which features Native American art. Built in 1889, the Waterstreet has maintained its charm and, in places, shows its age. For those looking for uniqueness rather than a generic hotel, this is a good choice. The rooms are clean and some offer great views of the city and the water. An added bonus: Children 12 and under stay free.

Centrally located in the Seaport district, the **Port Townsend Inn** (2020 Washington St., 800/216-4985, www.porttownsendinn.com, $68-168 d) has a year-round indoor heated pool and spa in a pretty parklike setting. The rooms here, however, could use some work.

The Palace Hotel (1004 Water St., 360/385-0773 or 800/962-0741, www.palacehotelpt.com, $59-109 s or d) was built in 1889 and has a lot of history behind it. Over the years, it has been a saloon, a hotel, and a brothel nicknamed "The Palace of Sweets." The hotel features unique guest rooms, a relaxing lobby, a coffeehouse on the bottom floor, and Victorian-themed rooms with high ceilings. Those high ceilings come with a bit of a price: Stairs. There are lots of them here, so be prepared.

The only bed-and-breakfast in Port Townsend actually located on the beach, the **Commander's Beach House** (400 Hudson St., 888/385 1778, www.commandersbeachhouse.com, $120-170 d) is also an easy walk from restaurants, shops, the Northwest Maritime Center, and Fort Worden's Marine Science Center. This definitely is a house, with a shared living room and uniquely furnished guest rooms.

An elegant five-bedroom Victorian house in the heart of Port Townsend's Uptown district, the **Holly Hill House** (611 Polk St., 800/435-1454, www.hollyhillhouse.com, $108-190) features extensive gardens with more than 80 rosebushes, and the Camperdown Elm, which is listed on the Historic Tree Register.

The Quimper Inn (1306 Franklin St., 800/557-1060, www.quimperinn.com, $98-160 d) mixes the historical with the modern. With several themed rooms, including the Library (a bedroom with 1,200 books), the Quimper also has free wireless Internet access for guests.

Tucked in the middle of the many shops and eateries that line Port Townsend's popular Water Street, **The Belmont** (925 Water St., 360/385-3007, www.thebelmontpt.com, $79-129 d) is housed in downtown's Sterming building, which was built in 1889 by a local saloon keeper. The building housed many businesses over the years and in 1992 reopened as The Belmont. Today, it is the only remaining restaurant and saloon that dates back to the 1880s. The rooms here have character and are spacious and charming. There's also an adjoining bar and restaurant, highlights of which include Oysters Rockefeller, pan-seared scallops, and 16-ounce Meyer Ranch red Angus rib eye, seasoned with The Belmont's own steak butter. Dinners are in the $15-27 range and the food receives high marks from locals and visitors alike. Of course you'll want to leave your hotel on your visit, but if you don't this is the perfect place to stay.

Located right next to the Port Townsend Boat Haven, the **Harborside Inn** (330 Benedict St., 800/942-5960, www.harborside-inn.com, $119-179 d) has 63 rooms, all which have views of the harbor and Admiralty Inlet. There's also a meeting room that can accommodate up to 70 people.

$150-200

The home of an imperial German consul from 1908 to 1911, the **Old Consulate Inn** (313 Walker St., 800/300-6753, www.oldconsulate.com, $120-230 d) is filled with Victorian antiques, has an extensive library, and has a music room with a grand piano and Celtic floor harp for guests to play and enjoy.

Built as a farmhouse in 1885, the **Thornton House** (1132 Garfield St., 360/385-6675, www.thorntonhousept.com, $155-175 d) has only three guest rooms. The innkeepers here are super friendly and the rooms elegant.

A classic seaport bed-and-breakfast, the **Ravenscroft Inn** (533 Quincy St., 855/290-8840, www.ravenscroftinn.com, $150-250 d) has a Great Room for meetings, weddings, and receptions, as well as guest rooms with French doors opening onto a large upper-story veranda with a view of the port.

With free access to the Port Townsend Athletic Club and a pet-friendly policy, the ★ **Bishop Victorian Hotel** (714 Washington St., 800/824-4738, www.bishopvictorian.com, $140-235 d) has 16 rooms with fireplaces, space for wedding receptions and conferences, and extensive gardens.

Famous for being one of the locations shot for the film *An Officer and a Gentleman,* the **Tides Inn** (1807 Water St., 800/822-8696, www.tides-inn.com, $72-287 d) has rooms with private decks overlooking Port Townsend Bay, in-room whirlpool tubs, and even a special bridal suite. This place has rooms available in just about every price range.

Built in 1889 by a wealthy contractor as a home for his new bride, the ★ **Ann Starrett Mansion** (744 Clay St., 800/321-0644, www.starrettmansion.com, $115-225 d) has a central grand spiral staircase with an eight-sided domed tower, inside of which are painted portraits of the former lady of the house. The master suite has a canopy bed and a cot-like piece of furniture called a "fainting couch."

The former home of the first mayor of Port Townsend, **Manresa Castle** (7th and Sheridan, 800/732-1281, www.manresacastle.com, $109-229 d) also has been a training college for Jesuit priests. Today, it boasts 43 rooms, meeting and conference facilities, and the **Castle Key** restaurant.

Featuring an 18-hole golf course, the ★ **Resort at Port Ludlow** (1 Heron Rd., Port Ludlow, 877/805-0868, www.portludlow-resort.com, $119-259 d) also has a full-service marina, as well as vacation condo rentals and a large rental guest house.

Over $200

Featuring gardens, a backyard waterfall, and a game room as well as modern amenities, the **Inn at McCurdy House** (405 Taylor St., 360/379-4824, www.innatmccurdyhouse.com, $150-250 d) will also make dinner reservations for you in town. And afterward, they've got a large library of DVDs and wireless Internet access to occupy your evening.

Located downtown, the **Swan Hotel** (222 Monroe St., 800/766-1718, www.theswanhotel.com, $105-280 d) has both hotel rooms and guest cottages, high-speed Internet connectivity, high-definition televisions, and free access to the Port Townsend Athletic Club.

Camping

With two campgrounds bordering a historic coastal fortress, ★ **Fort Worden State Park** (200 Battery Park Way, 360/344-4431, www.parks.wa.gov, $14-42) takes reservations up to a year in advance, and both campgrounds have full-service water and sewer hookups as well as restrooms with showers.

Another site with a rich military history, **Old Fort Townsend State Park** (two miles south of Port Townsend on Old Fort Townsend Rd., 360/385-3595, www.parks.wa.gov, $12-31) has 40 campsites and a group lodge that can accommodate up to 80 guests.

Able to accommodate RV groups of all sizes, the **Jefferson County Fairgrounds** (4907 Landes St., 360/385-1013, www.jeffcofairgrounds.com, $15-20) has 80 camping sites, dump stations, and showers, and it hosts special events year-round. Camping is on a first-come, first-served basis.

In addition to 32 slips and 800 feet of docks for boaters, the **Point Hudson Marina and RV Park** (103 Hudson St., 360/385-2828, www.portofpt.com, $20-52) has 48 RV spaces and is adjacent to the Northwest Maritime Center.

FOOD

American

The **Fountain Café** (920 Washington St., 360/385-1364, 11am-4pm and 5pm-9pm Sun.-Thurs., 11am-4pm and 5pm-9:30pm Fri.-Sat., $15-26) sits atop many people's "best of" lists for a reason. The small interior's eclectic decor filled with beautiful works of art on brightly colored walls and sparkling lights can be off-putting to some, but the food is great, presented well, and worth it. Vegetarians should try the black bean cakes; meat eaters, the lamb burger.

If it's lunch you're after, head to **Jordini's on the Water** (929 Water St., Ste. D, 360/385-2037, www.jordinis.com, 11am-5pm Mon.-Thurs., 11am-6pm Fri.-Sat., $7-11) and grab a sub sandwich and a pint of Port Townsend Brewing Company's beer as you look out over the water.

Cafés and Delis

Tucked away on a downtown side street, **Lehani's Deli and Coffee** (221 Taylor St., 360/385-3961, $6-10) is a hidden gem despite its cramped quarters. Locals come for coffee, sweets, and breakfast. Then they come back again. And again.

The name of ★ **Sea J's Café** (2501 Washington St., 360/385-6312, 6am-8pm Mon.-Sat., 7am-8pm Sun., $7-10) is a little misleading, because this place isn't what one typically would think of in a café. The menu at this local staple is filled with greasy burgers. The lobby is filled with used books. The walls are covered with bumper stickers. Combined, these elements make for a great atmosphere and a memorable meal.

Those in the know are willing to make the drive out of Port Townsend to the **Chimacum Café** (9253 Rhody Dr., Chimacum, 360/732-4631, 6am-9pm daily, $13-25) when they're looking for a good breakfast or a slice of fresh blackberry pie. A similar out-of-town option exists at the **Ajax Café** (21 N. Water St., Port Hadlock, 360/385-3450, www.ajaxcafe.com, 5pm-9pm Tues.-Sun. $12-24). It's only open for dinners, but they're good ones. Blue cheese and fig ravioli, oysters on the half shell, and stuffed pork chops at a deli? Yep, at least at this one.

Fancy food neatly presented in a clean environment is what the ★ **Silverwater Café** (237 Taylor St., 360/385-6448, www.silverwatercafe.com, 11:30am-3pm and 5pm-9pm Sun.-Thurs., 11:30am-9:30pm Fri.-Sat., $13-29) has to offer diners. The café has come a long way since its beginnings as a small fish-and-chips shack. They still serve fish-and-chips here, but the expansive menu now also includes more upscale fare, including truffled duck and braised lamb.

French toast, pork loin sandwiches, and poulet roti chicken. **Sweet Laurette Café & Bistro** (1029 Lawrence St., 360/385-4886, www.sweetlaurette.com, 8am-dinner Wed.-Sun., closed Mon.-Tues., $15-30) has something for the upper-end-seeking diner at any time of day.

Fine Dining

Housed in a building that was built in 1885, **The Belmont** (925 Water St., 360/385-3007, www.thebelmontpt.com, 11am-close daily, $14-29) is the only waterfront restaurant in the city that dates back to the 1880s. The decor is a tad dated, though charming, but the service and the excellent Black Angus filet mignon ($26.95) more than make up for any visual shortcomings. Toss in a waterfront deck that allows for access to the beach and it's easy to see why this place is often full.

Alchemy Bistro and Wine Bar (842 Washington St., 360/385-5225, www.alchemybistroandwinebar.com, lunch 11am-3pm, dinner 5pm-9pm daily, $16-26) has a small but sweet dinner menu filled with seafood, steaks, and lamb. Try some new blends in the wine bar, which is open 4pm-11pm every day. You'll see a few locals on the wine list here, but most are European.

Italian and Pizza

For a taste of authentic Italy in a Victorian town, try **Lanza's Ristorante** (1020 Lawrence St., 360/379-1900, www.lanzaspt.com, 5pm-10pm Tues.-Sat., $15-21). With always-full plates, you won't leave here hungry, even if you didn't know to ask for a slice of the awesome Italian wedding cake they serve for dessert. Before dessert, try a calabrian salad with angel hair pomodoro or tortellini carne.

There's no better place in the area for a slice of pie than ★ **Waterfront Pizza** (915 Water St., 360/385-6629, 11am-8pm Sun.-Thurs., 11am-10pm Fri.-Sat., $12-20), which uses a 100-year-old sourdough starter to make its crust. Expect a lot of people and a load of fun. A street-level storefront serves pizza by the slice for those who want a quick bite to eat and don't want to wait for service.

The claim made by the **Pizza Factory**'s (1102 Water St., 360/385-7223, $15-20) sign ("We Toss 'em, They're Awesome") is a bold one. Depending on your definition of awesome, it may be a claim that is met, especially for families with children looking to be entertained in a play area while dining. The best is the captain's special, which is loaded with pepperoni, ham, onions, bacon, mushrooms, and green peppers. But what's truly awesome here are the sub sandwiches, especially the meatball.

Mexican

Earth-toned colors and Mexican art is what you'll see at **El Sarape** (628 Water St., 360/379-9343, www.elsarapept.com, 11am-9pm Mon.-Thurs., 11am-10pm Fri.-Sat., closed Sun., $9-16), as well as plenty of standard Mexican fare and stiff drinks, including a tasty homemade sangria.

La Isla (1145 Water St., 360/385-1714, 11am-9pm Sun.-Thurs., 11am-10pm Fri.-Sat., $10-14) is also a pretty standard Mexican restaurant, although the waterside views here separate it from the rest.

Quick Bites

Elevated Ice Cream (631 Water St., 360/385-1156, www.elevatedicecream.com, 10am-9pm Sun.-Thurs., 10am-10pm Fri.-Sat., $3-6) is an old-fashioned ice cream parlor and candy shop. They make their own ice cream here, and offer neat flavors such as Blind Love, Cardamom, and Sequim Strawberry. The colorful shop is nearly as enticing as what's offered inside it.

Thai

Though **1-2-3 Thai Food** (2219 E. Sims Way, 360/344-3103, 11am-9pm daily, $8-14) may look like the typical restaurant you could find in any strip mall in the United States, one thing separates this place from many others: an extremely large menu. The salmon curry is an interesting dish, blending locals' favorite fish with the traditional Asian dish. The restaurant is geared toward the takeout crowd, so it's not the place for a fancy sit-down meal—but there are seats to be had for those who like to take their spiciness sitting down. Meanwhile, **Banana Leaf Thai Bistro** (609 Washington St., 360/379-6993, www.bananaleafthaibistro.com, 11am-9pm Mon.-Sat., noon-9pm Sun., $10-16) is a pricier but fancier Thai food option complete with outdoor seating, weather permitting. The desserts here are unique and delicious: The mango sticky rice paired with a pint of Reel Amber from the Port Townsend Brewing Company (on tap here) can make even the best of days a little better.

INFORMATION AND SERVICES

More information about this historic port city can be found at the **Port Townsend Public Library** (1220 Lawrence St., 360/385-3181). Travel information is provided at the **Jefferson County Chamber of Commerce** (440 12th St., 360/385-7869 or 888/365-6978).

Visitors needing emergency medical assistance may find it at the **Jefferson Healthcare Emergency** department (834 Sheridan St., 360/385-2200) or at the walk-in clinic (934 Sheridan St., 360/379-0477, 10am-7pm daily) next door.

GETTING THERE AND AROUND

Port Townsend is one of the stops for the **Washington State Ferry** (206/842-2345 or 888/808-7977, www.wsdot.wa.gov), which connects the city to Keystone on Whidbey Island. They run roughly every 45 minutes and cost $3.25 one-way for walk-ons and $13.40 one-way for cars, which includes the driver's fare.

Many people also arrive in Port Townsend by car, though it can be difficult to find parking, especially during summer. There are basically two driving routes to get to Port Townsend from Sea-Tac Airport. You can head north on I-5 and take a ferry to Bainbridge Island and drive from there, or you can drive south to Tacoma and cut across to the Olympic Peninsula through Gig Harbor. Either way, the trek takes 2-3 hours.

Jefferson Transit (360/385-4777 or 800/773-7788, www.jeffersontransit.com) offers park and rides, which are large parking lots where travelers leave their cars while riding the bus and later return to pick them up. It is smart to take advantage of park and rides around here, especially during busy times of the year. Port Townsend, particularly its downtown core, is an easy city to navigate on foot once you get there.

Carless travelers coming directly from Sea-Tac Airport should call **Olympic Bus Lines** (360/417-0700 or 800/457-4492, www.olympicbuslines.com, $49 one-way) to take advantage of one of its two daily trips on the **Dungeness Line.**

Sequim-Dungeness Valley

Sequim (pronounced S'kwim) is best known for two things: lavender and the sunshine that helps the purple plant produce in such abundance. The sunshine part is surprising to many, considering the town of approximately 7,000 is indeed a part of the Olympic Peninsula. But Sequim, and the Dungeness Valley that surrounds it, lies in a rain shadow created by the Olympic Mountains and air currents, which blow clouds right around the town. The result is an average of 17 inches of rainfall a year, in an area where triple-digit yearly accumulations aren't out of the ordinary.

The S'Klallam Indians called this area along the Strait of Juan de Fuca home long before the first white settlers came here in the mid-1850s. The city's name is a derivative of the S'Klallam word *skwim,* which means "place for going to shoot," as in hunting, which the Native Americans did here in abundance. Today, the mild weather makes Sequim

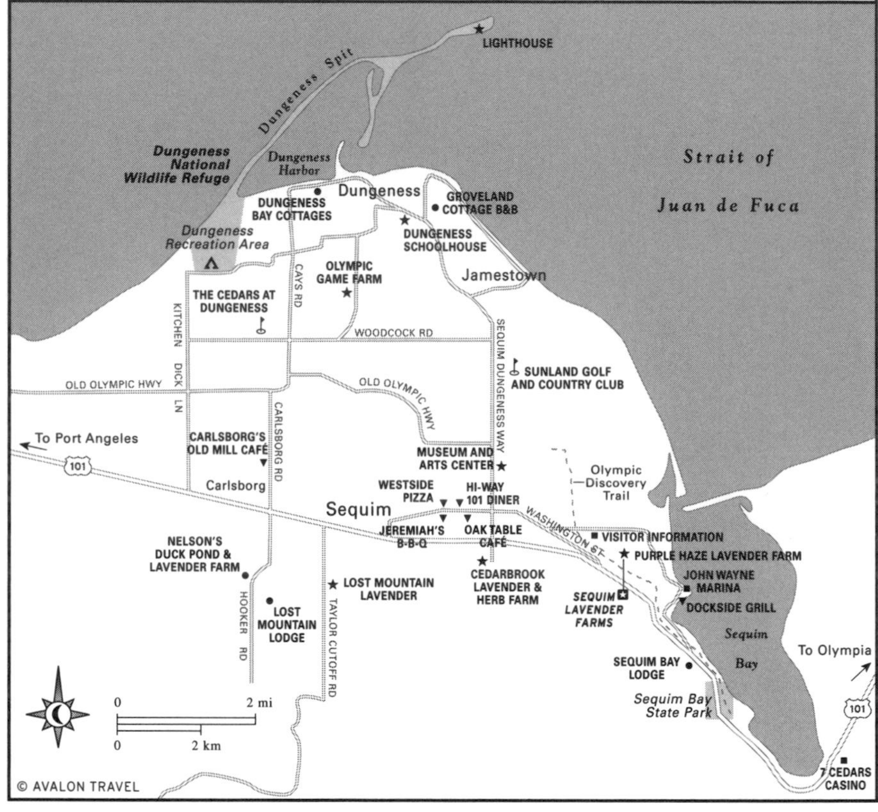

a popular retirement area as well as a popular place for recreationists. And, of course, those who love lavender farms and shopping for the plethora of products the plant is turned into.

SIGHTS

★ Sequim Lavender Farms

That lavender plays a large role in the Dungeness Valley is easy to see from the windows of an automobile as you drive around. Each of the massive fields of the fragrant purple plant is part of a network of area farms called the **Sequim Lavender Farmers Association** (www.sequimlavenderfarms.com). Though all the farms produce lavender, each farm is developed from the vision of its owners, and each owner has different harvesting techniques and uses for lavender. With creative names such as **Purple Haze Lavender Farm** (180 Bell Bottom Ln., 360/683-1714, www.purplehazelavender.com), it's difficult not to be curious as to who the people responsible for such farms are and exactly what they have to offer. At Purple Haze, for example, there are more than 15,000 lavender plants and more than 50 varieties. Visitors are encouraged to walk through the gardens, taking in not only the colors (not all lavender here is purple), but also the rich scents.

The Sequim Lavender Farmers Association produces a driving guide to local farms, as well as various events throughout the year, including the **Sequim Lavender Festival** each July, which includes a tour of local farms, a community celebration, and an opportunity to pick your own plants.

Dungeness National Wildlife Refuge

The **Dungeness Spit,** the world's largest natural sand spit, is responsible for the creation of **Dungeness Bay** and **Dungeness Harbor.** Both the bay and the harbor—and the spit itself—are important habitat areas for the wildlife that spurred President Woodrow Wilson to establish the **Dungeness National Wildlife Refuge** (Voice of America Rd., 360/683-5847, www.fws.gov, open sunrise-sunset daily, $3 per family, under 16 free) in 1915. Today, more than 250 species of birds use the area to rest and feed, and many briefly stop here during migration from Alaska to South America. Some 40 species of land mammals also call the refuge home.

Though pets aren't allowed in the refuge, humans are, at least in most spots. A half-mile trail easily accessible from the main parking lot leads to an overlook above the spit, and you can pay your entry fee here before setting off on the trail. You can walk on the spit, too. The interesting 4.5-mile beach trek ends at the **New Dungeness Lighthouse,** one of the oldest lighthouses in the state. It was lit for the first time in 1857. The lighthouse is open to the public and tours are offered daily. That doesn't mean the area is crowded. Reaching the lighthouse from the refuge parking lot requires a 10-mile round-trip walk along the spit, and the tide also plays a factor in whether or not many of the areas are passable. You also can take a boat from Sequim to get to the lighthouse, but reservations (360/683-6638, www.newdungenesslighthouse.com) are required in advance to dock at the landing near the lighthouse. The lighthouse is housed year-round by volunteers, who serve weeklong shifts at their own expense. Camping is not allowed in the refuge.

Olympic Game Farm

Want to get face-to-face with the area's animals from the safety of your own car? The **Olympic Game Farm** (1423 Ward Rd., 360/683-4295, www.olygamefarm.com, 9am-5pm daily late May through first week of Oct., 9am-4pm rest of year, $12 adults, $11 ages 6-14 and seniors, ages 5 and under free) affords visitors an opportunity to do just this by offering a driving tour of its grounds. You can cruise over the park's winding gravel roads past bison, elk, llamas, bears, and even a zebra. The animals often come right up to your car. Founded in 1972, the farm—which has been featured in many Disney films—recently added a walking tour ($5) that includes access to its petting area, freshwater aquarium, and a guided tour through the educational area. The farm once worked exclusively with Disney for many years and was closed to the public, before opening as the Olympic Game Farm in 1972. The farm's founders then began concentrating on offering needy animals that were bred in captivity a place to call home. However, most of the animals at the farm today are offspring of the former animal actors.

Museum and Arts Center in the Sequim-Dungeness Valley

The **Museum and Arts Center in the Sequim-Dungeness Valley** (175 W. Cedar St., 360/683-8110, www.macsequim.org, 11am-3pm Wed.-Sat., $2 suggested donation) opened in 1979 and features exhibits related to local history (way back history). The museum's prized exhibit is a mastodon mural, over which real bones from a local archaeological find called the Manis Mastodon (after discoverer Emanuel Manis) are overlaid. The bones date back some 14,000 years.

The mastodon isn't the only highlight owned by the center. Another of the center's highlights is located across town at the separate **Dungeness Schoolhouse** (2781 Towne Rd., Sequim), a school building that originally opened in 1893 and closed in 1955. The two-story, red-and-white building features a tower with a working school bell. On the first floor of the building, there are actual desks and books from its days as a school. The schoolhouse is a first-rate complement to the photographic history displayed in the Sequim Schools Exhibit at the center.

SPORTS AND RECREATION

Hiking and Biking

Without a doubt, the most popular multiuse trail in the region is the **Olympic Discovery Trail** (begins south of the ferry dock in downtown Port Townsend, www.olympicdiscoverytrail.com), a system of trails built mostly on an old railroad path that eventually will be a paved, 130-mile-long path connecting Port Townsend on the northeastern portion of the Olympic Peninsula to the Pacific Ocean at La Push. Scenery along the trail, which is open to most nonmotorized uses, including horses, runs the gamut and is spectacular and varied. Depending on how long you want to walk or ride, and where your starting point is, you can see deer, eagles, and many other types of wildlife, and cross a restored railroad trestle over the Dungeness River. The trail is busiest around the towns of Sequim, Port Angeles, and Port Townsend, particularly during the summer months. Currently, 55 miles of the trail are paved, with the rest being done in sections as time and funds permit.

Mountain biking in area forests is a popular outdoor activity. The **Gold Creek Trail** (located 14.5 miles south of Sequim down Palo Alto Rd. then Forest Service Rd. 2880) and the **Lower Dungeness Trail** (located 12 miles south of Sequim off Palo Alto Rd. then Forest Service Rd. 2880) are two popular starting points. Gold Creek is heavily wooded and offers great viewpoints of the Dungeness River. Lower Dungeness is six miles long, also heavily forested, and offers some views of valleys and mountains.

One of the best ways to explore Sequim and its surrounding areas is by bike. Rent one, buy one, or get parts for yours from **All Around Bikes** (150 West Sequim Bay Rd., 360/681-3868, www.allaroundbikes.com, 10am-6pm Mon.-Fri., 10am-5pm Sat., $30 half-day rental, $60 for 24 hours). Owner Mike Wanner is a former bike racer turned shop owner who knows whereof he speaks.

Water Sports

As might be expected in an area located on a large body of water, boating and kayaking enthusiasts will have no shortage of spots they'll

the Dungeness Schoolhouse in Sequim

The Olympic Discovery Trail is full of beautiful sights, such as this bridge near Sequim.

want to visit for some water-inspired serenity. **Dungeness** (north of Sequim at Dungeness Spit), **Sequim** (southeast of downtown Sequim), and **Discovery** (off Hwy. 101 between Port Townsend and Sequim) Bays offer opportunities, and there are access points at several other places. Those access points include **Port Williams Beach** (Port Williams Rd.), **John Wayne Marina** (West Sequim Bay Rd., 360/417-3456), and **Cline Spit** (Cline Spit Rd).

Several companies rent gear and offer stellar advice, including **Dungeness Kayaking** (5021 Sequim-Dungeness Way, Sequim, 360/681-4190, www.dungenesskayaking.com) and **Olympic Raft & Kayak** (123 Lake Aldwell Rd., Port Angeles, 888/452-1443, www.raftandkayak.com).

Golf

Sequim's abundant sunshine is a golf lover's dream come true. If you're willing to brave a little chill, you can golf here year-round. The area has a few courses to choose from, including top-notch **The Cedars at Dungeness** (1965 Woodcock Rd., 360/683-6344, www.7cedarsresort.com, $40-47 for 18 holes), a par-72 course in a tree-lined, creek-filled setting. Each hole here is named, including one called "Ole Crabby," which features a difficult bunker shaped like a Dungeness crab. **Skyridge Golf Course** (7015 Old Olympic Hwy., 360/683-3673, www.skyridgegolfcourse.com, $27-29 for 18 holes), on the other hand, is a nine-hole, par-36 links-style course that's also lined with trees. **Sunland Golf and Country Club** (109 Hilltop Dr., 360/683-6800, www.sunlandgolf.com, $35 for 18 holes) is a semiprivate, par-72 course that's open to the general public on weekends.

ENTERTAINMENT AND EVENTS

Nightlife

There's a lot of fun packed into the **Oasis Sports Bar and Grill** (301 E. Washington St., 360/582-3143, www.theoasissequim.com, $10-13). There are TVs displaying live sports contests, dart boards beeping when someone nails a bull's-eye, live music most nights of the week from local bands and DJs, and even a "Taco Tuesday," with unlimited tacos for $1 each. There's other excellent food here, too, including Janny's Turkey Burger, topped with caramelized onions. Swiss cheese and mushrooms cost extra but are fantastic additions to the sandwich.

Casinos

Feeling lucky? Check out the **7 Cedars Casino** (270756 Hwy. 101, 360/683-7777 or 800/458-2597, www.7cedarsresort.com) that's run by the S'Klallam tribe near the Blyn town border. They have video gaming machines and table games such as blackjack and poker. Maybe you'll win a jackpot. Eat pasta, seafood, burgers, and more at one of several restaurants inside the casino. Listen to live music, comedy, and more at **Club SEVEN** (360/683-7777, hours vary by event) if you're over 21. The club welcomes various entertainers, including comedy, jazz bands, and dance bands.

The Dynamic Rain Shadow

Yes, there is one area of the Olympic Peninsula where the sun shines year-round, thanks to a natural phenomenon called a rain shadow, which is a dry area on the downwind side of a mountain or range of mountains. The way the peninsula's rain shadow works is fairly straightforward. Prevailing winds carry moist air from the Pacific Ocean toward the Olympics, where it is pushed up over the mountains. As it climbs, the moisture is pulled from the air and falls as rain on the western side of the peninsula. That's the reason the awesome rain forests exist here. As the air descends down the eastern side of the Olympics, much of the moisture already has been pulled from it, leaving little left to fall.

The prevailing winds on the peninsula do not travel west to east, but rather southwest to northeast, which means the northeastern cities of Port Angeles, Sequim, and Port Townsend are the ones in the rain shadow, rather than the Hood Canal area or even Tacoma and Seattle, which would be the case if the winds blew directly from the west.

Also here is the **Cedar Boughs Art Gallery** (360/681-6728, 10am-10pm daily).

Art Galleries

The Blue Whole Gallery (129 W. Washington St., 360/681-6033, www.bluewholegallery.com, 10am-5pm Mon.-Sat., 11am-3pm Sun.) features about 35 artists in a 2,000-square-foot gallery in downtown Sequim. See photography, woodcarvings, jewelry, paintings, and more from established and new artists alike.

At **Jamestown S'Klallam Tribe Northwest Native Expressions Gallery** (1033 Old Blyn Hwy., 360/681-4642, www.northwestnativeexpressions.com, 9am-5pm Mon.-Fri.) appreciate or buy art by area artists from the S'Klallams and other tribes, including masks, paddles, baskets, clothing, framed prints, music, jewelry, and plaques.

Sequim Arts (www.sequimarts.org) is a great Internet resource to locate local artists individually. Some have art galleries you can visit. The website is also brimming with art event news in the area.

Festivals and Events

The **Sequim Irrigation Festival** (downtown Sequim, www.irrigationfestival.com) is one of the longest-running festivals in the state. It all started in 1896 to celebrate irrigation ditches that were designed to bring water from the Dungeness River to the thirsty land. The festival is still a big deal in the town and is held for several days during the first full week of May. There are parades, an arts and crafts show, fireworks, a carnival, a logging show complete with pole falling, hand-bucking (sawing logs by hand), and tractor pulls.

Every July, Sequim rolls out the purple carpet, so to speak, for the annual **Lavender Festival** (877/681-3035, www.lavenderfestival.com) that features free farm tours, you-pick opportunities and a two-day street fair (downtown Sequim on Fir St.) and food court. The town comes alive with activities, too, including live music, art tours, salmon bakes, and more. It's one of the biggest lavender festivals in the nation, according to organizers.

Music and family-friendly activities can be found at the **Dungeness River Festival** (at Railroad Bridge Park, 2151 W. Hendrickson Rd., www.dungenessrivercenter.org). The free two-day event usually takes place toward the end of September and is organized by the Olympic Peninsula Audubon Society. The festival is free, but donations are accepted and go to supporting the Dungeness River Center and Railroad Bridge Park. The event features nature walks, bird-identification courses, nature activities, crafts, storytellers, food, and games.

Sequim Open Aire Market (Cedar St. between 2nd Ave. and Sequim Ave.,

360/460-2668, www.sequimmarket.com, 9am-3pm Sat. spring and summer, 10am-2pm Sat. fall and winter) has been held since 1996, allowing the area's farmers, artisans, and restaurateurs to come together every week. Buy recycled and reclaimed items, handmade Belgian chocolates, organic produce, sea glass jewelry, gourmet street food, and more. The market is open year-round.

SHOPPING

There are a lot of lavender-inspired shops to explore, such as **Lost Mountain Lavender** (1541 Taylor Cutoff Rd., 360/681-2782, www.lostmountainlavender.com), **Nelson's Duck Pond & Lavender Farm** (73 Humble Hill Rd., 360/681-7727, www.nelsonsduckpond.com), **Port Williams Lavender Shop** (1442 Port Williams Rd., 360/582-9196), and **Olympic Lavender Farm** (1432 Marine Dr., 360/683-4475, www.olympiclavender.com), to name a few. Most sell dried lavender bouquets, lotions, bath salts, and other sweet-smelling treats—lavender lovers rejoice. The gift shop at the **Cedarbrook Lavender & Herb Farm** (1345 S. Sequim Ave., 360/683-7733 or 800/470-8423, www.cedarbrooklavender.com) is one of the many shops that stand out. This one is located in a historic farmhouse that's more than a century old. The home was built by John Bell, who came from Scotland in the late 1800s, and many locals believe Bell was the area's first white settler. Today, more than 70 kinds of lavender can be found here.

Find all kinds of home decor at **Over the Fence** (112 E. Washington St., 360/681-6851, www.overthefencesequim.com, 10am-5:30pm Mon.-Sat., 11am-4:30pm Sun.). There's wooden furniture for the home and garden, baskets for serving and storage, dishes, linens, towels, and hemp-based rugs even the biggest dogs would have a hard time chewing through.

ACCOMMODATIONS

$50-100

Sequim Bay Lodge (268522 Hwy. 101, 360/683-0691 or 800/622-0691, www.sequimbaylodge.com, $55-140 s or d) is a lodge-style hotel located off the main drag. It's a good, budget-friendly option just outside of Sequim. They have some pet-friendly units. Their most expensive units have whirlpool tubs and are not pet-friendly.

Sequim West Inn & RV Park (740 W. Washington St., 360/683-4144, www.sequimwestinn.com, $59-139 s or d) doesn't offer anything fancy, but it's easy on the wallet and clean. There's a cottage ($85-189) here, as well as RV sites ($32-41), as the name implies.

Bring the family for a stay on an eight-acre farm complete with animals, duck ponds, and a view of the Olympics at **Kinder Farm Vacation Rentals** (1074 Hooker Rd., 360/683-7397, $80-95 s or d).

Clark's Chambers (322 Clark Rd., 360/683-4431, $90 s or d) is housed in an old charming farmhouse with heirloom furniture. There are four rooms, all with private baths.

$100-150

Diamond Point Inn Bed and Breakfast (241 Sunshine Rd., 360/797-7720, www.diamondpointinn.com, $119-149 s or d), a cottage house located on 10 acres, is simple and offers comfy, homey rooms. A gourmet breakfast is included in your room rate, and they offer complimentary mountain bikes to ride.

Helga's Edelweiss (235 Roberson Rd., 360/681-2873, $120-150 s or d) offers two rooms in a spacious home.

Built in 1886, ★ **Groveland Cottage Bed & Breakfast** (4861 Sequim-Dungeness Way, 800/879-8859, www.grovelandcottage.com, $125-155 s or d) has charm and each room has its own bathroom. The rooms have interesting and sometimes appropriate names, such as Mr. Seal's, French, and The Secret Room, which is a detached cottage located next to the ground's gardens.

The cottages, hotel rooms, and suites of **Juan de Fuca Cottages** (182 Marine Dr., 360/683-4433, www.juandefuca.com, $130-315 s or d) are located on a private beach on Dungeness Bay.

For a unique adventure, stay the night

on a real train caboose at the **All Aboard Caboose Inn** (434 Bear Creek Estates, 360/683-5864, www.allaboardcabooseinn.com, $100 s or d). There is a two-night minimum here.

Get away from it all at the rental at **Nelson's Duck Pond & Lavender Farm** (73 Humble Hill Rd., 360/681-7727, www.nelsonsduckpond.com, $275 for two-night minimum), which can accommodate up to six people. Plus you get lemon lavender pound cake with your stay.

$150-200

There is a water view from every room and a two-night minimum stay at **Dungeness Bay Cottages** (140 Marine Dr., 360/683-3013, www.dungenessbay.com, $145-200 s or d).

John Wayne's Waterfront Resort (2634 W. Sequim Bay Rd., 360/681-3853, www.johnwaynewaterfrontresort.com, $130-229 d) has eight cabins with full views of the Dungeness Bay that vary in size and can accommodate two to six guests. Minimum stay is two nights in the cabins. There are 41 RV sites ($38-42); long-term stay options up to six months are available.

The views and beach access will make you not miss the lack of TVs or phones at **Sunset Marine Resort** (40 Buzzard Ridge Rd., 360/591-4303 www.sunsetmarineresort.com, $145-260 s or d). There are eight cabins, all with their own character and along a private road.

Over $200

The **Lost Mountain Lodge** is one of the most romantic places to stay in Sequim (303 Sunny View Dr., 888/683-2431, www.lostmountainlodge.com, $259-349 s or d).

Dungeness Barn House Bed & Breakfast (42 Marine Dr., 360/582-1663, www.dungenessbarnhouse.com, $195-215 s or d) is an actual barn built in 1924 and has views of the Strait of Juan de Fuca, Dungeness Bay, and New Dungeness Lighthouse.

If you want to experience agritourism, stay at ★ **Purple Haze Lavender Farm's Farmhouse** (180 Bell Bottom Rd., 360/683-1714 or 888/852-6560, www.purplehazelavender.com, $260). The farmhouse can accommodate up to six people for your stay (additional people or pets are subject to additional fees), and there is a two-night minimum here.

J & J Golf Retreat (290 Meadow Lark Ln., 360/808-8833, $300) is a 2,145-square-foot home that can accommodate up to four guests. It's located at the almost-always sunny Cedars at Dungeness golf course. Weekly rates and other specials may be available. There is a two-night minimum here.

It will feel like the waterfront view is exclusively yours at **Lighthouse Manor** (Three Crabs Rd., 800/879-8859, www.lighthouse-manor.com, $300), a fully furnished home rental that can accommodate up to six people.

Camping

Get up close and personal with birds and other aspects of nature at the ★ **Dungeness Recreation Area** (554 Voice of America W., 360/683-5847, $20). There are 64 campsites here that are open Feb. 1-Sept. 30. The campground is on a bluff high above the Strait of Juan de Fuca and offers great views and a mile-long bluff trail from which birds frequently can be spotted flying out of the tall grass and out over the water. The campground has restrooms with coin-operated showers and firewood for sale, but there are no utility hookups here. The campground is located just outside the Dungeness National Wildlife Refuge.

Sequim Bay State Park (269035 Hwy. 101, 360/902-8844 or 888/226-7688, www.parks.wa.gov, $20-28) is open year-round for overnight camping. It has 60 tent spaces, 16 utility spaces, and a couple of RV sites. The 92-acre park features nearly 5,000 feet of saltwater shoreline on generally calm Sequim Bay and a few large picnic areas right next to the water, including one with a watercraft launch area. As a bonus, the Olympic Discover Trail carves right through the center of the park, giving children (and other riders, too) a place to safely ride their bikes, as long as they keep an eye out for more serious riders who are quickly passing through.

Sequim's RV parks include **Rainbow's End RV Park** (261831 Hwy. 101, 360/683-3863, $40), **Olympic Paradise RV Park** (137 Pierson Rd., 360/683-1264, $40), and **Gilgal "Oasis" RV Park** (400 S. Brown Rd., 360/452-1324 or 888/445-4251, www.gilgaloasisrvpark.com, $36-42), from which you get a great view of the Olympic Mountains, access to a clubhouse with a game room, and a free continental breakfast every Saturday in July and August.

FOOD

American

At ★ **Oak Table Cafe** (292 W. Bell, 360/683-2179, www.oaktablecafe.com, 7am-3pm daily, $12) you can get breakfast all day and lunch is served Monday through Saturday after 11am. Here, the pancakes, crepes, waffles, and more are made from scratch, not from premade batters from a package. And they aren't afraid of butter! In fact, they boast that they only serve the finest, most pure butter available. Try one of their house specialties such as the fruit blintzes, crepes filled with a creamy filling and topped with a fruit of choice. Brandied peaches, please.

Organic, locally sourced, and sustainable food is the name of the game at the **Alder Wood Bistro** (139 W. Alder St., 360/683-4321, www.alderwoodbistro.com, 4:30pm-9pm Tues.-Sat., $20). Menu items include fresh seafood, salads, wood-fired pizzas, and a variety of Northwest-inspired American favorites, from planked fish to meatloaf.

Don't just drive by **Tootsie's** (537 W. Washington St., 360/683-9524, 7am-10pm Mon.-Sat., 8am-10pm Sun., $10); make sure you stop. This little pink place serves up juicy burgers, crispy onion rings, and thick shakes. They also serve breakfast, espresso, and fresh-squeezed juice.

Hi-Way 101 Diner (392 W. Washington St., 360/683-3388, 6am-9pm Mon.-Sat., 7am-9pm Sun., $12) is a 1950s-style diner with a light-blue facade, a black-and-white checkered floor, and a '57 Chevy on its sign that specializes in serving breakfast the old-fashioned way: with filling portions and friendly service.

★ **Carlsborg's Old Mill Café** (721 Carlsborg Rd., Carlsborg, 360/582-1583, www.old-millcafe.com, 8am-3pm Tues. and Sun., 8am-close Wed.-Sat., closed Mon., $22) serves hearty portions of American fare for breakfast, lunch, and dinner to satisfy big appetites. The menu offers a bit of everything, with pasta, seafood, burgers, and steak, including an Old Mill prime rib served slow-roasted with horseradish.

Breakfast is served all day (and you can get lunch, too) at **Sequim's Sunshine Café** (145 W. Washington St., 360/683-4282, 8am-3pm Wed.-Mon., $8-10). Kids 10 and under eat free. The cinnamon rolls are fresh, as are the marinades and dressings they use. Try the lavender vinaigrette.

Barbecue

Get finger-lickin' goodness at ★ **Jeremiah's B-B-Q** (825 W. Washington St., 360/681-4227, hours vary by season, www.jeremiahsbbq.com, $10-20). In addition to ribs, brisket, and everything else you'd expect to find at a barbecue place, they offer beer-battered fries, sweet potato fries, fried okra, hush puppies, and more.

Chinese

Fortune Star (145 E. Washington St., 360/681-6888, 11am-9:30pm Sun.-Fri., noon-9:30pm Sat., $9-12) isn't located in a fancy setting like you'd see downtown in a bigger city, but the food served here is presented as well as many such places. It's one of those places where when you see others being served before your food comes, you look at their plates and say, "Wow, that looks good!" Then your plate arrives and you say, "Wow, that tastes good!"

Moon Palace (323 E. Washington St., 360/683-6898, 11:30am-8:30pm Tues.-Thurs., 11:30am-9pm Fri., 1pm-9pm Sat., noon-8pm Sun., $11-14) is a favorite among locals who enjoy the authentic, MSG-free food, as well as the Lotus Room, a full-service bar with a good happy hour and an entrance that's separate from the main restaurant.

Fine Dining

When you're craving oysters on the half shell, salmon cakes, or fresh paella, head to the **Dockside Grill** (2577 W. Sequim Bay Rd., 360/683-7510, www.docksidegrill-sequim.com, lunch 11am-3pm, dinner 4pm-9pm Wed.-Sun., $25-40). Reservations are recommended at this waterfront restaurant in Sequim on John Wayne Marina that has received several "Best Of" accolades from regional media.

Mexican

As goofy as some restaurants' names can be, there really is something legitimate behind the name at **Jose's Famous Salsa** (126 E. Washington St., 360/681-8598, www.joesfamoussalsa.com, 11am-7pm daily, closed Sun. and Mon., $6-8). The restaurant's namesake sauce can be found in many markets throughout the area—assuming you can find the popular item on shelves. If not, there's always the restaurant, where not only will you get great salsa (and guacamole) dips, but you'll also get good deals on and large portions of taqueria-style Mexican food.

Las Palomas (1085 E. Washington, 360/681-3842, 11am-9pm daily, $8-14) is another local favorite.

Quick Bites

For fresh, chewy, soft bread, sink your teeth into a loaf from **Pane d'Amore** (104 E. Washington St., 360/681-3280, www.panedamore.com, 8am-4pm Mon.-Sat.), an artisan bakery that also offers pastries but mostly focuses on baking high-quality breads from scratch.

★ **Westside Pizza** (540 W. Washington St., 360/683-3100, www.westsidepizza.com, 11am-11pm Fri.-Sat., 11am-10pm Sun.-Thurs., $10-20) is a regional chain whose specialty pizzas include the frightening, but delicious, Death by Pizza, which includes pepperoni, Canadian bacon, sausage, pineapple, beef, mushrooms, olives, onions, green peppers, and bacon bits.

Thai

Thai food lovers should try **Sawadee Thai Cuisine** (271 S. 7th Ave., 360/683-8188, lunch 11am-3pm and dinner 4:30pm-9pm daily, $13), an unassuming restaurant with a high quality of both service and food that seems a bit out of place in such a small town. It's always busy here during rush times, and the yellow curry is fabulous.

INFORMATION AND SERVICES

The Sequim-Dungeness Valley Chamber of Commerce (1192 E. Washington St., 360/683-6197 or 800/737-8462, www.sequimchamber.com, 9am-5pm daily) is a busy one, but its staff is friendly and helpful and its convenient location off the main drag makes it even more beneficial to travelers.

The area's weekly paper, the ***Sequim Gazette,*** offers up-to-date information on local events.

GETTING THERE AND AROUND

To get to Sequim from Sea-Tac Airport, you can either head north on I-5, take a ferry to Bainbridge Island, and drive northwest on Highways 3, 4, and 101 from there, or you can drive south to Tacoma and cut across to the Olympic Peninsula through Gig Harbor. Either way, the trek is 2-3 hours.

Carless travelers coming directly from Sea-Tac Airport can take one of two daily trips on the Dungeness Line of **Olympic Bus Lines** (360/417-0700 or 800/457-4492, www.olympicbuslines.com, $49 one-way). Once you're in the area, **Jefferson Transit** (360/385-4777, www.jeffersontransit.com) will take you through Sequim and connect you to the eastern city of Port Townsend. Meanwhile, **Clallam Transit** (360/452-4511, www.clallamtransit.com) routes west from Sequim to Port Angeles and beyond.

Port Angeles

Port Angeles represents different things to different people. To some, it's a booming and important harbor guarded by a spit of land called **Ediz Hook** and shared by commercial ships, fishing boats, and ferries. To others, it's a gateway to the Olympic Peninsula and the largest city in its northern section—a convenient and sort-of-happening stopover on the way to Hurricane Ridge, Lake Crescent, Victoria, British Columbia, and points beyond.

Port Angeles is also home to some 19,000 permanent residents, an active art community, and a ton of history. That history—at least the modern part of it—began in the late 1700s, when a Spanish explorer dubbed the area "The Port of Our Lady of the Angels," which later evolved into the town's current name. It was some 150 years later that the town actually was settled. In 1862, President Abraham Lincoln signed an order that made Port Angeles a township, then, in 1890, the United States Board of Trade called Port Angeles the second national city (Washington DC being the first). Several of the city's land marks are named after Lincoln, including a park, a school, and a main street.

Foresight, however, was not a strong point of the city's founding fathers. Port Angeles was built so close to the Strait of Juan de Fuca and Port Angeles Harbor that the city often flooded during high tide. In 1914, an engineering plan used seawater to move dirt from a hillside to raise the level of the city more than a dozen feet. In doing so, many former main floors became underground basements, and second floors now became streetside storefronts. Some of the underground areas still can be toured by the public.

SIGHTS

Museum at the Carnegie

Those who love to find out about the history of the area they are visiting need to stop by the **Museum at the Carnegie** (207. S. Lincoln St., 360/452-6779, www.clallamhistoricalsociety.com, 1pm-4pm Wed.-Sat., $2 suggested donation adults, $5 suggested donation families). Not only are the exhibits historic in nature, but the restored 1919 building itself is historic. The permanent exhibit on the second floor, *Strong People: Faces of Clallam County,* focuses on the area's early tribes and settlers. The downstairs is dedicated to temporary exhibits that change a few times each year.

Port Angeles Fine Arts Center

The **Port Angeles Fine Arts Center** (1203 E. Lauridsen Blvd., 360/457-3532, www.pafac.org, 11am-5pm Thurs.-Sun., free) isn't exactly something you'd expect to find in a city the size of Port Angeles. Since it's a bit off-the-beaten path, you might not even find it, if you didn't talk to someone in the know before venturing out. The art gallery here is a hillside semicircle and mainly features works from Northwest-based artists. The gallery's windows themselves also serve as frames, their works being the excellent views of water and mountains you can see outside. The center specializes in contemporary art from both established and up-and-coming artists from across the region and beyond. Also outside the gallery, you'll find **Webster's Woods Art Park** (1203 E. Lauridsen Blvd.), a five-acre "museum without walls" located in a second-growth forest. Roughly 100 outdoor pieces line the park trails. It's a fascinating concept and inspiring to see what artists come up with when nature is their canvas. There's a face carved into a decaying tree stump and a carved-wood fire hydrant. There's a tree that's pierced with a larger-than-life silver belly-button ring. The artwork here is amazing, is unique, and couldn't occur in exactly the same way anywhere else. The center also hosts special programs, concerts, readings, and more.

Port Angeles

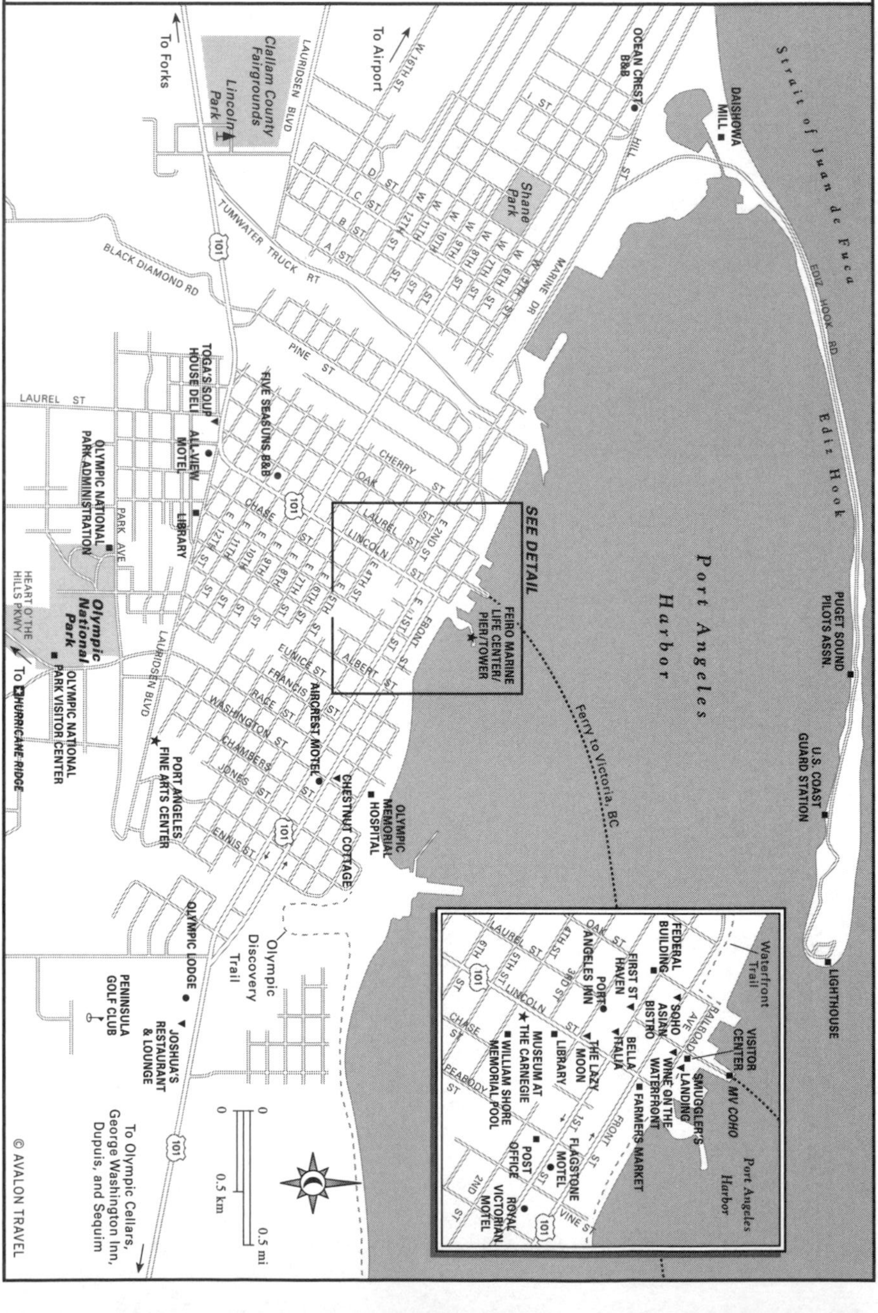
Strait of Juan de Fuca
Port Angeles Harbor
Ediz Hook
EDIZ HOOK RD
DAISHOWA MILL
PUGET SOUND PILOTS ASSN.
U.S. COAST GUARD STATION
LIGHTHOUSE
Ferry to Victoria, BC
To Forks
To Airport
Clallam County Fairgrounds
Lincoln Park
LAURIDSEN BLVD
W 16TH ST
OCEAN CREST B&B
I ST
HILL ST
Shane Park
D ST
C ST
B ST
A ST
W 12TH ST
W 11TH ST
W 10TH ST
W 9TH ST
W 8TH ST
W 7TH ST
W 6TH ST
W 5TH ST
MARINE DR
TUMWATER TRUCK RT
BLACK DIAMOND RD
PINE ST
LAUREL ST
TOGA'S SOUP HOUSE DELI
FIVE SEASONS B&B
ALL VIEW MOTEL
CHERRY ST
OAK ST
LIBRARY
OLYMPIC NATIONAL PARK ADMINISTRATION
PARK AVE
HEART O' THE HILLS PKWY
Olympic National Park
OLYMPIC NATIONAL PARK VISITOR CENTER
To HURRICANE RIDGE
SEE DETAIL
FEIRO MARINE LIFE CENTER/ PIER/TOWER
FRONT ST
E 1ST ST
E 2ND ST
LINCOLN ST
E 4TH ST
E 5TH ST
E 6TH ST
E 7TH ST
E 8TH ST
E 9TH ST
E 10TH ST
E 11TH ST
E 12TH ST
CHASE ST
ALBERT ST
EUNICE ST
FRANCIS ST
RACE ST
WASHINGTON ST
CHAMBERS ST
JONES ST
ENNIS ST
AIRCREST MOTEL
CHESTNUT COTTAGE
OLYMPIC MEMORIAL HOSPITAL
PORT ANGELES FINE ARTS CENTER
Olympic Discovery Trail
OLYMPIC LODGE
PENINSULA GOLF CLUB
JOSHUA'S RESTAURANT & LOUNGE
101
0 0.5 mi
0 0.5 km
To Olympic Cellars, George Washington Inn, Dupuis, and Sequim
© AVALON TRAVEL
Waterfront Trail
FEDERAL BUILDING
VISITOR CENTER
MV COHO
SMUGGLER'S LANDING
WINE ON THE WATERFRONT
FARMERS MARKET
RAILROAD AVE
SOHO ASIAN BISTRO
FIRST ST HAVEN
BELLA ITALIA
PORT ANGELES INN
THE LAZY MOON
LIBRARY
MUSEUM AT THE CARNEGIE
WILLIAM SHORE MEMORIAL POOL
POST OFFICE
FLAGSTONE MOTEL
ROYAL VICTORIAN MOTEL
VINE ST
PEABODY ST
3RD ST
5TH ST
6TH ST
2ND ST
1ST ST
Port Angeles Harbor

Feiro Marine Life Center and Port Angeles City Pier

Named after a local high school science teacher who spearheaded its construction, the **Feiro Marine Life Center** (Port Angeles City Pier, 360/417-6254, www.feiromarinelifecenter.org, 10am-5pm daily summer, noon-4pm daily winter, $4 adults, $2 ages 3-17, free ages 2 and under) is full of tanks featuring local marine wildlife, and touch tanks full of sea creatures. Highlights include a giant Pacific octopus and her tank mates, the Pacific sea nettles. There are knowledgeable volunteers aplenty here, all willing and capable of answering even the most difficult questions. This is a colorful and educational experience for all ages.

The marine center is located on the **Port Angeles City Pier,** which is next to the terminal for ferries traveling to Victoria, Britist Columbia. The pier offers beach access, restrooms, a playground, a covered pavilion where outdoor shows are often held, and a viewing tower (open 24 hours) from which you can see the Olympic Mountains and the city of Port Angeles. On a clear day, of course.

SPORTS AND RECREATION

Hiking and Biking

Downtown's 6.5-mile-long **Waterfront Trail** connects with the 120-mile-long **Olympic Discovery Trail**—55 miles of which is currently paved—giving even the most hardcore bicyclists plenty of terrain to satisfy their needs. Both trails provide ample scenic opportunities, too, so casual cyclists even find joy in pedaling here. These trails are where a large majority of recreational cyclists head when they are looking to get out for a ride. The nine-mile-long **Foothills Trail** (south of Port Angeles off Heart of the Hills Rd.) is a Department of Natural Resources Trail that is fun to ride but best-suited for hard-core mountain bikers.

Those who didn't bring their own two-wheelers with them can rent from **Sound Bikes and Kayaks** (120 E. Front St., 360/457-1240, www.soundbikeskayaks.com, 10am-6pm Mon.-Sat., closed Sun.) for a price of $10 per hour or $45 per day. Helmets, water-bottle holders, and locks are available to rent, too. Mountain bikes, BMX bikes, and road bikes are available. The shop even rents kayaks, at the rate of $15 per hour or $50 per day.

People looking to simply watch riders can attend one of the three NW Cup Downhill Cycling Series (www.nwcup.com) mountain bike races held throughout the year on Dry Hill. The NW Cup is one of the premier events in the country, and national and international racers compete during each race. The cup's other two events are held at Mount Hood, Oregon.

Swimming

The **William Shore Memorial Pool** (225 E. 5th St., 360/417-9767, www.williamshorepool.org, 5:30am-8:30pm Mon.-Thurs., 5:30am-9pm Fri., 7:30am-4pm Sat., 10am-4pm Sun., $5.25 adults, $3.25 ages 2-18) is a good option for those who want to guarantee some time in the water in the warm confines of a heated indoor pool. The water at **Lake Sutherland** west of town is a bit colder, but it does tend to heat up as the summer wears on, which brings out swimmers, wakeboarders, and tubers en masse.

Golf

Peninsula Golf Club (824 S. Lindberg Rd., 360/457-6501, www.golfinportangeles.com, $36 for 18 holes) is a semiprivate, par-72 course with excellent views of the Olympic Mountains and the Strait of Juan de Fuca. The course is open to the general public every afternoon except Thursdays.

ENTERTAINMENT AND EVENTS

Casinos

The **Elwha River Casino** (631 Stratton Rd., 360/452-3005, www.elwharivercasino.com, 10am-midnight Sun.-Thurs., 10am-2am Fri.-Sat.) is about the size of a large suburban home and sort of difficult to find. But for casino lovers, it's worth the effort. Especially if you like casino food—the deli here is one of the best. For seniors, the deli becomes even better on Wednesdays, when all food items are 30 percent off.

Wineries

It used to be only hot climates came to mind when the subject of wineries popped up in conversation, but not anymore. There are plenty of them on the Olympic Peninsula, including several in Port Angeles.

Check out this fabulous female-owned and -operated winery, **Olympic Cellars** (255410 Hwy. 101, 360/452-0160, www.olympiccellars.com, 11am-6pm daily Apr.-Oct., 11am-5pm Nov.-Mar.). Try the house-made chocolate sauce, too, and relax in the outdoor garden with a glass or two on nice days.

Camaraderie Cellars (334 Benson Rd., 360/417-3564, www.camaraderiecellars.com, 11am-5pm weekends May-Oct.) is a great place to visit to try award-winning wines. Winemaker Don Corson has been practicing his craft since 1981.

A former logging truck shop has been transformed into the **Harbinger Winery** (2358 Hwy. 101 W., 360/452-4262, www.harbingerwinery.com, 11am-6pm Mon.-Sat., 11am-5pm Sun.). As with most Western Washington wineries, Harbinger gets its grapes from the eastern part of the state and, from them, makes approximately 3,000 cases of wine a year here.

Performing Arts

The **Port Angeles Community Players** (1235 E. Lauridsen Blvd., 360/452-6651, www.pacommunityplayers.com, $12 adults, $6 students) put on five shows a year. Examples of past performances include *Damn Yankees* and *On Golden Pond.*

The **Port Angeles Symphony Orchestra** (Port Angeles High School auditorium, 304 E. Park Ave., 360/457-5579, www.portangelessymphony.org, $20 and up) performs several concerts from September through May in the Port Angeles High School auditorium, oftentimes with world-class performers sitting in. Each year, there are five symphony concerts, two pops concerts, and six chamber orchestra concerts. The **Port Angeles Light Opera Association** (360/457-5630, $10-16) performs year-round, also at the Port Angeles High School auditorium. Past shows include *Once Upon a Mattress, Oliver!,* and *Hello Dolly.*

Art Galleries

Art on the Town is a year-round, outdoor sculpture gallery in downtown Port Angeles. There are more than 40 pieces on display, spread throughout the town from City Hall in the east to Cherry Street in the west, and more than $350,000 has been spent on the project. Bob Stokes's multipiece *Avenue of the People* is one of the permanent highlights, as it tells the story of everyday life in a small town through abstract sculptures.

The Landing Art Gallery (115 E. Railroad Ave., 360/452-2604, www.landingart.com, 11am-5pm Tues.-Sat.), located in the Landing Mall near the ferry dock, features a variety of works in many forms of media, including acrylics, oil, metal, and wood. **Waterfront Art Gallery** (120 W. 1st St., 360/452-8165, www.thelandingmall.com/art) is a co-op that's home to works of roughly 30 local artists.

Festivals and Events

Memorial Day Weekend in Port Angeles means it's time for the **Juan de Fuca Festival** (360/457-5411, www.jffa.org), a four-day party that includes workshops; dance, musical, and theater performances; a street fair; and even a "Juan de Fuca After Hours," where performers take over local clubs as night sets in.

When school lets out for the year, the annual **Concerts on the Pier** (City Pier on the waterfront, 360/452-2363, www.portangeles.org/pages/concertsonthepier) series begins, and they run each Wednesday evening until school opens again in the fall. The concerts are free, and a variety of musical styles are

Catching Dungeness Crab

Even first-time visitors who have no idea how to pronounce any of the native-inspired area names are familiar with the term "Dungeness." Their familiarity is due to the popular crab with the same name, of course. It's a delicacy you can find in abundance in these parts if you know when, where, and how to fish for the tasty crustaceans.

Where: Sequim, La Push, Neah Bay, Grays Harbor, and the Hood Canal are all popular places to find crabs.

When: The Dungeness crab season varies from location to location, and the rules are strictly enforced in most popular fishing areas. To find exactly where you are allowed to go crabbing at any time of the year, visit wdfw.wa.gov/fishing/shellfish/crab.

How: The best way to catch a crab is from a boat or pier. You simply set your baited trap, called a crab pot, and drop it into the water. The pot is attached to a rope and, sometimes, a buoy so you can return and, if you're lucky, pull up your crabs after some time has passed. How long you wait before checking your pots is up to you, and depends on how the crabs are feeding that day. It's illegal to catch female crabs, so make sure you know the difference before you go. Permits and Catch Cards are required for everyone who plans to catch a crab. Visit wdfw.wa.gov/fishing/shellfish/crab to learn more about the exact rules you'll need to follow.

Don't want to catch your own but want to sample the best recipes that the area has to offer? Consider visiting during the **Dungeness Crab & Seafood Festival** (www.crabfestival.org), held in Port Angeles every October. Restaurants are another option for those who aren't interested in catching their own. **Toga's Soup House Deli and Gourmet** and **Dupuis** restaurants in Port Angeles are two great options.

highlighted, including bluegrass, jazz, folk, blues, rock and roll, and more. With water, boats, and the Olympic Mountains as a backdrop, this is a perfect setting to listen to music.

The **Clallam County Fair** (1608 W. 16th St. next to Fairchild International Airport, 360/417-2551, www.clallam.net/countyfair) is held the third week of August and features all the standard goodies of a small-town fair, including food, games, rides, entertainment for all ages, and more. The always-popular demolition derby sells out quickly each year.

October in a waterfront town is a perfect time for a big seafood festival, and that's exactly what the **Dungeness Crab & Seafood Festival** (City Pier on the waterfront, 360/452-6300, www.crabfestival.org) is. More specifically, it's a free event with all kinds of vendors, entertainment, and, of course, loads of fresh-caught food.

Depending on your perspective, the **Forest Storytelling Festival** (Peninsula College, 1502 E. Lauridsen Blvd., 360/417-5031, www.clallamstorypeople.org) can be one of the neatest, unique festivals you'll ever come across or one of the strangest. It's three days of stories told by master storytellers from across the United States. The event takes place in mid-October.

The Port Angeles Community Market (123 E. Front St., 360/417-0486) is a market/street fair that's open for a few hours each Sunday. Special events are sometimes held in conjunction with the market, including a popular pet parade. **The Port Angeles Farmers Market** (Front St. and Lincoln St., 360/460-0361, www.portangelesfarmersmarket.com) is open year-round on Saturdays, and also is open Wednesdays during the summer. The undisputed highlight of this market is the locally grown produce.

SHOPPING

Clothing and Accessories

Find cute, stylish clothes and accessories at the **Sassy Kat Salon and Boutique** (105 E. 1st St., 360/417-0800, www.sassykatsalon.com, boutique hours, 9am-6pm Mon.-Sat., noon-4pm Sun.). The shop offers big names you've heard of and up-and-comers, too.

Port Angeles Baby Store (313 W. 1st St., 360/565-1210, www.pababystore.com, 10am-5:30pm Mon.-Sat.) is a great place to find new and gently used clothing for little ones. And there's also maternity wear for moms.

Gifts and Supplies

Swain's General Store (602 E. 1st St., 360/452-2357, www.swainsinc.com, 8am-9pm Mon.-Sat., 9am-6pm Sun.) began as an army surplus store in the 1950s. Now it offers everything from hardware to men's and women's clothing, shoes, sporting wear, and sundries.

Get reminded of the good old days of childhood at **Pacific Rim Hobby** (138 W. Railroad Ave., 800/994-6229, www.olypen.com/prhobby, 10am-6pm Mon.-Sat., noon-5pm Sun.). Find model trains and more.

Books

Port Book and News (104 E. 1st St., 360/452-6367, www.portbooknews.com, 8am-7pm Mon.-Thurs., 8am-8pm Fri.-Sat., 9am-5pm Sun.) has a huge magazine selection as well as new and used books and several author readings every month.

ACCOMMODATIONS

$50-100

With 20 rooms and free continental breakfast, the ★ **Royal Victorian Motel** (521 E. 1st St., 866/452-8401, www.royalvictorian.net, $59-109 d) is conveniently located in the heart of Port Angeles. You'll have no trouble locating this bright-yellow, 20-room hotel. And while it's definitely not extravagant, it is great for its price point and offers a view of the Olympic Mountains, which likely are at least one of the reasons you're in the area in the first place.

With rooms containing as many as four queen-size beds, the **Flagstone Motel** (415 E. 1st St., 888/304-3465, www.flagstonemotel.com, $80-170 d) is ideal for larger families and groups. The motel is also an easy walk from the Victoria ferry.

Located on Highway 101 just outside of Port Angeles, the **All-View Motel** (214 E. Lauridsend Blvd., 888/457-7779, www.all-viewmotel.com, $89-159 d) includes free wireless Internet, in-room refrigerators, and microwave ovens. It's also family-owned and -operated.

Just minutes from the entrance to the Olympic National Park, the **Aircrest Motel** (1006 E. Front St., 360/452-9255 or 888/832-6303, www.aircrest.com, $54-88 d) is a family-run operation that offers a lot of value for the budget-minded traveler: continental breakfast, free wireless Internet, and more.

For the traveler who wants a quiet environment, the **Indian Valley Motel** (235471 Hwy. 101, 360/928-3266, www.grannyscafe.net, $75-125 d) has no telephones in the rooms, and no TVs except in its suites.

$100-150

Adjacent to a golf course and featuring an outdoor heated pool, the **Olympic Lodge** (140 DelGuzzi Dr., 800/600-2993, www.olympiclodge.com, $107-199 d) includes meeting facilities, wireless Internet in every room, an on-site gym, and computers for free guest use in the lobby.

Situated on a hill in the middle of downtown Port Angeles, the ★ **Port Angeles Inn** (111 E. 2nd St., 800/421-0706, www.portangelesinn.com, $99-160 d) has mountain views on one side and the Strait of Juan de Fuca on the other. It's also within easy walking distance of the Victoria ferry.

Located in a Dutch Colonial-style mansion, the **Five SeaSuns B&B** (1006 S. Lincoln St., 800/708-0777, www.seasuns.com, $139-169 d) will arrange day trips for you ranging from whitewater rafting to sea kayaking.

$150-200

With more than two acres of extensive gardens, **Domaine Madeleine** (146 Wildflower Ln., 360/457-4174, www.domainemadeleine.com, $160-355 d) features haute cuisine breakfasts, including a Dungeness crab omelet and spanakopita with eggplant pesto.

The only B&B actually situated on the

Elwha River, the **Elwha Ranch** (905 Herrick Rd., 360/457-6540, www.elwharanch.com, $145-165 d) is located on a 95-acre horse ranch and features guest rooms as well as a rustic log cabin for rent.

A Hidden Haven (1428 Dan Kelly Rd., 360/452-2719, www.ahiddenhaven.com, $175-315 d) has massage services, luxury suites with whirlpool tubs, and vacation cottages for rent.

At Home: A la Maison (240 Motor Ave., 360/461-6484, www.athome-portangeles.com, $175 with two-night minimum) is a tastefully furnished and decorated turn-of-the-20th-century house that also is a rental and vacation home.

Over $200

Situated between Port Angeles and Sequim, the ★ **George Washington Inn** (939 Finn Hall Rd., 360/452-5207, www.georgewashingtoninn.com, $250-300 d) is a bed-and-breakfast on a lavender farm. It was built as a replica of George Washington's home at Mount Vernon and sits directly on the Strait of Juan de Fuca.

With just three rooms and a contemporary motif, the **Ocean Crest B&B** (402 S. M St., $190-300 d) is more like staying in a contemporary home than the Victorian mansions more common in Port Angeles.

Camping

The Elwha Dam RV Park (47 Lower Dam Rd., Port Angeles, 360/452-7054 or 877/435-9421, www.elwhadamrvpark.com, $36 RVs, $21 tents) is keeping the "Dam" in its name, even though the Elwha Dam has been removed to restore the Elwha River back to its natural state. The 18-acre RV park is near the dam and the river, and there are 40 spaces at the RV park. This RV park actually looks like a park, with towering trees, the river, ponds, ferns, and natural beauty all around.

FOOD

American

Smuggler's Landing (115 E. Railroad Ave., Ste. 101, 360/452-9292, www.smugglerslanding.com, 6:30am-10pm daily, $9-16) has a view of the water and a menu that includes steak, burgers, and seafood, but it's best known locally for its crispy fries.

Corner House Restaurant (101 E. Front St., 360/417-0329, 6am-9pm daily, $7-12) offers all-American burgers in its all-American small-town diner. For something outside of the typical diner entrée, try the crab melt.

the Port Angeles Inn

Asian

Soho Asian Bistro (134 W. Front St., 360/417-8966, 11am-9pm Mon.-Thurs., 11am-9:30pm Fri.-Sat., 11am-9pm Sun., $10-15) serves everything from pho to pad thai. For something a little out of the ordinary, try the cranberry gingerbread pudding.

Bar and Grills

It isn't a Mexican establishment, but **The Lazy Moon** (130 S. Lincoln St., 360/452-2082, www.thelazymoon.com, 11am-close, $8-10) has fantastic nachos. Like, really big ones. It isn't a seafood joint, but the clam chowder is killer. It is a tavern, after all, and the beer is even better than the food here. There are many craft beers on tap here, the longtime site of Peaks Brew Pub.

LD's Woodfire Grill (929 W. 8th St., 360/452-0400, www.ldswoodfiregrill.com, 4:30pm-8pm Mon.-Thurs.,4:30pm-9pm Fri.-Sat., $12-25) has indoor and outdoor seating in a converted-home setting. It's known for its apple-smoked cuisine, and the wood-fired oven indeed is the heart of this place.

Breakfast

First Street Haven (107 E. 1st St., 360/457-0352, 7am-4pm Mon.-Sat., 8am-2pm Sun., $10-14) has the best breakfast in town. Try the blackberry walnut muffins or prosciutto omelet.

Joshua's Restaurant & Lounge (113 Del Guzzi Dr., 360/452-6545, 6am-9pm Mon.-Sat., 6am-8pm Sun., $7-12) has breakfast all day and all-you-can-eat fish-and-chips every Wednesday. Try the pecan-crusted French toast—it's a favorite of locals so you know it's good.

★ **Chestnut Cottage** (929 E. Front St., 360/452-8344, www.chestnutcottagerestaurant.com, 7am-3pm daily, $10-13) has traditional breakfast foods such as buttermilk pancakes and Belgian waffles as well as homemade bakery items. For lunch, enjoy the cottage's sandwiches, soups, and salads.

Cafés and Delis

Toga's Soup House Deli and Gourmet (122 W. Lauridsen Blvd., 360/452-1952, www.togassouphouse.com, 10am-6pm Mon.-Fri., $9-15) has soups and salads that might be a little more expensive than your typical deli shop but well worth it. For a taste of the Northwest, try the baked Dungeness crab melt panini or the salmon sandwich. Both are served with an interesting side: mango salsa.

Café Garden (506 E. 1st St., 360/457-4611, www.cafegardenpa.com, 6:30am-9pm Tues.-Sat., 6:30am-2:30pm Sun.-Mon., $11-27) is homey and quaint. The menu offers comfort food classics as well as unique dishes, such as a seafood croissant.

Fine Dining

C'est Si Bon (23 Cedar Park Rd., 360/452-8888, www.cestsibon-frenchcuisine.com, 5pm-11pm Tues.-Sun., $30-34) features an elegant dining room full of decorations, brightly colored walls, spacious seating, several chandeliers, and even a solarium. The menu offers traditional French cuisine, such as a Cornish game hen with mushroom stuffing that will pair beautifully with their eclectic wine selection.

Italian

★ **Bella Italia** (118 E. 1st St., 360/457-5442, www.bellaitaliapa.com, 4pm-9pm Sun.-Thurs., 4pm-10pm Fri.-Sat., $12-24) has everything from antipasti to piatti to pizza, and an extensive wine selection. The cute dining area set in the heart of downtown Port Angeles has European charm.

Mexican and Southwestern

Fiesta Jalisco (636 E. Front St., 360/452-3928, 11am-9:30pm Mon.-Thurs., 11am-11pm Fri.-Sun., $8-15) has inexpensive prices and huge plates of food, quick service, and a mean mole sauce.

Kokopelli Grill (203 E. Front St., 360/457-6040, www.kokopelli-grill.com, 11am-9pm Mon.-Thu., 11am-10pm Fri.-Sat., 2pm-9pm Sun., $17-31) has everything from grilled chicken salad to double-barrel whiskey ribs. Check out the extensive and original cocktail list here.

Steak and Seafood

Michael's (117-B E. 1st St., 360/417-6929, www.michaelsdining.com, dinner from 4pm daily, $13-49) has excellent seafood in a cozy, welcoming environment with booth seating and a bar. Come here for perfect Northwest-style dishes, including a hearty seafood stew and crab gnocchi pomodoro.

★ **Dupuis** (256861 Hwy. 101, 360/457-8033, opens daily at 5pm, $10-35) has been serving steaks and seafood in the same log building since 1920. The neon crab sign is a local landmark and the dinner a local favorite.

Wine Bars

Visit a swanky little wine bar at the Landing Mall called **Wine on the Waterfront** (115 E. Railroad Ave., 360/565-8466, noon-9pm Tues., noon-10pm Wed.-Thurs., noon-11pm Fri.-Sat., noon-5:30pm Sun.) and listen to some live music, too. Jazz, rock, blues, and other types of music are played here more than 100 nights a year.

INFORMATION AND SERVICES

The centrally located **Port Angeles Chamber of Commerce Visitor Center** (121 E. Railroad Ave., 360/452-2363, www.portangeles.org, 8am-9pm daily in summer) offers a visitors' guide, a travel planner, and a host of other helpful written and verbal advice for those seeking to learn about the area. Because many travelers leave Port Angeles for Victoria, British Columbia, by ferry, the city also is home to the **Port Angeles-Victoria Tourist Bureau** (121 E. Railroad Ave., 360/452-7084, 7am-5pm daily) for those needing advice about things to do and sights to see in the British Columbia capital. If a trip to British Columbia is in your plans, it's wise to check on travel regulations far in advance of your arrival on the peninsula. In all cases, a valid passport will allow you to cross the border, but some other forms of identification are accepted depending on country of origin. Visit www.travel.state.gov for more information.

GETTING THERE AND AROUND

Air

Kenmore Air Express (360/452-6371, www.kenmoreair.com) flies from Sea-Tac Airport to Fairchild International Airport several times a day and offers complimentary shuttles. **Rite Bros. Aviation** (Fairchild International Airport, 360/452-6226 or 800/430-7483, www.ritebros.com) offers charter flights from Port Angeles to many of the small airports throughout the Olympic Peninsula and beyond, and to international destinations such as Victoria, Britist Columbia.

Bus

Olympic Bus Lines (360/417-0700 or 800/457-4492, www.olympicbuslines.com, $49 one-way) offers two trips a day to and from Sea-Tac Airport. **Clallam Transit** (830 W. Lauridsen Blvd., 360/452-1315, www.clallamtransit.com) offers public transportation to all of Clallam County, which comprises most of the northern Olympic Peninsula from Sequim in the east through Port Angeles and Lake Crescent to Neah Bay, Forks, and La Push in the northwest.

Car

Getting to Port Townsend from Tacoma involves cutting through Gig Harbor and traveling north on Highways 16, 3, and 19 for 83 miles, which generally takes a little longer than 1.5 hours to achieve. From Seattle, you can simply travel the 30 miles to Tacoma and follow the same route or head north on I-5 and take a ferry to Bainbridge Island and drive northwest from there on Highways 305, 3, and 19. It takes a little longer that way, approximately 2-2.5 hours.

Ferry

There was a time when two ferries shuttled

passengers the 18 miles across the Strait of Juan de Fuca between Port Angeles and Victoria, British Columbia. These days, there's only one, the **MV *Coho*** (360/457-4491, www.cohoferry.com, $17.50 adults, $8.75 ages 5-11, children under 5 free, $62 for cars and drivers, all one-way), which makes it even more difficult to secure a ride across the water. The ferry carries passengers and vehicles (including bicycles) and makes the trip three times a day June-September and two times a day the rest of the year. It's difficult to predict when the ferries will be full, so it's important to make reservations in advance either online or by phone, or arrive at the terminal early. Parking spots near the terminal also are limited during certain times of the year.

The Elwha and Sol Duc River Valleys

This area once was known for its large river dams, and now is known for the recent movement to remove the dams in an effort to return the area to its natural state and restore passages for migrating salmon. Glacially carved Lake Crescent is a can't-miss attraction adjacent to Highway 101 and less than 20 miles west of Port Angeles. All the traditional water-based recreational opportunities are available here, including fishing, boating, and hiking. The name Sol Duc is linked to the hot springs that bear the same name, but the Sol Duc and Elwha River Valleys have much more to offer than hot sulfuric water, including a beautiful waterfall, several lakes, and plenty of hiking opportunities. The key sites in this area, including Olympic Hot Springs, Sol Duc Hot Springs, Lake Crescent, and Hurricane Ridge, all are located within Olympic National Park, though it's often difficult to distinguish whether or not you're actually in the park itself. There are some places, such as the road to Hurricane Ridge, where you must pay to enter. There are others, such as Lake Crescent, where you can simply visit for free.

SIGHTS

Olympic Hot Springs

"Magical" is a word that's tossed around a lot in **Olympic National Park,** and at **Olympic Hot Springs** (end of Boulder Creek Rd. off Elwha River Rd.) that word is heard more frequently than in many other places. And it pretty much fits. There are multiple springs, or seeps, at this now-undeveloped location. There once was a rather large resort here, but the buildings eventually were abandoned, collapsed, and were removed.

The springs still remain, however, and they're far less commercialized than their more-famous cousins at Sol Duc. Getting there requires an easy 2.5-mile hike across a couple of small creeks from the trailhead on Boulder Creek Road. Many parts of the year, there won't be any people here; other times, it's tough to find a spring to sit in. The most crowded times are the warmer months of July, August, and early September. Speaking of sitting in the springs, officials suggest not doing it (or going in the springs at all) due to high levels of bacteria that have been detected in the stagnant waters. The warning is posted at the trailhead, but, in actuality, it stops approximately 0 percent of people from stripping down and jumping in. And many of those who do so strip all the way down, so be warned, especially if you've got young children with you. The seeps vary in temperature, but typically hover around 100 degrees. The temperatures and semiremote location make them popular even in the winter months, when a hike through snow is necessary to get there. The site looks to be especially popular in the near future, because Olympic Hot Springs Road has only recently reopened, after a three-year closure while the Glines Canyon Dam was removed. There are still some access issues in the area due to ongoing construction, but you can easily get to the trailhead to Olympic Springs.

★ Hurricane Ridge

Though **Olympic National Park** offers a plethora of stunning views of land and wildlife, **Hurricane Ridge** (17 miles south of Port Angeles, off Hurricane Ridge Rd.) might be its most popular spot. It's easily accessible by car and becomes quite busy during summer season. Ease of access is hardly the only reason it is so popular. The ridge, named for the fierce winds that often hit the area, is perhaps the best place on the Olympic Peninsula to witness how quickly geography can change. In 17 miles and approximately 45 minutes by car, you can travel from a sea-level café at the Strait of Juan de Fuca to the **Hurricane Ridge Visitor Center** (top of Hurricane Ridge Rd., 9am-4pm daily summer, 9am-4pm weather permitting winter) where you're a mile high in the air and capable of glancing back down on the area from which you just came. The contrast can be breathtaking. The center isn't one that should be skipped; in fact, it should be considered an integral part of the whole experience. It is open every day in the summer, and during the winter on weekends and on days when Hurricane Ridge Road isn't snowed under. The standard tourist brochures from the National Park Service are here, as are displays and exhibits. Register for guided walks during the summer, or take a guided snowshoe trip during winter. Many of Hurricane Ridge's best hikes begin at the visitors center. The ridge is a place where many people wishing to explore the inner portion of the park begin their treks. There's also a gift shop and a snack bar on-site.

Hurricane Ridge offers spectacular views regardless of the season. In summer, you'll see a panorama of blue skies, blooming wildflowers in the subalpine meadows, deer, and snowcapped mountains. In winter, Hurricane Ridge is covered with snow, but the peaks and valleys are still there—and when you're a mile high there are plenty of both peaks and valleys. It's hard to believe you're less than 20 miles south of Port Angeles and the Strait of Juan de Fuca, where receiving any snowfall at all is a rarity. Hiking gives way to cross-country skiing, snowshoeing, downhill skiing, and sledding.

Checking the two Hurricane Ridge webcams at www.nps.gov before you drive up to the ridge can help you plan your trip around clear skies, or at least attempt to, for the best views once you reach the top. Tuning into 550 on your AM radio dial is another way to find out what's going on with area roads.

More daring adventurers can venture off from the visitors center onto **Obstruction Point Road** and drive the 7.8 miles, weather permitting, to **Badger Valley.** There is a parking area at the end of the road that is a jumping-off point for several hikes, including one to **Grand Pass Trail.**

★ Lake Crescent

Lake Crescent is a prime example of how powerful nature can be. Its waters used to be connected with those of adjacent **Lake Sutherland** until a massive landslide roughly 7,000 years ago came roaring down a hillside, filling the waters and splitting the body of water. The lake's trout populations became isolated as a result of the slide, and today there are two types of trout in the lake, Beardslee and Crescenti, that do not exist anywhere else in the world. Glacially carved, Lake Crescent is cold and clear, thanks to water that lacks a lot of nitrogen and thus plant life, and it is some 600 feet deep.

Native Americans tell a different, though strikingly similar, tale on how 8.5-mile-long Lake Crescent was formed. According to their legend, the area's Klallam and Quileute tribes had constantly been fighting each other. This warring angered a mountain spirit called Mount Storm King, who picked up a gigantic rock and threw it down the mountain at the tribes, killing all who were fighting. The boulder, according to the legend, is what caused the formation of the two lakes. The Indian spirit, or at least his name, still is very much a part of the area today. The tiny **Storm King**

Ranger Station (360/928-3380) is listed on the National Register of Historic Places and is open from May to September.

The **Olympic Park Institute** (111 Barnes Rd., Port Angeles, 360/928-3720 or 800/775-3720, www.naturebridge.org/olympic-national-park) is an area treasure. It's a nonprofit educational facility whose mission is to facilitate one-on-one connections with nature with a goal of helping sustain it. To achieve its goals, the institute offers a range of educational opportunities for youths and adults, such as several field science programs and teacher training. A variety of nature trips and talks are offered. This is not the type of place one just randomly stops in at, however. You'll need to call in advance to see what programs are being offered that may fit in with your travel schedule.

★ Sol Duc Hot Springs

First-time visitors to **Sol Duc Hot Springs** (32 miles west of Port Angeles, off Hwy. 101 and Sol Duc Hot Springs Rd.), especially those who don't research first, often are surprised by exactly what the springs are. They're not some isolated, rock-walled ponds such as can be found a short distance to the east at Olympic Hot Springs. Sol Duc's springs are far more commercialized, encapsulated in three soaking pools and one chlorinated and freshwater-infused swimming pool. The layout here looks like what you might find at any large resort. But these are mineral pools, and the temperature varies from pool to pool. Also, unlike at Olympic Hot Springs, lounging in these pools will cost you. Whether the pools are therapeutic or not depends on your definition. Certain times of the year, you can (sort of) be alone here; other times, relaxation is often difficult with kids screaming and full pools. People-watching, however, is always good here. Day-use privileges are free to those staying at the resort. For others, it's $12.25 for adults, and $9.25 for those ages 4-12, those 62 and older, and veterans.

According to legend, the name *Sol Duc* derives from a Quileute Indian term that means "people living where there's sparkling water." The springs are part of the **Sol Duc Hot Springs Resort** (12076 Sol Duc Hot Springs Rd., Port Angeles, 360/327-3583, www.olympicnationalparks.com). There's a gift shop, restaurant, and general store here, as well as massage therapists on-site, and you don't need to be staying at the resort to use any of its amenities. Grab lunch at the **Poolside Deli** (360/327-3585, 11am-4pm daily); the resort's **Springs Restaurant** (7:30am-10:30am and 5pm-9pm daily) offers northwestern fine dining in a casual atmosphere.

SPORTS AND RECREATION

Hiking on Hurricane Ridge

Hiking is the most popular activity on Hurricane Ridge during summer months, and there are plenty of trails to take advantage of. Shortest are the paved or partially paved Big Meadow Trail, Cirque Rim Trail, and High Ridge Trail, all of which are wheelchair-accessible, are less than a mile round-trip, and have negligible elevation gains. **Hurricane Hill** also is very popular, with its paved path leading 1.6 miles out (and up) to a stellar panoramic view. There are two picnic areas on the ridge with restrooms and running water.

To reach the trailheads beginning at Hurricane Ridge Visitor Center, take Highway 101 out of Port Angeles and turn south on Race Street. Take this road for one mile and then continue onto Mount Angeles Road. Take a slight right on East Lauridsen Boulevard and continue on Hurricane Ridge Road for 17.5 miles and then make a sharp left onto Obstruction Point Road after entering Olympic National Park. The visitors center is approximately 5.5 miles from there.

Big Meadow Trail

Distance: 0.5 mile round-trip
Duration: 0.5-1 hour
Elevation gain: None
Effort: Easy

Trailhead: Hurricane Ridge Visitor Center

Wheelchair-accessible and super short, Big Meadow Trail offers novice hikers a quick glimpse into the Hoh Rain Forest, with views of meadows and mountains. Ranger-guided tours also are available for travelers who would like to learn about the region's flora and fauna in a condensed and direct fashion.

Cirque Rim Trail

Distance: 0.5 mile round-trip
Duration: 0.5-1 hour
Elevation gain: None
Effort: Easy
Trailhead: Hurricane Ridge Visitor Center

This paved trail, like the Big Meadow Trail, offers a short-and-sweet overview of everything the Hoh has to offer. You'll see plants and wildlife (mostly deer) on this easy trek, and when the skies are clear, you'll also catch glimpses of both the city of Port Angeles and the Strait of Juan de Fuca.

High Ridge Trail

Distance: 1 mile round-trip
Duration: 0.5-1 hour
Elevation gain: None
Effort: Easy
Trailhead: Hurricane Ridge Visitor Center

The overlooks on paved High Ridge Trail allow you to look down upon the visitors center from whence you came, and also feature a super-short spur trail at the end that leads you to a site called Sunrise Point. This may be the best of the several short hikes that begin at Hurricane Ridge Visitor Center. You get views of meadows and mountains as well as panoramic views of the Olympics, Port Angeles, and the Strait of Juan de Fuca.

Klahhane Ridge Trail

Distance: 5 miles round-trip
Duration: 2-4 hours
Elevation gain: 1,700 feet
Effort: Moderate
Trailhead: Hurricane Ridge Visitor Center

Klahhane Ridge Trail is the most popular hike in the area, although it's much more difficult than the other short ones with trailheads at the visitors center. Still, there's hardly any elevation gained as the trail mostly follows the summit of the ridge. The ridge itself is a wide-open, switchback trail, which is great for the fabulous views. But the ridge also has its downside, as you're exposed to the elements most of the hike. To avoid them, try to start your day as early as possible.

Hiking Around Lake Crescent

Marymere Falls Nature Trail

Distance: 1.8 miles round-trip
Duration: 45 minutes-1.5 hours
Elevation gain: 500 feet
Effort: Easy-moderate
Trailhead: Storm King Ranger Station
Directions: About 20 miles west of Port Angeles, turn off Highway 101 and follow signs for Lake Crescent Lodge and Marymere Falls. Follow the road about 0.2 miles and turn right to park at the Storm King Ranger Station.

There are several hikes in the hills surrounding Lake Crescent's valley. Marymere Falls Nature Trail is easily the most popular, as it requires less than a mile-long jaunt up a hillside and across a bridge over Barnes Creek to reach the destination—a 90-foot-high waterfall. There's more flow during the early spring and winter months, which makes the falls more impressive then, although there's flow year-round.

Barnes Creek Trail

Distance: 6 miles round-trip
Duration: 2-3.5 hours
Elevation gain: 800 feet
Effort: Moderate
Trailhead: Off Marymere Falls Nature Trail

The Barnes Creek Trail veers off the Marymere Falls Nature Trail and offers a quieter, longer, and more difficult 7-mile round-trip hike up the Aurora Ridge and into the backcountry. Though there isn't much elevation on this trail and it's not all that long, some difficult challenges await. Foremost among them is a creek crossing (although it's fairly easy).

Mount Storm King Trail

Distance: 3.8 miles round-trip
Duration: 2-5 hours
Elevation gain: 1,700 feet
Effort: Difficult
Trailhead: Off Marymere Falls Nature Trail

The Mount Storm King Trail veers off the Marymere Falls Nature Trail and heads 2.2 miles and 2,000 feet up Mount Storm King. There's an excellent view of Lake Crescent partway up the climb, though the climb itself through the forest doesn't offer a ton of viewpoints. The view you get of the lake, however, is spectacular.

Spruce Railroad Trail

Distance: 8 miles round-trip
Duration: 3-4 hours
Elevation gain: 250 feet
Effort: Moderate
Trailhead: Off Boundary Creek Road
Directions: Head west out of Port Angeles on Highway 101 for 17 miles. Follow signs for the East Bench of the Log Cabin Resort and turn right onto East Bench Road. In three miles, turn at the sign for the Spruce Railroad Trail (Boundary Creek Rd.). You will see the trailhead in less than a mile.

The Spruce Railroad Trail on the north shore of Lake Crescent follows the Spruce Railroad path and comes across an old railroad tunnel. The railroad was built in 1918 to transport spruce trees cut for the war effort, but it wasn't completed until the war had ended. The trail follows the lake for most of its length, and you can either hear or see Lake Crescent during most of your hike, which will wind through forests filled with all types of trees, including the Sitka trees the railroad used to haul out of here.

Pyramid Peak Trail

Distance: 7 miles round-trip
Duration: 3-5 hours
Elevation gain: 2,400 feet
Effort: Moderate-difficult
Trailhead: North Shore Picnic Area
Directions: From Port Angeles, drive 30 miles west on Highway 101, then 3 miles down North Shore Road.

Pyramid Peak Trail is a steep, 3.5-mile climb to an old spotting tower used during World War II. Across Lake Crescent from the Mount Storm King Trail, it offers similarly excellent views and treks through a forest filled with various types of trees. However, unlike Mount Storm King Trail, this trail is often prone to landslides and occasionally has to be closed and rerouted for safety reasons.

Hiking in Sol Duc Hot Springs

Sol Duc Falls Trail

Distance: 5.3 miles round-trip
Duration: 2-4 hours
Elevation gain: 400 feet
Effort: Easy
Trailhead: Sol Duc Hot Springs Resort
Directions: Follow Highway 101 west from Port Angeles for about 29 miles and turn left onto Sol Duc Hot Springs Road. At about milepost 219, turn left on Sol Duc Hot Springs Road. Park at the resort.

You don't need to stay in the resort to park onsite and experience either the pools or the simple—and free—beauty of the area. From the parking lot, it's only a mile down well-worn, flat Sol Duc Falls Trail to Sol Duc Falls. The falls flow year-round, though you may need to don snowshoes to see them in the winter. Rather than return the same way, you can loop back to the parking lot through old-growth forest via **Lover's Lane Trail.**

Deer Lake Trail

Distance: 7.5 miles round-trip
Duration: 3-5 hours
Elevation gain: 1,700 feet
Effort: Moderate-difficult
Trailhead: Off Sol Duc River Trail

From Sol Duc Falls, you can take Deer Lake Trail up 3.8 miles through thick forest to small Deer Lake. Backpackers looking for an overnight excursion can grab a backcountry permit from the Eagle Ranger Station (360/327-3524) and head up from Deer Lake past the intersection of the Appleton Trail to **High Divide** in the **Seven Lakes Basin** area. Deer Lake Trail isn't an easy one as it's mostly uphill, rocky, and filled with switchbacks. Great opportunities to interact with wildlife (mostly deer and birds) and trips through meadows and old-growth forests—not to mention a nice lake at the end—are the reward.

Appleton Pass Trail

Distance: 15 miles round-trip
Duration: 6-10 hours
Elevation gain: 3,100 feet
Effort: Moderate-difficult
Trailhead: at the end of Olympic Hot Springs Road
Directions: From Port Angeles, drive nine miles west on Highway 101, then turn left on Olympic Hot Springs Road.

High mountain meadows, old-growth trees, waterfalls, deer, and mountain goats are just some of the treats that await hikers advanced enough to try the lengthy and steep Appleton Pass Trail, which meanders for miles along the Sol Duc River. Early-season hikers might experience some snow along the way, but the trail is mostly snow-free from July to early fall.

WINTER SPORTS

The **Hurricane Ridge Ski and Snowboard Area** (off Hurricane Ridge Rd., 360/457-2879, www.hurricaneridge.com, $32 all day, all lifts) offers one of only three ski lift operations in all of the U.S. National Parks. This one is small and geared toward families, but it's also cheap and out of the way with a few difficult black runs for advanced skiers and snowboarders. The area gets 400 inches of snow a year, has two rope tows and one Poma lift, and averages about 5,000 visitors a year. You can rent snowshoes and cross-country and downhill skis here.

ACCOMMODATIONS

The Lake Sutherland Lodge B&B (430 S. Shore Rd., 360/928-2111 or 888/231-1444, $65-90 d) isn't as well-known a lodging option as those located on Lake Sutherland's sister lake, Lake Crescent, but this log home has four guest rooms, is a lot cheaper, and offers a full breakfast.

★ **Lake Crescent Lodge** (360/928-3211, www.olympicnationalparks.com, $99-239 s or d) was built along the south shore of the lake in 1916 by Avery J. Singer who called the business Singer's Lake Crescent Tavern. The tavern, which also was part resort, eventually became a full-fledged resort, and President Franklin D. Roosevelt stayed here during a 1937 visit to the area. Today, the popular Roosevelt Fireplace Cottages are named after FDR, and the resort's other rooms also have historic names. There's the Singer Tavern Cottages, Pyramid Mountain Rooms, Marymere Rooms, Storm King Rooms, and Historic Lake Crescent Lodge Rooms. Many of the rooms have views of the lake, and there's a comfortable lobby with a stone fireplace.

As difficult as it may be to believe, ★ **Log Cabin Resort** (3183 E. Beach Rd., 360/928-3325, www.olympicnationalparks.com, $66-161 cabins, $40 RVs) has an even better setting than that of Lake Crescent Lodge. Located on the northeast side of the lake, the resort is more secluded and features rustic cabins, lodge-style rooms, chalets, and RV hookups. There's also a gift shop and a restaurant here with a fairly extensive menu full of burgers and seafood.

Sol Duc Hot Springs Resort (12076 Sol Duc Hot Springs Rd., 360/327-3583, www.olympicnationalparks.com, $163-193 d, mid-May-mid-Oct. only, $36 RVs) offers cabins with and without kitchens, and one River Suite, which has three bedrooms, two baths, and sleeps 10. Including the pools, the site truly is a resort, with a café, gift shop, restaurant, store, and massage therapists on-site. Despite such modern conveniences, the resort doesn't offer phones or TVs in its cabins.

Camping

Klahowya Campground (360/374-7566, $17) is a 55-unit campground located 35 miles west of Port Angeles off Highway 101. Many of the sites are located along the Sol Duc River. The campground is a cheap place to stay in a location central to many Olympic Peninsula attractions.

The closest campground to Hurricane

Ridge that allows vehicles is **Heart O' the Hills,** which is 12 miles below the summit off Hurricane Ridge Road. There are 105 campsites here set among old-growth forest, and the cost is $12-25 per day.

Fairholme Campground (360/565-3130, $12) on the west end of Lake Crescent is open from April through mid-fall and offers 88 campsites and running water. A boat launch and the **Fairholme General Store** (360/928-3020) are nearby.

The **Sol Duc Campground** (360/327-3583, $14-25) is open year-round and offers 82 campsites. There's running water in the summer, but none in the winter. The sites are located along the Sol Duc River.

GETTING THERE AND AROUND

Getting to Hurricane Ridge from Port Angeles is a simple, quick endeavor. Simply head south from the city via Hurricane Ridge Road for 19 miles. Getting to Lake Crescent from Port Angeles is just as simple: Drive 22 miles west on Highway 101 until you reach the lake. Both trips take about 20 minutes from the city.

Strait of Juan de Fuca Highway

As the direct route between Port Angeles and Neah Bay, the Strait of Juan de Fuca Highway (Hwy. 112) cuts across the northern peninsula and through the towns of Joyce, Clallam Bay, and Sekiu. Cliffs line the south side of the roadway, while water dominates the north. It's an alternative route many travelers choose to skip, instead opting to continue on Highway 101 west of Port Angeles toward Lake Crescent and Forks. However, the best option is to allow enough time to accommodate both routes. Though there aren't a ton of things to see or do along most of the road, it's the only path that leads to Neah Bay on the Makah Indian Reservation, and to beautiful Cape Flattery, the northwesternmost point in the continental United States. Winding Highway 112 is designated a National Scenic Byway for a reason, as it's a beautiful drive, the scenery of which changes with the seasons.

SIGHTS

Historic Joyce Depot Museum

The single-story log building doesn't look like much from the outside, but the **Historic Joyce Depot Museum** (50993 Hwy. 112, 360/928-3568, 10am-4pm Thurs.-Mon. summer, 10am-4pm Fri.-Sun. winter) is itself, well, historical. It originally was built as a train depot in 1914 and now holds many locally relevant artifacts. Most unique is the collection of the area's historic voting rolls.

Shipwreck Point

Located between the towns of Sekiu and Neah Bay, Shipwreck Point is a 472-acre Natural Resources Conservation Area. The area is divided by Highway 112. To the north, there's everything you'd expect to see at a saltwater beach, including many fascinating and mostly untouched rock formations, such as a spiral sea stack and tide pools. Lucky visitors will catch an occasional whale spouting in the Strait of Juan de Fuca. The southern part of the area is home to old-growth hemlock and spruce trees.

Salt Creek Recreation Area

Salt Creek Recreation Area (three miles northeast of Joyce off Highway 112) was home to Fort Hayden during World War II, and its gun batteries were used to guard the entrance to the Strait of Juan de Fuca. Remnants of several bunkers still exist here, though it's the nature—not decades-old history—most come here to see. There's plenty of diversity in the 198 acres here, including forests, beaches, and trails, and panoramic views of Vancouver Island, and the strait it resides on. Technically, Salt Creek is a county park, but it sure doesn't look or feel like one. Sure, there are basketball and volleyball courts, a playground, and a softball field, but there's also 90-site **Salt Creek Campground** (360/928-3441, www.clallam.net/Parks/SaltCreek.html, $22-27); a majority of the sites have water views. Bluff Creek Trail, which is roughly one mile long and offers excellent views of Crescent Bay, is a favorite here, as are the access points to adjacent Striped Peak Recreation Area.

FESTIVALS AND EVENTS

Each July, the communities of Clallam Bay and Sekiu come together to produce the very fun three-day-long **Clallam Bay Sekiu Fun Days** (www.clallambaysekiufundays.com), featuring a fun run, grand parade, photo contest, vendors, and more. The event initially began as a way to give hardworking loggers some fun things to do, but since has evolved into a day for the entire family.

ACCOMMODATIONS

Mostly due to its location on the water on the west side of Clallam Bay, the community of Sekiu is home to most of the best lodging options Highway 112 has to offer.

Winter Summer Inn B&B (16651 Hwy. 112, Clallam Bay, 360/963-2264, www.wintersummerinn.com, $85-140 d) only has four rooms, but they are well taken care of. Breakfast is only served in three of the rooms.

Curley's Resort and Dive Center (291 Front St., Sekiu, 360/963-2281 or 800/542-9680, www.curleysresort.com, $55-110 d) is part diving center, part kayak- and boat-rental shop, and part hotel, and does it all equally well. All rooms have TVs and wireless Internet, and many have kitchens with stoves. There also are three cabins ($80-105) for rent. Pets are not allowed in any of the units here.

Straitside Resort (241 Front St., Sekiu, 360/963-2100, www.straitsideresort.com, $73-109 d) has suites, cabins, and studios available. It does not allow pets.

Van Riper's Resort (280 Front St., Sekiu, 360/963-2334, $70-190 d) is a beachside motel, an RV park, and a campground, and also offers boat rentals and has a grocery store on-site.

Middlepoint Inn (15526 Hwy. 112, Sekiu, 360/963-2788, www.middlepointinn.com, $135-200 d) isn't fancy or modern by any means, but the deck has a water view.

★ **Chito Beach Resort** (7639 Hwy. 112, Sekiu, 360/963-2581, www.chitobeach.com,

Salt Creek Recreation Area

$125-160 d) has six themed cabins with full kitchens, HDTV, wireless Internet, a communal fire pit, and more. All the cabins are located on the beach.

★ **The Beaver Creek Cabins** (272 Rixon Rd., Beaver, 360/327-3867, www.thecabinsatbeavercreek.com, $150-180) are closer to Forks than they are to Clallam Bay or Sekiu, but for those who don't mind a 15-minute drive down a scenic highway or for those on their way to Forks anyway, the accommodations here are top-notch and in a comfortable and serene setting.

Camping

Shadow Mountain Campground & RV Park (232951 Hwy. 101, 877/928-3043, www.shadowmt.com, $22.50-35) has 40 full hookup sites for RVs, several grassy tent sites, showers, and laundry facilities, and **Shadow Mountain General Store** is nearby.

FOOD

Get homemade cooking (and desserts such as a towering slice of carrot cake or a hunk of homemade blackberry pie) at **Granny's Café & Motel** (235471 Hwy. 101, 360/928-3266, www.grannyscafe.net, 8am-9pm daily, $8-13).

Devour a full-pound Logger Burger complete with cheese, bacon, and more at **The Family Kitchen** (50800 Hwy. 112, Joyce, 360/928-9777, 11:30am-8pm Mon.-Fri., 9am-8pm Sat.-Sun., lounge open as late at 2am, $7-15). It looks like a house on the side of the busy highway, and it's worth a stop if you have the appetite to tackle the biggest burger around or other hearty menu items.

If you like blackberries, head to the **Blackberry Café** (50530 Hwy. 112, 360/928-0141, 7am-8pm daily, $6-12), where the menu is inspired by the fruit. Try the blackberry barbecue burger and save room for a slice of the heavenly blackberry pie.

GETTING THERE AND AROUND

The best way to travel between Port Angeles and Neah Bay along scenic Highway 112 is by car. **Clallam Transit** (360/452-4511, www.clallamtransit.com) also travels between Clallam Bay, Sekiu, and Neah Bay, and from Port Angeles to Joyce.

The Logger Burger at The Family Kitchen in Joyce is indeed tops.

Neah Bay and Lake Ozette

The northwesternmost point of the contiguous United States is at Neah Bay, which isn't officially a town but a census-designated place, located on the Makah Indian Reservation. Only two of the reservation's beaches are open to the general public, but a world-class museum and other attractions such as glistening Lake Ozette help make the area one worth checking out. Lake Ozette is technically located in the western portion of Olympic National Park but only can be reached, by car at least, via Hoko-Ozette Road, which branches off Highway 112 a mile west of Sekiu.

SIGHTS

★ Lake Ozette

Lake Ozette is the third-largest natural lake in Washington, eight miles long, and three miles across at its widest point. Located at the northwestern tip of **Olympic National Park**'s coastal section, the lake is only accessible by one main road, Hoko-Ozette, which connects to Highway 112 just west of Sekiu. In the 1800s, the lake was surrounded by homesteaders who would travel by foot or on horseback around the area. The homesteads now all have been reclaimed by the land and are part of Olympic National Park. In the 1960s and 1970s, archaeologists took advantage of the erosion caused by a major storm and found more than 50,000 artifacts from early settlers dating back at least 2,000 years.

Today, the 21-mile road into Lake Ozette ends at the **Ozette Ranger Station** (360/963-2725, open daily in summer, hours vary in winter), where two popular trails begin. **Cape Alava Trail** is the more popular of the two. It's a 3.1-mile-long boardwalk through prairie and coastal forest to a rocky beach just south of the small Ozette Indian Reservation. Here, you're at the westernmost point in the contiguous United States. The 2.8-mile **Sand Point Trail** leads to much the same type of area, but a little south. You can walk 3.1 miles on the beach from the end of Sand Point Trail to Cape Alava Trail during low tide, or hike overland when the tide is in, for a hike totaling nine miles. There are roughly three dozen petroglyphs along the beach between the two trails, carved hundreds of years ago. The more adventurous hikers can continue down the coast for several miles, passing many noteworthy sites along the way. Expect to see many sea otters: This place has the largest concentration of them in the United States.

Cape Flattery

Cape Flattery is one of those places where you can meet just about anybody. As the northwesternmost point in the contiguous United States, the cape draws adventurous souls from across the United States and the world, cross-country trekkers who chose Cape Flattery as either the beginning or end of their journeys, and people who just want to say they've been to this remote corner of the United States. Most every visitor, even first-timers, have some sort of story to tell as to why they're here. Many are told in languages other than English.

For some, the main draw is simply the area's beauty and spectacular views. To get to the best of those views, it's necessary to hike the **Cape Flattery Trail.** Until recently, doing so meant undergoing a muddy, sometimes dangerous, trek out to the cape. But in the 2000s, several road and trail improvements were made by the Makah tribe, who own the land here. Traffic in the area has increased accordingly, but the 0.75-mile trail is now easy to navigate. There are plenty of lookouts along the way before you reach the final one at the end of the cape. The end is not anticlimactic: You'll see sea stacks rising out of the ocean, several types of birds flying over them, and waves hitting the shores of rocky **Tatoosh Island.** The island once was home to Makah fishers and whalers and, later, to members of the U.S. Coast Guard, who helped run the lighthouse there, **Cape Flattery Light.**

The **Olympic Coast National Marine Sanctuary** (360/457-6622, www.olympic-coast.noaa.gov) begins at Cape Flattery and extends to the mouth of the **Copalis River** in the south. It also extends 25-50 miles seaward for a total coverage area of 3,310 square miles. The sanctuary is administered by the **National Oceanic and Atmospheric Administration.** Its goal is to protect the zone, which is important to many marine mammals, and also the area's many cultural resources. The sanctuary offers many educational programs in conjunction with state and federal agencies.

★ Makah Cultural and Research Center

The Makah Indians are perhaps the best-known tribe that calls the Olympic Peninsula home, though not only for positive reasons—recent battles with environmentalists and the federal government over whaling rights has kept the Makah name in the headlines for years. It's a shame the tribe has become best known for such an issue, while the hundreds of years of fascinating tribal history on display in Neah Bay at the **Makah Cultural and Research Center** (360/645-2711, www.makahmuseum.com, 10am-5pm daily, $5 adults, $4 students and seniors) goes virtually unnoticed. The museum's permanent exhibit consists of artifacts that are 300-500 years old; the artifacts were excavated from a former Makah village on Lake Ozette. The museum also is home to a language program that's goal is to preserve the Makah language. This is one of the finest cultural museums in the country.

Shi Shi Beach

Primitive Shi Shi (pronounced "shy-shy") Beach was among the last additions to **Olympic National Park,** and its admission did not come easily as locals fought its inclusion. As beautiful as the area is, it's hardly surprising that those who lived there would not want to allow the public access to their semisecret paradise. The beach still is relatively people-free, however, thanks to its distance from the state's major cities. Those who do visit will find dramatic sea stacks, including **Point of Arches,** a striking group of ocean-carved, tunnel-filled, green-topped sea stacks that is unparalleled on the Pacific Coast. Fascinating and life-filled tide pools can be found on the beach itself. Access them via the **Shi Shi Beach Trail,** a three-mile trek through thick forest to the beach. The trail is part wooden boardwalk and part muddy road. You can camp here with a permit, which is obtainable either from the Wilderness Information Center by phone (360/565-3500) or in person in Port Angeles (3002 Mount Angeles Rd.). Those brave souls hoping to camp here from October through May likely won't have any trouble getting a permit on short notice, but those wanting to camp here the rest of the year should call far in advance.

FESTIVALS AND EVENTS

For nearly 90 years, the **Makah Days** celebration has been held during the last week in August, showcasing the tribe's culture and the Makah's U.S. citizenship to whoever wishes to attend the free three-day event. The first Makah Days was held in late August 1913, the first day an American flag was flown over the town of Neah Bay. Today, there are canoe races, a softball tournament, salmon bakes, fireworks, and more than 100 vendors. A grand parade, which draws participants from across the area, also is held each year.

ACCOMMODATIONS

Neah Bay

The Cape Motel & RV Park (1510 Bay View Ave., 360/645-2250, $65-95 s or d, $15 tents,

$25 RVs) features a campground that's open from April to September. Call the motel before you go to see if it is open during the late fall and winter months, because it can close for the season almost on a whim.

★ **The Hobuck Beach Resort** (2726 Makah Passage, 360/645-2339, www.hobuckbeachresort.com, $150-200 cabins, $20 tents, $30 RVs) has RV park cabins and campground cabins that have private baths, kitchenettes, and other conveniences. For tent campers, there are approximately 500 unmarked spots in an open, grassy area. There are some restroom facilities and portable toilets. RV camping is first-come, first-served. Much of the Hobuck Beach Resort has a view of the Pacific Ocean.

Lake Ozette Area

There are 30 tent sites and three cabins set on 10 acres of forest and sparkling Lake Ozette at **The Lost Resort** (20860 Hoko-Ozette Rd., 360/963-2899 or 800/950-2899, www.lostresort.net, $15 tents, $65 cabins). The tent sites are first-come, first-served, but reservations are recommended for the cabins. There is a general store that offers a deli, and a big selection of microbrews that may make you want to start singing "99 Bottles of Beer" by the campfire.

Take in the view at **Ozette Campground** ($12-25) where there is tent and RV camping, running water during summer months, and pit toilets in winter. Get permits and make reservations at the Wilderness Information Center in Port Angeles (360/565-3100) or at the Forks Recreation and Information Center (360/374-7566). There is a free boat-in campground halfway down the lake at Erickson's Bay, which has some good fishing spots, but you can only access it by boat.

FOOD

Washburn's General Store (1450 Bayview Ave., Neah Bay, 360/645-2211, 9am-7pm Mon.-Sat., 9am-6pm Sun.) has some groceries, a soda fountain, and a little of this and some of that. It may not be a five-star restaurant, but a store like this comes in quite handy in this small Indian reservation area. You also can get prepared food with a view at **Warm House Restaurant** (1471 Bay View Ave., 360/645-2077, 7am-8pm Mon.-Sat., 7am-7pm Sun.).

INFORMATION AND SERVICES

More information about the area can be found at several sites online. The website for the **Neah Bay Chamber of Commerce** (www.neahbaywa.com) is among the best. It offers trip itineraries and a detailed map; its FAQ section deals with the complications unique to visitors to an Indian reservation, such as the one located here.

GETTING THERE AND AROUND

Traveling between Port Angeles and Neah Bay along scenic Highway 112 is best done by car, although **Clallam Transit** (360/452-4511, www.clallamtransit.com) travels between Clallam Bay, Sekiu, and Neah Bay, and from Port Angeles to Joyce. There are basically three driving routes to get to Neah Bay from Sea-Tac Airport. You can head north on I-5 and take a ferry to Bainbridge Island and drive north, then west, on Highway 101 from there; or drive south to Tacoma and cut across to the Olympic Peninsula through Gig Harbor; or you can drive farther south on I-5 and cut through Olympia. Depending on traffic and route taken, the trip will take you 4-5 hours.

Hoh Rain Forest and the Coast

Everyone knows about the rain. Stand anywhere on the western half of the Olympic Peninsula and you can hardly escape it. In 1931, more than 184 inches of the wet stuff was recorded at the Wynoochee Oxbow weather station in the foothills of the Olympic National Forest. In many areas, yearly totals of 110 inches or more—enough to cover the tallest man that ever lived—are more norm than exception. At the Quinault Ranger Station, one foot of rain once fell in a 24-hour period. A large outdoor gauge at the Lake Quinault Lodge measures rain in feet rather than inches. At the area's higher elevations, the precipitation translates into massive amounts of snow. At Blue Glacier near the summit of Mount Olympus in Olympic National Park (elev. 7,980 feet), for example, 542 inches of snow once fell in a year.

The impact such large amounts of precipitation has on the Olympic Peninsula is breathtaking and makes for a geologically unique environment. Without it, the area would not be the amazing place it is. In the middle of the Hall of Mosses Trail in the Hoh Rain Forest, it feels like another world, one where fairies could at any moment pop out from the thick undergrowth of ferns and moss-covered cedar, fir, spruce, and hemlock trees. Plastic ponchos sell well here for a reason. Kids often are shocked when their parents encourage them to go play in the rain.

Or if it isn't fairies you spot in the forests, how about vampires and werewolves? There's a reason author Stephenie Meyer chose to set her popular *Twilight* books on the Olympic Peninsula. She said she was looking for someplace ridiculously rainy and surrounded by forest. With a quick search of the Internet, she found her dark and ominous setting here.

Explore on foot small towns such as Hoquiam, Ocean Shores, and Forks, and then take in the journey from a car window, where you'll see shorebirds pecking away in muddy estuaries and hip-wader-clad anglers braving cold, rushing rivers—both hoping to catch their dinner. There are the forests and snow-capped Olympic Mountains and the many

Previous: hiking trail in Hoh Rain Forest; sea stacks at Rialto Beach. **Above:** Cape Disappointment Lighthouse.

Look for ★ to find recommended sights, activities, dining, and lodging.

Highlights

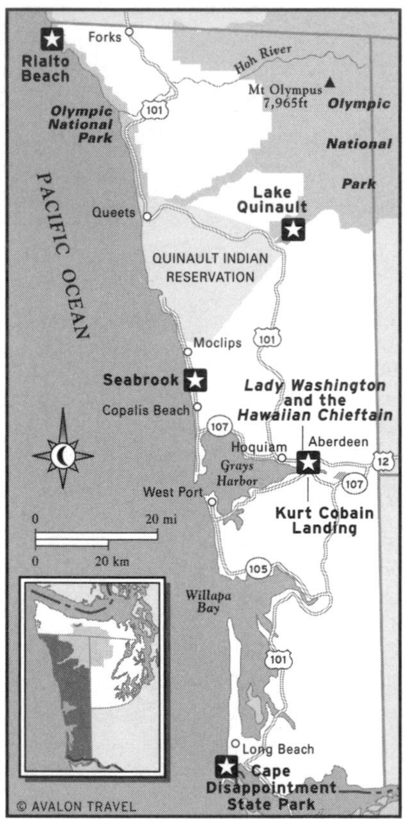

★ **Rialto Beach:** Located in the coastal section of Olympic National Park, this popular beach boasts breathtaking views of offshore islands known as sea stacks (page 121).

★ **Lake Quinault:** Lake Quinault is surrounded by rain forest, waterfalls, and giant trees. Come here to hike, fish, or spy a herd of Roosevelt elk (page 132).

★ **Seabrook:** A beach town built to attract idyll-seeking tourists, Seabrook features New England-inspired architecture and pathways of crushed oyster shells (page 139).

★ ***Lady Washington* and the *Hawaiian Chieftain*:** Take a tour of these full-scale replica tall ships, or watch them engage each other in battle—real gunpowder and all (page 150).

★ **Kurt Cobain Landing:** The honorary designation describes the area surrounding Young Street Bridge in Aberdeen, where Kurt Cobain spent some of his time writing songs. It is also the home of a left-handed guitar sculpture commemorating the singer's life and career (page 152).

★ **Cape Disappointment State Park:** This park marks the endpoint of the Lewis and Clark Expedition. An interpretive center chronicles the expedition's trials, tribulations, and discoveries (page 168).

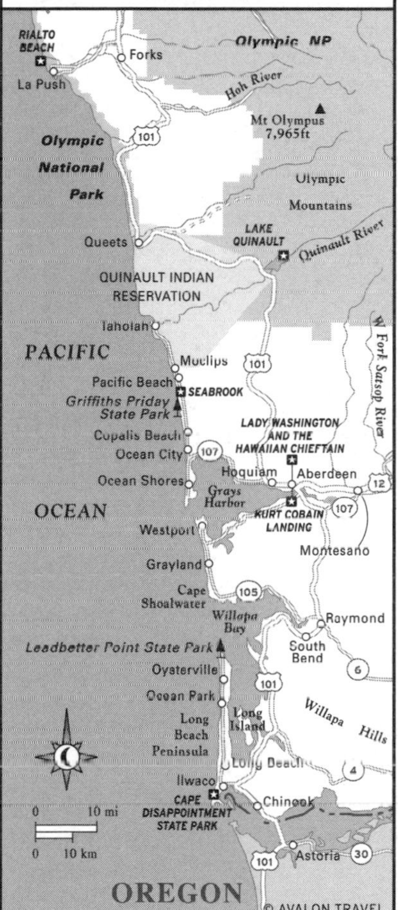

rivers, creeks, and waterfalls that flow down toward the Pacific Ocean.

HISTORY

When iconic musician Kurt Cobain moved from his home in Aberdeen he said he was searching for, in part, the culture he believed his mostly blue-collar homeland lacked. It's doubtful Cobain ever considered the irony in his decision. Archaeological evidence shows Native Americans have lived in the region for more than 10,000 years, farming its seemingly endless supply of natural resources for food, clothing, and supplies, and developing languages to communicate with each other and their gods. It may not be the edgy art scene Cobain was looking for, but fascinating culture it was and continues to be.

It wasn't until the 16th century that Europeans began exploring the area. The first white settlements didn't begin to pop up until the mid-1850s. Today, from the moment you enter the western Olympic Peninsula you begin to feel, even adopt, the laid-back attitude of the locals in this once-booming—now somewhat sleepy and struggling—former logging mecca.

Although harvesting the area's natural resources still provides a major source of income for many locals, tourism now also plays a major role. Despite the uptick in tourists, the area has maintained its small-town feel. Sensory overloads don't come from Starbucks here (there are only two in the entire area, both in Aberdeen)—it's the sounds (or lack thereof), fresh air, and awe-inspiring wonders of Mother Nature that perk up even the most caffeine-desperate travelers.

PLANNING YOUR TIME

The variety of landscapes offered here—beaches and forests literally minutes apart—make the area an outdoor lover's paradise during the summer season, although with the amount of rain that hits the area annually, recreating even in the warm months can be challenging. If the weather is warm, the area becomes a popular playground for visitors from Tacoma, Seattle, and elsewhere in the more-populated Puget Sound region. If the weather is rainy, the beaches, trails, and even some cities, can virtually be all yours. It's a guessing game as to which situation you'll encounter on your visit as the weather can quickly turn here.

The most interesting section of Olympic National Park, at least as far as diversity is concerned, is undoubtedly the western portion (which is covered in this chapter), namely because there are two sections of that portion—the coastal section and the non-coastal section—separated by a few miles of land and a coastal Highway 101. The western section also is farthest from any major city, meaning, if you time it correctly, you can have some places all to yourself. But timing it correctly here means avoiding the summer months. If you attend during that season, you're going to have to share. An **Olympic National Park pass** ($25 per vehicle, $12 pedestrians and bicyclists, valid for 7 days) is required for many of the Olympic National Park sights listed in this chapter, although some of the coastal beach sections can be accessed without a pass.

Visitors heading north on Highway 101 are greeted with this sign when they enter Forks.

ORIENTATION

Traveling through the area is fairly simple. While it's easy to get lost if you leave your car, if you are in it, navigation is straightforward—even without a GPS. Highway 101 is the main thoroughfare. It runs north-south through Forks, Aberdeen, Raymond, and the eastern portion of the Long Beach Peninsula on its way through Oregon all the way down to Southern California. Several smaller state roads branch off Highway 101 to take travelers to the beaches. Highway 110 begins at Forks and extends west toward La Push. Highway 109 begins west of Hoquiam and runs out to the North Beach and up to the Quinault Indian Reservation at Taholah. Highway 105 begins south of Aberdeen and runs along the South Beach, where it ends at Westport, and Highway 103 breaks off Highway 101 near Ilwaco, and runs to the coast and through the Long Beach Peninsula to Leadbetter State Park. Outside Aberdeen, Highway 12, then Highway 8, takes travelers through East Grays Harbor County to Olympia.

Although a ferry used to allow people to cross from Westport to Ocean Shores, ferries no longer serve any parts of this region.

Forks, La Push, and Vicinity

Now known worldwide as the setting for Stephenie Meyer's *Twilight* books and movies, Forks (pop. 3,200) once was solely known as a logging mecca that drew its name from its location near forks in the Bogachiel, Calawah, and Sol Duc Rivers. Today, however, it's the *Twilight*-related highlights most visitors under age 50 come to see. Many of those, particularly the shops, can be found within a three-block radius of the main thoroughfare, Forks Avenue. There's even a portable toilet downtown painted red and black called a "Twilight Twoilet."

During summer, downtown often is teeming with camera-toting fans. Shhh . . . don't tell them all the films were shot elsewhere and Meyer hadn't even visited the area prior to writing her first book.

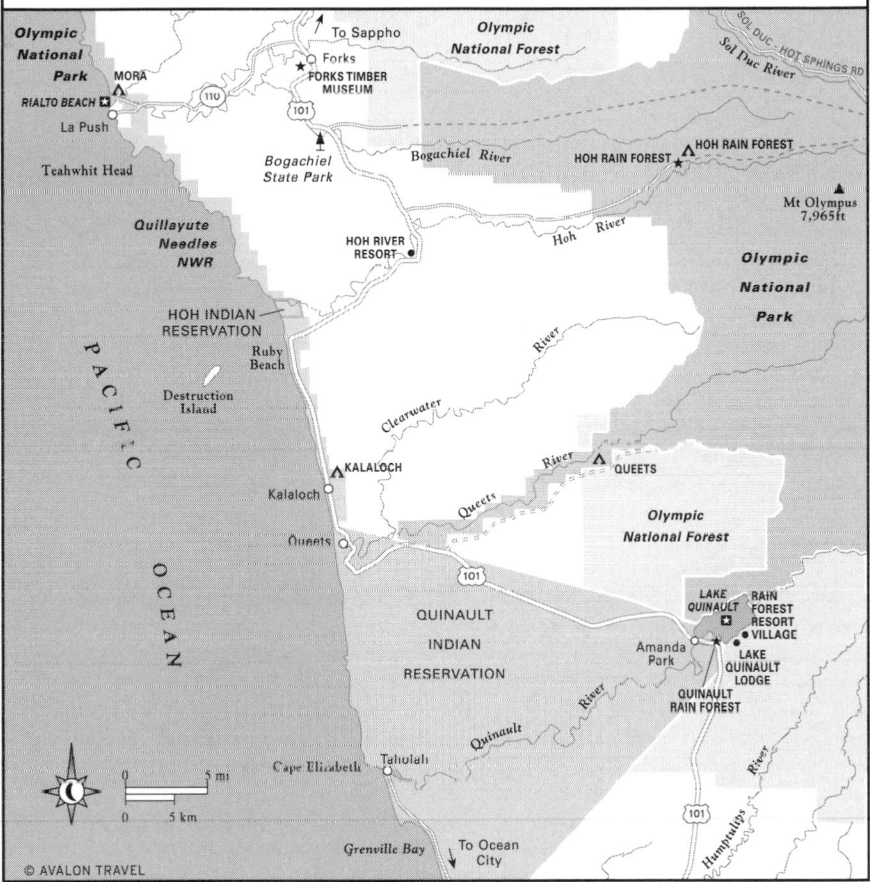

Though the timber industry has declined in recent decades, logging still plays a key role in the city's economy, and evidence of Forks' vibrant past, when it was nicknamed "The Logging Capital of the World," still can be found at parks, memorials, and museums, including the Forks Timber Museum at the south end of town and the circa-1930 Shay locomotive at Tillicum Park in the north end. The city's close proximity to the popular Hoh Rain Forest and Olympic National Park, as well as several beaches in and around the Quileute tribe's unincorporated village of La Push (where *Twilight* werewolf Jacob Black "lives"), helps keep the area busy during the summer months. Sometimes, thanks also in large part to *Twilight*, there are even tourists after the rainy season begins.

SIGHTS

★ Rialto Beach

Due mainly to the convenience of the paved road leading into it, Rialto Beach is arguably the most popular beach located on **Olympic National Park**'s coastal strip (or anywhere in Western Washington, for that matter). But easy access isn't the only reason this beach is so popular with visitors. There are some spectacular views here, and you can only see them by trekking down a short trail from the parking lot. Piles of easily traversed driftwood separate the end of the trail and the beach. For those who can't or don't want to travel down to the beach, there are two slightly obscured-view lookouts at various points along the trail. Those who do make the short trip are rewarded with face-to-face views of sea creatures such as starfish and sea anemones, and spectacular views of offshore islands commonly referred to as sea stacks. Hike roughly 1.5 miles north along the beach at low tide to visit **Hole in the Wall,** a giant monolith at the mouth of the Hoh River with a cave door-like hole carved through it by the sea. For all its beauty, the rugged shoreline still is dangerous and many people have died there. Most notably, in January 1903, 18 people were killed when a Norwegian ship ran aground here, and 20 people died in November 1920 when a Chilean boat slammed into the treacherous coastal rocks. Today, monuments marking both incidents can be found in the area. Camping along the coast is also an option, and necessary for those set on making the 20-mile hike from Rialto Beach north to Lake Ozette.

Forks Timber Museum

Those who want to know the true, pre-*Twilight* history of Forks can find numerous logging-related relics dating as far back as the 1870s at the 3,200-square-foot **Forks Timber Museum** (1411 S. Forks Ave., Forks, 360/374-9663, 10am-4pm daily, Apr.-early Oct., free). Here, visitors can glimpse into the history of an industry that once made the town famous. Highlights include a re-created bunkhouse, an evolutionary exhibit featuring tools of the trade, and an outdoor logging memorial guarded by an 11-foot-tall carving of an ax-wielding logger created by local chainsaw artist Dennis Chastain.

Bogachiel State Park

Heavily forested Bogachiel State Park, located on the western tip of the Hoh Rain Forest roughly six miles south of Forks on Highway 101, is a 123-acre camping park on the Bogachiel River. The Indian word *bogachiel* roughly translates to "turbulent waters," but the river is relatively calm most of the summer. In the winter, however, it earns its name. That's when the river kicks it up a notch, and the park becomes a base camp for anglers. The park's campsites (360/374-6356, www.parks.wa.gov, $12 primitive site, $31 full-utility site) are available year-round. Fishing and camping aren't the only activities available at the park. Many come here to float the river, when it's warm, and also to picnic and search for mushrooms. Because massive Olympic National Park is nearby, Bogachiel often is overlooked. It shouldn't be. There may not be as many, but there are massive trees here, too, including a large stand of hemlock near the park's entrance.

SPORTS AND RECREATION

Beaches

Much of the same breathtaking scenery found north of La Push at Rialto Beach also can be found both in and south of the village at not-so-creatively named **First Beach, Second Beach,** and **Third Beach.** Though their indistinct boundaries connect, you can't hike directly between any of the three beaches, due to headlands that protrude into the ocean and block the way. First Beach, located at the end of La Push Road in La Push on the Quileute Indian Reservation, is best known for its views of tree- and bird-covered James Island and for being the spot where *Twilight* characters Jacob Black and Bella Swan first met. The beach is on the reservation, but no special permits are required to access it. In real life, there is a marina and a few small businesses here.

A 0.75-mile hike over a forest trail is necessary to get from the trailhead off La Push Road down to Second Beach, located just south of La Push and 13 miles off Highway 101, but it is worth it. The end of the hike is marked by a steep descent to the ocean. In

Twilight Time

Twilight fans will be familiar with this truck, a replica of the one from the movies.

The tiny town of Forks, on the Pacific Coast, was once known as a jumping-off point for fishing and hunting expeditions into the western reaches of the Olympic Mountains, as well as one of the biggest logging towns in the country. Then an author named Stephenie Meyer started writing books about teenage vampires and werewolves that were set in and around Forks, the books got made into movies, and an entire tourist industry was born.

Since the release of the first book in the series in 2004, thousands of fans have come to the Washington coast, hoping to see some of the books' settings, and the massive success of the movies has only increased the flood. They find out quickly that all is not as it seems. Scenes in the film at Forks High School actually were shot elsewhere, and some shooting was done on sets in Hollywood. Forks locals have their share of memorabilia and sites for *Twilight* tourists to view, however. For example, you can have your picture taken in the pickup truck driven by Bella, the main character in the books and movies, at the **Forks Chamber of Commerce Visitor Center.** The **Miller Tree Bed & Breakfast** in Forks has been designated by the locals as the "official" home of the Cullen family from the books and films, and has a signboard out front on which the innkeepers write what the Cullens are up to each day. Forks Hospital even has a parking spot reserved for the fictional Dr. Cullen.

It's also easy to find other major settings from the books and films. **First Beach,** where Bella first finds out the truth about her blood-sucking boyfriend, is located in nearby La Push. And farther inland, there's **Bella Italia,** an Italian restaurant in Port Angeles where Bella and Edward had their first date. The red sauce is recommended.

the distance, a mass of coastal rock and reefs called the **Quillayute Needles** (an alternate spelling of Quileute) can be seen. The needles are part of a 100-mile-long section of coast called the **Quillayute Needles National Wildlife Refuge,** where sea lions rest and more than a dozen species of shorebirds nest and raise their young in a place where humans are not allowed to roam. You can easily see the needles from the beach, but binoculars are necessary to spot any of the wildlife. Until recently, Second Beach was closed due to territorial disputes between the Quileute tribe and the federal government. The disputes, which chiefly center on the tribe's desire to be granted more land so it can move its village to higher ground and out of a tsunami-prone zone, continue. However, access to the beach has been restored.

The trailhead to Third Beach is only about a mile east of the trailhead to Second Beach, but the two beaches offer much different viewing opportunities. Getting to Third Beach requires a two-mile hike down an old road and through hemlock and spruce trees. As you get close you will begin to hear the water and after a descent, you will see the ocean. The beach is trapped by two large headlands. The headlands to the south are called Taylor Point, off which a waterfall drops directly into the ocean during rainy season.

Hiking

Bogachiel River Trail

Distance: 12 miles round-trip
Duration: 4-5 hours
Elevation gain: 400 feet
Effort: Moderate
Trailhead: Undi Road
Directions: Five miles south of Forks on Highway 101 (across the highway from Bogachiel State Park), turn east on Undi Road. The trailhead is 5.6 miles down the road, the latter portion of which is unpaved and can be tricky to navigate during and immediately following the rainy season.

Those who trek to this trail are rewarded with a quiet stroll through moss-covered, old-growth spruce and fir trees into Olympic National Park. There, the trail snakes along the river and connects with several other trails before eventually ending nearly 30 miles in at Seven Lakes Basin.

Hoh Head Trail

Distance: 3.5 miles round-trip
Duration: 1.5-2 hours
Elevation gain: 400 feet
Effort: Difficult
Trailhead: Oil City
Directions: Heading south from Forks, turn west on Oil City Road, and follow it to the end.

The Hoh Head Trail begins at Oil City in the south and heads north. Oil City itself has an interesting story. It once was slated to be a deep-water oil port and, in 1913, two test wells were drilled here. A substantial amount of oil and gas was found, but nowhere near as much as would be needed to sustain even one operation. Future oil-seekers drilled more wells and began to plot a city, but again there wasn't enough oil for anyone to stick around for the long haul. The often-muddy trail winds north through Jefferson Cove into a section near Hoh Head that one must use ropes and ladders to pass. This is not an easy hike, but when you end at Mosquito Creek, where camping is allowed with a backcountry permit, you'll feel like you've accomplished something.

Fishing

Located seven miles north of Forks, 500-acre **Lake Pleasant** (West Lake Pleasant Rd., Beaver) is one of the few lakes open to fishing year-round. It offers anglers the opportunity to catch several species of fish, including kokanee and cutthroat trout. Swimming and boating also are allowed on the lake, which is unique in that it is surrounded by private property. But it still can be accessed via a community beach, where there's a small parking lot and a boat ramp.

Those looking for an off-season fishing adventure need look no further than the **Bogachiel River,** a steelhead angler's paradise with its hatchery steelhead, as well as some natives. Winter steelhead fishing usually takes place from late November to January, while summer steelhead fishing typically peaks in early September and October. For an excellent guided steelhead- or salmon-fishing trip on the "Bogey" and other local rivers, check out the friendly guides at **Three Rivers Resort** (7765 La Push Rd., 360/374-5300, www.threeriversresortandguideservice.com, $275/day).

Surfing

Surfing in often-chilly Western Washington may not seem like a smart thing to do, but La Push happens to be fairly popular for those who like to ride some gnarly waves. Good surfing can be hit-and-miss here, however,

Catch Your Own Meal

As might be expected in an area rich in unspoiled wilderness and complex micro-ecosystems, the Olympic Peninsula has excellent fishing, especially toward the coastal areas. There are many river systems inland with major fish runs as well. Before *Twilight* was produced and a score of vampire fans came to town, the tiny town of Forks was primarily known as a base camp for anglers trying their luck on the Sol Duc, Bogachiel, Hoh, Quileute, and Calawah river systems. Species include salmon and steelhead in season, while fly fishers in particular may be looking at the cutthroat trout runs.

If you prefer digging your dinner instead of casting for it, there also are a number of beaches with razor clam seasons; just be sure to check with local authorities for open harvest dates and permit rules.

There's also excellent hunting in the dense forests of the central and coastal Olympic Peninsula. Deer and Roosevelt elk are common—in fact, the elk are so common that at times the Department of Fish & Wildlife has to relocate entire herds that wander into farmland areas.

Or if it's dangerous trophy game you're after, Washington also allows deer hunters with a valid cougar license and transport tag to hunt cougars during deer season. Whether you eat the big cat or not is up to you. Black bears also are common on the peninsula and often hunted for trophies. The annual Bear Festival, held each July in the town of McCleary, even serves bear stew.

so check current surf reports (www.swell-info.com) before investing the time to drive out. **Wilderness Creative** (51 N. Forks Ave., Forks, 360/640-0571, www.wildernesscreative.org, 10am-6pm daily) is the best place in the area to rent boards and wetsuit, as well as skateboards and more.

ENTERTAINMENT AND EVENTS

Nightlife

La Push has no nightlife to speak of and, though it's technically the largest incorporated city on the western side of the Highway 101 loop, Forks really doesn't either. Your best option in Forks for late-night food, drink, and socializing is **Blakeslee's** (1222 S. Forks Ave., Forks, 360/374-5003, 11am-10pm Mon.-Thurs., 11am-2am Fri., noon-2am Sat., noon-9pm Sun.). The former Mill Creek bar/restaurant doesn't look like much from the outside, but Blakeslee's is a rather neat and tidy joint inside, with a hardwood dance floor and a bar area that's decently separated from the general restaurant. Those who frequented the establishment when it was Mill Creek should note that it is now a 21-and-over establishment only.

Festivals and Events

Many communities across the United States host Independence Day celebrations each year. But for Forks, the **Old-Fashioned 4th of July** is a multiday affair filled with off-the-wall contests, including a frog-jumping competition, a memorial road race, shopping deals, food, a parade, and a demolition derby. Of course, there's fireworks, too.

Another multiday celebration held in July is La Push's **Quileute Days.** With its stick games, native art, and dancing, the festival is centered on tribal culture, but it also gives a nod to the present day by including a poker tournament and scheduling appearances by *Twilight* actors.

What exactly would a weekend held in your honor look like? If you're *Twilight* author Stephenie Meyer, you already know. **Stephenie Meyer Day** is actually three days of food and art vendors, music, scavenger hunts, and look-alike contests in Forks. It's all held during the second week of September to coincide with the birthday of *Twilight*'s main character, Bella Swan.

After the majority of tourists have high-tailed it back home, Forks gets back to basics by holding the **Forks Heritage/Hickory**

Shirt Days during the first week of October. Logging-related activities abound, including a pumpkin-carving contest, where participants create their works of art with chainsaws. The event's name comes from the striped, long-sleeved shirts worn by local loggers. During this time of year the shirts are resurrected, and you'll see them being worn all over town.

Be sure to browse **Forks Open Aire Market** (1421 S. Forks Ave., 10am-3pm Sat., mid-May-mid-Oct.) if you're in the area between May and October. The market is a great, albeit relatively small, place to check out interesting items produced by local artisans.

SHOPPING

Because most of the area's shops offer at least some sort of *Twilight*-related goods, it's difficult to tell people where to go if they want to exclusively shop for *Twilight* merchandise. One shop, however, is easy to categorize as such. **Native to Twilight** (10 N. Forks Ave., Forks, 360/374-2111, www.nativetotwilight.com, 10am-6pm daily) is a locally focused shop featuring *Twilight*-related merchandise. It shouldn't come as a surprise that some of the store's best sellers are *Twilight*-related clothes, but the quality of Native American-themed merchandise found here may surprise some. Of particular note are the paintings by local Shirley Owens and the wooden native eagle head carved by Rob Taylor of La Push. The shop once was just one of a handful of *Twilight*-centric stores in town, but now it's pretty much the only game left in town. A recent fire took out an even more popular shop and its owners decided—no doubt due to the shrinking popularity of *Twilight*—not to rebuild.

More of a catchall shop than a gallery (but there's *Twilight* merch here, too), **The Fern Gallery** (11 S. Forks Ave., Forks, 360/374-4300, www.theferngallery.com, 10am-5pm Mon.-Sat.) is a gift and flower shop that features a variety of items, some created by locals.

A Work in Progress & Café Paix (71 N. Forks Ave., Forks, 360/374-0330, 10am-5pm daily) sells antiques and coffee in the same spot, and features a variety of other goods, too.

A must-stop for outdoor enthusiasts looking for some gear, all kinds of gaming licenses, and stellar local advice is **Olympic Sporting Goods** (190 S. Forks Ave., Forks, 360/374-6330, 7am-4pm Mon.-Sat.). The shop has many name brands, and also has some used equipment for sale.

ACCOMMODATIONS

$50-100

The best motel choice in Forks, although from the outside it doesn't look like it would be, is the ★ **Pacific Inn Motel** (352 S. Forks Ave., Forks, 360/374-9400 or 800/235-7344, www.pacificinnmotel.com, $89 d). Standard rooms feature large, flat-screen TVs, microwaves, refrigerators, and wireless Internet. *Twilight*-themed rooms are decked out in red and black, and the property's executive suite has a full kitchen and its own washer and dryer.

Equally impressive is the **Olympic Suites Inn** (800 Olympic Dr., Forks, 360/374-5400 or 800/262-3422, www.olympicsuitesinn.com, $94-109 d), located north of Forks's city center. At 650 square feet, suites are as large as some small apartments, and all in a quiet, wooded setting off the main drag. Full-size refrigerators in every room make long-term stays easier on those who don't want to eat out every meal (not to mention there are limited restaurant choices in Forks).

$100-150

It typically only takes one night for guests at the **Misty Valley Inn** (194894 Hwy. 101, Forks, 360/374-9389 or 877/374-9389, www.mistyvalleyinn.com, $125-165) to realize why the place is named the way it is. Typical mornings from the back deck of the 6,000-square-foot, four-guest room home offer a picturesque view of a layer of mist topping the Sol Duc meadows.

If you like ample opportunity to fraternize with down-to-earth hosts in a rural setting, one of the two spacious rooms at the **Fisherman's Widow Bed and Breakfast**

(62 Steelhead Ave., Forks, 360/374-5693, www.fishermans-widow.com, $125 d) might be just the place for you. Mere feet from the Sol Duc River, the rooms feature whirlpool tubs and are great for families or groups of friends looking to crash for the night, wake to a fully prepared breakfast, and hit the road on an outdoor adventure.

At the **Forks Motel** (351. S. Forks Ave., Forks, 360/374-6243 or 800/544-3416, www.forksmotel.com, $99-159 d), there's even a whirlpool tub suite. Expect the outdoor pool to be full of kids, even when the weather isn't so hot.

Located just off the main drag in the southern end of Forks, **The Dew Drop Inn** (100 Fern Hill Rd., Forks, 360/374-4055 or 888/433-9376, www.dewdropinnmotel.com, $94-149 d) offers clean rooms and a free continental breakfast, and it's pet-friendly. The mostly red Bella Suite is a hit with *Twilight* fans, particularly because author Stephenie Meyer stayed here in 2004.

Located along First Beach in La Push, **Quileute Oceanside Resort** (330 Ocean Dr., La Push, 360/374-5267 or 800/487-1267, www.quileuteoceanside.com, $63-280 d) is more complex than resort, offering multiple lodging options, including 33 oceanfront cabins, two 14-unit hotels, a full-service RV park, and tent sites. The accommodations themselves are mostly excellent, although the luxury cabins are the best bet. There's the small-but-expensive **Lonesome Creek Grocery Store** and a laundry on-site.

$150-200

The address may say Forks, but the ★ **Manitou Lodge Bed and Breakfast** (813 Kilmer Rd., Forks, 360/374-6295, www.manitoulodge.com, $139-179 d) really is located in a remote wooded setting about halfway between the town and the beautiful beaches of La Push. Room names such as Pocahontas and Lily of the Mohawk reflect the lodge's proximity to the Quileute Indian Reservation a few miles to the west. A stone fireplace in the lodge's main room adds to the relaxation, as does the full breakfast each morning. Two small cabins ($69, $99) also are on-site, though they are not available during winter months.

A more expensive, in-town option can be found at **Miller Tree Inn Bed and Breakfast** (654 E. Division, Forks, 360/374-6806, www.millertreeinn.com, $130-225 d). Located in a 1916 farmhouse with a large deck out back that overlooks a forest, the inn is a favorite for those looking for a quiet night in a pastoral setting with a hearty breakfast to look forward to each morning, prepared by gracious innkeepers Bill and Susan Brager.

Camping

Those looking for a cheap, yet nice, camping spot close to the beaches in and around La Push will find it at ★ **Mora Campground** (14 miles west of Forks, 360/565-3130, open year-round, $12-25), which features 94 sites for tents or RVs up to 21 feet long. There are trails surrounding the wooded, mostly flat campsites, including a 0.3-mile trail around James Pond and the 0.9-mile Slough Trail. Rialto Beach, Second Beach, and Third Beach all are within two miles of Mora. Be warned, the campground fills up quick during summer months.

Nearby lies the **Three Rivers Resort** (360/374-5300, www.threeriversresortandguideservice.com, $14 tents, $18 full RV hookups, $93-189 cabins), where tents, cabins and RVs coexist in a peaceful setting located just beyond the self-proclaimed "Treaty Line," near which a sign reads: No Vampires Beyond This Point. The resort is located near a spot where the Quillayute, Sol Duc, and Bogachiel Rivers meet. There's a restroom with pay showers and a convenience store on-site, in addition to the Three Rivers Resort Restaurant (11am-7pm daily), best known for its burgers and milkshakes.

For RVers who don't want to venture far off the highway, **Forks 101 RV Park** (901 S. Forks Ave., 360/374-5073 or 800/962-9964, www.forks-101-rv-park.com, $39-50) is a good option, especially for those looking for a convenient place to do laundry and/or wash their campers. Twelve miles north of Forks, there's a cozy, free campground on the Sol Duc River outside Sappho called **Tumbling Rapids Park** (360/374-6565, free). The short Ron Smith Memorial Trail runs along the river, and the park is owned by Rayonier.

FOOD

American

The **Forks Coffee Shop** (241 S. Forks Ave., Forks, 360/374-6769, 5:30am-8pm daily, $4-10) name may be a little misleading and the light-blue booths a bit campy, but when a restaurant's motto is "Nobody Leaves Hungry!" it can be difficult not to try it at least once. Turns out, they're not joking about the large portions here. Dishes such as the Sol Duc Scramble leave diners scrambling to ask for a doggy bag, which the staff will happily provide.

Another local greasy spoon worth trying is **The In Place** (320 S. Forks Ave., Forks, 360/374-4004, 6am-9pm daily, $6-12), especially if you're in the mood for an easy-to-prepare item, such as a sandwich. Just north of town, the **Smoke House Restaurant** (193161 Hwy. 101, Forks, 360/374-6258, $8-16) has a local reputation for having slow service and overpriced food, but there are gems, such as the smoked salmon.

At the **River's Edge Restaurant** (off River Dr., La Push, 360/374-3236, 8am-8pm daily, $9-15), both the perfectly cooked, seasoned salmon and the view, to throw in a *Twilight* reference, are to die for.

Chinese

Golden Gate (111 S. Forks Ave., Forks, 360/374-5528, 11am-9pm Mon.-Sat., $7-12) is one of two places to get Chinese food. The dishes are typical Americanized fare, but the portions are decent. Better to satisfy your craving at **South North Garden** (140 Sol Duc Way, Forks, 360/374-9779, 11am-10pm, $8-12), where you can slip on over to the lounge for some stiff drinks and post-meal karaoke with the locals on weekends.

Italian

Fresh deep-dish pizza, several types of pasta, sandwiches, and salads make **Pacific Pizza** (870 Forks Ave., Forks, 360/374-2626, 11am-9pm Sun.-Thurs., 11am-10pm Fri.-Sat., $8-13) a good choice, whether you want to dine in or have the food delivered to your hotel room. Take a gander at, and sign, the *Twilight*-related guestbook before you leave.

Mexican

Twilight tacos? Yep, **Plaza Jalisco** (90 N. Forks Ave., Forks, 360/374-3108, 11am-9pm Sun.-Thurs., 11am-10pm Fri.-Sat., $6-12) has them, along with hot food, and plates customized with the restaurant's name. Fortunately, the tacos are made with beef or chicken.

Quick Bites

Soups, sandwiches, ice cream, and a fairly extensive (some might add expensive) candy selection are offered at **JT's Sweet Stuffs** (80 N. Forks Ave., Forks, 360/374-6111, 10am-6pm daily, $4-8). If the good eats and the location weren't enough to draw people inside, the favorable quote about the store from author Stephenie Meyer written on the store's window should. An equally sweet and even more unique place to satisfy a sweet tooth is **Sweet P's Bake Shop** (80 W. A St., Forks, 360/374-4332, 10am-5pm daily, $2-5).

Don't let the Bella Burger on the menu fool you. Family-owned ★ **Sully's Drive-In** (220 N. Forks Ave., Forks, 360/374-5075, 11am-9pm Mon.-Sat., $4-8) is steeped in tradition, having served hungry Forks residents and tourists its popular burgers, including the Spartan, Rainy Day, and Tall Timber, for decades. There's a reason people keep coming back.

INFORMATION AND SERVICES

The *Twilight* phenomenon helped lead to increased staffing levels at the **Forks Chamber of Commerce Visitor Center** (1411 S. Forks Ave., 360/374-2531 or 800/443-6757, www.forkswa.com, 10am-5pm Mon.-Sat.,

11am-4pm Sun. in summer), which already was known for its small-town hospitality.

The **Pacific Ranger District Forks Office** (437 Tillicum Ln., 360/374-6522, 8am-4pm Mon.-Fri.) are also helpful and provide information and maps on the area.

Several media outlets cover the area, including radio stations and the *Forks Forum* newspaper (www.forksforum.com).

GETTING THERE

There are basically three driving routes to get to Forks from Sea-Tac Airport. You can head north on I-5 and take a ferry to Bainbridge Island and drive north, then west, then south on Highway 101 from there, you can drive south to Tacoma and cut across to the Olympic Peninsula through Gig Harbor, or you can drive farther south on I-5 and head out to, and up, the coast through Aberdeen on Highway 101 north. Budget 3.5-4 hours, if you're driving directly there. But no one really does that, because there are so many sights to see either way that you have to stop.

Clallam Transit (360/452-4511 or 800/858-3747, www.clallamtransit.com) provides service north to La Push, Neah Bay, and Port Angeles, while **Jefferson Transit Olympic Connection** (www.jeffersontransit.com) covers Forks and Lake Quinault via stops in the Hoh Valley, Kalaloch, Queets, and more.

Hoh River Valley

Rain, of course, is what makes the Hoh River Valley special. Roughly 12 feet of it falls annually, contributing to the lush greenery of old-growth trees, ferns, and mosses that is prevalent throughout the area, located south of Forks off Highway 101. Only Native Americans have ever lived in this section of the valley that lies within Olympic National Park. Glaciers near Mount Olympus, including the Blue and the Hoh, are responsible for the creation of the valley and the milky-colored river that flows through it.

SIGHTS

Hoh Rain Forest

The Hoh Rain Forest, located at the end of the 19-mile-long Upper Hoh River, within **Olympic National Park,** is popular with visitors to the area thanks to its ease of access and its natural beauty. Upon entering, visitors discover an ethereal temperate rain forest adjacent to the Hoh River, where green is the dominant color, time seems to slow down, and words don't do justice, and often are unnecessary.

The adventure begins just 14 miles south of Forks, at the turnoff to the Upper Hoh Road. The road's first dozen miles are located outside Olympic National Park, run through second- and third-growth woods and open fields, and offer an occasional glimpse of the Hoh River. Inside the park, after passing through a pay station, it's old-growth forest all the way. The Hoh is a temperate rain for est, which means it needs mild weather and massive amounts of precipitation to thrive. These conditions help the trees grow quickly and for long periods of time. Indeed, some of the trees here are more than 500 years old, and many of them look the part. Green moss covers the massive Sitka spruce and Western hemlock trees here in much the same way a gray beard might an old man, and fallen trees known as nurse logs act in the same way fertilizer might in your garden. A fresh smell dominates the air. Water drips from moss-covered tree limbs above, allowing the "rain" to continue long after any clouds have passed from overhead.

Unlike some visitors centers, the **Hoh Rain Forest Visitor Center** (360/374-6925, 9am-7pm daily July-Aug., 9am-4pm Sat.-Sun. Sept.-June) is a place where you must stop, as there's so much to see and do here. The center offers interpretive exhibits, brochures, wilderness-use permits, and maps of the area and its trails. Some of those trails begin behind the center, including a 0.1-mile flat, paved, and unnamed mini-trail through old-growth forest.

Mount Olympus

At 7,965 feet, Mount Olympus is the tallest mountain in **Olympic National Park,** and as such, a focus of many climbers. Despite its relatively low elevation, Mount Olympus is covered in glaciers, thanks to the near-constant snowfall it receives. Summiting the mountain generally entails beginning at the head of the Hoh River Trail, hiking in 17.5 miles to Glacier Meadows, registering at the ranger yurt there, hiking to, then traversing, **Blue Glacier,** and ascending **Snow Dome** to the summit. The climb is considered technically difficult, and involves the use of climbing gear and the ability to rock climb. The fastest-known round-trip (car-to-car) hike-climb of Olympus is believed to have been done in less than 12 hours, though it generally takes the average climber that long just to go the 4.5 miles from Glacier Meadows to the summit. Mount Olympus climbers occasionally begin at other points, as well, but the Hoh River Trail is by far the most common.

Beginners and intermediate hikers may be wise to hire a guide service to assist them in their quest. Several options are available, including **Northwest Mountain Guides** (19215 SE 34th St., Camas), and **Mountain Madness** (3018 SW Charlestown St., Seattle, 206/937-8389 or 800/328-5925, www.mountainmadness.com). Both offer four-day round-trips to the summit.

SPORTS AND RECREATION

Hiking in the Hoh Rain Forest

The three trailheads below are right next to the Hoh Rain Forest Visitor Center, approximately 31 miles south of Forks on Highway 101.

Hoh Rain Forest in Olympic National Park

Hall of Mosses Trail

Distance: 0.8 mile round-trip
Duration: 0.5-1 hour
Elevation gain: 100 feet
Effort: Easy
Trailhead: Hoh Rain Forest Visitor Center

The Hall of Mosses Trail is the most popular trail in the Hoh Rain Forest for several reasons. Its location next to the visitors center means you can't miss it, and the little elevation gain the trail offers (less than 100 feet) isn't enough to deter many. Mostly, though, the trail is popular for what it offers from the moment you step onto it. In the middle of the trail it feels like being in another world. Fallen cedar, fir, spruce, and hemlock trees frequently line the path, and have become host to shrubs and seedlings. Ducks bathe in standing pools of water, partially obscuring the shiny reflection of tree limbs from above. Light peeks through the canopy here and there, allowing visitors to see just how many shades of green there are. It may take less than an hour to hike the trail, but in that time you get to see centuries of nature's work, untouched by man.

Spruce Nature Trail

Distance: 1.2 miles round-trip
Duration: 0.5-1 hour
Elevation gain: Less than 100 feet
Effort: Easy
Trailhead: Hoh Rain Forest Visitor Center

The Spruce Nature Trail travels through much of the same type of greenery found on the Hall of Mosses Trail, only this jaunt leads down to, and briefly runs alongside, the Hoh River. Deer are a common sight here, as are Roosevelt elk. A walk through moss-covered maple trees leads you back to the visitors center.

Hoh River Trail

Distance: 34.8 miles round-trip
Duration: 12-15 hours
Elevation gain: 3,700 feet
Effort: Moderate
Trailhead: Hoh Rain Forest Visitor Center

Visitors to the Hoh Rain Forest looking for a longer, less-crowded trip through the forest and along the Hoh River can veer off the Spruce Nature Trail onto the Hoh River Trail, which travels 17.4 miles all the way up to Glacier Meadows at the base of Mount Olympus. For day hikers, however, there are several points at which to turn around, including the meadows at Mount Tom Creek three miles in, and the campsites at Five Mile Island, which are, as the name suggests, five miles from the trailhead. More adventurous hikers can trek up the **Hoh Lake Trail** (6.5 miles), which veers off from the Hoh River Trail just east of the Olympus Ranger Station. However, at roughly 15 miles from the Hoh trailhead, it's more than a day hike. The trail passes through a spot where, in 1978, a massive fire tore through the area. There are several spots to camp along the way, but you need a permit to do so. You can obtain one at the Hoh Rain Forest Visitor Center.

Outfitters

The **Peak 6 Adventure Store** (4883 Upper Hoh Rd., 360/374-5254, 9am-6pm daily) offers most everything you'll need for hiking, climbing, and camping in this neck of the woods. Grab some advice about the area's hikes and rivers and learn about its history while you shop.

ACCOMMODATIONS

Located 16 miles south of Forks near where Highway 101 brushes up against the Hoh River, the quiet **Hoh River Resort** (175443 Hwy. 101, Forks, 360/374-5566) is both RV park and campground, with 15 full or partial RV sites ($25), five tent sites ($17), and four cabins with kitchens and bathrooms ($65). There's also a small store/gas station on-site, and easy access to a boat launch and a typically wide-open gravel bar on the river.

Twenty miles south of Forks off Highway 101 is the **Ho Humm Ranch Bed & Breakfast** (171763 Hwy. 101, Forks, 360/374-5337, $35 d), a 200-acre homestead in the Hoh River Valley. Accommodations are no-frills and rustic, but that's part of the appeal here. Guest rooms are just rooms in the ranch house, but there are farm animals to look at, and a filling breakfast to start off your morning.

If you know what you're getting into and are short on—or looking to save—cash, the **Rain Forest Hostel** (169312 Hwy. 101, Forks, 360/374-2270, www.rainforesthostel.com, $12 pp) might be just the place you're looking for. It is a private, rural home 24 miles south of Forks with two rooms (one for each gender) full of bunk beds. Here, you'll share a kitchen and a bathroom, and fraternize with the owners and fellow travelers, whose backgrounds and beliefs may be vastly different from your own. In exchange for completing a chore each morning, you only pay $12 per adult ($6 children 7 and under) per night.

Camping

Campgrounds are a traveler's best friend in the Hoh River Valley area, and there are plenty of spots to choose from, beginning with the popular ★ **Hoh Rain Forest Campground** (360/374-6925, www.nps.gov/olym), located in the middle of old-growth forest along the Hoh River some 19 miles off Highway 101 down the Hoh River Road. There are 88 campsites for tents or RVs up to 21 feet long. There also is running water. Cost is $12-25 per night.

Nearby campground options include **Cottonwood** (two miles west on Oil City Rd.), **Hoh Oxbow** (at milepost 176), **Minnie Peterson** (4.5 miles up Hoh Rain Forest Rd.), and **Willoughby Creek** (3.5 miles up Hoh Rain Forest Rd.). All are free, open year-round, and run by the Department of Natural Resources (360/374-6131).

FOOD

Don't be alarmed if you think you've spotted Bigfoot; that's just Harry the Yetti. He's a really nice guy and often found sitting on the deck of the **Hard Rain Café** (5763 Upper Hoh Rd., 360/374-9288, www.hardraincafe.com, 9am-7pm daily, $6-11). This itty-bitty restaurant is literally at the entrance of the Hoh Rain Forest and looks like a small house. As such, there only are a few seats, but there are souvenirs here and a wealth of information to be had by fraternizing with your fellow diners. Try the Mount Olympus burger, a meaty half-pounder slathered with special sauce and swiss cheese. They also offer picnic food to go and catering for large groups. The café doubles as a small grocery store and souvenir shop and will even mail letters and postcards for you.

GETTING THERE

Drivers have three options for getting to the Hoh River Valley from Sea-Tac Airport. You can head north on I-5 and take a ferry to Bainbridge Island and drive north, then west, then south on Highway 101 from there, you can drive south to Tacoma and cut across to the Olympic Peninsula through Gig Harbor, or you can drive farther south on I-5 and head out to, and up, the coast through Aberdeen on Highway 101. Budget four hours.

Queets, Quinault, and Kalaloch

The lands here are a continuation of the greenery found up north in the Hoh Rain Forest, though without as much fanfare. The Olympic Peninsula's two other major rain forests, Queets and Quinault, are here, and filled with the same type of old-growth trees, river valleys, flora, and fauna, as can be found up north. The **Quinault Rain Forest,** located on the south side of Lake Quinault, is part of the **Quinault Indian Reservation** but is open to the general public. To the west on the coast, Kalaloch and other beaches in the area serve to highlight just how small a distance separates the area's mountains from its flat Pacific Ocean coastline.

One warning from the locals: Truck drivers on Highway 101 do not drive slower than passenger cars. Oftentimes, in an effort to get in an extra load of lumber before darkness sets in, they will drive faster. It's important to be alert as you drive through this area.

SIGHTS

★ Lake Quinault

If there was a main attraction of the southwestern section of **Olympic National Park,** Lake Quinault certainly would be it. Located in a glacier-carved valley and enclosed by the Quinault Rain Forest, the steep-banked lake and its surrounding area is a favorite of hardcore hikers and anglers, and big-city sightseers in search of a relaxing getaway.

The steep hills surrounding the lake are filled with waterfalls, many of which can be viewed from the South Shore and North Shore Roads that connect east of the lake to form a 31-mile-long, oftentimes rough and hilly,

Tall Trees

Once the site of ancient-growth forests, with trees so enormous a single trunk would fill an entire log truck, there are few truly old-growth trees left on the Olympic Peninsula, the legacy of nearly two centuries of industrial logging, tree farming, and the odd natural disaster. But there are places where giant trees still grow. The Hoh Rain Forest in Olympic National Park, less than an hour inland from Forks, has Sitka spruce trees as tall as 300 feet, and some have a diameter of nearly 25 feet. These trees grow so huge that sometimes younger trees literally will grow on them like conjoined twins.

The Quinault Rain Forest, on the Quinault Reservation, has several of the largest-known examples of different species of trees. That's the reason it's sometimes referred to as the "Valley of the Rain Forest Giants." The Quinault Lake red cedar, for example, is the largest red cedar in the world, at more than 165 feet high and 20 feet in diameter, and the Queets spruce is one of the largest in the world at nearly 250 feet tall and 15 feet in diameter.

There also are hundreds of thousands of acres of farmed trees on the Olympic Peninsula, and these are generally cut on a 100-year cycle. The most popular farmed tree is the Douglas fir, but ancient-growth Douglas firs often don't even branch as close to the ground as the very tops of farmed trees. Five of the 10 largest known Douglas firs are ancient-growth trees still living in the Quinault Rain Forest. Only coastal redwoods are known to grow larger.

Not all of the record trees on the Olympic Peninsula are ancient-growth, however. Softwood trees tend to grow faster. The tallest cottonwood known to exist is 188 feet tall, lives at the campground in Queets . . . and is only 40 years old.

mostly unpaved loop around the largest body of water in Grays Harbor County. Trailers are not permitted on some sections of the loop and it's not an easy drive for any vehicle, but those who dare drive it have a great chance of witnessing herds of Roosevelt elk grazing in one of the many open meadows along the way. One particularly good spot for elk viewing is **Bunch Fields** off North Shore Road.

The Quinault Valley is nicknamed "The Valley of the Rain Forest Giants" due to the record-setting trees found here. Two such giants, the largest Sitka spruce in the world and the largest western red cedar in the United States, are located just off the shores of Lake Quinault and are easily accessible.

Ruby Beach

Ruby Beach gets its name from the reddish pebbles you can find sprinkled along the shore. Although the pebbles aren't really rubies (they're fragments of garnet), the beach is a jewel of the southern portion of **Olympic National Park**'s coastal section. Here, rock formations jut up from the beach. Ruby Beach's sea stacks and driftwood-lined access points are reminiscent of what you might find off the northern beaches near La Push, but here it's a much easier trek from parking spot to beach (only 0.25 mile). Swimming isn't advised, and you aren't allowed to pitch a tent for the night, but stay a while and enjoy the views.

SPORTS AND RECREATION

Hiking

The ability to hike through beautiful settings draws many people to the area. The trails here are more plentiful and scenic than anywhere else on the Olympic Peninsula. Many of them are easily accessible, too.

Beginning at the U.S. Forest Service Ranger Station (353 South Shore Rd., 360/288-2525), **Trail of the Giants** passes through several large Douglas fir trees before looping back, all in under three miles. A short drive down South Shore Road will take you to the **world's largest Sitka spruce,** which is 191 feet tall and roughly 18 feet wide.

Hard-Core Hiking

Don't be fooled, as countless people are each year, into thinking that hiking is a one-size-fits-all activity. Sure, there are plenty of trails on the Olympic Peninsula that can be traversed in flip-flops and a T-shirt, all while holding a toddler in one arm and pushing a baby stroller with the other. But there are just as many hikes in the peninsula's backcountry that can be dangerous to undertake, and also can turn deadly if you're not properly prepared.

Exactly what that preparation entails depends on what type of hike you're taking. Preparation for an overnight or multiday hike is far different than getting ready for an out-and-back from sunup to sundown. Still, there are a few general tips that should be followed by hikers who are braving the backcountry, no matter how long they are doing so.

Most important, your backpack should always carry what are called the **10 essentials.** Exactly what those 10 things are vary depending on who's telling you, but they often include a map and a compass, a flashlight, extra food and clothing, a fire starter, rain gear, a first-aid kit, a knife, sunglasses, and water. Cell phones also can come in handy when they work, which isn't a given in the mountains. Backcountry hikers also need to be aware of some of the dangers that they might encounter on their journey. Things such as how to sanitize fresh water so it can be consumed, what to do if you encounter a cougar or a bear, how to dispose of garbage, how and where to go to the bathroom, and how to store your food all need to be figured out before you head out. The best bet for backcountry first-timers is to travel and plan with someone who has done it before.

Quinault Rain Forest Nature Trail

Distance: 0.5 mile round-trip
Duration: 0.5-1 hour
Elevation gain: 40 feet
Effort: Easy
Trailhead: Off South Shore Road
Directions: Take Highway 101 to Lake Quinault then head east on South Shore Road. Drive 1.4 miles to the trailhead, which will be on the right.

This easily accessible, family-friendly loop begins in a large parking lot, and heads off into massive old trees and thick underbrush, with interpretive signs scattered about. For a short distance, the trail even parallels Willaby Creek and is wheelchair-accessible. The trail is connected to the **Cedar Bog Trail** and the primitive **Big Cedar Trail.**

Backcountry Hiking

Colonel Bob Trail

Distance: 12 miles round-trip
Duration: 6-8 hours
Elevation gain: 4,292 feet
Effort: Difficult
Trailhead: South Shore Road
Directions: From Lake Quinault, travel east along South Shore Road for six miles.

South Shore Road continues after the lake ends, and takes you to access points for more trails into the forest, including Colonel Bob Trail. Colonel Bob is a mountain named after Civil War veteran Colonel Robert Ingersoll, who actually never visited the spot that's named after him. A steeper-but-shorter route (8.2 miles round-trip) to the summit begins at **Pete's Creek Trailhead,** which is accessible from forest service roads off Highway 101 south of Quinault. Either route you take, the trip is a quad burner due to its elevation gains. But the views of shiny Lake Quinault, the valley, and snowcapped Mount Olympus are worth the effort.

Queets River Trail

Distance: 10 miles round-trip
Duration: 3.5-5 hours
Elevation gain: 200 feet
Effort: Easy
Trailhead: Upper Queets Road
Directions: On Highway 101, drive halfway between Forks and Hoquiam. Turn east on Forest Road 21 and travel eight miles before making a left turn on Forest Road 2180. Follow this road for two miles then turn left onto Forest Road 2180-011. Stay on this road for

1.5 miles, then turn right onto Upper Queets Road and drive three miles to the trailhead.

The Queets River Trail is a popular hike north of Lake Quinault, though it's now even more of a bear to get to thanks to a recent landslide that blocked access from Queets River Road. You can still get there, but it involves a somewhat confusing trip off Highway 101 down newly opened forest service roads that allow you to bypass the area of the landslide and get back onto Queets River Road. A river ford, which can be impassible during winter months, is necessary to reach the trailhead. Whether the headache is worth it depends on who you ask. In addition to the beautiful natural sights of the Queets Valley, there is evidence of old homesteads along the path, and you can rest assured there won't be a crowd.

North Fork Quinault River Trail

Distance: 32 miles round-trip
Duration: 12-15 hours
Elevation gain: 3,100 feet
Effort: Moderate
Trailhead: Upper Queets Road
Directions: On Highway 101, drive halfway between Forks and Hoquiam. Turn east on Forest Road 21 and travel eight miles before making a left turn on Forest Road 2180. Follow this road for two miles then turn left onto Forest Road 2180-011. Stay on this road for 1.5 miles, then turn right onto Upper Queets Road and drive three miles to the trailhead.

Trails on the north side of Lake Quinault and the Quinault River, including North Fork Quinault River Trail, are generally less used. This trail follows the river through its valley and, if the timing is right, offers views of salmon migrating upstream to spawn. You can turn around at any point, of course, but the trail continues for miles into the middle of Olympic National Park, eventually meeting up with the **Skyline Ridge Trail** at Low Divide, near 6,246-foot-high Mount Seattle. Just west of North Fork's trailhead is the **Irely Lake Trail,** a 1.1-mile hike to a shallow, marsh-like lake that is a favorite of beavers and waterfowl. As with many of the local trails, insect repellant is a must here. You can continue onto **Big Creek Trail** past Three Lakes to hook up to Skyline Ridge Trail and into the middle of the park.

Fletcher Canyon Trail

Distance: 4 miles round-trip
Duration: 2-5 hours
Elevation gain: 1,100 feet
Effort: Easy
Trailhead: Off South Shore Road at Lake Quinault
Directions: On Highway 101, 35 miles north of Hoquiam, turn east onto South Shore Road and follow it for 12 miles. The trailhead will be marked in a small turnoff.

Remote Fletcher Canyon Trail offers a window into a canyon full of moss-covered trees and fern-filled forests, as well as a chance to see elk—and possibly a cougar or a bear. The trail can get very wet and multiple water crossings often are necessary.

Maple Glade Rain Forest Trail

Distance: 0.5 mile round-trip
Duration: 0.5-1 hour
Elevation gain: None
Effort: Easy
Trailhead: Across bridge from the Park Service Ranger Station
Directions: From Highway 101, take the North Shore Road at Lake Quinault for six miles.

Maple Glade Rain Forest Trail is an easy loop across Kestner Creek through big-leaf maple trees and moss-covered old growth. There are opportunities to see deer and plenty of flora on this well-maintained trail. It's a popular one, so those seeking solitude may wish to get here early in the morning. Another benefit of an early morning visit is the beautiful view as the sun begins to break through the tree leaves and onto the trail.

Kestner Homestead Trail

Distance: 1.3 miles round-trip
Duration: 0.5-1.5 hours
Elevation gain: None
Effort: Easy

Trailhead: Maple Glade Rain Forest Trail at the Park Service Ranger Station

Directions: From Highway 101, take the North Shore Road at Lake Quinault and follow it for six miles. The trail is at the Park Service Ranger Station. You will find the trailhead by starting down the shorter Maple Glade Rain Forest Trail.

Kestner Homestead Trail is a loop through the former property of Anton Kestner, an early settler of Lake Quinault Valley. You can see all the grounds, including his barn, home, and a neat rusted delivery truck by taking the hike on your own, or see the same sights and get an intimate lesson on the area by taking a guided tour of this trail. For tours, inquire at the ranger station.

Fishing

Motorized boats are not allowed on **Lake Quinault,** but you can canoe, kayak, and row to your heart's content. Rentals are available at several of the lodging options.

Because Lake Quinault is on the Quinault Indian Reservation, you need a tribal permit to fish it. The cold lake does have some cutthroat trout and Dolly Varden if you know what you're doing. **Denny Theel Guide Service** (360/288-2640) is a good place to contact for professional fishing guidance.

Rules, regulations, and seasons vary greatly and change frequently, and tickets for illegal fishing aren't cheap, so it's best to check with the Washington Department of Fish & Wildlife (360/902-2500, www.wdfw.wa.gov) for current information. They can give you information on how and where to get a fishing license, which you'll also need.

ACCOMMODATIONS

Plenty has been written about the best-known place to stay on Lake Quinault, the ★ **Lake Quinault Lodge** (345 South Shore Rd., 360/288-2900 or 800/562-6672, www.nationalparkreservations.com/olympic_lakequinault.php, $156-309 d). With the funding of Hoquiam businessman Ralph Emerson and Augustus Morck of Aberdeen, the lodge was built in 1926—in just 53 days. It was designed by Seattle architect Robert Reamer, who also had designed the Old Faithful Inn at Yellowstone National Park. Eleven years later, President Franklin D. Roosevelt dined here, and he was so inspired by the scenery that he signed a bill creating Olympic National Park less than a year later. In the years since, the lodge has earned a spot on the National Register of Historic Places. Through the years, the rustic lodge lost much of its original shine, but in doing so gained more charm. The high ceiling beams in the lobby are decorated, and seating areas located around the large brick fireplace comfortable and relaxing. There is a heated pool and sauna. Internet access is hard to come by, which can be a good thing here, and while there are no TVs in any of the main lodge's rooms, the family-friendly Lakeside Rooms annex has some. The rates here may seem a bit spendy, but the trendiness of the destination, as well as the name recognition it holds, will score major nods of familiar "Hey, I've been there too!" when you relay the stories back home.

The Lake Quinault Lodge is managed by the Aramark Parks and Destinations corporation, the same company that operates the **Kalaloch Lodge** (157151 Hwy. 101, 360/962-2271 or 800/204-3116, www.thekalalochlodge.com, $164-300 d), located about 40 miles northwest of Quinault and 35 miles south of Forks off Highway 101. There isn't as much history here as at Lake Quinault, but the main lodge (built in 1953) is located on a bluff above the ocean and does offer rooms with ocean views. The property also includes a gas station, a gift shop, and public telephones. Like the Lake Quinault Lodge, there are no TVs or telephones in any guest rooms. There also are several wooden cabins available, some on the bluff overlooking the ocean and some with kitchens.

Those looking for a cheaper but equally excellent spot in the area need look no further than the ★ **Rain Forest Resort Village** (516 South Shore Rd., 360/288-2535 or 800/255-6936, www.rainforestresort.com, $119-245 d). The resort sits on the banks of Lake Quinault, a little more than a mile up South Shore Road from the lodge. The variety of lodging options here can make choosing where to stay difficult. There's the 16-room Village Inn, a variety of Fireplace Cabins with lake views, fully furnished Parkside Suites with bedroom, jetted tub, and decks overlooking the lake, and the large Lakeside RV Campground ($35). Toss in the fine Salmon House Restaurant & Lounge, a laundry, grocery store/gift shop, free Wi-Fi, and the tiny Quinault Post Office, and it's difficult to find a reason to leave.

Across the lake off the North Shore Road is the **Lake Quinault Resort** (314 North Shore Rd., 360/288-2362 or 800/650-2362, www.lakequinault.com, $179-199 d). This place is even farther from the crowds than the previous two options on the lake, and its facilities, in most cases, are shinier on the outside. Inside, the rooms are hit-and-miss, but there are two townhouse suites and one- and two-room kitchenette rooms for families. The kitchens are a good thing, because the resort's restaurant hasn't been built yet, so you have to travel to the south side of the lake if you want to dine out. A covered deck overlooks the beautiful grounds and lake.

Farther down the road is **Lochaerie Resort** (638 North Shore Rd., 360/288-2215, www.lochaerie.com, $155-165 d), a group of private, mismatched cabins built during the Great Depression from whatever lumber and other materials the builders could cheaply salvage. Each cabin has a fireplace, kitchen, and bathroom with shower. Some of the cabins are more rustic than others, but each one is charming and they all blend perfectly with their setting.

Located just off Highway 101, sandwiched between the North Shore and South Shore Roads in the pit stop of Amanda Park, is the **Quinault River Inn** (8 River Dr., 360/288-2237 or 800/410-2237, www.quinaultriverinn.com, $134 d). The Inn is a year-round favorite for hunters and anglers, and in the summer its relatively affordable, recently renovated rooms with queen beds, cable TV, and microwaves are a hit with sightseers, as is the fire pit near the river. There isn't much else in Amanda Park, but the inn is just a short distance from the amenities and activities at Lake Quinault. A small RV park ($29) is also on-site.

Camping

While cabins, hotels, and resorts are nice and convenient, those who want to get the complete nature experience and save some money can pitch tents or park their RVs and camp at

the Kalaloch Lodge near Forks

any of the public campgrounds the area has to offer. Near the ocean and Kalaloch, there's the **Kalaloch Campground** (www.olympicnationalparks.com, year-round, $14-25), which sits on a bluff overlooking the beach and has the distinction of being the only National Park Service campsite in the park that allows reservations (www.recreation.gov), at least during the summer months. A bit farther down the coast, there's also the primitive **South Beach Campground** (summer only, $10-25), located in an open field with little shade or privacy.

In addition to the RV sites at the Rain Forest Resort Village and Quinault River Inn, campers in the Quinault area have several other options, including the **North Fork Campground** (year-round, $10-25), and the walk-in **July Creek Campground** (year-round, $10) on the north side of the Lake Quinault, which it overlooks. On the south side of the lake, campers can stay among the old-growth spruce trees at **Willaby Campground** (mid-Apr.-mid-Nov., $14), **Falls Creek Campground** (mid-May-mid-Sept., $15-20), and the tent-only **Gatton Creek Campground** (year-round, $11).

In the Queets Valley, the 20-site **Queets Campground** (year-round, $10-25) is a nice, quiet place, if you dare deal with the alternative route you'd need to take to get there, thanks to a landslide that washed out the regular road.

FOOD

If there ever was a place where it's smart to pack your meals and not rely on restaurants, this area would be it. There are a few exceptions, however, especially for those staying on the south side of Lake Quinault. The ★ **Salmon House Restaurant** (516 South Shore Rd., 360/288-2535, 4pm-9pm daily, $13-38) at the Rain Forest Resort Village has excellent appetizers and an entire page of its menu devoted to seafood entrées, including a baked salmon topped with garden-fresh dill sauce ($18.95). Up the road at the Lake Quinault Lodge, there's the **Roosevelt Dining Room** (360/288-2900, breakfast 8am-11:30am weekdays, 7:30am-11:30am weekends, lunch 11:30am-2pm weekdays, 11:30am-3pm weekends, dinner 5:30pm-8:30pm weekdays, 5pm-9pm weekends, $18-36). The menu here is a little fancier than at the Salmon House, and entrées are a tad more expensive. Still, the sesame-crusted ahi tuna and oysters fresh from Hood Canal ($28) are outstanding.

The **Creekside Restaurant** (360/962-2271 or 866/525-2562, $12-30) at the Kalaloch Lodge has an excellent view and fairly expensive, but good, menu items, including a seafood-filled pasta and your typical breakfast fare. Portions are generous.

GETTING THERE AND AROUND

Getting the 120 miles to Lake Quinault from Tacoma takes approximately 2.5 hours and is accomplished by heading south on I-5, veering off to the west on Highway 8 in Olympia, then traveling north when you get to Aberdeen.

North Beach

Not long ago, the northern section of the deepwater port of Grays Harbor was only a hub of trade for several Native American tribes, including the Quinault, Chinook, and Chehalis, which could hop into wooden canoes to make the trek up the Chehalis River to meet others and exchange goods. In 1792, that all began to change, when American merchant Captain Robert Gray sailed into the bay, opening the door for much exploration and settlement.

Today known as the North Beach area, this section of the Washington coast consists of several smaller beach towns, as well as the area's hub, the relatively new city of **Ocean Shores.** Most of the towns are underdeveloped, with Ocean Shores and the planned community of **Seabrook** being the exceptions. Much of the area is empty during the off-season, and many of the shops close altogether or chop their hours, but during the peak season, they all fill up—especially when the weather is warm and residents of the Puget Sound area decide to escape the heat and hit the beach.

SIGHTS

Coastal Interpretive Center

A seven-room box of wonders, the **Coastal Interpretive Center** (1033 Catala Ave. SE, Ocean Shores, 360/289-4617, www.interpretivecenter.org, 11am-4pm daily Apr.-Sept., 11am-4pm Sat.-Sun. Oct.-Mar., free) is packed with beautiful natural and human-made treasures. The center offers educational, hands-on activities and video presentations, and volunteers constantly refresh exhibits on beachcombing, beach safety, birds, geology, history, mammals, and more. The "beach to the mountains" display of local birds and animals, the demonstration garden, and the 8- by 4-foot chunk of the famous SS *Catala* shipwreck help underscore the uniqueness of the center—and the city it's named after.

★ Seabrook

Founded in 2004, the postcard-perfect, intentionally built vacation beach town of Seabrook (360/276-0099, www.seabrookwa.com) in Pacific Beach offers a picturesque setting for a refreshing afternoon or a getaway weekend. New England-inspired cottages with beautiful woodwork, gables, and generous front porches are carefully arranged around village greens and walking paths of crushed oyster shells, which connect the community with the beach. The walking path, shops, spa, and community events, such as an annual salmon bake, are open to the public. To stay longer, rent a cottage in town or in the woods through the Seabrook Cottage Rental Program (www.seabrookcottagerentals.com). The town is so Mayberry-like, it's almost surreal.

Mill 109 Restaurant & Pub (14 Front St., Pacific Beach, 360/276-4884, www.mill109.com, 11am-9pm Mon.-Thurs., 11am-10pm Fri., 8am-10pm Sat., 8am-9pm Sun., $14-24) is the main place to eat at Seabrook. Breakfast is served on weekends, while lunch, dinner, and happy hour are offered every day of the week. For lunch, there's traditional pub food, such as fish-and-chips, burgers, and sandwiches; the dinner menu includes razor clams, grilled salmon, and steak.

Museum of the North Beach

The **Museum of the North Beach** (4658 Rte. 109, Moclips, 360/276-4441, www.moclips.org, 11am-4pm Thurs.-Mon. May-Oct., 11am-4pm Sat.-Sun. Nov.-Apr.) presents the history of North Beach and its 10 coastal communities: Aloha, Carlisle, Copalis Beach, Copalis Crossing, Moclips, Ocean City, Ocean Shores, Oyehut, Pacific Beach, and Taholah. Founded in 2001, the museum is home of the 1910's NPRY caboose from the last train to Moclips. The museum is raising funds to rebuild a Northern Pacific train depot in Moclips, and eventually will relocate there.

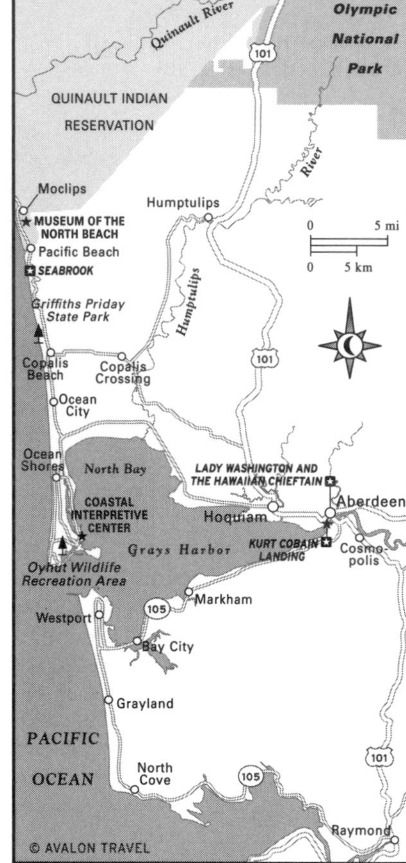

SPORTS AND RECREATION

Beaches

The area may be called North Beach, but it's actually a collection of several beaches/beach towns. Each offers a slightly different feel and vibe, and activities available differ from spot to spot.

Sunset Beach, down the Analyde Gap Road at the Pacific Beach/Moclips boundary, is a good place for storm watching, beachcombing, kite flying, and bonfires. The beach extends north past Moclips to the Quinault Indian Nation boundary, where a tribal beach pass is required to enter. To the north in the ocean, you can see the towering rocks of Point Grenville.

Copalis Beach (www.parks.wa.gov) is a popular spot for clam digging when the sport is open, and the **Oyhut Wildlife Recreation Area,** 682 acres of wildlife habitat at the south end of the peninsula, is known for its wetlands, tide flats, and world-class bird-watching. Blue herons, brown pelicans, pheasants, and snowy plovers can be seen here.

The **North Jetty/Point Brown,** at the southwesternmost tip of the Ocean Shores peninsula, is an iconic spot for storm watching, kite flying, surfing, and surf fishing. The rock jetty is an easy, six-mile drive south from the gates of the Ocean Shores city limits. Abundant parking and public restrooms are available. Just down the road to the east, **Damon Point State Park** is a one-mile-long, half-mile-wide stretch of land jutting out into Grays Harbor. The 61-acre day-use park is also known as "Protection Island" because it's a refuge for many species of birds and wildlife and one of the few remaining nesting sites of the snowy plover. People come here hoping to see that bird, as well as peregrine falcons and others. The park is open to the public, but there are no parking and no restroom facilities. Opportunities for beachcombing, bird-watching, and agate searching are plentiful. Surf fishing is best at Damon Point State Park near the Ocean Shore Marina.

Hiking

Damon Point State Park Trail

Distance: 4 miles round-trip
Duration: 1-2 hours
Elevation gain: 0-10 feet
Effort: Easy
Trailhead: South of Yesterday's RV Park
Directions: Take State Route 115 to Ocean Shores. Turn south on Point Brown Avenue and continue for 4.5 miles. Park off the road in a grassy area and hike east to reach the spit.

World-class bird-watching, wildlife, and spectacular views of Grays Harbor, the Olympic

Mountains, and Mount Rainier are why many people visit the Damon Point State Park Trail. The flat loop trail around Protection Island is frequently full of water and subject to washouts. The point is named for early settler A. O. Damon, and for years there was a half-buried ship, the SS *Catala*, visible there, but it was scrapped out in 2006 for environmental reasons after it began to leak oil.

Copalis River Spit Trail

Distance: 4 miles round-trip
Duration: 1-2 hours
Elevation gain: 0-40 feet
Effort: Easy
Trailhead: Griffiths-Priday Ocean State Park
Directions: Take State Route 109 north from Hoquiam for 21 miles. Turn left on Benner Road and drive a short distance to Griffiths Priday State Park.

The Copalis River Spit Trail is at Griffiths-Priday Ocean State Park, a 364-acre marine park with about 8,300 feet of saltwater shoreline on the Pacific Ocean and about 9,950 feet of freshwater shoreline on the Copalis River. The trail itself travels directly near or on the beach. Snowy owls are often spotted here at certain times of the year, and the trail sometimes is washed out during high tides and inclement weather. A designated wildlife refuge is also part of the park.

Biking

The Ocean Shores peninsula is only about six miles long, but with about 120 miles of mostly flat roads in the city, bicycling is one of the best ways to get around. There are special bike lanes on the main drag (Point Brown Ave.) from downtown to the North Jetty, typically the best route to take for those looking to see most of the city in one shot. You also can veer off to the beach or inland on many of the side roads along the way. Rent bikes and gear at **Apollo Activities** (172 W. Chance A La Mer Ave., 360/289-3830, $10/hour).

Fishing

Whether you're into freshwater fishing, surf fishing, or crabbing, you'll probably find something in the area that will interest you. Take advantage of the tuna, halibut, salmon, and bottom-fishing charters that are offered in season at the **Ocean Shores Marina** (southern tip of Ocean Shores peninsula, six miles south of downtown, 360/289-4789). For freshwater fishing, try **Duck Lake** (off Chance A La Mer Ave., three blocks south of downtown). The **North Jetty** (southern tip of Ocean Shores peninsula, six miles south of downtown) and **Damon Point State Park** near the marina is best for surf fishing. Crabbing is ideal near Damon Point (or Protection Island) marina. Salmon can be found at the marina and at the Copalis and Humptulips Rivers in season. Be sure to check the current regulations pamphlet to be sure you know what's open and when (www.wdfw.wa.gov).

The **Humptulips River** is the place to catch winter and summer steelhead, fall chinook, coho, and chum salmon, and sea-run cutthroat trout. Boat fishing offers advantages here, and there are a few boat ramps. There also are plenty of good places to fish from the bank, including under the Humptulips River Bridge off Highway 101.

The 65-acre, modest-sized **Failor Lake** is a favorite of many anglers because it's restocked each year with about 6,000 rainbow and cutthroat trout. The season is late April through October, and there is a boat ramp. Good local fishing also can be had at the North Jetty in Ocean Shores.

Boating

With 23 miles of interconnecting freshwater lakes and canals in the city of Ocean Shores and the Ocean Shores Marina, boating opportunities are everywhere. On **Duck Lake,** you can launch your watercraft at **North Bay Park** (on Albatross and Chance A La Mer Ave., by the airport) or **Chinook Park** (Duck Lake Dr., 2.5 miles south of the airport). Boat launch maps and other related information are available at the **Ocean Shores Visitor Information Center** (360/289-9586 or 866/602-6278, www.tourismoceanshores.

com). Additionally, the **Ocean Shores Marina** is home to many private fishing and crabbing boats.

You can rent boats from the **Electric Boat Company** (952 Point Brown Ave. SE, 360/289-0487, www.oselectricboat.com). Their motor boats hold up to 10 people, and paddleboats also are available here.

Surfing

Surfing in Ocean Shores is considered more dangerous than many other places along the Washington coast, but those who know what they're doing and how to deal with the area's often-strong undertow like to surf at the North Jetty. The **North Coast Surf Shop** (773 Point Brown Ave. NW, 360/289-0651, 10am-6pm daily) is a great place to check in to pick the brains of the pros working there, and also to grab some gear if you need it.

Golf

Ocean Shores Golf Course (500 Canal Dr. NE, 360/289-3357, www.oceanshoresgolf.com, $40 for 18 holes) offers the fun challenge of a Scottish links-style front nine and a wooded back nine. A practice range, pro shop, and clubhouse with a snack bar complete the facility. Tournaments are planned and organized by resident golf pros.

Moped Rentals

With smooth beaches, beautiful scenery, and over 120 miles of mostly flat roadway, Ocean Shores is a playground for moped riders. Mopeds are great for transportation and exploration, and you can rent by the hour or by the day. They can be driven both on the beach and through town. A valid driver's license and helmet are required. Rent mopeds at **Apollo Activities** (172 W. Chance A La Mer Ave., 360/289-3830, $20/hour) and **Affordable Mopeds** (896 Ocean Shores Blvd., 360/289-0919, $10-30/hour).

Horseback Riding

Horseback riding on the beach can be one of the most memorable outdoor experiences. Beginners and experts are welcome year-round, although the weather does play a role in when the horses are available. Lessons and day camps are also offered.

Local stables include **Chenois Creek Horse Rentals** (on the beach at Damon Rd., 360/533-5591), **HoneyPearl Ranch** (on the beach at E. Chance A La Mer Ave. beach approach, 360/580-1150, www.honeypearlranch.com), and **Nan-Sea Stables** (255 Rte. 115, 360/289-0194, www.horseplanet.com). Costs vary by company and time of year, but typical rates are in the $20-per-hour range.

Kite Flying

Home to open skies, open beaches, steady winds, and the large Ocean Shores International Kite Festival, the North Beach area offers some of the best kite flying in Washington. The wide selection of beach toys, kites, and windsocks in local shops make beautiful keepsakes and gifts. Kites and advice are available at **Cloud Nine Kites** (380 Hwy. 115, 360/289-2221) and **Ocean Shores Kites** (849 Point Brown Ave. NW, 360/289-4103, www.oceanshoreskites.com).

ENTERTAINMENT AND EVENTS

Nightlife

In the off-season you may find yourself asking, "What nightlife?" but during peak season there's generally something going on somewhere on the North Beach. As a bonus, most places are within walking distance, so if the scene at one place goes dead, it's easy enough to move on to another without getting in a car.

Galway Bay Irish Pub (880 Point Brown Ave. NE, 360/289-2300, www.galwaybayirishpub.com, 11am-10pm Sun.-Thurs., 11am-midnight Fri.-Sat.) is one of those places in Ocean Shores that often has something going on, whether it's locals gossiping over a pint of Guinness with omnipresent owner Bill Gibbons or out-of-towners enjoying some shepherd's pie from the pub's rather large menu. There's always music on the weekends, and the pub hosts an Irish music festival each October.

Pirates Cove Pub (789 Ocean Shores Blvd. NW, 360/289-4400, 11am-8pm Mon.-Thurs., 7am-10pm Fri.-Sun.) is across the street from the Sands Resort and has plenty of beer on tap and food as well. Don't forget to say hello to Captain Curley, a six-foot-tall pirate statue near the door. Rumor has it he's a sucker for having his picture taken.

Within eyesight down the road is the **Shilo Beachfront Restaurant & Lounge** (707 Ocean Shores Blvd. NW, 360/289-0567, 7am-10pm daily), which has music on the weekends; Shilo closes later than its stated times often on weekends and during busy times. **Waves Restaurant & Bar** (491 Damon Rd., 360/289-2311, www.bwlighthouse.com, 4pm-close daily) also is located in a chain hotel but can be a fun place to hang out whether you're staying there or not. The award-winning clam chowder is the house specialty, and the view is the best in Ocean Shores.

Beer lovers must check out the **Elk Head Tap Room** (739 Point Brown Ave. NE #5, 360/289-8277, 3pm-7pm Thurs., noon-7pm Fri.-Sat., noon-4pm Sun.). The beers here come from the Elk Head Brewery, located a few hours away in the small town of Buckley. The decor is unique and the beers, including the popular Hempinator, even more so. **The Porthole Pub** (893 Point Brown Ave., 360/289-4469, www.portholeoceanshores.com, 8am-1:30am daily) is another place locals go to hammer down a cold one or two, especially because it's always happy hour here and very down-to-earth.

Casinos

There isn't a casino in Washington State with a better location than the **Quinault Beach Resort & Casino** (78 Hwy. 115, 360/289-9466 or 888/461-2214, www.quinaultbeachresort.com). It's on the beach and offers entertainment, fine dining, and gaming throughout the year, along with a hotel. There are table games, plenty of slots, an award-winning restaurant, a deli, a full-service spa, a pool, and live music on the weekends in the Ocean Lounge. Special larger events are held throughout the year.

Art Galleries

Small as it may be, Ocean Shores has a neat little art scene, thanks in part to the creative souls drawn to the area for its natural beauty.

Fusions Art Gallery (834 Point Brown Ave. NW, 360/289-2811, www.fusionsgallery.com, 10am-6pm daily) may be in isolated Ocean Shores, but much of the art on display here—everything from glassworks, paintings, pottery, jewelry, and photography—could be placed in many big-city shops. Stuart May's nature photography, for example, is some of the best of its kind in the world.

Gallerie Timbuktu (818 Point Brown Ave. NE, 360/289-4595) doesn't feature Native American art like many of the museums and galleries around the area do. No, Africa is the theme here, and masks, textiles, and sculptures dominate. There's also vintage jewelry.

Gallery Marjuli (865 Point Brown Ave. NW, 360/289-2858, 10am-5pm daily) has been around almost as long as Ocean Shores has been a city thanks in part to its originals, prints, and custom-framing service.

Festivals and Events

The relatively new **Chocolate on the Beach Festival** is held at the end of February in the communities of Pacific Beach, Moclips, and Seabrook. The event features recipe contests, bake sales, chocolate raffles, vendors, "wine and dine" specials at area restaurants, and more, all to benefit the **Museum of the North Beach.**

In early March, the **Beachcombers' Fun Fair** offers food and examples of local art, including driftwood creations, at the Ocean Shores Convention Center.

The **International Kite Festival** is held the first week of June and brings world-champion kite flyers to the beach. The **Sand and Sawdust Festival** is held the same month in Ocean Shores. Competitions are held in sand sculpting and wood carving. There are free lessons, and some competitions are open to all.

The biggest July celebration in the Quinault Indian Nation town of Taholah isn't Independence Day. Here, it's **Chief Taholah Days** everyone looks forward to. Held the first week of July, the event celebrates the 1855 signing of the Quinault Treaty with cultural events, canoe races, a parade, and, of course, fireworks.

An event where the Fourth of July is at the forefront is **Fire O'er the Water,** held each year at Ocean City. The real main event is a professional fireworks show on the beach that is second to none in the state. The unofficial undercard features thousands of boozed-up revelers parked on the beach, partying and blowing up their own fireworks, which is OK here. Some enjoy the latter show more than the main event, but both have their merits.

Bonfires, fireworks, music, parades, and, of course, motorcycles, all are part of the **Sun and Surf Run,** held at the end of July in Ocean Shores.

More than 100 booths inside and outside the Ocean Shores Convention Center highlight the **Ocean Shores Arts & Crafts Festival** each September.

The Kelpers Festival and Shake Rat Rendezvous is an event unlike any other in the world and held Labor Day Weekend in the Moclips and Pacific Beach areas. Shake rat is a term used to describe timber salvagers who harvest cedar wood blocks to be turned into shakes. The event features two parades and competitions galore.

The **Dixieland Jazz Festival** brings jazz musicians and those who enjoy dancing to it from across the country to Ocean Shores each November.

SHOPPING

If there's a downside to shopping in Ocean Shores, it's the layout of the town, which generally involves traveling some distance to get from store to store. If that works for you, there are some good places to hit, and a few strip-mall-style spots, too, such as the **Shores Mall,** located just off the Chance A La Mer beach approach. You'll find a variety of items, including food, clothing, moped and bike rentals, and a kite shop. The **Driftwood Plaza** and the **Catala Mall** house similar shops.

The kids—and the kid in you—will thank you profusely for even a brief visit to the **Pacific Paradise Family Fun Center** (767 Minard Ave. NW, 360/289-9537, 11am-6pm Mon.-Tues., and Thurs.-Fri., 10am-6pm Sat.-Sun.). Dozens of arcade games, a 36-hole miniature golf course, and bumper boats await. Another option is **Playtime Family Fun Center** (748 Point Brown Ave. NE, 360/289-2702, www.playtimefamilyfun.com, 9am-9pm Sun.-Thurs., 9am-10pm Fri.-Sat), which also has games, in addition to bumper cars and a good go-kart track with fast karts. **Shores Bowl** (125 W. Chance A La Mer, 360/289-9356, 11am-close daily) is another family entertainment option.

Creative souls will enjoy the one-of-a-kind jewelry, beads, and specialty fragrances available at **Tsunami Beads & Gems** (732 Point Brown Ave. NE, 360/289-0389, 10am-4pm daily).

Mermaid Cove (739 Point Brown Ave. NW, 360/289-2985, www.mermaidcovegallery.com) features some enchanting mermaid-themed artwork, and some lighthouse works, too.

One store that caters to pets is **Scurvy Dog** (172 W. Chance A La Mer, 360/289-2414), located in the Shores Mall. It's a good thing this store exists here, too, as many hotels in the area have pet-friendly rooms and services (such as dog washes!).

Those searching the area for eclecticism and oddities will find them in Pacific Beach at the **Wacky Warehouse** (48 Main St., 360/276-4200, 10:30am-5:30pm Mon., Wed.-Sat., 10:30am-3pm Sun., closed Tues.). Former cab driver James "Mr. Wacky" Preisinger's shop resembles a cluttered garage sale but is fun, and, as the saying goes, one person's trash. . . .

ACCOMMODATIONS

$50-100

Lodging in Pacific Beach is a good choice for those who want a nighttime respite from the crowds of Ocean Shores. There are a few options to choose from here. The **Sand Dollar Inn** (56 Central Ave., 360/276-4525, www.sanddollarinn.net, $85-110 d) is a good choice, with seven rooms, five of which are pet-friendly, a penthouse with full kitchen and an ocean view ($129/night), and three cottages ($189-239).

$100-150

A June 2011 fire temporarily wiped out the restaurant, but the resilient folks at the ★ **Ocean Crest Resort** (4651 Hwy. 109, 800/684-8439, www.oceancrestresort.com, $69-207 d) in Moclips kept the rest of the business open while they rebuilt their restaurant. The restaurant is now open and back on track. Guests who want to take a dip in the water here have two options: Step out the front door and hop the stairs down to the ocean or walk across a state highway to the resort's recreation center, where a warm indoor pool, sauna, and an outdoor play area await. Lodging options include studio rooms, as well as one- and two-bedrooms. Many rooms feature full kitchens and fireplaces, a perfect choice for those who want to harvest (or buy) their own local food and save money by cooking it themselves. Oceanview rooms are available.

There are beach views awaiting you at the 12-room **Pacific Beach Inn** (12 1st St., Pacific Beach, 360/276-4433, www.pbinn.com, $85-155 d).

An in-town, oceanfront option in Ocean Shores is **The Polynesian Resort** (615 Ocean Shores Blvd. NW, 360/289-3361 or 800/562-4836, www.thepolynesian.com, $97-229 d). There's an indoor pool and separate sauna area with a hot tub, a game room with a pool table and vending machines, an outdoor play area with a swing set, and a restaurant, Mariah's, located in the same parking lot. Room options range from basic motel rooms to two-bedroom suites.

On the outskirts of what could be considered downtown Ocean Shores is the **Grey Gull Motel** (651 Ocean Shores Blvd. SW, 360/289-3381 or 800/562-9712, www.thegreygull.com, $135 d), which has 37 ocean-facing condo units with fireplaces and full kitchens. Viewed from overhead, the hotel in fact looks like a gray seagull, with its wings spread in a V. At the center of it all are a heated outdoor pool and an outdoor fire pit on the beach side.

A few miles outside the Ocean Shores city limits is the modern **Quinault Beach Resort and Casino** (78 Hwy. 115, 360/289-9466 or 888/461-2214, www.quinaultbeachresort.com, $134-159 d). Those searching for everything in one place—including food, entertainment, pool, and beach access—will find it here. Standard rooms overlook the busy and sometimes noisy parking lot. View rooms in back of the complex are much nicer and quieter. All rooms include fireplaces, and the Grand Suite has a 50-inch flat-screen TV.

$150-200

Guests who want to stay in isolated, fully furnished, oceanfront condos should consider the **Hi-Tide Ocean Beach Resort** (4890 Railroad Ave., 360/276-4142 or 800/662-5477, www.hi-tide-resort.com, $150 d). Hi-Tide is the northernmost beachfront accommodation on the North Beach, just outside the boundary for the Quinault Indian Reservation. As such, peaceful doesn't begin to describe the setting.

Floating Feather Inn (982 Point Brown Ave. SE, 360/289-2490, $119-175 s or d) overlooks the city's freshwater-filled Grand Canal in Ocean Shores, and for years was known as Silver Waves B&B. All five rooms feature feather beds, and breakfast is served each morning in the dining room overlooking the canal.

★ **Judith Ann Inn** (855 Ocean Shores Blvd. NW, 360/289-0222 or 888/826-6466, www.judithanninn.com, $160-205 d) is hands down the prettiest—and according to *South*

Ocean Shores

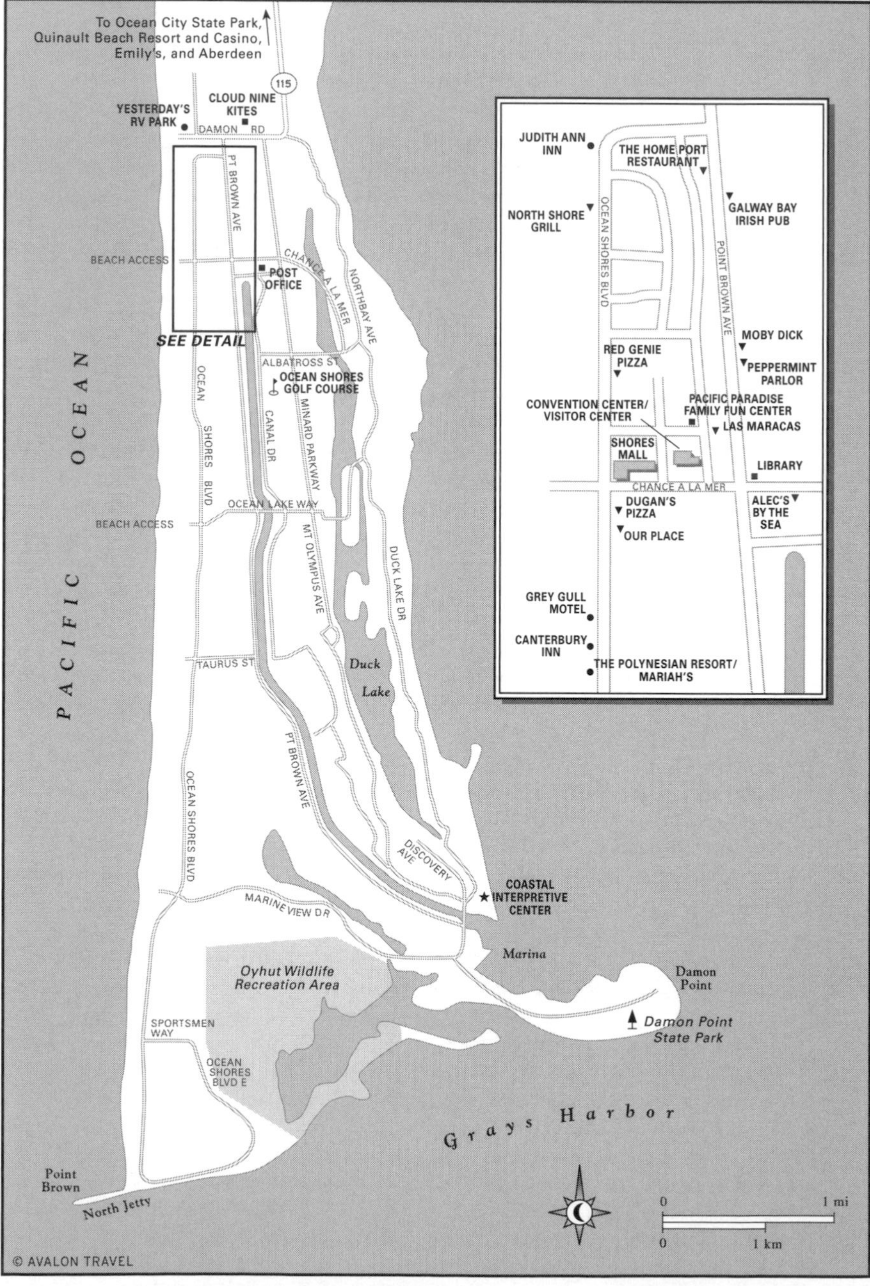

Sound magazine, the most romantic—place to stay in Ocean Shores. Each of its 10 Victorian-inspired suites is ornately decorated yet still unique, and all rooms have full-size kitchens, fireplaces, and more than 900 feet of living space with elevated, jetted tubs.

Calling itself a "luxury beach resort," **Canterbury Inn** (643 Ocean Shores Blvd. NW, 360/289-3317 or 800/562-6678, www.canterburyinn.com, $151-189 d) is a decent option for those who want to be on the beach and also near the heart of it all in Ocean Shores. Sure, there's an indoor pool, spa, and other amenities, but with some dingy, outdated rooms it's debatable whether or not a stay here is worth the hefty price tag.

Over $200

Just north of the more popular vacation destination of Ocean Shores, lies perhaps the best-kept lodging secret on the coast, that being ★ **Iron Springs Resort** (3707 Hwy. 109, Copalis Beach, 360/276-4230, www.ironspringsresort.com, $239-339). The recently remodeled resort is actually five groups of fully equipped cabins nestled on a cliff overlooking the ocean and the only official beach airport in the state. Planes may regularly come and go here, but those visitors who have come here since the cabins were renovated really never want to leave. Like the cabins, the grounds also have been renovated. The place is pet-friendly, offers beach access, and there's even a food truck on the grounds. This used to be a place worth only a glance out the car window as you drive by to your lodging elsewhere, but no more. If you can afford it, there's no better option in the area.

Camping

Set between the edge of Pacific Beach and the ocean, **Pacific Beach State Park** (49 2nd St., Pacific Beach, 360/276-4297 or 888/226-7688, www.parks.wa.gov) is a 10-acre, year-round camping park that's popular with families. The 2,300 feet of ocean shoreline features plenty of room for beach walking, bird-watching, paddling, picnicking, surf fishing, and uninterrupted views of the ocean. There is no shade and no fire pits. The park is open for camping on a first-come, first served basis until construction of the park office is complete.

Ocean City State Park (148 State Rte. 115, 360/289-3553 or 888/226-7688, www.parks.wa.gov, $22-36) is a year-round, 170-acre camping park of dunes and dense thickets of shore pine. It is located at the entrance to

the award-winning restaurant at Ocean Crest Resort in Moclips

the Ocean Shores peninsula, about one mile north of the city of Ocean Shores. You will see people beachcombing, bird-watching, kite flying, picnicking, and relaxing here. Camping is free, but reservations are required. There is no direct vehicle access to the beach.

Just past the entrance to Ocean Shores, **Yesterday's RV Park** (512 Damon Rd., 360/289-9227, $19 tent, $32 full RV hookup with cable TV) has hot showers and is just across the street from the Best Western hotel, where there's a full restaurant and lounge.

FOOD

Because it's a touristy area whose visitors often travel from long distances, Ocean Shores and the surrounding towns are loaded with all types of dining options.

American

Paddie's Perch (41 Main St., 360/276-8144, $8-12) is in Pacific Beach, doesn't look like much from the outside, and features a small menu. Three strikes? Maybe, but this place deserves a chance, if only for its spectacular homemade pies.

Located at the Ramada Inn, the **North Shore Grill** (845 Ocean Shores Blvd. NW, 360/289-7710, 8am-8pm Sun.-Thurs., 8am-9pm Fri.-Sat., $10-18) has a family-friendly menu with decent prices.

Moby Dick (788 Point Brown Ave. NE, 360/289-2777, 11am-9pm Sun.-Thurs., 11am-10pm Sat.-Sun, $6-15) has the best deep-fried foods in Ocean Shores, including deep-fried bread. The hamburgers here also are good.

★ **Our Place** (676 Ocean Shores Blvd. NW, 360/940-7314, 6am-2pm daily, $12-27) is best known for its filling breakfasts—almost too well known for some. Its convenient location and excellent food means the small place can easily fill up on busy weekends.

International

Las Maracas Mexican Restaurant (729 Point Brown Ave. NW, 360/289-2054, 11am-10pm Sun.-Thurs., 11am-11pm Fri.-Sat., $9-17) is fairly expensive, even for a tourist town, but the food is authentic, hearty, and good.

The restaurant's name may be Italian for "take a break," but the best food at **La Pausa** (825 Point Brown Ave. NW, 360/289-3070, 11am-8pm daily, $12-25) is Greek. Try the stifado (Greek stew) in a merlot base served on a bed of mashed potatoes.

Pizza

In Pacific Beach, the **Windjammer**

The Hi-Tide Ocean Beach Resort is the northernmost place to stay in Moclips.

Restaurant (131 N. 1st St., 360/276-8199, $8-15) has good pizza and clam chowder, and its lounge is a good place to chat with locals or watch a college football game on a Saturday afternoon. The restaurant is located at the Pacific Beach Resort & Conference Center, which is run by the U.S. Navy.

Dugan's Pizza (690 Ocean Shores Blvd. NW, 360/289-2330, 11am-11pm daily, $10-20) offers delivery and dining-in options. The owners are heavily involved in the community and occasionally host charitable events.

The best pie at **Red Genie Pizza** (766 Ocean Shores Blvd. NW, 360/289-8144, 11am-8pm Sun.-Thurs., 11am-10pm Fri.-Sat., $10-20) is created with a little dark local humor. It's called the Tsunami, and features several toppings thrown together and placed on the pie the way a tsunami might treat local structures, were one to strike the area.

Quick Bites

Sweet tooths will love the area for its numerous candy shops and ice cream parlors, including **Peppermint Parlor** (742 Point Brown Ave. NW, 360/289-0572, $3-5) and **Murphy's Candy & Ice Cream** (172 W. Chance A La Mer, 360/289-0927, $3-6).

Steak and Seafood

The steaks, seafood, and a full bar highlight the **Home Port Restaurant & Lounge** (857 Point Brown Ave., 360/289-2600, 8am-8:30pm Sun.-Thurs., 8am-9:30pm Fri.-Sat., $14-22). Prime rib is available for dinner on weekends, and locally harvested razor clams are available all week long. Breakfast and lunch also are served here.

Located at the Polynesian hotel, **Mariah's Restaurant & Lounge** (615 Ocean Shores Blvd. NW, 360/289-3315, 4pm-9pm daily, 9am-1pm Sunday brunch buffet, $16-24) has a wide range of seafood dishes on its menu, including a Cajun halibut with blackberry bourbon sauce.

Alec's by the Sea (131 E. Chance A La Mer NE, 360/289-4026, 11:30am-8pm Sun.-Thurs., 11am-8:30pm Fri.-Sat., $12-26) is home to some of the best seafood in the area, including oysters collected from nearby Willapa Bay. The restaurant's main downside is its off-the-beach location.

Located inside the Quinault Beach Resort, ★ **Emily's** (78 Rte. 115, 360/289-9466, 8am-9pm Sun.-Thurs., 8am-10pm Fri.-Sat., $14-35) has a five-star ambience and setting and quality gourmet food, but the real deals are the restaurant's buffets,

the Iron Springs Resort in Copalis Beach

especially the Land and Sea, available Friday nights for $24.95.

INFORMATION AND SERVICES

If it's happening in town or elsewhere in the area, it's likely someone at **The Ocean Shores/North Beach Chamber of Commerce** (873 Point Brown Ave. NW, Ste. 1, 360/289-2451, www.oceanshores.org, 9am-5pm Mon.-Fri., 10am-4pm Sat.-Sun.) will know about it.

GETTING THERE AND AROUND

From their garage in Hoquiam, the buses of **Grays Harbor Transit** (360/532-2770 or 800/562-9730, www.ghtransit.com) serve the entire North Beach area, including in and around Ocean Shores, and also provide routes from the North Beach cities to Aberdeen, Hoquiam, and Lake Quinault. The best driving route to get to North Beach from Sea-Tac Airport is to head south on I-5, drive south to Olympia and cut across to the coast through Aberdeen. Budget 2.5 hours.

Grays Harbor

Both the county of Grays Harbor and the body of water are named after American Captain Robert Gray, the same explorer/fur trader who first "discovered" many other coastal areas. Gray originally named the bay Bullfinch Harbor, though it was later named after him. Many places in the area now bear Gray's name, though—for some unknown reason—the apostrophe is missing from Grays Harbor.

Divided only by a nondescript street named Myrtle, the twin cities of **Aberdeen** and **Hoquiam** were once among the most powerful logging communities in the United States and now are trying to reinvent themselves with the help of tourism. To the towns' benefit, there are plenty of significant features to work with, including excellent waterfronts and a claim to fame as the birthplace of legendary musician Kurt Cobain and home to a movie-star tall ship. East Grays Harbor County is made up of a few smaller towns, including tidy **Montesano, Elma,** and **McCleary.** Less-informed sources frequently advise bypassing the area on Olympic Peninsula trips, but those opinions generally are based on the condition of the area's main thoroughfares. They're loaded with weathered homes and dilapidated shops, all of which admittedly could use some TLC. But don't be misled; there's plenty to see and do here if you venture off the beaten path.

SIGHTS

★ *Lady Washington* and the *Hawaiian Chieftain*

If you're lucky, you might catch a glimpse of history and Hollywood docked behind the Aberdeen Walmart on the Chehalis River. The tall ship ***Lady Washington*** (813 E. Heron St., 360/532-8611, www.historicalseaport.com) appeared in *The Pirates of the Caribbean: The Curse of the Black Pearl* with Johnny Depp. The Grays Harbor Historical Seaport built the *Lady Washington* in Aberdeen; it's now the official ship of Washington State. The ship is a full-scale replica (with a crew always in full costume) of the original *Lady Washington,* the first American ship to reach Japan in the 1700s, and the one originally captained by Grays Harbor's namesake, Captain Robert Gray.

When the ship is docked in Aberdeen, it is often open for walk-on tours (free, but a $3 donation is requested) and various sails ($35-60). The Lady also spends a lot of time at sea, stopping in large cities and small towns up and down the West Coast to make appearances at festivals and for educational trips and tours. It often travels with its companion and fellow

Aberdeen and Hoquiam

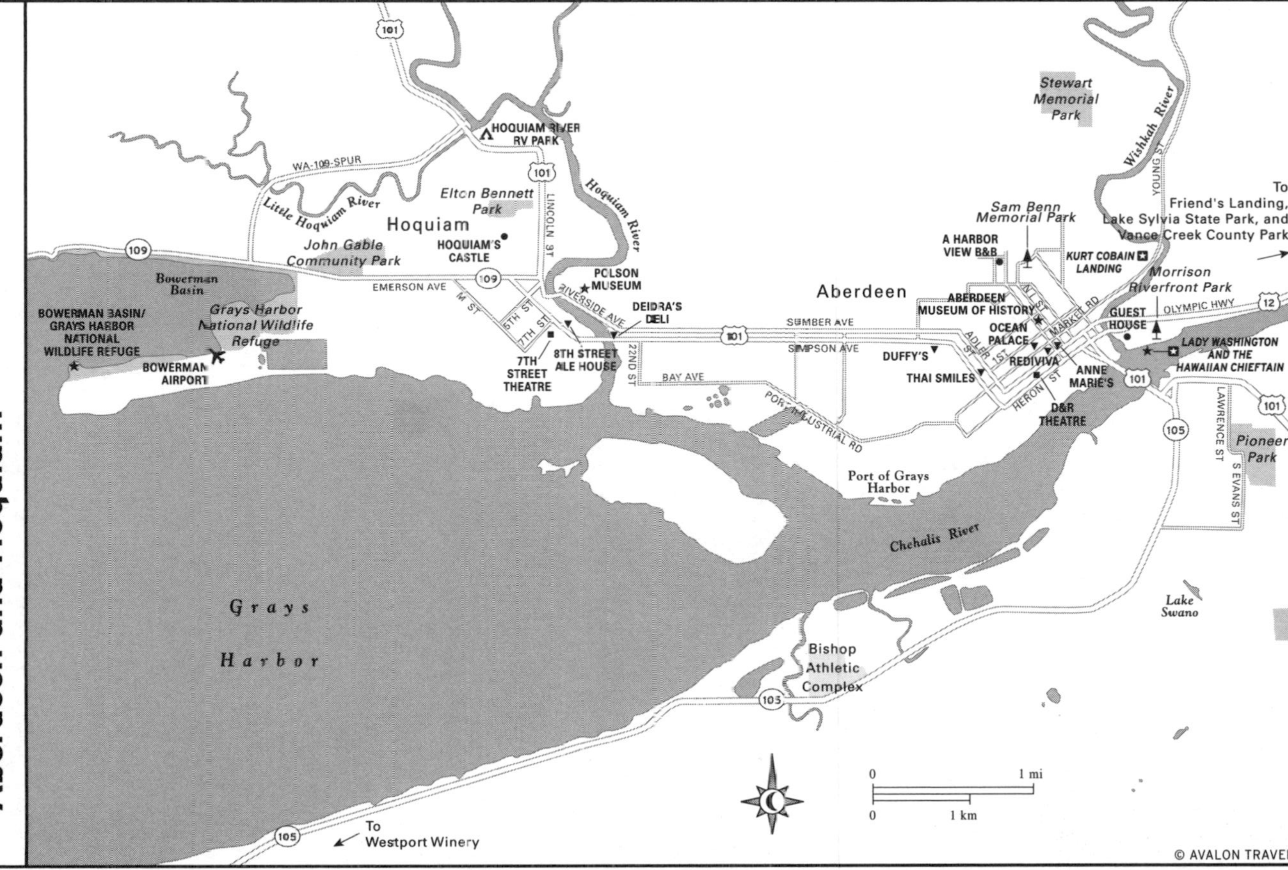

tall ship, the ***Hawaiian Chieftain.*** The two engage in "battles" where the crews shoot cannons (blanks, but with real gunpowder). It's just like you'd imagine an 18th-century battle to be—minus the actual damage. The Grays Harbor Historical Seaport Authority is currently raising funds to build Seaport Landing in South Aberdeen, which eventually will be the new home to the ships. Plans also include a multiuse visitors' destination center with exhibits, classrooms, a gift shop, and more.

Aberdeen Museum of History

Tucked inside the historic Armory Building in the heart of town, the **Aberdeen Museum of History** (111 E. 3rd St., 360/533-1976, www.aberdeen-museum.org, 10am-5pm Tues.-Sat., noon-4pm Sun., closed Mon., suggested donation $2 adults, $1 students/seniors, $5 families) is an educational and interesting place to visit. Permanent exhibits include a blacksmith shop, an old general store, a historical fire engine, and a Model T car. Several large community events also are hosted here. In addition to the Aberdeen Museum of History, which was founded in 1981, the old Armory also houses the Aberdeen Senior Community Center and the Grays Harbor Genealogical Society.

★ Kurt Cobain Landing

Thousands of people head to Aberdeen every year to visit the hometown of legendary rocker Kurt Cobain, the singer/guitarist of the seminal rock-and-roll band Nirvana. The Young Street Bridge, which the late Cobain is said to have spent some time under writing lyrics, always has been a popular stop on pilgrimages. Recently, the area surrounding the bridge has been designated Kurt Cobain Landing by the City of Aberdeen, and there is a large sculpture of a left-handed guitar there—designed by local artist Lora Malakoff—to commemorate Cobain, as well as hundreds of graffiti dedications to him written underneath the bridge from fans across the world. The landing, sculpture, and bridge are located at the end of East Second Street in Aberdeen.

Polson Museum

The 6,500-square-foot **Polson Museum** (1611 Riverside Ave., Hoquiam, 360/533-5862, www.polsonmuseum.org, 11am-4pm Wed.-Sat., noon-4pm Sun., closed Mon.-Tues., $4 adults, $2 students, $1 under 12, $10 families) was built in 1924 and was a wedding gift to Arnold Polson, a prominent lumber businessman, from his bachelor uncle, Robert. It had 26 rooms, six bathrooms, and four fireplaces. The family eventually donated the home to the city and it has been a museum ever since. The museum now occupies 17 of the 26 rooms, and there are various exhibits, including a replica of a 1920s kitchen, period clothing, logging and Native American exhibits, and more. The home sits on about two acres of parklike land and has a replica of the former Polson Logging Company's blacksmith shop, two steam donkeys, a rose garden, and more. A replica railroad camp is being built on the property to house heavy machinery artifacts. The museum is curated by Grays Harbor native John Larson, who's as knowledgeable as it gets when it comes to local history and a friendly chap, to boot.

Grays Harbor National Wildlife Refuge

People flock to Bowerman Basin in Hoquiam to see the wildlife at the **Grays Harbor National Wildlife Refuge** (Airport Way, off Hwy. 109, Hoquiam), especially the various birds that stop to feed in the rich and muddy estuary located on tidal flats. You can park near Bowerman Field or across from Lana's Hangar Café and walk on the boardwalk to get a pretty good view. Some birders consider the area one of the top 10 places in the country to go bird-watching. Although birds can be spotted year-round, late April and early May are the best times for viewing. That's when migrating shorebirds often stop here to take a break. More than 200 species of birds have been spotted here, and often in massive numbers. By one count in the early 2000s, nearly 100,000 dunlins were seen at once.

A Musical Nirvana

The makeshift memorial to Kurt Cobain under a bridge in Aberdeen draws music fans from all over the world.

Nirvana may have become known as the standard-bearers for the Seattle-centric grunge sound, but the band was created on the Olympic Peninsula in the town of Aberdeen. Consisting of Aberdeen native Kurt Cobain on guitar and vocals, Croatian-born Aberdeen transplant Krist Novoselic on bass, and a succession of local drummers including Dave Foster, Aaron Burckhard, and Chad Channing, Nirvana blew out of the Olympic Peninsula in 1988 with its debut album *Bleach*.

The band quickly gained a regional and international following, leading to a major-label recording contract, the recruiting of powerhouse drummer Dave Grohl, and the recording of 1991's *Nevermind,* which included the massive breakthrough hit single "Smells Like Teen Spirit." World tours, massive success, and controversy over Cobain's drug use followed, but Nirvana's musical status was firmly established on January 11, 1992, when *Nevermind* replaced Michael Jackson's *Dangerous* at number one on the *Billboard* albums chart.

Tragically, Cobain took his own life less than three years later. Novoselic had limited success with other bands in the years after Nirvana ended, but he still lives in Southwest Washington and is involved with politics. He has served as the president of the Wahkiakum County Democrats and once considered running for lieutenant governor of Washington. Grohl is still making music with his own band, the Foo Fighters.

There are several landmarks in Aberdeen that are significant to the Nirvana story. Cobain is rumored to have slept under the Young Street Bridge, for example, and the Nirvana song "Something in the Way" is said to have been written about his time spent there. There is a small memorial park adjacent to the bridge, and the city's eastern entrance greets visitors with a large sign that reads, "Welcome to Aberdeen: Come As You Are," in honor of one of Nirvana's biggest hits.

Other bands from the Grays Harbor area have had international success, too, albeit none on the scale of Nirvana. The Montesano-centered Melvins have had an international cult following for 30 years and were one of Cobain's first big inspirations in the business. And Aberdeen's Metal Church has sold millions of records and continues to soldier on, reforming periodically for an album or tour. Patrick Simmons of the 1970s band The Doobie Brothers also is from Aberdeen.

Lake Swano

Created in the 1940s when adjacent Alder Creek was dammed, Aberdeen's **Lake Swano** (1620 Edward P. Smith Dr.) is part of the Model Watershed Project located in a second-growth forest area on the Grays Harbor College campus. Nearby is the John P. Smith Aquaculture Building and a student-run fish hatchery. The entire area is often used for educational purposes, and there are trails around the lake filled with interpretive signs.

Morrison Riverfront Park

Take a stroll along the Chehalis River waterfront at **Morrison Riverfront Park** (1401 Sargent Blvd., Aberdeen) and have a picnic at this 11-acre park located just down the hill from the Come As You Are sign near the east entrance of Aberdeen. There are big toys for kids to play on, too.

Sam Benn Memorial Park

On a hill in the heart of Aberdeen lies the 14-acre **Sam Benn Memorial Park** (300 Hanna Ave.). The wooded park has tennis courts, a large playground, and a lot of green grass perfect for kicking back on a blanket with a good book on a sunny afternoon.

Friends Landing

Just a few minutes from the highway east of Montesano, Friends Landing is a recreational area that features forest trails, boat launches, picnic areas, fishing, hiking, and camping along the Chehalis River and a human-made lake. It is one of the few recreational areas in the United States that is entirely wheelchair-accessible. Take the Devonshire Road exit off of Highway 12 and follow the signs.

Lake Sylvia State Park

Lake Sylvia State Park (1813 Lake Sylvia Rd., www.parks.wa.gov) is located one mile north of Montesano at the site of an old logging camp. This 233-acre camping park boasts 15,000 feet of shoreline and is great for fishing, picnicking, and exploring the many trails that wander through the forest. There's even a half-mile-long trail that's wheelchair-accessible. The campground is open mid-March through October, but the day-use area is open year-round.

Vance Creek County Park

There are two small lakes at Vance Creek County Park, just west of Elma, and nature trails that are a favorite among local joggers and casual bicyclists. When it's hot outside, this place really fills up. From Highway 12, you often can see children running along the beach and bobbing in and out of the water.

SPORTS AND RECREATION

Fishing and Water Sports

North of Hoquiam on Highway 101, **Failor Lake** (2.5 miles down Failor Lake Rd.) is stocked with rainbow trout and has some resident cutthroat. Both facts make it a fishing favorite for locals. Head north about nine miles from Hoquiam on Highway 101 and turn left on Failor Lake Road. There's a boat ramp here, and the lake is open for fishing from the last Saturday in April through October 31.

It's not exactly natural, but the **YMCA of Grays Harbor** (2500 Simpson Ave., 360/537-9622, www.ghymca.net) in Hoquiam is a popular water destination, especially for an area that sees so much rain. There is a waterslide, wave pool, lazy river, and diving board, and a variety of group classes such as yoga, spinning, Zumba, and Pilates. Day passes are available and range from $5 for young kids and seniors to $15 for families.

The 4.4-mile **Wynoochee Lake** is surrounded by giant trees and is a great out-of-the-way place for fishing, boating, swimming, and hiking. The **Wynoochee Dam** (tours 253/502-8759) is about 28 miles from Montesano on the Wynoochee River and is the reason the lake exists. The river was dammed in 1972 to help control flooding in the Wynoochee Valley, and the dam is now managed by Tacoma Power.

Golf

People have been golfing at the 18-hole **Highland Golf Course** (2200 1st St., 360/533-2455, $26 for 18 holes) in Cosmopolis since 1931. It is a "Highland" course filled with hills and trees. It's a pretty course to walk, but if you're not up for dealing with the hills, you should rent a cart here.

In contrast, **Oaksridge Golf Course** (1052 Monte-Elma Rd., 360/482-3511, $48 for 18 holes) in nearby Elma is an extremely flat public 18-hole course. There's also a nine-tee driving range here.

Dirt Bikes and ATVs

If you like things muddy and to ride your dirt bike or ATV, the **Straddleline ORV Park** (literally located at the line between Grays Harbor and Thurston Counties, 360/495-3054) is a good place to do so. Sometimes trails are shut down for routine maintenance, so it's recommended to call first. There also are several spectator events, and RV camping and tent sites are available.

ENTERTAINMENT AND EVENTS

The Arts

If you're hoping to catch a big-name act in a small-town setting, be sure to check the schedule at Aberdeen's **D&R Theatre** (205 S. I St., 360/532-9348). Built in 1923, the historic theater recently was restored to its original grandeur and opened its doors to the public in 2009 to a live show by rockers Candlebox for a benefit for the Kurt Cobain Memorial Foundation. The theater holds 1,200 and has since provided a gorgeous backdrop for performances by such stars as Bill Cosby, Wynonna Judd, LeAnn Rimes, Clint Black, Queensryche, Soul Asylum, and many others.

Built five years after the D&R Theatre, the **7th Street Theatre** (313 7th St., 360/537-7400, www.7thstreettheatre.com) in Hoquiam focuses more on quality local entertainment and classic movies than national acts, though several of those also have performed at the venue. The 1,022-seat theater also has been remodeled over the years and today operates as a nonprofit.

A small gallery with a gift shop full of interesting art, **Six Rivers Gallery** (210 6th St., 360/532-9979, 10am-5pm Fri.-Sat., 1pm-5pm Sun.) in Hoquiam hosts several art-related events and poetry readings.

The **Chehalis Valley Historical Museum** (703 W. Pioneer Ave., 360/249-5800, noon-4pm Sat.-Sun., free but donations

the historic 7th Street Theatre in Hoquiam

accepted) in Montesano is located in a 1906 Scandinavian Lutheran Church and is full of historical items mostly pertaining to the Chehalis River Valley and the area from Oakville to Aberdeen.

Wineries

Family-owned and -operated **Westport Winery** (1 S. Arbor Rd., Aberdeen, 360/648-2224, www.westportwinery.org, $5 wine tasting) is the only winery in Grays Harbor County and definitely worth a visit. The Roberts family purchased their "Vineyards-By-The-Sea" in 2007 and opened the winery in 2008. They have been winning awards for their wines since. Stop by for a fun and lively wine tasting. Many of the wines feature local flavors such as Little Blackberry and Bog Berry Blush, and a portion of the proceeds from every bottle sold goes to a select local charity. The family recently opened a restaurant at the winery, located along Highway 105 between Aberdeen and Westport, that serves gourmet lunches and dinners. The vineyard grounds feature grapes, berries, and fruit trees, as well as several sculptures created by local artists.

Festivals and Events

The **Grays Harbor Shorebird Festival** (www.shorebirdfestival.com) takes place the last week of April. It celebrates the thousands of birds that come to Bowerman Basin in Hoquiam to feast. Bird-watchers travel from near and far to witness the event. The festival features keynote speakers, a banquet, live auction, field trips, a birding marketplace, and more. Visit the website for a current schedule of events.

The biggest Fourth of July celebration in the area is Aberdeen's free **Splash Festival.** Held at Morrison Park, the festival features food vendors, live music, games, and, of course, fireworks.

For more than 50 years, the **McCleary Bear Festival** has been feeding its fabulous bear stew to anyone fortunate enough to come out and try it. Held in early July, the event is three days long and includes a softball tournament, dance, concerts, two parades, and more. This is one of the most unique small-town events around.

Grays Harbor County Fair brings national talent to the fairgrounds in Elma each August. Just because it's a typical small-town fair doesn't mean it's short on charm. Food vendors are scattered throughout the grounds, and there's a decent number of rides here.

The granddaddy of Grays Harbor County events, Hoquiam's **Loggers Playday** features a grand parade through the city's streets, vendor fair, salmon bake, pancake breakfast, and road race. But the highlight is the logging show held in historic Olympic Stadium, where competitors from all over the country square off in competitions such as ax throwing, saw bucking, choker setting, pole climbing, and more. It is held in early September.

Montesano's **Festival of Lights** is held in the middle of each December and features tours past many of the spectacular light displays exhibited on the homes of prideful residents. There's also a parade through downtown, food vendors, a road race, and more.

The **Driftwood Players** (www.aberdeendriftwood.com) began performing in the 1950s and have offered quarterly plays at various locations around Grays Harbor County since. In 1982, the players found a permanent home at the charming **Driftwood Playhouse** (120 E. 3rd. St.) in Aberdeen.

Open year-round, the **Grays Harbor Public Market** (1956 Riverside Ave., 360/538-9747, www.ghpublicmarket.com) in Hoquiam is home to **Nancy's Bakery,** where you will find some of the best fresh-baked pies you've ever tasted. The market also features locally produced jams, salad dressings, honey, and more.

SHOPPING

Beer, Wine, and Specialty Food

Grays Harbor Wine Sellers (206 S.

Broadway, Aberdeen, 360/532-0555, 3pm-9pm Mon.-Thurs., noon-9pm Fri.-Sat.) is also a family-owned affair, and it offers specialty wines by the glass or by the bottle in a beautiful downtown setting. Owners Karen and Ryan Rowe are community activists who aren't opposed to spending time with their guests, educating them on the wines they offer for sale or the area in which they call home.

Literally right around the corner at **The Tap Room** (103 E. Wishkah St., Aberdeen, 360/589-3311, 3pm-close Mon.-Tues., 11:30am-close Wed.-Fri., 3pm-close Sat., hours vary Sun.), you'll find more family-owned fun, a host of on-tap craft beers, and great soup and sandwiches. The latest piece in what many are calling the "revitalization of downtown Aberdeen" is another good fit that's doing well.

Gifts and Home Decor

Grand Heron (200 E. Heron St., Aberdeen, 360/532-5561, www.grandheron.com, 10am-5pm Mon.-Fri., 10:30am-4pm Sat.) is a high-end home decor store you'd probably not expect to find in a small town such as Aberdeen. Still, the locals flock here for all kinds of upscale goods, as do a large number of out-of-towners.

Opal Art Glass (1232 1st St., Cosmopolis, 360/532-9268, www.opalartglass.com, 10am-5pm Mon.-Fri., 10am-4pm Sat.) is the place to go if you are looking for interesting paper weights, light fixtures, glass sinks, and more. They also have live demonstrations and teach classes. The gallery is sometimes closed during regular business hours, so call before you go.

Country Tyme (316 S. Main St., Montesano, 360/249-5588) is a cute little gift shop in Montesano that has candles, cards, and other small items.

Clyde & Sylvia's Frames-N-Things (113 E. Wishkah St., Aberdeen, 360/537-5755, 10am-6pm Tues.-Fri., 10am-5pm Sat.) does an excellent job of custom framing, and there's original art and engravable gift items, too.

Clothing

Pure Clothing (317 7th St., Hoquiam, 360/533-9670, 11am-6pm Thurs.-Sat.) sells mostly used clothing and has a large selection of premium jeans, band T-shirts, and Levi's. They don't accept just any item, so their selection is stellar.

Jewelry

There are several family-owned jewelry stores in the area, including **Wiitamaki Jewelry Store** (201 E. Wishkah St., Aberdeen, 360/532-6280, 10am-5:30pm daily) and **Herbig Jewelers** (601 W. Wishkah St., Aberdeen, 360/532-8232, 10am-5pm Mon.-Fri., 10am-3pm Sat.). Both have gifts that will sparkle.

ACCOMMODATIONS

The **Guest House Inn and Suites** (701 E. Heron St., Aberdeen, 360/537-7460, www.guesthouseintl.com, $100-150 d) is one of the cleaner, nicer places in Aberdeen to stay the night. It has a pool and continental breakfast, and some of the rooms are pet-friendly.

The historic ★ **Hoquiam's Castle** (515 Chenault, Hoquiam, 360/533-2005, www.hoquiamcastle.com, $145-195 d) is a bed-and-breakfast set in a neat location. It is perched on a hill overlooking Hoquiam and is a stately, 10,000-square-foot Victorian-style home built in 1897. The three-floor, five-bedroom castle was built by lumber baron Robert Lytle, who made a fortune running one of the first electric sawmills on the West Coast. The castle features period furniture, down comforters, and private baths in each room. The princess room has an original toilet designed by Thomas Crapper's company.

A Harbor View Bed and Breakfast (111 W. 11th St., Aberdeen, 360/533-7996, www.aharborview.com, $129-225 d, no kids under 12) is located in a 1905 Colonial Revival-style home that sits high on a hill and offers views of the Chehalis and Wishkah Rivers, as well Grays Harbor and the city of Aberdeen.

In Montesano, you'll find the ★ **Abel House Bed and Breakfast** (117 Fleet St. S.,

360/249-6002, $100-130 d) that was built in 1908. It has four rooms including the Abel Suite, which is a large room with a private bath. Massage and reflexology services are available upon request.

If you're on a budget, check out the **Grays Harbor Hostel and Guest House** (6 Ginny Ln., Elma, 360/482-3119, www.ghhostel.com, $18 s shared bath, $35 s or d private bath). This is a clean, affordable place to stay and even has a disc golf course on-site. It's open daily from April 15 to October 15 and by reservation the rest of the year.

If you want to stay in a really old hotel, head to the **Old McCleary Hotel** (42 Summit Rd., McCleary, 360/495-3678, $55-65 s or d). It's on the National Register of Historic Places and originally was the home of Henry McCleary, for whom the town is named. It was built in 1912, and most rooms have private baths and original furniture and fixtures.

Camping

A newcomer to the local camping scene, **Hoquiam River RV Park** (425 Queen Ave., 360/538-2870, www.hoquiamriverrvpark.com, $18 tents, $28.50 RVs) has more than 75 sites with full hookups, wireless Internet, a clubhouse, laundry, showers, and cable TV. Not a bad start for a location that has access to 500 feet of Hoquiam River waterfront.

If a quiet location is what you're looking for, **Lake Sylvia State Park** (www.parks.wa.gov, $22-36) will fit the bill nicely. Located just one mile north of Montesano, the park is a former logging camp set in a heavily wooded area. There are 35 tent sites here and, one of the reasons the park is so quiet, no RV spots.

The 119-acre **Schafer State Park** (12 miles north of Elma, www.parks.wa.gov, $21-31) on the Satsop River offers all the amenities of a typical camping location. There are picnic areas, hiking trails, fishing, and much more. There are 42 tent sites, several sites for RVs, and a handful of primitive and walk-in sites. The park was donated to the state in 1924 by the Schafer Brothers' Logging Company, whose owners used to hold picnics at the location.

There's also the **Coho Campground** and its 56 sites for tents, trailers and motor homes, and walk-in tent camp units. It's about 38 miles north of Montesano, so make sure you're prepared with plenty of gas, snacks, and other supplies before heading out.

FOOD

Although the Aberdeen-Hoquiam-Montesano area isn't flush with accommodations, mostly due to the more-attractive, beachfront settings located just minutes away at Ocean Shores and Westport, there are better food choices here than there are at the beaches. Smart visitors will want to take advantage of these places on the way to or from their ultimate destination.

American

★ **Deidra's Deli** (1956 Riverside Ave., Hoquiam, 360/538-9747, www.ghpublicmarket.com, 9am-5pm Mon.-Sat., 11am-4pm Sun., $6-8) is a gem of a place tucked inside the blink-and-you'll-miss-it Grays Harbor Public Market. If you want a seriously stacked deli sandwich, Deidra and her sandwich artists will hook you up. The taco soup here is so popular, Deidra's now serving it three days a week instead of one. If you arrive early, the bakers may let you in and make you an espresso; however, the rest of the vendors won't be there until normal business hours.

If you're looking for really good local burgers, fries, shakes, and malts, head to **Al's Humdinger** in Hoquiam (104 Lincoln St., 360/533-2754, 10am-10pm daily, $4-9). The food is cooked fresh to order. There is no seating except for two picnic tables outside, but it's still a local favorite not to be missed. Just down the street is another local burger joint, **The Grizzly Den** (300 W. Emerson Ave., 360/537-9840, 10:30am-8pm daily, $7-10). Try the peanut butter shake, waffle fries, and a burger, of course. Both the Humdinger and The Grizzly Den have special sauce, too. You be the judge as to which one's better.

Another fast-food fried treasure is **The**

Crow's Nest (441 S. Main St., Montesano, 360/249-5505, 9am-8pm daily, $6-9). They have tater tots, cotton candy ice cream, tacos, burgers, and hot dogs. The question is, what don't they have? Oh, and the shakes are super thick.

The Bee Hive (300 S. Main St., Montesano, 360/249-4131, 6am-8pm daily, $9-14) has hearty servings and friendly service, though the decor is a bit outdated. The drink prices are outdated as well, which makes it easier to overlook aesthetics. The Bee Hive offers basic burgers and greasy-spoon fare, although their Monte Cristo sandwich is as sweet as you'll find in the area.

Want a hearty breakfast? Go to **Anne Marie's** (110 S. I St., Aberdeen, 360/538-0141, 7am-2:30pm Mon.-Fri., 8am-2pm Sat.-Sun., $7-13) for a big, fat omelet. Lunch also is served here, and the bread is homemade.

Bar and Grills

The **8th Street Ale House** (207 8th St., Hoquiam, 360/612-3455, www.8thstreetalehouse.com, 11am-midnight daily, $12-16) is a newer local watering hole with good food. It's owned by the same person who owns the successful Galway Bay in Ocean Shores, and he knows what he's doing. It features local art and music, and has outdoor seating for when the weather is nice. Lunch and dinner is served here.

Billy's Bar & Grill (322 E. Heron, Aberdeen, 360/533-7144, 7am-11pm Mon.-Thurs., 7am-midnight Fri.-Sat., 7am-9pm Sun., $7-16) offers visitors a glimpse into Aberdeen's past. This building housed a brothel once upon a time, and the restaurant is named after Billy Gohl, who was rumored to have killed more than 100 men during the late 1800s. In the upstairs windows, you'll see some "ladies of the night." Standard American fare such as burgers, steaks, and a lot of fried foods are served here, and beer, of course.

Barbecue

If you're looking for a mouthwatering rack of ribs or lip-smacking barbecue brisket, head to the award-winning ★ **Ranch House BBQ & Steakhouse** (10841 Kennedy Creek Rd. SW, between Elma and Olympia, 360/866-8704, www.ranchhousebbq.com, 11am-8pm, closed Tues., $10-18). This off-the-beaten-path place was even featured on the Food Network. Make sure you order some french fries; I promise you'll be happy with the decision.

Chinese

Ocean Palace (112 E. Wishkah St., Aberdeen, 360/533-6966, 11am-9:30pm Mon.-Sat., $7-13) is a place where you can get all your Asian food favorites, and the fried rice is yellow and super delicious. The service is great, too.

Italian and Pizza

If pizza is what you're craving, get a gooey slice of it at **Casa Mia** (2936 Simpson Ave., Hoquiam, 360/533-2010, 11am-10pm daily, $8-15). Try the award-winning Pizza Strada Susina: It has tomato and gorgonzola parmesan sauce topped with roast chicken, cashews, onions, and basil. There's also manicotti and more.

Mangiamo (116 W. Heron St., Aberdeen, 360/533-2442, 11am-9pm Mon.-Thurs., 11am-10pm Fri.-Sat., 11am-8pm Sun., $14-28), a newer restaurant, owned by the same person who owns the nearby D&R Theatre, serves pasta, upper-crust gourmet pizzas, and more.

Mexican

Spice things up at **El Rancho Family Mexican Restaurant** (216 S. Main St., Montesano, 360/249-5500, $9-18) or get something sweet at **La Unica Bakery** (307 S. Park St., Aberdeen, 360/533-9902), an authentic Mexican bakery that also serves excellent burritos at a great price. Definitely a local secret.

Steak and Seafood

If you have a hankering for some local fare such as fried razor clams, a grilled cheese and Dungeness crab sandwich, wild blackberry pie (a house specialty), or something else hearty that seems like it came out of Grandma's kitchen, head to locally owned **Duffy's** (1605

Simpson Ave., Aberdeen, 360/532-3842, www.duffysaberdeen.com, 6am-9pm Sun.-Thurs., 6am-10pm Fri.-Sat., $10-18). They also have a large selection of local books for sale.

Aberdeen's **Breakwater Seafoods and Chowder House** (306 S. F St., 360/532-5693, 10am-7pm Mon.-Thurs., 10am-8pm Fri.-Sat., 11am-6pm Sun., $9-14) is a great place to pick up your own fresh catch. Or order some halibut fish-and-chips and clam chowder. If it's sunny, eat on the deck overlooking the Wishkah River.

The newest restaurant on the local scene, ★ **Rediviva** (118 E. Wishkah St., Aberdeen, 360/637-9259, www.redivivarestaurant.com, 3pm-11pm, Mon.-Sat., closed Sun., $20-40), almost instantly established itself as one of the best in the area. For those who know the history of chef and owner Andrew Bickar, that should come as no surprise. Bickar was chef at the Ocean Crest restaurant in Moclips when it burned down in 2011, and he decided in 2013 to start his own place a couple dozen miles away in his hometown. He's been successful so far, with craft cocktails, and a to-die-for black pepper beef loin among the highlights.

Thai

Don't dismiss the **Thai Carrot** (412 S. Boone St., Aberdeen, 360/532-2044, 11am-8:30pm Mon.-Thurs., 11am-9pm Fri.-Sat., 4pm-8:30pm Sun., $8-13) just because it doesn't have the most attractive facade. The atmosphere may not be dazzling, but the food is so tasty it really doesn't matter. It rivals that of any large city. Try the pad see ew or the pad thai—heck, any of the noodle dishes are good. And you even get free refills on the Thai tea.

There's still signage from its former life as a hot dog shack, but don't let that, or its tiny shop, fool you into not stopping in at ★ **Thai Smiles** (100 N. Park St., Aberdeen, 360/637-9434, 11am-7pm Mon.-Sat., closed Sun., $6-12). The portions here are enormous, the taste more than adequate, and the price, well, the price is at least half of what you'd pay in a larger city. The aesthetics here might be quirky and off-putting, to say the least, but the food and value are excellent.

INFORMATION AND SERVICES

For information on the cities in the area, visit the **Grays Harbor Chamber of Commerce** (506 Duffy St., Aberdeen, 360/532-1924 or 800/321-1924, www.graysharbor.org).

GETTING THERE AND AROUND

Grays Harbor Transit (360/532-2770 or 800-562/9730, www.ghtransit.com) provides service throughout Grays Harbor County, including to the cities of Aberdeen, Hoquiam, Montesano, Elma, and McCleary. To get to the area from Sea-Tac Airport, head south on I-5 and cut across to the coast through Aberdeen. Budget two hours typically, and up to three on weekends.

South Beach

Today, South Beach is the locals' name for the southwestern portion of Grays Harbor. The town of Westport, a tourist draw for its beaches, surfing, and fishing opportunities, is the area's hub, and the lodging options that have sprouted up in recent years indicate tourism here is doing quite well. Still, for the most part, Westport has escaped the inundation experienced by its neighbor across the water, Ocean Shores, and remains a fishing village populated by hardworking locals who make their living off the sea.

SIGHTS

Westport Maritime Museum

Housed in an old Coast Guard lifeboat station, the **Westport Maritime Museum** (2201 Westhaven Dr., 360/268-0078, www.

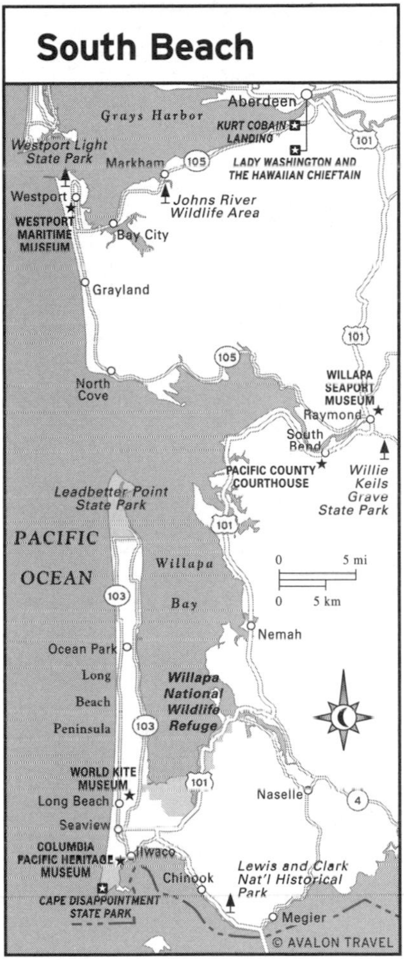

westportwa.com/museum, 10am-4pm daily June-Sept., noon-4pm Wed.-Sun. rest of year, $5 adults, $3 ages 13-18, $2 ages 6-12, children 5 and under free) stands out in the city of Westport, not only for the uncommon-to-the-area structure, which features several gables and a widow's tower, but also for its two outdoor whale houses, one that holds an entire whale skeleton. The fun continues indoors, and an entire building was built just to hold a gigantic lens created in 1888 in France and designed by Augustin Fresnel. For years, the lens was in operation at Destruction Island off the coast of Washington, but it was replaced by a modern light and given to the museum in 1998. In the main building, there's information on the history of the area. McCausland Hall, the museum's lecture center, is named after celebrated editorial cartoonist Bob McCausland and his wife, Ruth, a noted historian and author.

Westport Light State Park

The unique jewel at Westport Light State Park (www.parks.wa.gov), as the sight's name might suggest, is the **Grays Harbor Lighthouse,** a 107-foot-tall lighthouse—the tallest in the state—built in the late 1890s and now listed on the National Register of Historic Places. Its light marks the entrance to Grays Harbor. The lighthouse is closed to the public but sometimes is available for tours coordinated by the Westport Maritime Museum. The rest of the 212-acre park is open year-round for day-use purposes, such as kite flying and hiking of the scenic 1.3-mile concrete boardwalk, which links up with the smaller **Westhaven State Park,** where there are good clam digging and fishing spots next to the South Jetty.

SPORTS AND RECREATION

Hiking

Johns River Trail

Distance: 1 mile round-trip
Duration: 0.25-1 hour
Elevation gain: 0-40 feet
Effort: Easy
Trailhead: Johns River Road
Directions: Travel west on Highway 105 from Aberdeen and turn left onto Johns River Road, approximately 11 miles outside of Aberdeen, then left onto Game Farm Road. Continue one mile to the parking area.

The paved Johns River Trail begins in the parking lot off Game Farm Road and continues a half mile along the river. From there, the trail continues, unpaved, through the Johns River Wildlife Area, a 15-unit, 6,700-square-acre estuary and wetlands located in and around Grays Harbor. The 1,500 acres are full of birds, deer, elk, bear, and all sorts of flora.

Fishing, Clamming, and Crabbing

Whether you want to leave it to the professionals and take a charter boat excursion or you want to go it alone with a pole, clam gun, or crab ring, there are several opportunities to fulfill your food-gathering desires in the South Beach area. The **South Jetty** is a great spot to fish for rockfish, perch, cod, and salmon. The docks at the Westport Marina are a little more family-friendly, and the fishing pier located at the end of **Float 20** even has holes drilled in it for anglers to rest their poles while waiting for a bite. Adventurous sorts can do two activities at once: fishing and crabbing, all at Float 20. The key is to drop your crab rings or pots into the water, secure them to the dock, and make your way out to the pier to fish for 30 minutes or so before returning back to check your crab gear to see if you caught any keepers.

When open, **Westhaven State Park** is a prime spot for digging razor clams, as is most of the beach in Grayland except a quarter-mile section that's closed off as a razor clam sanctuary.

Those who want to leave their fishing to the pros, or at least let them help you, can visit any of the many charter companies located next to the **Westport Marina** along Westhaven Drive. Most charter boats leave early in the morning and return in the late afternoon. Some even guarantee catches and, for a charge, will fillet your catch for you. When gray whales are migrating from Baja California in March, April, and May, many of the same charter boat operators use their vessels to take customers on whale-watching excursions with a goal of catching a glimpse of these magnificent creatures as they make their way to the Bering and Chukchi Seas.

All three sporting activities require licenses and have specific seasons and regulations. Local shops that sell licenses also will have copies of the state's rules and regulations pamphlet, or you can visit www.wdfw.wa.gov to read all about the sports online.

Catching (and eating!) Dungeness crab is a popular pastime at the Westport Marina.

Surfing

Some of the best surfing in the state can be found at **Half Moon Bay** in Westhaven State Park. The reason: the human-made South Jetty just above the bay. This isn't your stereotypical California beach, however. The best waves of the year often come during the coldest months, so wetsuits are typically a necessity. Advice from those in the know, as well as whatever gear you may need, can be had at the **Surf Shop** (207 N. Montesano St., Westport, 360/268-0992, www.westportsurfshop.com) and the **Steepwater Surf Shop** (316 N. Montesano St., Westport, 360/268-5527, www.steepwatersurfshop.com).

ENTERTAINMENT AND EVENTS

Casinos

The **Shoalwater Bay Casino** (4112 Hwy. 105, Tokeland, 360/267-2048 or 888/332-2048, www.shoalwaterbaycasino.com, 10am-midnight, Sun.-Thurs., 10am-2am Fri.-Sat.), at the turnoff to Tokeland, is tiny, but it's also a fun place to visit. There are more than 300 slot machines, a small card-table section, a bar, and even a nice (and cheap) buffet.

Festivals and Events

Mid-April, Westport plays host to the **World Class Crab Races,** a quirky festival where competitors pay to rent a crab (or bring their own) and race it down a slide-like chute in order to win prizes, including cash. Simultaneously, an all-you-can-eat crab feed is held.

A more traditional and far more subdued event is the annual **Blessing of the Fleet,** held each May in Westport as people gather to bless the anglers and pray for a bountiful season. The day kicks off with a grand parade through town.

Another unique festival is Westport's **Rusty Scupper's Pirate Daze,** held each June at the Westport Marina. The festival is three days long and features dozens of vendors, games, look-alike competitions, and more.

The popular and long-running (more than 60 years) **Westport Seafood Festival** is held each Labor Day Weekend at the Westport Maritime Museum. Local crafts are on sale, there's live music, and, of course, there's fresh seafood. Other key events in the area include the **Cleanwater Classic** surfing contest each May, the **Windriders Kite Festival** in July, and the **Grayland Open** Jet Skiing competition each August.

For the kid in everyone, the **Westport Aquarium** (321 E. Harbor St., Westport, 360/268-0471, 10am-4pm Fri.-Sun., $5.50 adults, $3.50 children, under 3 free) has several exhibits, including a touch tank. Lovers of odd facts and local history can visit the **Furford Cranberry Museum** (2395 Hwy. 105, 360/267-3303, free, donation suggested) in Grayland and learn how one machine, developed by Julius Furford, forever changed the cranberry industry. Tours are by appointment only, so call in advance.

SHOPPING

If one had to pick a center to Westport's shopping district, it would be located on Westhaven Drive across from the marina. During the winter months, the street often is filled with water that's washed over the jetty and into town. During the summer months, the street is filled with cars and pedestrians looking for lunch and souvenirs.

Fudge-loving tourists love to stop to get their fix at **Gifts Ahoy Sea Shanty** (2563 Westhaven Dr., Westport, 360/268-0426) and farther up the street at **Granny Hazel's Candy & Gift Shop** (2329 Westhaven Dr., Westport, 360/268-0033), where they also can get other types of candy, various local trinkets, and more.

Bay West Emporium (300 E. Dock St., Westport, 360/268-5494, www.westportflowershop.com, 10am-4pm daily) is an excellent flower shop that also has a good selection of wine and gifts. Another local option for flowers is **Bayside Floral** (316 N. Montesano St., Westport, 360/268-5494).

Those who weren't successful catching their own seafood but still want fresh food have a few good options. In Westport, they can swing by **Merino's Seafood** (301 E. Harbor St., 360/268-5009, www.merinoseafoods.com, 9am-5pm daily) to pick up some fresh, or even canned, goods, or they can venture out to the end of Float 8 at the marina and visit the floating fish store that is **Seafood Connection** (360/268-1328, 9:30am-5:30pm Thurs.-Mon.), where boats pull up right at the store to sell their catch.

Make the short trek down Highway 105 toward Aberdeen and visit **Brady's Oysters** (3714 Oyster Pl., 360/268-0077 or 800/572-3252, www.bradysoysters.com, 9am-5pm daily) to pick up some fresh food. The shop features other seafood, too, but oysters are its specialty. Its semi-naughty bumper stickers ("Shuck Me, Suck Me, Eat Me Raw" and "Eat Oysters and Keep It Up," among them) are almost as popular as the food itself and can be seen proudly displayed on cars throughout the region and beyond.

The **Pomegranate** (1767 Hwy. 105, 360/267-0701, 11am-5pm Thurs.-Sun.) gift shop in Grayland seems somewhat out of place in its location. Not for any bad reason, but because its merchandise is almost too good to be sold off a coastal highway lined with driftwood, fishing nets, and buoys. But co-owners and sisters-in-law Heather and Hollie Tucker have found a niche that somehow works, and their shop features a wide variety of quality goods, including candles, house wares, furniture, and more, all at reasonable prices. There's more home decor a short distance down the road at **Rose Cottage** (360/267-0205, hours vary).

Antiques sold in a 1920s schoolhouse with a nautical theme? That's the **Olde Mercantile** (1820 Hwy. 105, Grayland, 360/267-0121, 10am-5pm daily) in a nutshell.

ACCOMMODATIONS

$50-100

A small and quiet family-oriented motel on the beach in Westport, **Ocean Avenue Inn** (275 W. Ocean Ave., Westport, 360/268-9400, www.oceanavenueinn.com, $99-159 d) has individual rooms, suites, and a guest cabin called The Salty Seahorse ($150) to accommodate larger groups. This is one of the closest hotels to Westport Light State Park.

If having a go-kart track immediately in front of your hotel room sounds like a good idea, **Breakers Boutique Inn** (971 Montesano St., Westport, 360/268-0848 or 800/898-4889, www.breakersboutiqueinn.com, $99 d) might just be for you. Whirlpool tub suites also are available from $210 a night. And don't worry, the go-kart track does close early enough for everyone to catch some peaceful ZZZs.

Mariners Cove Inn (303 Ocean Ave., Westport, 360/268-6000 or 877/929-9096, www.marinerscoveinn.com, $69 d) isn't fancy by any means, but it's neat and serves the needs of anglers and less-demanding tourists quite well with its convenient barbecue gazebo and convenient location next to a grocery store.

For those whose main interest is fishing, the best location in town is the **Harbor Resort** (871 Neddie Rose Dr., Westport, 360/268-0169, $69-99 d). The resort is at the very edge of town, right next to Float 20 at the Westport Marina. There are cottages available ($149-189) here, too, and the on-site store has food, fishing tackle, and snacks.

Located in the middle of the South Beach in the quiet town of Grayland, **Grayland Motel and Cottages** (2013 Hwy. 105, 360/267-2395 or 800/292-0845, www.westportwa.com/graylandmotel, $59-97 d) is ideal for beach lovers, storm watchers, or those who just want to be near the water.

With a variety of accommodation styles and prices, the **Walsh Beach Motel** (1593 Hwy. 105, 360/267-2191, www.walshmotel.com, $65-139) in Grayland is an oceanfront resort with a unique personality and spectacular views of the Pacific.

First built as a farmhouse in 1885, and since designated a National Historic Landmark, the venerable ★ **Tokeland Hotel** (100 Hotel Rd., Tokeland, 360/267-7006, www.tokelandhotel.com, $55-65 d) overlooks both Willapa Bay and the Pacific Ocean in the tiny fishing village of Tokeland. Legend has it the place may be haunted. The place certainly is old enough to fit the haunted stereotype. The hotel first opened for guests before Washington even became a state. There's a restaurant here, too.

$100-150

Just a short walk from the Pacific Ocean, the ★ **Chateau Westport** (710 Hancock, Westport, 360/268-9101, www.chateauwestport.com, $119-299 d) offers spectacular views and a homelike atmosphere with kitchenettes and fireplaces in many rooms. Rooms are not modern by any means, but the staff is friendly and the ability to cook whatever you may catch in your room is a big bonus in this area. The Chateau's suites sleep 4-6 people and cost $197-299 per night.

Perched at the end of Neddie Rose Drive like it's protecting Westport's Marina, the

Islander Resort (421 E. Neddie Rose Dr., Westport, 360/268-9166, www.westport-islander.com, $109-119 d) overlooks an active and picturesque fishing port and has plenty of space for RVs, including full hookups. Many rooms are pet-friendly.

An ecofriendly spot offering full breakfasts, the **Westport Bayside B&B** (1112 S. Montesano St., 360/268-1403 or 888/318-8868, www.westportbayside.com, $115-160 d) sits on four acres on the shores of Grays Harbor and has beautiful rooms, hiking trails, gardens, and deer on the grounds.

$150-200

If direct beach access is a must, **Vacations By The Sea** (260 E. Dock St., 360/268-1119, www.vacationbythesea.com, $179-259 d) rents condominium units for vacation stays. Amenities include an outdoor hot tub and heated swimming pool, mini-golf, kids' play area, and a large communal fireplace room.

Vacation Rentals

With dozens of properties across the South Beach area, **Beachy Day Vacation Properties** (360/267-3234, www.beachyday.com) likely has something for most every traveler, including bungalows, cabins, houses, and condos.

Camping

Centrally located in Westport, the **Pacific Motel & RV Park** (330 S. Forrest, Westport, 360/268-9325, $20-74) has everything for the active traveler, including fish-cleaning stations and tent sites available for as low as $20 per night. There's also a pool, fire pits, laundry, and more.

Located just south of Westport, ★ **Twin Harbors State Park** (3120 Hwy. 105, www.parks.wa.gov, $12 primitive tent site, $36 premium hookups) is the most popular camping spot in the area. There are 219 tent sites, 42 utility sites, and nine restrooms scattered throughout the 172-acre site. The sites are close together, which is fine when it's not busy, but can be a headache when it is.

Kenanna RV Park (2959 Hwy. 105, 360/267-3515 or 800/867-3515, www.kenannarv.com, $19-35) in Grayland offers full hookups for RVs and tent sites for both individuals and groups, as well as a variety of cabins ($45-59).

FOOD

American

Inn of the Westwind (2119 N. Nyhus St., Westport, 360/268-1315, 5:30am-4pm daily, $6-10) is best known for its hearty breakfasts and favored by locals.

Good prices and good food are the words that pretty much sum up the **Blue Buoy Café** (2323 Westhaven Dr., Westport, 360/268-7065, 8am-4pm daily, $10-15). The basic double-pattied Blue Buoy Burger is a local favorite.

The **Mermaid Deli & Pub** (200 Patterson, 360/612-0435, www.mermaiddeli.com, 11am-10pm Sun.-Thurs., 11am-2am Fri.-Sat., $7-16) is just a few steps off Westport's main drag and offers more than a dozen submarine sandwiches, including the spicy Blazin' Cajun. The pub frequently features live music, and there's an outdoor patio and fire pits.

The newest game on the South Beach might arguably be the best. That's the ★ **Sand Verbena** (4115 Hwy. 105, Tokeland, 360/267-2048, www.sand-verbena.com, 11:30am-8pm Sun.-Thurs., 11:30am-9pm Fri.-Sat., $12-22). Located near the Showalter Bay Casino, the restaurant has all the seafood options you could want, and specials certain nights of the week. Willapa steamer clams in citrus butter, and steamed in beer and honey? More, please. Fast service and nice, clean interior with a water view should seal the deal for most.

Fine Dining

Located at Westport's Islander Resort, the dining room at the **Half Moon Bay Bar & Grill** (421 E. Neddie Rose Dr., Westport, 360/268-9166 or 800/322-1740, www.washingtonsbestbloodymary.com, 11am-9pm Sun.-Thurs., 11am-10pm Fri.-Sat., $12-28) looks out over the marina and serves award-winning cuisine and drinks, including the confidently named Washington's Best Bloody Mary.

Pizza

Original House of Pizza (1200 N. Montesano St., Westport, 360/268-0901, 11am-8pm Mon.-Thurs., 11am-9pm Fri.-Sat., closed Sun., $10-15) has great customer service and even better food. They also offer takeout for those who want to get back to their hotel room or activities.

Quick Bites

The name **Little Richard's House of Donuts** (2557 Westhaven Dr., Westport, 360/268-9733, $2-4) is a bit misleading, only because the shop offers more than just doughnuts. But, rest assured, it's the doughnuts and other pastries that are best here. They melt in your mouth and, thanks to the typically chilly weather here, not in your hand.

Seafood

It might be the large waterwheel out front that first grabs your attention, but the food is the thing that's going to keep it at ★ **Bennett's Restaurant** (1800 Hwy. 105, 360/267-2350, www.bennettsdining.com, 10:30am-9pm daily, $12-22) in Grayland. The restaurant, and its fantastic food, has been compared to fine-dining options in bigger cities such as Seattle and Tacoma, although with prices even locals can afford. Try the wild salmon fillet.

Another Grayland hot spot is the **Mutineer Restaurant** (2120 Hwy. 105, 360/267-2077, $10-15), where trying the fish-and-chips at least once (which will get you hooked) is almost mandatory. The restaurant was closed for renovation in 2014 but planned to open bigger and better than ever.

INFORMATION AND SERVICES

All the information you need to know about the area can be obtained at the **Westport-Grayland Chamber of Commerce** (2985 N. Montesano St., Westport, 360/268-9422 or 800/345-6223, www.westportgrayland-chamber.org).

GETTING THERE AND AROUND

Grays Harbor Transit (360/532-2770 or 800/562-9730, www.ghtransit.com) serves the entire South Beach area, including Westport and Grayland, as well as the rest of Grays Harbor County and beyond. The best driving route to get to the South Beach from Sea-Tac Airport is to head south on I-5 and cut across to the coast from Olympia through to Aberdeen. Budget 2.5 hours.

All it takes to navigate the area successfully and to keep your travels on schedule is to remember the 20-minute rule. That is, it takes 20 minutes (or a factor thereof) to get from most any place to another. Ocean Shores to Aberdeen is 20 minutes, and Aberdeen to Westport is 20 minutes. Westport to Raymond is 20 x 2 (40) minutes.

Long Beach Peninsula

Visitors traveling from the Olympic Peninsula to the Long Beach Peninsula via windy Highway 101 will pass through two towns located on Willapa Harbor. First up is **Raymond** (pop. 2,800), a once-bustling but now down-on-its-luck mill town; in its heyday in the 1910s and 1920s Raymond boasted double its current number of residents. Six miles to Raymond's south is the Pacific County seat of **South Bend** (pop. 1,600), whose history is similar to Raymond's albeit a bit more based on the fishing industry. The state's official song, "Washington, My Home," was penned by South Bend's Helen Davis. Getting to these two towns from Aberdeen in the north requires driving a windy, hilly, 20-mile stretch of Highway 101 that, at times, can be nerve-wracking, thanks both to the narrow, tree lined roads on which deer and other wildlife occasionally pop onto out of nowhere, and to the speed-watching police cars that also sometimes seem to appear out of the blue. The scary part of the drive is over when you come down the steep hill into the safety of the Raymond city limits. It's a good time to stop and explore, and there are gems to be found in and around the two main towns here. Both cities lie near the mouth of the Willapa River, which feeds into Willapa Bay. The bay is home to one of the largest estuaries in the world and also produces record numbers of oysters.

Originally named Tinkerville after its founder, Henry Harrison Tinker, the city of **Long Beach** is considered by some to be the only "real" beach town in Washington. It's the flag- and shop-filled walkable downtown area, half-mile-long wooden boardwalk, and, of course, the beach that make it so. There are 28 miles of uninterrupted beaches on the Long Beach Peninsula, and signs all around the area proclaim its home to the "World's Longest Beach." The claim isn't true, but the sentiment is certainly there. Long Beach and the cities surrounding it fill with tourists from the Puget Sound area during the summer. Most come for the beaches or to visit the incredible Cape Disappointment State Park. To the east of the peninsula are the pristine waters of Willapa Bay, and the northern end of the peninsula is home to Leadbetter Point State Park and the Willapa National Wildlife Refuge.

SIGHTS

Willapa Seaport Museum

The unheralded **Willapa Seaport Museum** (310 Alder St., Raymond, 360/942-4149, 10am-4pm Thurs.-Sun., suggested donation of $3 adults, $2 seniors and veterans, $1 children, $5 families), located on the South Fork of the Willapa River, is one of the area's best-kept secrets. Curator Pete Darrah has meticulously gathered and displayed historical materials related to the military, logging, shipbuilding, fishing, Native Americans, and, of course, life on the high seas. There's even a bust of President Theodore Roosevelt. To say this museum is packed would be an understatement.

Northwest Carriage Museum

The second half of Raymond's excellent waterfront historical twosome, the **Northwest Carriage Museum** (314 Alder St., Raymond, 360/942-4150, 10am-4pm Wed.-Sat., noon-4pm Sun. in summer, $4 adults, $2 ages 6-18, under 6 free) is home to 27 restored horse-drawn carriages, many of which at one point were owned by rich Americans or Englishmen, who had purchased the pre-car vehicles not only as a means of transportation but also as a way to publicly display their wealth. Children are encouraged to try on the museum's period costumes during their visit. This museum is an unexpected find in such a small town, and one that's definitely worth a look.

Pacific County Courthouse

Yes, the **Pacific County Courthouse** (300

Memorial Dr., South Bend) is an actual courthouse, where legal proceedings take place during business hours. Locals come to get their car tabs renewed, register for marriage licenses, and gather information on various permitting processes. But this also is a place where travelers, many of which first spot the hilltop building while puttering by on Highway 101, like to roam. The building, opened in 1911, features a Tiffany glass dome and has been on the National Register of Historic Places since 1977. It cost $132,000 to build: a cost so large that the building became known as "The Gilded Palace of Extravagance." The view of the city and the water from the courthouse grounds is the best you'll find in the area. Not bad for a place that may not have existed, were it not for the bold moves of a few South Bend residents in the late 1800s. At the time, the Pacific County seat was located at Oysterville on the Long Beach Peninsula. A year earlier, voters had decided South Bend should be the county seat, but Oysterville didn't want to give it up. So, in February 1893, a group of South Bend residents took two Steamers to Oysterville, removed the county records, and brought them back to South Bend where they have remained since.

Columbia Pacific Heritage Museum

Located in the quiet fishing town of Ilwaco at the southern end of the Long Beach Peninsula, the **Columbia Pacific Heritage Museum** (115 Lake St. SE, 360/642-3446, 10am-4pm Tues.-Sat., noon-4pm Sun., $5 adults, $4 seniors, $2.50 ages 12-18, under 12 free, free admission every Thurs.) does as good a job of telling the story of the area it's located in as any museum in the state. It would be easy to overlook this place as another small-town, understaffed museum, but those who do so are missing out. This is a large museum, full of exhibits on the varied lifestyles and cultures that helped form this area where the Columbia River and Pacific Ocean meet. Permanent galleries include ones dedicated to the Chinook, the Lewis and Clark era, pioneer life, and local natural resources. This museum is a can't-miss—the Discover Garden and Mariner's Memorial particularly so.

★ Cape Disappointment State Park

It's doubtful names of places could be more depressing—even ominous—than they are at **Cape Disappointment State Park** (360/642-3078, www.parks.wa.gov), a two-mile stretch of beach south of Ilwaco. Of course, there's a reason why this area is a must-see for all those visiting the Long Beach Peninsula, and it's the history behind those names that help make it so.

The park's name stems from a 1788 incident during which English fur trader John Meares was searching for the mouth of what was to become the Columbia River and instead bumped into this cape of land that juts out at the southern end of the Long Beach Peninsula. Meares dubbed the area "Cape Disappointment." Some 17 years later, explorers Meriwether Lewis and William Clark ended their journey to the Pacific Ocean at this spot, writing in their journals of the "Great joy" they felt to finally be "in View of the Ocian" they had been longing to see.

That historic moment, as well as the rest of Lewis and Clark's fascinating story of discovery and survival, can be revisited at the **Lewis and Clark Interpretive Center** (360/642-3029, 10am-5pm daily, $5 adults, $2.50 ages 7-17, children under 7 free). The center sits on top of a cliff some 200 feet above the mouth of the mighty Columbia. There are several interactive exhibits here for those of all ages to enjoy, and the views from the center's large windows are some of the best around. Each November, there is an "Ocian in View" cultural weekend held at the Columbia Pacific Heritage Museum.

The 1,882-acre park also is home to the **Cape Disappointment Lighthouse,** which was completed in 1856 and still today helps guide northbound vessels into the mouth of the Columbia. The lighthouse is the oldest functioning lighthouse on the West Coast.

Across the peninsula near Seaview is the **North Head Lighthouse,** completed in 1898, which helped southbound vessels navigate into the Columbia. The lighthouse is perched above Dead Man's Hollow, a rocky area named after the sailors who lost their lives here in 1853 when their ship, the *Vandelia,* crashed nearby. The ship's captain, E. N. Beard, also has a hollow named after him. Beard's Hollow is where his body was found. The North Head Lighthouse is no longer operational, but tours are available ($2.50).

Cape Disappointment State Park also operates the **Colbert House** (360/642-3078, corner of Spruce St. and Quaker St., $1, by appointment only). The historic house is listed on the National Register of Historic Places and originally was built in 1872 in Chinookville, a town that no longer exists. Eleven years later, the former home to a fishing family was moved to its current location, where it was restored in 1994.

There are nearly seven miles of trails in Cape Disappointment State Park. Watch for water on all the trails in this area.

World Kite Museum and Hall of Fame

In Long Beach, the **World Kite Museum and Hall of Fame** (303 Sid Snyder Dr., 360/642-4020, www.kitefestival.com, 11am-5pm daily May-Sept., 11am-5pm Fri.-Tues. rest of year, $5 adults, $4 seniors, $3 children) is the only museum in the United States dedicated to kites. It's hard to imagine a better location for such a place than Long Beach, where there are more kites visible on storefronts than there are people during some portions of the year. The museum houses pretty much what you'd expect: an enormous collection of kites from around the world, as well as exhibits, workshops on all kinds of kite-related subjects, and a gift shop.

Leadbetter Point State Park and Willapa National Wildlife Refuge

Located at the northern tip of the Long Beach Peninsula, **Leadbetter Point State Park** is—if it's a clear day, that is—home to some of the most-scenic views on the West Coast. A portion of the **Willapa National Wildlife Refuge** lies to the north of the park. One word you'll hear used a lot around here is "pristine," and the refuge is just that. It's an estuary where ecosystems remain untouched, and migratory birds can rest in virtual peace in the vast wetlands. That doesn't mean you can't catch a glimpse of them.

SPORTS AND RECREATION

Hiking in Cape Disappointment State Park

To reach the two trailheads below, take Highway 101 to Ilwaco and head west at the stoplight to Cape Disappointment State Park.

North Head Trail

Distance: 3.4 miles round-trip
Duration: 1-2 hours
Elevation gain: 160 feet
Effort: Easy
Trailhead: McKenzie Head parking lot, Cape Disappointment State Park

North Head Trail travels through a marshy area and up an often-slippery rocky ridge to a parking lot, where you'll find the trailhead that leads down past the lighthouse keeper's quarters to the 65-foot-tall North Head Lighthouse. That there's often water on the trail shouldn't be much of a surprise, given that the trail is adjacent to the ocean and it's surrounded by coastal old-growth trees.

Discovery Trail

Distance: 8.5 miles round-trip
Duration: 1-2 hours
Elevation gain: 300 feet
Effort: Easy
Trailhead: Cape Disappointment State Park

The Discovery Trail is by far the most-used

path on the Long Beach Peninsula. Depending on what you're looking to see, it's arguably the most interesting. The trail runs from Ilwaco to Long Beach, but there are several spots along the way you can either jump on, or off, it. Starting near a bronze condor at the Port of Ilwaco, the trail heads west on Main Street, traveling through town and through the Beard's Hollow parking lot. When you hit the beach, you'll be wandering across sand dunes into Long Beach. The end of the trail is located a short distance from Clark's Tree, a bronze sculpture commemorating a carving explorer William Clark made in a pine tree in 1805. For a current view from the spot, check out the tree cam (www.funbeach.com/treecam). Other sights along the trail include the skeleton of a gray whale and a sculpture of Clark watching over a 10-foot-long sturgeon.

Hiking in Willapa National Wildlife Refuge

To reach the two trailheads below, head south on Highway 101 out of Aberdeen for 57 miles to the Willapa National Wildlife Refuge at Leadbetter Point. Both trailheads are at the western end of the parking lot.

Bearberry Trail

Distance: 1.8 miles round-trip
Duration: 30 minutes
Elevation gain: None
Effort: Easy-moderate
Trailhead: Willapa National Wildlife Refuge

Also known as the Yellow Trail, this path cuts east to west across the refuge, taking hikers through sand and thick salal to the beach and an opening where you can view a spot where snowy plover birds nest during certain times of the year. The snowy plover nesting area is beautiful to look at if the birds are there.

Dune Forest Loop Trail

Distance: 2.8 miles round-trip
Duration: 1 hour
Elevation gain: None
Effort: Easy-moderate
Trailhead: Willapa National Wildlife Refuge

Dune Forest Loop Trail (Red Trail) is the longest in the area and connects to **Weather Beach Trail** (Blue Trail) to create a 0.9-mile path to the coast. When you hit the coast, you sometimes can walk up it all the way to the tip of Leadbetter Point, although tides and flooding often make this trek impossible. The Dune Forest Loop Trail takes you exactly where its name implies—through dunes and forest—and offers frequent views of pristine Willapa Bay.

Water Sports

Those who feel tempted to venture out in the water that's surrounding them here have plenty of options in addition to simply wading out into the ocean from approaches such as the one at popular **Waikiki Beach** near the Lewis and Clark Interpretive Center.

For razor clam diggers, being on the "World's Longest Beach" simply means more spots to dig for the sharp-shelled bivalves. A license is required to do so, and clamming must be open for digging, so it's necessary to check with the state Department of Fish & Wildlife (www.wdfw.wa.gov) before heading out. The same goes for other recreational fishing, including crabbing, which can be done at the jetty at Cape Disappointment State Park and the **Port of Peninsula** in Nahcotta, located at the end of 273rd Street and Sandridge Road.

If you're in the area, or the state, for only a short period of time, consider purchasing a two-day nonresident license (www.wdfw.wa.gov) and head to the water to fish for sturgeon, halibut, perch, and more. Beard's Hollow is one good place to fish for surf perch. Oftentimes, the best bet for newcomers looking to make those fish tales come true is to hook up with the pros and let them do most of the work. The fishing village of Ilwaco is where you'll find such places. **Beacon Charters** (322 Elizabeth St., 360/642-2138, www.fishbeacon.com), **Coho Charters** (237 Howerton Way SE, 360/777-8475, www.cohocharters.com), and **Pacific Salmon Charters** (191 Howerton Way SE,

360/642-3466, www.pacificsalmoncharters.com) are three good options.

Golf

Willapa Harbor Golf Course (2424 Fowler Rd., Raymond, 360/942-2392, $26 for 18 holes) is a nine-hole course with several sets of tees, which keeps the course fresh for those wishing to play a full 18.

Peninsula Golf Course (9604 Pacific Hwy., 360/642-2828, www.peninsulagolfcourse.com, $25 for 18 holes) is a nine hole public course one mile north of downtown Long Beach.

Near Ocean Park, **Surfside Golf Course** (31508 J Pl., 360/665-4148, www.surfsidegolfcourse.com, $32 for 18 holes) is another nine-hole, regulation-length course that's open to the public. There is a driving range, putting green, and pro shop here.

ENTERTAINMENT AND EVENTS

Raymond

The first weekend in August in Raymond means it's time for the **Willapa Harbor Festival** (360/942-5419), also known as Wet and Wild on the Willapa. The event kicks off Saturday with a pancake breakfast and includes a car show, salmon barbecue, parade, street dance, entertainment, and more, before ending with brunch Sunday.

In the neat and supposedly haunted Hannan Playhouse, **The Willapa Harbor Players** (518 8th St., 360/934-8329, $10) stage several shows a year, and have been doing so for decades.

South Bend

Labor Day Weekend is South Bend's time to shine, and to capture the attention of the thousands of motorists passing through the city, with its **Come and Play on Labor Day** (360/942-5419) festival. A mile-long parade of floats takes over Highway 101, taking the two-lane road down to just one lane. Even when the parade isn't happening, it's impossible to miss the activities here. Large signs over the road inform drivers as to what's going on, and festivities line the roadside downtown. It's part celebration, part opportunity for local politicians to campaign, and part tradition: The event has been held for roughly 50 years.

Ilwaco

The Saturday Market (360/642-3143, 10am-4pm, Apr.-Sept.) at the Port of Ilwaco features vendors selling produce directly from the farm, art, flowers, crafts, and a variety of food.

Labor Day Weekend means garage sales, 28 miles of them, to be exact. That's what the **World's Longest Garage Sale** is. There's no central location, no guide to take you to the sales. Just look for signs throughout the area and search for treasures.

Mid-August, when it's actually sunny here, may not be the time to think about the actual blues, but it is the time to think about the **Blues and Seafood** festival, held at the Port of Ilwaco. The Friday-Saturday event kicks off a weekend full of music in the area, as the annual **Jazz and Oysters** festival is held that Sunday up the road in Ocean Park.

In mid-October, during the local cranberry harvest, the **Cranberrian Fair,** a tradition that's been going on for more than 90 years, is held. Many of the festivities are held at the Columbia Pacific Heritage Museum, and that's also where you can catch the Cranberry Trolley to visit the Pacific Coast Cranberry Research Foundation and the **Cranberry Museum** (360/642.5553, www.cranberry-museum.com, 10am-5pm daily Apr. 1-Dec. 15, appointment only rest of year) in Long Beach, where you can take a self-guided tour of a cranberry farm and see how the popular fruit is grown and harvested.

Long Beach

Those who happen to be in the vicinity of Long Beach on the Fourth of July generally do one of two things: Vacate the area so as to avoid the mass of humanity set to descend upon it, or buck up and go along for the crazy ride that is the city's **Fireworks on the Beach** celebration. The fireworks are set off just after dark in front of the half-mile-long Long Beach Boardwalk, but the thousands of people hoping to see them crowd Highway 103 into town much earlier than that. Those in the know arrive far in advance of the spectacular show. Those even smarter, rent a hotel room within walking distance, and do so far in advance.

The third full week of August—yes, the entire week—is devoted to the **Washington State International Kite Festival,** which draws tens of thousands of kite-loving spectators and renowned kite flyers from all over the world for various competitions. A similar, yet smaller, two-day festival, **The Windless Kite Festival,** is held every January inside the Long Beach School Gym.

Every Thanksgiving Day weekend, a tree-lighting ceremony and a birthday celebration for Frosty the Snowman is held during **Holidays at the Beach.**

Ocean Park

North of Long Beach along Highway 103 lies the much quieter town of Ocean Park, where the **Northwest Garlic Festival** draws dedicated bulb lovers from across the area the third week of every June. Live entertainment, garlic-related crafts, games, and foods, including garlic soup, are highlights.

Ocean Park also holds its **Old Fashioned Fourth of July Parade** each year to coincide with the large fireworks show at Long Beach. During the second week of September, the **Rod Run to the End of the World** fills the town with music, parades, people, and classic cars.

SHOPPING

Long Beach

Half-reptile, half-man, 75-year-old (or so) Jake the Alligator Man is the face—and scaly body—of **Marsh's Free Museum** (409 S. Pacific Ave., 360/642-2188, www.marshsfreemuseum.com, 9am-6pm daily), an eclectic, kitschy, and outright fun place to spend a couple hours' time. There are century-old machines on which you can view a peep show, play baseball, or get your fortune told. There are antiques and trinkets for sale, taxidermy experiments, and even a bowl made from human skin and a human tapeworm in a bottle. But Jake the Alligator Man is the real attraction here. He even has his own fan club, line of merchandise, and song (set at a bar in Long Beach and written and performed by Seattle's Ghetto Monks). Was the now-mummified Jake once really alive? Find out more at his website (www.jakethealligatorman.com). He even has a blog.

Many visitors come to Long Beach to slow down, and oftentimes the best place to do that is just by sitting down with a book in one hand and a cup of coffee in the other. **Banana Books** (114 3rd St. SW, 360/642-7005, noon-5pm Mon.-Tues. and Fri., 11am-6pm Sat.-Sun.) is a great place to do that here. Books of all genres are literally spilling from the shelves here. Sit outdoors and relax.

Another good, possibly great, cup o' joe as well as a place to relax and enjoy it, can be found at **Long Beach Coffee Roasters** (811 Pacific Ave. S., 360/642-2234, www.longbeachcoffee.com, 7am-4pm Mon.-Sat., 8am-4pm Sun.). The coffee here is roasted on-site, so it doesn't get much fresher. For about $14, you can purchase bags of coffee to take home with you. There's even one medium roast called Beards Hollow, named after the area where a boat captain died in the 1800s.

For more than 25 years, **The Candy Man** (115 Pacific Ave., 360/642-2666, www.shopcandyman.com) has been producing its candy, chocolate, and taffy for sweet tooths near and far. There are 16 flavors of fudge here, including a unique cranberry variety.

Ocean Park

There's truly a little bit of everything at **Jack's Country Store** (26006 Vernon Ave., 888/665-4989, www.jackscountrystore.com, 7am-8pm daily), from groceries to hardware, outdoor gear to toys and games. But that's not necessarily its main appeal. Built in 1885, four years before Washington was a state, the store's main appeal is its infrastructure: stained

Heidi's Inn in Ilwaco is conveniently located.

glass ceilings, oak cabinets, and rolling track ladders.

Adelaide's Books and Coffee (1401 Bay Ave., 360/665-6050, www.adelaidescoffee.com, 7am-4pm Tues.-Sat.) is almost as old as Jack's. Well, at least the building is. It was built in 1887 as the Taylor Hotel, and today it is home to books, coffee, and various events.

Art lovers will find plenty of places to choose from in Ocean Park. Among the best are **Bay Avenue Gallery** (1406 Bay Ave., 360/665-5200, www.bayavenuegallery.com, 10am-5pm Wed.-Sat., 10am-4pm Sun.) and **Willapa Bay Tile and Design** (360/665-4763, www.willapabaytile.com), artist Renee O'Connor's custom tile-design business. O'Connor's work can be seen at various places across the Long Beach Peninsula.

ACCOMMODATIONS

Ilwaco

Heidi's Inn (126 Spruce St., 360/642-2387 or 800/576-1032, www.heidisinnilwaco.com, $49-105 d) in Ilwaco probably is the best deal on the peninsula for those simply looking for a basic place to stay with little frills attached. It's a short distance from activity central in downtown Long Beach and right near the nation's newest state park, Cape Disappointment, and Lewis and Clark National Historic Park. Recent remodels have made this property a more appealing choice than it was in the past—and it wasn't bad before.

Want to have a small wedding near the beach, hold your reception, and have a place for your guests to crash on-site after all is said and done? ★ **Inn at Harbour Village** (120 Williams Ave. NE, 360/642-0087 or 888/642-0087, www.innatharbourvillage.com, $115-185 d) in Ilwaco is one place where you can do so. That's because there's a 120-seat chapel here. There are only nine guest rooms and one suite here, however, so if you're pushing capacity at the chapel, some of your out-of-town guests may have to stay elsewhere.

Long Beach

Unless you're visiting the area in the off-season or traveling in an RV, cheap lodging isn't easy to come by on the Long Beach Peninsula. One decent option is **Our Place at the Beach** (1309 S. Ocean Beach Blvd., 360/642-3793 or 800/538-5107, $94-119 d). The 23-room property is newly remodeled and conveniently located just south of the World Kite Museum and Hall of Fame. Two family suites have full kitchens and baths.

This modern-looking hotel seems a bit out of place in Long Beach, but **Adrift Hotel and Spa** (409 Sid Snyder Dr., 360/642-2311, www.adrifthotel.com, $115-270 d) is a great bet for those looking for decent prices and modern rooms like you'd find in downtown hotels in bigger cities. Some of the rooms have ocean views. There's even a bunk bed suite with two bunk beds and a king-size bed.

Spacious 1930s cottages at the approach to Bolstad Beach, **Akari Bungalows** (203 Bolstad Ave., 360/214-3222, www.akaribungalows.com, $178-230 d) offers king-size beds, fireplaces, and jetted tubs in each bungalow.

★ **The Breakers** (210 26th St.,

360/642-4414 or 800/219-9833, www.breakerslongbeach.com, $129-139 d) has at least one distinct advantage over most of its competitors: land. The beachfront resort is spread out across 24 acres of it, and has been around for more than 100 years. The apartment-style rooms actually are condos, and for a little more money ($199-289) you can rent an entire condo.

A Rendezvous Place B&B (1610 California Ave., 360/642-8877, www.rendezvousplace.com, $129-169 d) has rooms named after flowers that can be found in the beautiful gardens that surround the property. The Jasmine Suite ($219) has a two-person soaking tub and large living room.

Boreas B&B Inn (607 N. Boulevard St., 360/642-8069 or 888/642-8069, www.boreasinn.com, $179-199 d) may be somewhat hidden from view among the dunes, but it certainly isn't hidden from people's minds when they're thinking about finding a place to stay. The oceanfront inn offers three-course breakfasts, large common areas with fireplaces, and five guest rooms, all with private bathrooms. On the grounds, there's even a jetted spa located inside a wooden gazebo that's for private use and overlooks the sand dunes and the ocean. Romance and solitude at its finest. You won't get breakfast if you stay at the cottage next door, but the Yett Beach House ($150/night), another offering of the inn, does allow pets.

The name of **Lighthouse Oceanfront Resort** (12417 Pacific Way, 360/642-3622 or 877/220-7555, www.lighthouseresort.net, $89-189 d) pretty much sums up what there is to offer here. Yes, there is a small lighthouse onsite. Yes, the lodging (at least some of it) is next to the ocean. And, yes, this is a resort. There's a conference center with pool and hot tub, indoor tennis courts, and a dune trail leading down to the beach. Choose from one-, two-, or three-bedroom townhouses with fireplaces and full kitchens or semi-rustic cottages.

Perched atop sand dunes overlooking the ocean between Seaview and Long Beach, ★ **Inn at Discovery Coast** (421 11th St. SW, 360/642-5265 or 866/843-5782, www.innatdiscoverycoast.com, $125-199 d) is a boutique inn with simple rooms painted in earth tones. Each one has a TV, a large tub, and a deck overlooking the ocean. Opened in 2004, the inn is clean and modern.

Seaview

The ★ **Shelburne Inn** (4415 Pacific Way, 360/642-2442 or 800/466-1896, www.shelburneinn.com, $149-199 d) opened in 1896 as a retreat and has remained open since, reportedly making it the oldest, continuously running lodge in the state. There are 16 rooms (numbered 1-17, skipping "unlucky" 13) and each is uniquely Victorian-themed. Full breakfasts are provided each morning. A restaurant/pub is attached to the inn. Stained glass windows throughout help keep the retreat private though not always quiet.

Camping

Located five miles south of South Bend on Highway 101, **Bruceport County Park** (7807 Hwy. 101, 360/875-6611, $12 tents, $21 full hookups) offers 40 lots on Willapa Bay.

You can reserve campsites at **Cape Disappointment State Park** up to nine months in advance, and if you want a spot here during some of the busier summer festivals such as the Washington State International Kite Festival or the Fourth of July, it's best to count back nine months from the date of the event and, um, campout by your computer (www.parks.wa.gov) or phone (888/226-7688). And that's with more than 250 campsites, including some 75 utility sites, and several one-room cabins and yurts available. If you're lucky and willing to spend quite a bit more, you can stay at one of three **Lighthouse Keeper's Residences** here. Residence 1 ($291 night) is a pretty, red-roofed, fully furnished house with three bedrooms and full kitchen that sleeps six. Residence 2 ($291) also has three bedrooms and is fully furnished. The Head Lighthouse Keeper's Residence is $412 a night, has hardwood floors and, as one might expect, offers an excellent view of the ocean. It also sleeps six.

Private campsites are abundant in the area. Most are located along Pacific Highway and have advertising signs along the way to their site.

Located three miles north of Long Beach near Oceanside, **Andersen's RV Park** (1400 138th St., 360/642-2231, $38 standard sites, $46 ocean sites) doesn't allow tenters, but it does feature a laundry room, free wireless Internet, a fish-cleaning station, and restrooms with showers, all just a short stroll down windswept Dunes Trail to the ocean.

Those hoping to escape both the crowds—and children and young adults—would do best to choose **Cranberry RV Park** (1801 Cranberry Rd., 360/642-2027, www.cranberryrvpark.com, $25-35). The pet-friendly park doesn't welcome anyone under the age of 40.

FOOD

Raymond

The place for hungry families to eat in Raymond is **Slater's Diner** (124 7th. St., 360/942-5109, www.slatersdiner.com, 11am-8pm Mon.-Thurs., 11am-9pm Fri.-Sat., noon-8pm Sun., $9-14), a restaurant with 1950s decor, and an oyster burger that's superb.

Long Beach

Guarded by a larger-than-life parrot, the bar at **Castaways Seafood Grille** (208 Pacific Ave. S., 360/642-4745, www.castawaysseafoodgrille.com, 11:30am-close daily, $13-23) is nearly as colorful as the town it calls home. The restaurant is family-friendly and has a menu especially for kids.

You'll first notice the bright yellow surfboard out front with the word "Smoothies" painted on it, but it's sandwiches that **Surfer Sands** (1113 Pacific Ave. S., 360/642-7873, 11am-4pm Mon.-Sat., $9-14) does best, especially the grilled steak ones.

For lovers of simple seafood, a trip to any beach generally means at least one cup of clam chowder, and what better place to get one than the small house that is ★ **Captain Bob's Chowder** (609 Pacific Way S., 360/642-2082, www.captainbobschowder.com, $5-11), where chowder is its main focus. **Dooger's Seafood & Grill** (900 Pacific Ave. S., 360/642-4224, 11am-8pm daily, $6-10) also has an award-winning chowder.

A spicy plate of pad thai and many other excellent noodle dishes await diners at **Long Beach Thai Cuisine** (1003 Pacific Ave. N., 360/642-2557, 11:30am-8pm Thurs.-Tues., $9-14).

Entering the town, you'll see the signs. "Grand Tsunami Burger: Can You Survive It?" If you'd like to try, you'll need to head to **The Corral Drive-In** (2506 Pacific Ave., 360/642-2774, 11:30am-8:30pm daily, $7-11), a basic-looking burger stand with no seats inside but with a covered ordering area. And the Tsunami Burger? Let's just say it truly is "the big one" capable of wreaking mass destruction to your heart and, if you're not careful when you eat it, to your clothing.

Take a quick glance into the well-lit glass display cases at the **Cottage Bakery** (118 S. Pacific Ave., 360/642-4441, 8am-4pm daily, $2-4) and next thing you know, you're walking out of this tidy shop off the main drag with a box full of cookies, donuts, and maybe a peanut butter muffin or two.

Probably the most popular place to eat on Long Beach nowadays, especially for families, is **The Lost Roo** (1700 S. Pacific Hwy., 360/642-4329, www.lostroo.com, 11:30am-close, $10-16). The kangaroo-themed restaurant is a spacious place that has something on the menu for nearly all types of diners.

Ocean Park

Full Circle Café (1024 Bay Ave., 360/665-5385, 7am-5:30pm Wed.-Sun., $8-22) claims to be Ocean Park's best-kept secret. While the "secret" part certainly isn't true, the restaurant is close to being the best, if for no other reason than its fresh-baked pastries.

Seaview

★ **The 42nd Street Café** (4201 Pacific Way, 360/642-2323, www.42ndstcafe.com,

8:30am-4pm daily, $15-25) is open for all three meals and has won multiple local and regional awards for its food. There are seafood specials each day, and many items on the menu are made from scratch. A fine selection of Northwest wines also are available, many from Oregon's Willamette Valley. As the café's slogan states, this is gourmet comfort food.

Housed in a former train station, ★ **Depot Restaurant** (1208 38th Pl., 360/642-7880, www.depotrestaurantdining.com, 5pm-10pm daily, $20-34) may only serve dinner, but it does what it does very well. The entrées aren't cheap, but the food you get isn't, either. French-cut veal chops glazed with Jack Daniels whiskey and Southern Comfort pork (notice the alcohol theme here?) are two favorites.

Chico's Pizza Parlor (4301 Pacific Hwy., 360/642-3207, noon-9pm Mon.-Fri., noon-10pm Sat.-Sun. $10-15) is what a pizza joint should be: a not-so-stuffy place where you can get a little loud and crazy while noshing on some thin-crust specialties. Chico's is a little spendy, though, for what you get.

INFORMATION AND SERVICES

The **Willapa Harbor Chamber of Commerce** (415 Commercial St., Raymond, 360/942-5419, www.willapaharbor.org) is the place to visit for those seeking information on the northern portion of Pacific County, including the towns of Raymond and South Bend.

Long Beach is so popular during summer months that it has its own activities hotline. The **Long Beach Info-Line** (800/835-8846) plays a recorded message of what's coming up in the area. To speak with an actual person, contact the **Long Beach Peninsula Visitors Bureau** (3916 Pacific Way, Seaview, 360/642-2400 or 800/451-2542, www.funbeach.com).

GETTING THERE AND AROUND

There are two good driving routes to get to Long Beach from Sea-Tac Airport. You can either drive south on I-5 to Olympia, head west to Aberdeen and south on coastal Highway 101 from there (three hours) or drive south on I-5 to Longview and cut across into Oregon and back north (3.5 hours). To get to the Long Beach Peninsula from Raymond, head south on Highway 101 to Seaview. The driving distance is 47 miles and it takes roughly 1.5 hours to get there, especially during busy seasons because the highway is difficult to pass on.

Pacific Transit System (360/642-9418 or 800/642-9418, www.pacifictransit.org) serves nearly every city in Pacific County, including the Long Beach Peninsula, Raymond, and South Bend. It connects to the north to Aberdeen, and even makes a run south to Astoria, Oregon. But take note, buses do not run through the Long Beach Peninsula on Sundays.

Background

The Landscape

Defining the Olympic Peninsula is not as easy a task as it might seem at first glance. Even cartographers disagree as to exactly where the southern border of the Olympic Peninsula is. A peninsula, by definition, is a body of land surrounded by water on three sides. To the north, the land here is bordered by the Strait of Juan de Fuca. To the west, it's bordered by the Pacific Ocean. To the east, there's the Hood Canal and Puget Sound. All bodies of water. But to the south, there's only land, so it's difficult to determine where that "body of land" begins. Liberal definitions include towns such as Elma, Aberdeen, Westport, and Ocean Shores, while conservative definitions exclude them. For the record, though its name makes it sound as if it might be, no definition of the peninsula includes the state capital of Olympia, as it's too far east. The capital and the peninsula are both, however, named after the Olympic Mountains, which are part of the peninsula and are a prominent backdrop often seen north of the city.

Those mountains are some of the youngest in the world, and part of the Coast Range, which runs along the entire coast of North America, from Alaska into Mexico. The most common theory says they arose from the sea, when the mountainous sea floor plate pushed up against the continental plate and the underwater mountains ended up on top of the continental plate.

The Olympics aren't particularly tall, as are the Cascades to the east. The Olympics also aren't volcanic, as the Cascades are. During the Pleistocene era, massive sheets of ice helped carve the mountains, as did alpine glaciers. Today, there are some 266 glaciers in the Olympics, most of them so small that they are hardly noticed. The glaciers are remnants of what used to be the massive glaciers that carved the area's waterway and created many of the area's lakes. Not surprisingly, the largest glaciers here are located on the highest peak, nearly 8,000-foot-high Mount Olympus. Of those, Blue Glacier is the largest and the most-studied. It's roughly two square miles, and has been shrinking for the past several hundred years, its melted waters eventually ending up in the Hoh River. Between 1987 and 1996, Blue Glacier lost 100 feet of thickness. Other glaciers on Mount Olympus include the Hoh, which is the longest glacier in the Olympics and also feeds into the Hoh River, Hubert, Jeffers, and White. Many of the peninsula's glaciers are accessible via the myriad trails that circle through and around the Olympics.

CLIMATE

First-time visitors to the Olympic Peninsula often come away shocked at how varied the climate here actually is, and how nice the weather can be during certain parts of the year. Summer temperatures, in fact, average in the 70s, sometimes hit 80, and occasionally climb into the 90s. Then, marine air typically cools things down in the evenings to somewhere in the 40s or low 50s. A typical summer day on the peninsula, if there were such a beast, would begin with a low morning fog that would burn off by midday and stay gone most of the day while things heat up. Lower elevations near the water see more fog than do inland areas and areas of higher elevation. That doesn't mean summers are rain-free, but major accumulations do not typically occur during this time of year, at least not at the same levels they do the rest of the year.

Early fall is when things begin to cool down and the rain begins to drop. Beginning

Previous: driftwood on Rialto Beach; Cline Spit, Sequim.

in October, winds also begin to pick up. While it's not out of the question for an early-October day to hit a high of 70°F, it's more likely the high will be somewhere in the 50s or 60s. Nighttime temperatures often dip into the 30s during fall, and sometimes drop below freezing, which can make driving treacherous on the peninsula's many icy, shady roads. Winter temperatures average in the 40s during the day, and fall to the 30s, or even the 20s, during the night. At lower elevations, snow is rare and when it does fall, it seldom stays around long. However, the opposite is true at higher elevations inside Olympic National Park. Hurricane Ridge, for example, sits a mile high and has a snowpack deeper than 10 feet for most of the winter. More than 400 inches of snow falls there annually.

What snow does accumulate begins to melt in the spring as the temperatures start their rise and rain begins to fall. Temperatures rarely drop below freezing, even on the coldest of nights, and rarely top 60°F on the warmest of days.

Tornadoes, while extremely rare, have touched down on the peninsula. In January 1921, a storm featuring winds estimated at 150 mph blew down eight billion board feet of old-growth timber in the Hoh River Valley and across the rest of the western peninsula. Storms of that magnitude are atypical, but high winds do occur each year, and they often topple trees and power lines. In some areas along the ocean beaches and in the Quinault Valley, for example, residents lose electricity to their homes several times a year, sometimes for days at a time.

Visitors need to keep in mind that there are some areas where "typical" weather patterns do not necessarily apply. Cities located in the northeastern portion of the peninsula, such as Sequim, Port Angeles, and Port Townsend, benefit from being located in a rain shadow created by the Olympic Mountains and see significantly less rain each year than do places nearer to the Pacific Ocean such as Hoquiam, Quinault, and Forks.

History

PREHISTORY

The Olympic Peninsula may have been "known" to the rest of the world for only a few hundred years, but plenty of evidence has been uncovered showing that humans have inhabited the area for at least 14,000 years.

The biggest proof of early human existence on the peninsula was uncovered in August 1977 by Emanuel "Manny" Manis, who was using a backhoe to excavate his property in Sequim. Manis's goal was to build a permanent pond in which to store water for his cattle and his garden. After digging up what he initially thought were old logs, Manis quickly realized those logs were instead the eight-foot-long tusks of some unknown animal. Manis contacted a team of experts, and his backhoe soon gave way to the more-delicate tools of archaeologists.

Several bones were recovered at the site, including one rib bone that had another, smaller bone protruding out of it. The smaller bone was analyzed and determined to be the tip of a spear. The bones, which were determined to be from an ancient mastodon, dated back 14,000 years, proving that humans were living in the area and hunting animals at least that long ago.

Less than six months after Manis's discovery, his property was placed on the National Register of Historic Places. More digging was done at the site, and further evidence of human habitation was found. Cactus also was uncovered, suggesting that the Sequim Valley once was much drier than it is today. The mastodon's bones and tusks are now on display at the Museum and Arts Center in Sequim. In 2002, Manis's property was donated to The Archaeological Conservancy.

Exactly how those Native American mastodon hunters got to North America in the first place has for generations been a source of debate. One theory is that they came from Asia to Alaska during the end of the last ice age via a land bridge that once connected the two continents but now, thanks to a rise in sea level, lies underwater in the Bering Strait. From there, the theory contends, the Native Americans spread throughout the new continent, splitting into tribes and settling in places such as the Olympic Peninsula, where the climate was mild and natural resources were abundant. Over the years, evidence of ancient Native American villages has been uncovered elsewhere throughout the peninsula, including at James Island off the coast at La Push and near Port Angeles Harbor.

Native Americans don't necessarily subscribe to the land bridge theory. Their cultural records—not written, but oral—often mention times when their people lived among the animals, and that the land they live upon is the same place they have lived for all time. As such, most tribes teach their members to be stewards, not abusers, of the land and all that lives and grows upon it.

What archaeological evidence has shown, regardless of where it was found, was that the daily lives of the various indigenous tribes were similar. Most tribes resided near the coast, which allowed them access to the ocean, and the fish, clams, crab, seal, and whales provided them with ample food. For example, the Makah Indians, residing on the northwestern tip of what is now Washington State, carved canoes from massive cedar trees and used them not only to navigate local rivers but also to traverse the choppy saltwaters of the Strait of Juan de Fuca and the Pacific Ocean, which bordered their territory. They even hunted whales far out in the open ocean. During summer, camps were set up near various bodies of water so the Native Americans could harvest as much food as possible. Much of the food was dried or smoked, and little of the killed animal was wasted. Skin became clothing. Bones and teeth became tools and weapons. Blubber became cooking oil. After each kill, the Makah would say a prayer of thanks. During the wetter months, the Makah would move inland to drier settlements less prone to flooding and live off their harvest.

Around 1700, a large mudslide on the shores of Lake Ozette buried an entire Makah village. In the 1960s, remnants of the village were uncovered by storm-related erosion and archaeologists began excavating. That work continued for years, and uncovered more than 55,000 artifacts, many in great shape thanks to the clay and mud they were buried in, which had protected them for centuries. Evidence uncovered at the site suggested the Makah had lived there for thousands of years. The well-preserved artifacts included several Makah homes, or longhouses. Many of the artifacts are now on display at the Makah Cultural and Research Center in Neah Bay. Though the Makah living on the reservation today utilize modern conveniences such as computers, cell phones, and store-bought clothing, they also learn about the history and practice the ways of their ancestors in order to preserve their unique culture. The history of the Hoh, Quinault, Quileute, and other coastal tribes is similar to that of the Makah.

EARLY EXPLORERS AND STATEHOOD

Juan de Fuca, a Greek explorer who adopted a Spanish name, often is given credit as being the first nonindigenous human to sail around the Olympic Peninsula. He did so in 1592, as captain of a Spanish vessel searching for the Strait of Anian. The strait commonly was believed to be the mythical Northwest Passage, a direct link between the Pacific and Atlantic Oceans. When he returned home, de Fuca claimed he had found the Anian and claimed it for the viceroy of Mexico. Historians, however, question whether de Fuca found any strait at all. If he did, it certainly wasn't the Northwest Passage, which doesn't exist, but rather a waterway that paralleled the

Indigenous Past and Present

The history of people living on the coastal Olympic Peninsula goes back at least 14,000 years—a fact that was handily confirmed in 1977 when a Sequim resident dug up the skeleton and tusks of an ancient mastodon. Toolmarks were found on the animal's bones and a spear point was embedded in one of its animal's ribs.

Most of the coastal tribes settled for easier prey, living on a diet heavy in fish and shellfish. The Makah, however, have a whaling tradition that goes back centuries, a tradition halted for nearly 70 years by international anti-whaling treaties, briefly revived in the 1990s, and then put on hold again thanks to the threat of legal action.

The treaties establishing the current reservations on the Olympic Peninsula were mostly signed in the 1850s, including the treaty that established the Makah Indian Reservation at Neah Bay and the treaty establishing the much larger Quinault Indian Reservation around Taholah and Lake Quinault. The Quinault Indian Reservation includes members of the Quinault, Chehalis, Quileute, Queets, Chinook, and Cowlitz tribes. The Quileute and Hoh tribes also have smaller reservations of their own to the north of the Quinault, as does the Lower Ozette branch of the Makah tribe. The tiny Shoalwater Bay Tribe Reservation (which sports a casino) lies to the south, and to the east toward Puget Sound are the Lower Elwha and Jamestown S'Klallam Reservations.

Most of the reservations have annual festivals and events, and some have museums and tribal centers open to the public. Stop by the following reservations to learn about Native American history and culture:

JAMESTOWN S'KLALLAM TRIBE

The small Jamestown S'Klallam reservation is a mere blip of land located off Highway 101 on Sequim Bay. The tribe operates the **Jamestown S'Klallam Tribe Northwest Native Expressions Gallery,** which has two locations: one inside the tribe's casino and one on the tribal campus. The campus location features a wall of masks and wood carvings, as well as shirts, hats, artwork, boxes, music, and jewelry. Some of the artwork and handicrafts are for sale.

MAKAH NATION

The entire northwestern tip of the Olympic Peninsula is home to the Makah Nation. Visit the fascinating **Makah Cultural and Research Center,** which features 18 showcases of tribe relics. Rotating exhibits in the past have included basketry, carvings, and photographs. There's even an outdoor botanical garden. The annual **Makah Days** celebration, held the last week of August, boasts traditional dancing and singing and canoe races.

QUINAULT INDIAN NATION

The Quinault Indian Nation is by far the largest reservation on the Olympic Peninsula. Tribal headquarters are located in the village of Taholah, which is the site of the annual **Chief Taholah Days** held the first week of July. This event serves to teach attendees about the Quinault Treaty, signed in 1855. The celebration features canoe races, a salmon bake, a parade, and fireworks.

SKOKOMISH TRIBAL NATION

The Skokomish Tribal Nation, also known as the "Big River People," has a reservation at the southwestern tip of Hood Canal at the mouth of the Skokomish River. The tribe operates the **Skokomish Tribal Center and Museum,** which is home to carvings, totem poles, masks, and tools, many of them hundreds of years old.

northern portion of what is known today as the Olympic Peninsula before making near-90-degree turns south toward present-day Canada and south into Puget Sound.

Whether de Fuca's story was true or not, English explorer Charles Barkley named the waterway the Strait of Juan de Fuca when he visited in 1787. By that time, the Olympic Peninsula had been fully discovered by Russians and Spaniards. Other English explorers followed, including Captain James Cook. American Captain Robert Gray was a fur trader who, in 1792, discovered the important deepwater harbor on the coast, which today bears his name, as well as the Columbia River to the south. The same year, English explorer Captain George Vancouver conducted a highly detailed trip of his own to the area. He visited modern-day Alaska, British Columbia, Washington, and Oregon, charting in detail each point he visited. Vancouver and his crew made their way through the Strait of Juan de Fuca and into Puget Sound (named after crewmember Peter Puget) and Hood Canal (named for Royal Navy Captain Lord Samuel Hood).

Those early expeditions opened the door for permanent settlers, who came to the area from far and wide. In November 1889, the same year Washington became a state, the *Seattle Press* newspaper led a call for "hardy citizens" to explore the Olympic Mountains. The exterior of the Olympic Peninsula was, by then, fairly well explored, but not much was known about its rugged interior. A 35-year-old Scotsman living in Yakima named James Christie answered the newspaper's call. He rounded up five other men (one who quickly dropped out), and traveled to Port Angeles, where they began their journey in December. While common sense would have indicated it would be better to begin such a trek in the spring rather than during the harsh winter, Christie was in a hurry. Many others were interested in making the trip, and he wanted to be first. His team traveled south by boat up the Elwha River. But the boat leaked and was abandoned. Then one of the team's two mules fell from a cliff and died. The men hiked slowly through one of the worst winters in recorded history, and made it to the headwaters of the Quinault River and into the Quinault Rain Forest in May 1890. They built a raft to float down the Quinault, and lost much of their supplies to the swift waters. When the men reached Quinault, they rented a horse-drawn wagon that drove them down to Aberdeen. From there, they returned to Seattle. The trek was considered a success, and today a small neighborhood park in Seattle even bears Christie's name.

OLYMPIC NATIONAL PARK CREATED

The Press Expedition paved the way for further exploration into the middle of the Olympic Peninsula, and soon it seemed as if everyone was heading off into the Olympic Mountains. Some went looking for gold. Some were fur trappers. Others simply wanted adventure. Homesteads popped up throughout the peninsula. Those homesteads concerned President Grover Cleveland enough that he decided to put an end to such land claims by declaring more than 2.1 million acres of forest, nearly two-thirds of the entire Olympic Peninsula, as the Olympic Forest Reserve in 1897. Cleveland's concern was simple: He wanted to protect the land from the development settlers would inevitably cause. Pressured by timber companies, President William McKinley reduced by 712,000 the number of acres in the reserve in 1900 and 1901. In 1907, the Olympic Forest Reserve was renamed the Olympic National Forest. In 1909, President Theodore Roosevelt created 610,000-acre Mount Olympus National Monument, located within the Olympic National Forest, in an effort to create a preserve for the area's threatened elk herds, which today are named after him. Again due to pressure from timber companies, President Woodrow Wilson removed 170,000 acres from the Mount Olympus National Monument.

After visiting the area, a fifth president, Franklin D. Roosevelt, signed an act creating

Waterfalls for All

Because there is snow runoff from the Olympic Mountains, and the coastline is often steep and full of jagged cliffs, there are literally hundreds of small waterfalls along the Pacific Coast and farther inland on the Olympic Peninsula, ranging from the majestic and remote Enchanted Valley to tiny seasonal falls that can be seen along nearly any highway in the backcountry. There are even falls that can only be seen by boat, most prominently the Hi Hi Kwitht Falls off the Makah Indian Reservation. Many of the more impressive and visually arresting falls are accessible to hikers, but waterfalls can be found from the Hood Canal's 420-foot Vincent Creek Falls all the way to the Pacific Coast's Fall Creek Falls, which are only 40 feet high but sometimes become level with the surf at high tide.

Wynoochee Falls at the Wynoochee Lake Campground is one of the few that empties into a swimming hole, albeit a cold one. Beaver Falls, near Forks, is only 20 feet high but is more than 70 feet wide, and resembles a miniature version of Niagara Falls.

The Olympic Peninsula Visitor Bureau and Grays Harbor Tourism have collaborated to produce the **Olympic Peninsula Waterfall Trail** project, a website listing some of the prominent waterfall features on the peninsula and grouping them for driving and day hike expeditions. The website (www.olympicpeninsulawaterfalltrail.com) includes maps, photos, and descriptions of the waterfalls and their locations.

Olympic National Park in 1938. In 1953, a large, mostly rugged strip of the Pacific Coast was added to the park by President Harry S. Truman to help protect Lake Ozette and much of the coast from development. Today, the park encompasses more than 922,000 acres, nearly 150,000 more than the state of Rhode Island, and includes mountains, beaches, and everything in between. The majority of the park lies directly in the middle of the Olympic Peninsula, which is surrounded by water on three of its four sides.

Plants and Animals

The Olympic Peninsula is a lush, green paradise full of flora and fauna that depend on the abundance of rain that falls on the area. The geographic diversity here, from the rocky Pacific Ocean beaches to the muddy river banks, mossy rainforests, grassy meadows, and snowcapped peaks of the Olympics, creates a variety of climates and, thus, is home to a variety of wildlife.

VEGETATION ZONES

Along the miles of Pacific Ocean shoreline known as the Olympic Peninsula's **Coastal** zone, you can find many coastal forests filled with Sitka spruce, western hemlock, and alder trees, as well as bunches of salal, which often is picked and sold to local floral businesses for use in their flower arrangements. Inland a bit, you'll find the **Lowland** zone, areas such as the Sol Duc and Elwha Valleys, and the Staircase area around Lake Cushman, where you can see some old-growth forests filled with Douglas firs and the sword ferns and trillium that line the floor from which they're growing. The **Temperate** zone includes the Hoh and Quinault Rain Forests, unique ecosystems where plants called epiphytes, such as licorice fern and cat-tail moss, smother the branches and trunks of ancient Sitka spruce, Douglas fir, western red cedar, alder, and maple trees. In the **Montane** zone, located at 1,500-4,000 feet, slower-growing trees such as the Alaskan yellow cedar and the silver fir begin to show up, as do various types of shrubs, including the huckleberry and the Oregon grape. Moving up into the **Subalpine** zone introduces colder conditions, which makes it more difficult for many types of trees and shrubs to grow. This is where many colorful wildflowers, such as wildgrass, lilies, heather, and violets, begin to stake their claim to the land. The **Alpine** zone is all but devoid of trees, but hearty and resourceful plants exist here, including the purple Piper's bellflower, which is unique to the Olympic Mountains and grows from cracks in rocks.

PLANTS

The state flower is the **rhododendron,** a hardy plant that boasts bright colors from red to shades of pinks, purples, and white. There are about 500 true species of the plant and several hundred more that are hybrids. Around the peninsula, you'll spot rhododendrons in landscaped yards, parks, and the wild. They are in full bloom in spring and early summer.

Deep in the Northwest forests, underneath the trees that provide them cover, you'll find shade-loving **ferns, moss,** and **mushrooms,** as well as wild **blackberry bushes** in summer and flowers such as the **western trillium** in spring. In the meadows where the sun shines brighter, wildflowers dot the tall green rolling hills from spring through summer. Common wildflowers on the Olympic Peninsula include **violets, lilies, alfalfa, honeysuckle,** and **mountain dandelions.**

TREES

Some of the world's biggest trees are rooted in the fertile grounds of the Olympic Peninsula; some are more than 300 feet tall, as tall as a 30-story building. The state tree, the **western hemlock, Sitka spruce, red cedar,** and **Douglas fir** literally are giants that only can be appreciated in person.

Two of the largest western hemlock and Sitka spruce trees can be found in the Quinault Valley. The largest Douglas fir is in Queets and it stands more than 300 feet tall. There's also a large red cedar near Kalaloch. It's a big, hollow trunk with thick Medusa-like roots that snake around it. It's not so tall anymore, but it's still super wide, and you can tell it was once even grander. Other common trees you'll see here are **Pacific silver firs** and along the coast red-barked, twisty **Pacific madronas.**

MAMMALS

Many people who travel to Washington's coastal beaches do so mainly wanting to see one animal—a whale. The coast, especially from late spring to early fall, is a great place to see **gray** and **humpback whales,** or if you're lucky, a pod of orcas, better known as **killer whales.** They do visit the Olympic Peninsula on occasion, although the best chance of seeing them is off-the-beaten path near the San Juan Islands in Puget Sound.

However, gray whales are common on the peninsula. You can take a tour or see them from the beach as they migrate back and forth from the Bering and Chukchi Seas to the warm waters of Baja California. See them heading south in November and December and north in March, April, and May. Gray whales can easily be spotted from the coast because they travel so close to it. They are large, sometimes up to 42 feet long, and when they exhale, they blow plumes of seawater up to 15 feet high. A spectacular sight if you happen to see one!

Those who ride the ferry across the Strait of Juan de Fuca to Victoria, British Columbia, often see what they believe to be killer whales, but most likely are **Dall's porpoises.** The porpoises resemble whales and can reach six feet in length and typically weigh more than 300 pounds. They are black with white markings and don't usually leap or breach but instead like to swim fast, sometimes near the surface where they ride bow waves caused by the ferries. **Harbor porpoises** are smaller, gray animals that live in the Puget Sound, but they are rarely seen.

Harbor seals sunning themselves on rocks, dark-brown barking **California sea lions,** and light-colored **Steller sea lions** also can be seen throughout the Olympic

Peninsula on ocean beaches and in Puget Sound waters.

After President Theodore Roosevelt visited the Olympic Peninsula and created the Mount Olympus National Monument (now Olympic National Park), it was fitting that at least one thing in the area be named after him. That thing turned out to be the area's elk. **Roosevelt elk,** as they're now called, have slightly smaller antlers than their cousins across the state in the Cascade Mountains.

Chances of spotting the elk are good, especially in and around the Lake Quinault area. **Deer, rabbits, squirrels,** and **raccoons** also frequently pop up across the peninsula. So do **black bears** and **cougars,** though thankfully with much less frequency.

Sometimes called pumas or mountain lions, cougars live throughout the Olympic Mountains. Cougars are the largest North American members of the cat family, with adult specimens weighing in at upwards of 100 pounds. Cougars hunt deer, elk, and moose, and are not above taking the occasional domestic cow, sheep, or family dog. They're usually brown to tan, with lighter fur underneath and dark markings on the face and tail. Of course, if you see one, you'll know what it is, especially if it's coming toward you!

Human encounters with cougars are rare, but they do occur. The first thing to remember in a cougar encounter is that running away is the worst thing you can do, because the cougar will assume you are a prey animal and immediately come after you. If you're with a small child, pick the child up so the child doesn't try to run. Facing the animal, talking to it in a loud and firm voice, and making yourself look bigger if possible (opening your coat, standing on a rock to look taller, etc.) can convince the cougar that you are a threat. Also, if the cougar is trapped, you should immediately get out of its way. And much like bears, cougars are fiercely protective of their young, so if a cub is around stay far away. Mama is likely watching from nearby, and she'll be extremely upset if she thinks you're threatening her little one. If all else fails, and the cougar attacks, fight back. It may be hard to believe, but it's true that the cougar is likely more afraid of you than you are of it.

BIRDS

Some estimates say there are more than 500 species of birds in Washington State. In spring, the Grays Harbor National Wildlife Refuge in Hoquiam is probably the hottest of spots for bird-watching, and Ediz Hook in Port Angeles, John Wayne Marina in Sequim, and the Theler Wetlands on Hood Canal are also good places to visit. In summer, Friends Landing near Montesano is a great place to see **ospreys, cormorants,** and **cedar waxwings,** and La Push is ripe with **brown pelicans** and **bald eagles.** Waterfowl are prominent at Potlatch State Park and elsewhere along Hood Canal during fall, and Dungeness Bay at Sequim is one of the best year-round sites.

Just showing up at the spot and looking for birds works quite well when conditions are optimal and birds are plentiful. But to really get the most of your experience, you need a field guide of some sort, either a book or a mobile app. Binoculars also are a must-have, and a good camera, preferably with a zoom lens, will come in handy.

There are several annual festivals dedicated to birds on the Olympic Peninsula. The Grays Harbor Shorebird Festival and the Olympic Peninsula BirdFest, both held in April, are among the best.

Once listed as an endangered species, the **bald eagle** today often can be spotted flying high in the Olympic Peninsula skies. Identifying the bird is easy, especially if it's at least four years old. It's at that age that the eagles grow their distinctive white head feathers. You'll often see giant eagle nests at the tops of trees. Some nests are over eight feet wide!

The **northern spotted owl** nests in old-growth forests along the Pacific Coast. In the late 1980s and early 1990s, environmental groups pushed for the owl to be listed on the threatened species list and succeeded. As a result, loggers were required to leave old-growth forest intact within 1.3 miles of any reported spotted owl activity or nesting area. Even with such protective measures, spotted owl populations still are shaky at best. It's unlikely you'll see one on your travels, but many other owls call the area home, too. Other prominent birds include the **kingfisher, red-tailed hawk, seagull,** and **hummingbird.**

MARINE LIFE

If you're a diver you even might encounter a 30-pound octopus or two in the Puget Sound, home to some of the largest species of **octopus** in the world. But don't worry, they aren't dangerous. Washington waters also are brimming with wildlife including fish such as **salmon** and **smelt,** and **crabs, starfish, jellyfish, sea cucumbers,** and more. As for fish, there are more species here than can easily be mentioned. However, the two most popular, both by those who like to fish and those who like to eat fish, are salmon and steelhead. You can catch various types of **salmon** in coastal rivers, such as the Chehalis, Hoh, and Humptulips; in marine areas such as Neah Bay and Westport; and in some rivers that flow into the Strait of Juan de Fuca and Hood Canal. And, of course, in the Pacific Ocean itself.

Winter-run **steelhead** are perhaps the most-prized fish to be had here. Steelhead are rainbow trout that go out to sea and return upriver in spring to spawn. The winter runs spawn closer to the ocean than do the summer runs, which means they are vulnerable to be caught when they are returning from sea. Good rivers for steelhead fishing include the Hoh, Bogachiel, and Quinault.

Government and Economy

GOVERNMENT

Conservation efforts from late-19th-century and early-20th-century politicians have played key roles in making today's Olympic Peninsula what it is. The most important role, at least symbolically, was played by President Franklin D. Roosevelt who, on June 29, 1938, signed the act establishing Olympic National Park. Roosevelt's move was made possible by several prior political moves, including President Grover Cleveland's 1897 proclamation, which created an Olympic Forest Reserve in the area, and President Theodore Roosevelt's 1909 creation of the Mount Olympus National Monument.

In the years since, politics have impacted the parks in other ways, with certain factions calling for boundaries to be adjusted. Most recently, a coalition of conservation groups has put together what's being called a Wild Olympics Campaign. The campaign's goal is to protect more of the area's wilderness, especially watersheds, by acquiring state and private lands and adding them to the Olympic National Park, as well as designating certain lands as wilderness. Opponents say the move is just a half-cocked land grab that will mean the loss of jobs, private homes, and access to some of the most utilized areas of the Olympic Peninsula. Several noteworthy politicians have entered the debate, which is ongoing.

ECONOMY

As it has for thousands of years, the land still is firmly in control of the economy and industry on the Olympic Peninsula, though not necessarily in the same ways it once was. The logging and fishing industries have fallen from their respective heydays, but both still are vital to the area's economy. But in recent years, the land has been used in a different way: as a promotional tool to help draw tourists. Many cities, towns, and counties are redoubling their efforts to market whatever particular draws they may have to bring outsiders in to see them.

History of Logging

Logging as a commercial enterprise on the Olympic Peninsula goes back to the establishment of the first permanent settlements, Port Townsend and Port Ludlow, in the mid-1800s. But the industry didn't really take off until the 1880s, when the railroad finally reached Olympia, and between then and World War I, the annual board feet of timber cut on the peninsula grew at such an alarming rate that concern was expressed by the public that all the trees would simply be cut down and nothing would be left.

This sentiment led directly to the formation of Olympus National Monument, in 1909, which protected more than 900,000 acres from cutting. This was later expanded to the current Olympic National Park by President Franklin D. Roosevelt in 1938.

Because timber companies were able to get in and buy such vast tracts of land before development could take place, the Olympic Peninsula became something of a petri dish for tree production, and the first American monoculture tree farms were established in the 1930s. A monoculture tree farm differs from a regular forest. Whereas a regular forest consists of many species of trees, monoculture tree farms are all the same species. Douglas fir, prized for its relatively fast growth, strength, and straight grain, is a favorite among tree farmers. Spruce is another common species, and during World War II, billions of board feet of spruce planking, much of it grown in the Pacific Northwest, formed the decks of American aircraft carriers.

The industry boomed through the 1940s and 1950s, as millions of new homes were built across America for servicemen using their benefits under the GI Bill. But a growing environmental consciousness and new laws to protect wildlife and habitat started a steady decline in the industry in the 1980s. It's a decline that continues to this day.

Lumber

There was a time when nearly every town on the peninsula seemed as if it were a mill town, or at least had a mill located somewhere near its city limits. Timber barons such as Frederick Weyerhaeuser, who along with 15 other partners purchased 900,000 acres of state timberlands from the Northern Pacific Railroad for $5.4 million in 1900, grew gigantic empires by cutting down trees and turning them into lumber for homes, paper, and numerous other goods. Forests were logged at a breathtaking pace. New technology helped companies such as Weyerhaeuser log even quicker. Within a couple of decades, most of the old-growth timber, at least that which wasn't on protected lands, had disappeared from area forests, replaced by unsightly clear-cuts and much smaller second growth.

The speed further increased in the 1980s, when companies logged as fast as they could ahead of environmental regulations that would severely limit the number of areas that could be logged. At the center of those regulations was the northern spotted owl, which had been declared an "indicator species" for the general health of old-growth forests and declared a threatened species under the Endangered Species Act. Several lawsuits were filed and a regional war of words broke out between loggers, and those towns who depended on timber dollars, and environmentalists. By 2000, timber harvest on federal lands was down 90 percent from its peak. As a result, thousands of local jobs disappeared, likely to never return. Ironically, even with the anti-logging regulations, spotted owl numbers have continued to decline. The current theory is that the decline is because the spotted owl's natural enemy, the barred owl, has invaded the spotted owl's territory and has either driven the spotted owl away or has been killing it.

Fishing

The Olympic Peninsula's commercial fishing industry also has declined in recent years. On the whole, fishing never has been as vital to the peninsula's economy as logging, but in some coastal towns fishing was the economy. Salmon and steelhead numbers have been in constant decline for more than 100 years, thanks to dams, pollution, overfishing, poor ocean conditions, habitat destruction, and many other factors. Thus, restrictions have been placed on commercial fishing and locals who once made good livings off the sea have either moved on to other professions or now spend seasons in Alaska, where fishing opportunities are more abundant than they are here.

Shipping

The ports of Seattle and Tacoma, and to some extent Longview and Vancouver, may be the biggest and best-known shipping centers in Washington, but smaller ports throughout the peninsula also do their fair share of domestic and international trade. The Port of Grays Harbor, for example, has diversified from shipping mostly timber to dealing with other products, as well. Business is booming and the port is expanding. In 2006, the port exported 276,000 metric tons. By 2011, that number had jumped to 1.4 million metric tons. Other ports in the region also have begun to diversify.

Tourism

Exactly how big a role will tourism play in the Olympic Peninsula's ever-evolving landscape? Can cities and residents that once farmed and harvested the area's abundant natural resources for income and sustenance come full circle and use those same natural resources differently by promoting them to visitors as a way of creating income to pay the bills? Just how far it will go is unknown, but the shift already is happening throughout the area. The city of Forks, once only known for its logging prowess, now is touting itself as a place where tourists can come and see all things *Twilight*. The coastal town of Aberdeen finally is beginning to tout its charms, which include a movie-star tall ship and an iconic musician and his rock-and-roll band, to bring people to its city. Sequim is promoting its abnormally dry weather; Port Townsend and Poulsbo their Victorian and Scandinavian heritages, respectively. Even the Native American tribes are turning to tourism as a source of income. The Squaxin Island Tribe has a luxurious resort, casino, and championship golf course outside Shelton. The Quinault Indians have a similar resort and casino outside Ocean Shores, and the Suquamish Tribe's accommodations at the Clearwater Resort on the Kitsap Peninsula are dream inducing. The list continues.

People and Culture

DEMOGRAPHY

Although nearly seven million people call Washington State home, most of them live along the I-5 corridor and elsewhere in the Puget Sound region, in larger cities such as Everett, Seattle, Tacoma, Bellevue, and Federal Way. With roughly 220,000 residents, the Olympic Peninsula remains rural, a little more than 30 people occupying each square mile. When including Kitsap Peninsula as part of the Olympic Peninsula, the population doubles to about 450,000.

The peninsula is less racially diverse than the rest of Washington. Ninety-four percent of the residents here are considered white, approximately 4 percent are Native American, and the rest are mostly Hispanic and Asian. There are a number of Native American tribes on the peninsula, including the Hoh, Jamestown S'Klallam, Lower Elwha Klallam, Makah, Port Gamble S'Klallam, Quileute, Quinault, and Skokomish. The Quinault and Hoh are the two largest reservations, each with about 1,400 members living there.

The peninsula does have a relatively large population of retirees, thanks mostly to the slower pace of life, cheaper cost of living, and the extraordinary number of sunny days found in the rain shadowed-area of the northeastern peninsula.

RELIGION

As a whole, Washington State isn't a particularly religious one. In fact, it consistently ranks as one of least-religious states in the country. Of those declaring a religion, nearly half say they are Protestant, one-quarter say they are not affiliated with a particular sect, 16 percent say they are Catholic, and the rest are divided among several other religions. Those trends hold true on the Olympic Peninsula, as well. The religion practiced here by Native Americans varies. Some are strictly Christians, while many other practice Indian Shaker, a form of religion that combines elements of Christianity with elements of traditional native religion, including a respect for nature and the belief in the existence of spirits.

LANGUAGE

As might be expected, English is the overwhelming language of choice spoken in households throughout the peninsula. What might not be expected is that approximately 6 percent of all those living here have said Spanish is the language most frequently used in their homes. All the Native Americans here speak English, although some also use their tribe's language to communicate with each other. Many of the Indian languages have gone extinct as the last generation speaking them has died. Some, such as the Quileute language, are on the verge of extinction. Recently, Quileute tribal elders have redoubled their efforts to pass their language on to students by making sure the subject is taught in local schools.

THE ARTS

Pop Culture

Clearly, the two best-known links the Olympic Peninsula currently has with the world of popular culture are *Twilight* and Kurt Cobain (1967-1994). *Twilight*'s link is a cursory one, due to the fact that author Stephenie Meyer decided to set her popular books in the rainiest area she could find, which turned out to be the Olympic Peninsula's town of Forks.

Cobain's link is deeper, and likely to last far beyond the point at which *Twilight* fades in popularity. Indeed, the musician already has transcended fad level and now is considered an international icon, frequently mentioned in the same breath as people such as Elvis Presley and John Lennon. Cobain created a large number of his songs while living here. He doesn't mention the names of cities and towns in his songs, as some writers might, but instead indirectly refers to the peninsula's people, places, and things. The most well-known example of such is the song "Something in the Way," which Cobain wrote about living underneath a bridge in his hometown of Aberdeen.

Along with his band Nirvana, Cobain often is credited with popularizing a style of rock music the mainstream press calls "grunge," basically a more-melodic form of punk rock frequently played with sludgy-sounding guitars. If any band deserves credit for the creation of such a sound, it would be Cobain's mentors, the Melvins, another band from the area that has seen some commercial success. Cobain's popularity was so immense at its peak in the early 1990s that people across the world even began imitating his style of dress. The style included flannel shirts that Cobain began wearing as a child because they kept him warm from the chilly Olympic Peninsula weather. Ironically, blue-collar workers had been wearing such shirts here for decades, and continue to do so today.

Crafts

Native Americans here always have been master craftspeople, mostly due to necessity. For centuries, they have carved canoes to aid them in their hunting and gathering, forged tools from bone, jewelry from animal teeth, made baskets from the bark of cedar trees. They still do those things today, although often more for commercial purposes than practical ones. You can find such items and more on sale in shops, on reservations, and at farmers markets throughout the area.

Essentials

Transportation

GETTING THERE

Almost every means of transportation will take you to the Olympic Peninsula, or at least get you close to it. Trains follow the I-5 corridor through Olympia, Seattle, and Tacoma. Buses connect at most train stations and travel a variety of directions, including to the peninsula. Major airlines fly out of **Seattle-Tacoma International Airport** and **Portland International Airport.** Smaller airports are scattered throughout the peninsula. Boats can take you from points beyond to almost any marina along the peninsula's coast, and ferries travel from Seattle throughout Puget Sound to the Kitsap Peninsula, Port Angeles, and Victoria, British Columbia. Despite the abundant transportation options, however, cars remain the most practical method of fully exploring the vast territory here.

Air

Seattle-Tacoma International Airport, or Sea-Tac for short, is the primary airport in the region and handles approximately 32 million passengers per year. It is one of the 20 busiest airports in the United States and welcomes flights from most major carriers. It is the main hub for **Alaska Airlines.** Although it's common to hear people saying they're flying "into Seattle," that's actually not the case. The airport is located in the city of SeaTac (without the hyphen), which is about 15 miles south of Seattle and 25 miles north of Tacoma. Visitors arriving at Sea-Tac en route to the Olympic Peninsula, then, wouldn't necessarily ever need to enter Seattle and could, instead, travel by car south through Tacoma and Olympia directly to the peninsula. However, travelers arriving at Sea-Tac who want to visit Seattle can head north on I-5, and then take a ferry to either Bainbridge Island or Bremerton, and access the Olympic Peninsula that way.

Train

Western Washington is well-served by **Amtrak** (800/872-7245, www.amtrak.com). The **Cascades** route runs north-south from Vancouver, British Columbia, through Seattle, Tacoma, Olympia, Centralia, and Portland, Oregon, before ending in Eugene, Oregon. The **Coast Starlight** route also runs north-south, from Seattle through Portland and the rest of Oregon and much of California, ending in Los Angeles. Amtrak's east-west route is called **Empire Builder,** and runs from Chicago through Milwaukee, Minneapolis, North Dakota, Montana, and Spokane, at which point you can either continue on to Seattle or branch off to Portland.

Car

The names of three major highways, all which are well-marked, are all travelers need to know to navigate the Olympic Peninsula and, for that matter, most of Washington. **I-90** brings travelers into the state from Idaho and points farther east. **I-5** enters Washington from the north near Vancouver, British Columbia, and from the south near Portland, Oregon. The most important highway for navigating the Olympic Peninsula is coastal **Highway 101,** which crosses over into Washington from Astoria, Oregon, heads north through Raymond, Aberdeen, and Forks, and then heads east through Port Angeles and Sequim before turning south and following Hood Canal through Shelton to Tumwater. The highway ends there at a junction with I-5.

Previous: ferry to Port Townsend; on the road in the Olympic Peninsula.

GETTING AROUND

Car Rentals

As you might expect, Sea-Tac Airport is a hotbed for car rentals. It can be a little more expensive to rent cars here than elsewhere in the area, but for the convenience, it's well worth it. Nine rental car companies have information counters at baggage claim, five of which have pickup and drop-off areas in the parking garage. Those that don't have cars on-site provide shuttles from the airport to their lots. Car prices vary from company to company, but one good one that is well represented across the peninsula is **Enterprise** (206/246-1953, www.enterprise.com).

Bus

County bus systems are cheap and plentiful here, but also problematic, in that the land area here is so vast and the systems generally only serve one particular area. This means public transportation is a great way to get around in certain cities and areas, but traveling between regions using only public transportation isn't an easy task. It actually can be done, but it really isn't worth messing with.

Ferry

With all of the water in Western Washington, it should come as no surprise that the **state's ferry system** (206/464-6400, www.wsdot.wa.gov) is the largest in the United States. More than 22 million people ride the state-run ferries each year. The ferries' main purpose is to connect the big cities on the eastern side of Puget Sound with those smaller areas to the west on the Olympic and Kitsap Peninsulas. Much of the traffic, then, are commuters who use the ferries to commute to and from work each day. Some of the ferries are passenger-only; others allow vehicles. All are operated on a first-come, first-served basis, so early arrival at the point of departure can be critical, especially during peak commute times. The larger ferries offer food service and other amenities.

Currently, the **MV *Coho*** (360/457-4491, www.cohoferry.com), operated not by the State of Washington but by the **Black Ball Line,** is the only ferry running across the Strait of Juan de Fuca from Port Angeles on the Olympic Peninsula to Victoria, British Columbia, on Canada's Vancouver Island. The ferry carries passengers, vehicles, and bicycles, and makes the trip three times a day from June-September and two times a day the rest of the year.

Accommodations

For most of the year, accommodations are fairly easy to come by on the Olympic Peninsula. There are exceptions to this rule, of course, and most of those occur during the summer months. From June through September, many of the more popular lodging options fill up, leaving unprepared travelers scrambling for places to stay and often having to drive miles to find an adequate place to rest their head. Big local festivals, which happen at various times during the summer throughout the region, also put lodging in high demand. It's not only hotels that fill up, either. Many of the better-known campgrounds, and even many of the lesser-known ones, can fill up fast. The best bet for those who plan to travel to the peninsula in the summer is to reserve ahead of time. On the flipside, great deals can be had in the off-season, when rooms and campgrounds often are nearly empty.

HOTELS AND MOTELS

As is the case most everywhere, the established cities here, including Port Angeles, Bremerton, Port Townsend, and Ocean Shores, offer the most lodging options, though that doesn't mean they necessarily are the first place one should look for hotels. After all, it isn't typically those cities that draw visitors to the Olympic Peninsula, but rather the unique attractions of Olympic National Park. Many of the park's main attractions aren't close to any cities, so by necessity have their own lodging options nearby. Sol Duc Hot Springs, for example, has its own resort, Lake Crescent has its own lodge, and Lake Quinault has both a resort and a lodge. There aren't as many budget chains here as you might find in and around bigger cities, either. That doesn't mean deals don't exist, just that it takes a little work to find one that is of quality and has the amenities you desire.

Hotels listed in this guide include average high-season rates for either single or double occupancy. They do not include sales or other local taxes. An important note on this issue is that rates here can change quickly and often vary dramatically based on demand and season. It isn't uncommon for a hotel to lower its rates on a whim to try and make sure its rooms are as full as possible on any particular night. If, for example, it's early evening, you don't have a place to stay, and you drive past a hotel with a lit vacancy sign, feel free to enter and negotiate. As long as you're nice about it, you may find yourself the recipient of a cozy and well-priced room for the night.

BED-AND-BREAKFASTS

There are great bed-and-breakfasts scattered across the peninsula, though exactly what you'll be getting for your money (and how much of that money you'll be spending!) varies widely. The best B&Bs here typically are located in the bigger cities, where rooms in large century-old homes have been renovated and converted into places reserved for overnight guests. The highest concentration of such spots is located in Port Townsend, although the Grays Harbor towns of Aberdeen and Hoquiam also have neat, large B&Bs, the one in Hoquiam being a 20-room National Historic Site on a hilltop locals simply refer to as "The Castle." One good thing about B&Bs is that, although they may cost as much as a typical hotel room, most every one includes a full breakfast each morning. For free. One bad thing is that some of the B&Bs here require the sharing of a bathroom with other guests.

CAMPING

Perhaps nowhere else in the world does the term "camping" have as many definitions as it does here. Some campgrounds here have fully furnished cabins with electricity and paved roads leading to the door. Others require a map and a full day's hike just to reach them, and are so poorly marked you might not even know you've arrived once you do. Some get so crowded during the summer that you'll need to book months in advance just to get a spot. Others are so desolate and hard to reach that hardly anyone ever stays there. Some are privately owned, and others are owned by the park. There's also everything in between. Two good resources for those hoping to camp on the peninsula include the **National Park Service** (360/565-3130, www.nps.gov/olym/planyourvisit/campgrounds.htm) or the **Olympic National Forest** (360/956-2402, www.fs.usda.gov/recmain/olympic/recreation).

Geocache Me If You Can

Geocaching is a relatively new treasure-hunting game in which people use their GPS devices or smartphones to locate waterproof containers, called geocaches, others have hidden somewhere outdoors. The geocaches contain logbooks and a writing utensil. Those who find a geocache must sign the logbook. Geocaches also often contain various items, such as small trinkets. Finders are welcome to take something from the geocache, but only if they leave something of equal or greater value in its stead. Those are the game's basic rules, although there are variations for more advanced players. There's plenty of geocaching happening on the Olympic Peninsula, because the area is rich with great hiding spots.

You can obtain geocaching information from several places online—the best is www.geocaching.com. According to the site, there are thousands of caches waiting to be discovered on the peninsula. They can be found over and over again, and the website allows people to comment on what the cache contained, when they found it, how hard it was to reach, and more.

Recreation

One of the main reasons people visit the Olympic Peninsula is the multitude of diverse recreational opportunities the area offers. Where else in the world could you go snow skiing or snowboarding in the mountains then, in less than an hour, be on a beach (albeit a cold one) surfing? Other recreational opportunities available include backcountry hiking, mountain biking, mountain climbing, rock climbing, fishing in both freshwater and saltwater, kayaking, biking, camping, sailing, beachcombing, cycling, waterskiing, and rafting.

The Olympic Peninsula sparks a lot of pride in its citizens. People here, because of their intense love for the area, also feel protective of the peninsula. Nature is respected here, and the focus for many is on conserving and preserving the environment. On your visit to the Olympic Peninsula, it is important to follow the basic rules of the land: Don't pick things you shouldn't, stay on the trails, don't feed the wildlife, and don't litter. Following these tenets will guarantee a successful and earth-friendly trip.

OLYMPIC NATIONAL PARK

Even those who are familiar with the way America's national park system works would do well to learn one important thing about Olympic National Park prior to visiting. Unlike many of the other parks you may have visited, such as Yosemite in California and Yellowstone in Wyoming, you can't drive through Olympic National Park. You can drive into the park at several spots, but you can't get from the west side of the park to the east, or the north side of the park to the south, without hopping on Highway 101 and driving around the park's perimeter.

At those parts of the park that you can drive into, you must purchase an **Olympic National Park pass** ($25 per vehicle, $20 per motorcycle, $12 per pedestrian or bicyclist, good for 7 consecutive days). Children 15 and under are admitted free of charge. An annual Olympic National Park pass also is available for $50. Passes can be purchased at park entrances. At press time, national park fees were under review. Call ahead to confirm. Those who would rather plan ahead, or who plan on visiting more than one national park during the course of a year, may best be served by buying an annual **America the Beautiful Pass** (888/275-8747, www.store.usgs.gov) for $80, good for all federal lands for one vehicle, its driver, and up to three passengers.

Surf's Up

You would think no one would be crazy enough to go surfing in the frigid waters of the northern Pacific Ocean. But you'd be wrong. **Westport** and **Ocean Shores,** both located at the mouth of Grays Harbor, are prime surfing grounds, as are many other spots on the coast. True, the water is cold, but the surfers gear up with wetsuits to insulate against the chill and hit the breakers anyway.

Westport even has its own annual surfing competition, the **Cleanwater Classic,** which takes place every May. More hardcore surfers who are holding out for bigger waves say, however, that the best surfing on the coast is around the Makah Indian Reservation at **Neah Bay,** not coincidentally the site of the stormiest and most turbulent water conditions, thanks to it being the place where the Pacific Ocean and the Strait of Juan de Fuca meet.

Other hot spots for good surfing are the beaches around **La Push,** where small channels and bays will sometimes funnel wave energy in and create unexpectedly high breakers, and the beaches around **Point Grenville** and **Cape Elizabeth** on the Quinault Indian Reservation.

Surfers should bear in mind that there are often few developed beach approaches in the areas where surfing conditions are best, and that local beach-use rules may be very different on Indian reservations. Also bear in mind that should an injury occur or something else go wrong, once you're out on the wild Pacific Coast, help may be many miles away. This can be especially important when you consider that the weather conditions that produce the best waves also produce large and unpredictable storms.

BACKCOUNTRY PERMITS

Anyone wishing to hike into Olympic National Park's backcountry on an overnight trip must first purchase a permit from the National Park Service. The permits, which are good for an entire hiking group, are $5 plus $2-7 per night per person. They can be purchased at the **Wilderness Information Center** (3002 Mount Angeles Rd., Port Angeles, 360/565-3500), the **Quinault Wilderness Information Office** (360/288-0232, two miles off Hwy. 101 on South Shore Rd., Lake Quinault), or at the **Forks Information Station** (551 Forks Ave., Forks, 360/374-7566).

Travel Tips

WHAT TO TAKE

As varied as the terrain and weather are here, it is important to pack a variety of clothes. You can pretty much guarantee a **jacket** of some sort will be necessary regardless of the time of year you visit. Even if it's summer and the temperatures are high and the skies are clear, which isn't all that common, you'll still need the jacket for evening strolls along the beaches or for higher-elevation hikes. Locals like to dress in **layers,** with T-shirts underneath fleece pullovers, underneath sweatshirts, underneath flannel shirts, underneath jackets. That many layers aren't always needed, but the weather does change frequently. A **light raincoat** can come in awfully handy at times, especially for treks in the rain forest, although many of the local shops do sell cheap plastic pullover ponchos and other rain gear for those who forget or would rather save room in their suitcase for something else.

Dress is casual on the peninsula. Even in the bigger cities, **jeans** are appropriate almost everywhere. Proper footwear also is important. There may be a place for sandals on the beach or in the cities during warmer days, but sturdy shoes or even **hiking boots** are a must-have for exploring at many popular sites. **Sunglasses** are helpful: When the

Know Before You Go

Have you ever gone somewhere and, upon leaving, said to yourself, "It was a great trip, but I wish I would have known . . ."? Here are some things to know before you visit the Olympic Peninsula:

- **Pack smart.** The weather here can change on a dime all year long. Be prepared for inclement weather and sunshine.
- **Carry extra supplies.** Gas stations on the peninsula can be few and far between, as can stores, hospitals, and ATMs. Carry snacks, medications, and emergency preparedness kits with you.
- **Bring extra cash.** There are several businesses on the peninsula that do not take credit cards, so be prepared with a little more cash than you might otherwise carry at home.
- **Bring your camera.** There's lots to see that you won't find anywhere else in the world. It's always a good idea to pack a spare memory card and extra batteries, just in case.
- **Look for landlines.** Cell phones don't work everywhere on the peninsula, so you can't rely on them to bail you out of an emergency.
- **Pack a map.** Don't exclusively rely on your car's (or cell phone's) GPS system. Technology is a good thing, but there are areas on the peninsula where the GPS may not be accurate.
- **Brave the storms.** To look more like a local, you have to act like one. Here, that means keeping the umbrella stowed away when there's only a slight mist. Definitely don't take it out for a major windstorm!
- **Drive smart.** Slow down when driving down tree-lined highways, especially around dawn and dusk. Deer and other wild animals can pop out of nowhere onto the road in front of your car, and you'll need the time to react and avoid a collision.
- **Hike smart.** Know your own abilities, especially when hiking in the backcountry. People do get lost and die here. Always carry what seasoned hikers call the 10 essentials: map, compass, flashlight, a day's worth of food, extra clothing, rain gear, first-aid kit, knife, matches or lighter and a fire starter, and water. This list can expand to include a cell phone, sunglasses, and other necessities.
- **Watch for waves.** Waves are unpredictable on the coast. They can sneak up on you and riptides can suck you under the water and take you out to sea. Be observant of your surroundings.
- **Leave Fido at home.** Most of the popular trails here, as well as many popular campsites, lodges, and hotels, don't allow pets.

sun does shine, it can get very bright around these parts.

GAY AND LESBIAN TRAVELERS

Gay and lesbian travelers will be happy to know there are no special precautions they will need to take while visiting the Olympic Peninsula. That's not to say some homophobia doesn't still exist here and there, but overall attitudes on the peninsula have shifted toward acceptance (or at the very least ambivalence) over the past couple of decades. This is not an area where you'll find a plethora of gay bars or an annual gay pride parade, but it isn't a place where gay people need to walk in fear, either.

ACCESS FOR TRAVELERS WITH DISABILITIES

The National Park Service and most towns, cities, and counties on the peninsula have done an excellent job of making sure their major sites are accessible to all people, including those who have disabilities. Since the passage of the Americans with Disabilities Act of 1990, many of the most popular tourist spots on the peninsula have made adjustments to their layout to accommodate visitors with disabilities. For instance, wheelchair-accessible restrooms are now available in nine of the park's 16 campgrounds, and many of those parks have paved campsites and picnic tables with built-in extensions so they can be used by people in wheelchairs. Several of the park's lodging facilities, including Kalaloch and Lake Crescent Lodges, also have wheelchair-friendly options. Sol Duc Hot Springs also are accessible to those with disabilities.

Park admission is free to those who qualify to receive federal benefits based on a disability. Those wishing to take advantage of this option need to pay a $10 processing fee and fill out an application form for an **Access Pass** from the National Park Service (www.nps.gov/findapark/passes.htm). Pass holders also may receive discounts on certain amenity fees for facilities. The pass is good for the bearer's lifetime and can be used at more than 2,000 federal recreation sites.

SENIOR TRAVELERS

The Olympic Peninsula is a place where there's definitely an advantage to getting older. The purchase of a **Senior Pass** ($10) from the National Park Service (www.nps.gov/findapark/passes.htm) will get you into some 2,000 recreation sites managed by the federal government, including Olympic National Park, for the rest of your life. Many outside-the-park lodgings, attractions, and shops also offer discounts to seniors.

The peninsula is a place where hiking is necessary in order to see many of the attractions. If walking short to medium distances is an issue, you will want to make sure you plan your trip accordingly by bringing along any aids or assistance you anticipate needing.

FOREIGN TRAVELERS

Before entering the United States, most foreign travelers must obtain a Pleasure, Tourism, Medical Treatment visitor visa, also known as a B-2 visa. Note: There are currently 35 countries that participate in the Visa Waiver Program: Citizens of those countries may not need a visa in order to travel to the United States. Visit the U.S. Department of State's website (http://travel.state.gov/visa/temp/without/without_1990.html) to learn more about the program.

To apply for a visitor visa, you should visit the branch of the U.S. Embassy or Consulate in your home country. Documents required to apply for the visa are: visa application form DS-160; a passport that is valid for at least six months after your planned trip; a 2- by 2-inch photograph. Be sure to check with the U.S.

What's That Name?

The names of many of the towns, rivers, and areas on the Olympic Peninsula are derivatives of Native American words. As such, many visitors, and even many locals, often find the names challenging to pronounce. Here is a pronunciation cheat sheet to help you during your adventures:

Bogachiel	BOE-guh-cheel
Chehalis	shuh-HAY-lis
Copalis	co-PAY-lis
Dosewalips	DOSE-wall-ups
Elwha	EL-wah
Hoh	HOE
Hoquiam	HO-kwee-um
Kalaloch	CLAY-lock
Kamilche	KA-MILL-CHEE
Lilliwaup	LILLY-WOP
Makah	ma-KA
Montesano	MON-ta-SAY-no
Queets	KWEETS
Quilcene	KWILL-seen
Quileute	KWILL-E-oot
Quinault	kwin-ALT
Sekiu	CEE-kyoo
Sequim	SKWIM
Sol Duc	SAUL-duck
Squaxin	SQUAK-sin

Embassy or Consulate to see if you will need any additional documents when applying for your visa.

Foreigner travelers visiting the Olympic Peninsula generally begin their trek at one of four points: Victoria or Vancouver, British Columbia, Canada; Sea-Tac Airport (in the city of SeaTac, between Seattle and Tacoma); or from Portland, Oregon. From there, most travelers drive to the peninsula.

Upon entry to the United States, all travelers will go through customs. For foreign travelers, this process entails showing the customs officer your passport, visa, and Customs Declaration form (this will be given to you during your flight, shortly before landing), and telling the officer your reason for visiting the United States. This process is often straightforward and uncomplicated.

Health and Safety

HYPOTHERMIA

The weather doesn't need to be freezing for a person to die from hypothermia. All that needs to occur is for a person's body temperature to fall below 95°F. That can easily occur on the Olympic Peninsula, even during the summer months. Falling in the water or getting rained on and staying in wet clothes can cause it. So can not dressing warmly enough for conditions. The calendar may say summer, but on the Olympic Peninsula, especially at higher elevations in the Olympic Mountains, that doesn't mean it's T-shirt and shorts weather.

Uncontrollable shivering is one of the first signs of hypothermia. Other symptoms include clumsiness, slurred speech, confusion, drowsiness, a weak pulse, and shallow breathing.

Treatment includes removing any wet clothing, moving the person out of the cold, and warming the person by putting him or her in a warm spot. You also can share body heat by stripping your clothes and lying in a sleeping bag with the hypothermic person, making skin-to-skin contact. Seek professional medical help as quickly as possible.

TICKS

An unfortunate by-product of hiking through the forests of the Olympic Peninsula is that there are ticks here. The blood-sucking insects often fall from trees onto unsuspecting, and unknowing, individuals. They can burrow into the skin and can spread Lyme disease, a bacterial infection that causes arthritis-like symptoms. The disease is spread by deer ticks, which do exist here, especially in the northern portion of Olympic National Park. Fortunately, according to the National Park Service, no cases of Lyme disease have yet been reported. No one wants to be the first. Prevention—by covering exposed skin when hiking through areas that may have ticks, using insect repellant, and checking the skin shortly after hikes—is important. If you find a tick on your body, immediately remove it. Use tweezers if necessary.

GIARDIA

The peninsula's rivers and lakes may contain some of the clearest waters on the planet, but they still aren't safe to drink without first being treated. The reason: giardia, a parasite found in dirt or water that has been contaminated by the feces of infected animals or humans. Symptoms occur about a week after contact with the parasite, and they include diarrhea, bloating, abdominal pain, nausea, and headache. Giardia infection often goes away on its own, but medical treatment can be necessary and a health care professional should be consulted. The best way to treat water is by boiling it for at least a minute prior to using it for cooking, drinking, washing your hands or dishes, or brushing your teeth. There also are filters and tablets you can buy from sporting goods stores that will rid water of giardia.

MEDICAL SERVICES

There are several small hospitals and clinics located throughout the Olympic Peninsula, particularly in the larger cities. For emergencies, regardless of location, first dial 911.

The Kitsap Peninsula and Hood Canal

On the Kitsap Peninsula, there's **Harrison Medical Center** (2520 Cherry Ave., Bremerton, 360/744-3911, www.harrisonmedical.org) and **St. Anthony Hospital** (11567 Canterwood Blvd. NW, Gig Harbor, 253/530-2000). On the Olympic Peninsula, there are 24-hour emergency services available at **Mason General Hospital** (901 Mountain View Dr., Shelton, 360/426-1611, www.masongeneral.com).

Port Angeles and the Northern Peninsula

Olympic Medical Center (939 Caroline St., Port Angeles, 360/417-7000, www.olympicmedical.org) and **Jefferson Healthcare Hospital** (834 Sheridan St., Port Townsend, 360/385-2200, www.jeffersonhealthcare.org) are the two best hospitals here.

Hoh Rain Forest and the Coast

There are two hospitals in this area: **Grays Harbor Community Hospital** (915 Anderson Dr., Aberdeen, 360/532-8330, www.ghcares.org) and the smaller **Forks Community Hospital** (530 Bogachiel Way, Forks, 360/374-6271, www.forkshospital.org).

CRIME

Crime is low on the Olympic Peninsula, but that doesn't mean you can throw caution to the wind. The signs you will see in parking lots of popular attractions warning you to not leave valuables in your car are there for a reason: Things do get stolen here. Some common sense, such as not leaving valuables in plain sight, will go a long way, and most likely be all you need to keep from being a victim of crime here.

Information and Services

COMMUNICATIONS AND MEDIA

Telephone

The entire Olympic Peninsula uses the area code 360, although there are a few exceptions. Bainbridge Island, for instance, uses the 206 area code and Gig Harbor and the area surrounding it uses 253. The best emergency number here is 911. One area-specific tip: Don't rely only on cell phones to bail you out of tricky situations. There are many places on the peninsula, especially in the national park, where they won't work. In other places, even along Highway 101, reception will be spotty or nonexistent.

Newspapers and Magazines

Despite recent setbacks, newspapers are alive and well on the peninsula, and their print copies and their websites continue to be among the best places to learn about local goings-on. Some of the newspapers are dailies, and others here are weeklies. A large section of the western peninsula, including Aberdeen, Ocean Shores, Raymond, and Quinault, is covered by *The Daily World,* and the *Forks Forum* covers Clallam County. The *Peninsula Daily News* also covers Clallam County and the rest of the northern peninsula, including Port Angeles, Sequim, and Port Townsend. Port Townsend is covered even more directly by *The Leader.* The western Hood Canal area is covered by the weekly *Shelton-Mason County Journal.* On the Kitsap Peninsula, the *Bremerton Sun* is the main newspaper of record, but there are many smaller community-based newspapers here, too, including ones in Poulsbo, Bainbridge Island, Port Orchard, and Silverdale. Residents living in the south end of the Kitsap Peninsula, including Gig Harbor, get their news from the *Peninsula Gateway,* as well as *The News Tribune* of Tacoma.

There aren't as many magazines dedicated to the peninsula as there are newspapers. However, there are some good ones. Tacoma-based *South Sound* is a well-rounded, local lifestyle magazine that can be found on store shelves in Port Angeles, Port Townsend, Bremerton, Bainbridge Island, Shelton, Aberdeen, and elsewhere.

MAPS AND TOURIST INFORMATION

Local chambers of commerce, visitors centers, and ranger stations are the best places to obtain pertinent travel information here. Hours of operation vary widely, depending on season and location. Those located in cities, such as Aberdeen, Port Angeles, Port Townsend, and Shelton, generally are open during business hours year-round. Others in smaller areas fluctuate based on season. These sites are highly recommended for those who seek answers to questions, insider information, or maps. Most of the information centers here are well-stocked not only with information specific to their particular location, but also with brochures and maps for other areas on the peninsula, including the Olympic National Park. People here realize that by helping other agencies, you're also helping your own. A large number of hotels, restaurants, and stores also have entryway displays full of informational pamphlets on the peninsula. The **Olympic Peninsula Tourism Commission** (www.olympicpeninsula.org) has the best online source for information, although its focus is primarily on the northern half of the peninsula.

Resources

Suggested Reading

HISTORY AND CULTURE

Bentley, Judy. *Hiking Washington's History.* Seattle: University of Washington Press, 2010. This book is not only interesting for hikers, but for those interested in learning more about the state. It includes trail maps and directions to trailheads as well as interesting historical photos, diaries, and more. It's a fun read even if you never actually hit a trail.

Davis, Jefferson, and Al Eufrasio. *Weird Washington.* New York: Sterling, 2008. Every state has its share of spooky stories, legends, and folklore, and this book explores the strange sides of Washington State. Learn about the legends of the Soap People of Crescent Lake, the UFO landing on Maury Island, and more about famous hijacker D. B. Cooper. Even people who have called the state home for many years will likely learn something new.

Kirk, Ruth, and Carmela Alexander. *Exploring Washington's Past: A Road Guide to History.* Seattle: University of Washington Press, 1990 (revised 2003). This book is a great traveling companion. When you wonder to yourself what you are looking at as you travel roads and highways, chances are this book has some of those answers. It's a travel and history book all in one.

RECREATION

McQuaide, Mike. *Trail Running Guide to Western Washington.* Seattle: Sasquatch Books, 2001. Sometimes the best way to really appreciate nature is during a heart-pounding run. This book highlights some of the best places in the state to take your exercise routine to a whole new adventure level. There are three Olympic Peninsula trails featured in this book that are worth exploring.

Mueller, Marge and Ted. *Washington State Parks.* Seattle: The Mountaineers Books, 2004. This book is a comprehensive guide to parks across the state. It contains photos, maps, and activities. Use it to learn where to picnic, crab, hike, and scuba dive.

Pyle, Jeanne. *The Best in Tent Camping Washington.* Birmingham, Alabama: Menasha Ridge Press, 2005. The subtitle says it all, "A guide for car campers who hate RVs, concrete slabs, and loud portable stereos." The author picked 50 of the state's best campsites. Several of them are in Olympic National Park.

Romano, Craig. *Day Hiking Olympic Peninsula.* Seattle: The Mountaineer Books, 2007. You will be amazed at the hikes you can take in the area if you only have a day. The book also features stunning photographs of the Olympic Peninsula area.

Rudnick, Terry. *Moon Washington Fishing.* Berkeley, California: Avalon Travel, 2012. The state is full of lakes, streams, and saltwater: an avid angler's paradise. This guide tells you where to fish, how to get to the destination, and what to expect when you get there.

Stienstra, Tom. *Moon Washington Camping.* Berkeley, California: Avalon Travel, 2014. This is a thorough guide full of information not only about campgrounds throughout the state, but camping in general. From tips for catching fish and avoiding bears, to how to stay warm and get along with other campers, this book has you covered whether you are camping in a tent or an RV.

TRAVELING WITH KIDS

Smith, Roland, and illustrator Linda Holt Ayriss. *E Is for Evergreen: A Washington State Alphabet.* Ann Arbor, Michigan: Sleeping Bear Press, 2004. This colorful alphabet book will educate your little one about Washington, both fact and fiction. Or is it? B is for Bigfoot!

Internet Resources

HISTORY AND GENERAL INFORMATION

History Link
www.historylink.org

This free online encyclopedia of Washington State history is written by some of the state's best writers and is rich in information.

Olympic Peninsula
www.olympicpeninsula.org

This is a detailed website that is one of the best Olympic Peninsula resources with information about how to get around, places to stay, and things to do.

Washington Chamber of Commerce
www.wcce.org

Click on the "Biz & Tourism" tab on the state's chamber of commerce site to find a wealth of information including where to golf, bed-and-breakfast listings, and all about wine. You also can access regional chamber of commerce websites across the state, including those on the peninsula.

Washington State
www.access.wa.gov

This is Washington's official website. It has several links about how best to visit the state and available recreational opportunities, as well as additional information on topics such as employment, government, and education. There's also a link under the "Visiting & Recreation" tab that allows you to send a scenic e-card. How's that for speedy delivery?

TRAVEL

The Map Company
www.themapcompany.com

Here's a handy site that offers maps of the state that are updated often. Some of them are available for viewing online and many others are available for purchase.

Washington State Department of Transportation
www.wsdot.wa.gov

Here's all the information you need to better navigate the area, including links with details to bus, plane, and train travel, and information to help your drive (or your bike ride) go smoother.

Washington State Tourism
www.experiencewa.com

The state tourism site offers a wealth of information about everything from arts and entertainment, to dining and wine, festivals and fairs, and scenic drives. Plus, it is full of breathtaking photos that showcase the beauty of the area.

RECREATION

The Mountaineers
www.mountaineers.org

This Seattle-based organization hosts outdoor trips, supports a variety of environmental issues, promotes conservation, publishes books, and frequently guides hikes on the Olympic Peninsula.

National Park Service
www.nps.gov

Visit this site and scroll to Washington to learn more about the national parks here. Hint: Olympic National Park may be the biggest, but it is just one of many located in the state.

Recreation.gov
www.recreation.gov

This is a one-stop site to make reservations for public campsites around the state.

Washington Department of Fish & Wildlife
www.wdfw.wa.gov

Want to know when you can fish, clam, crab, or hunt? Learn about all the regulations before you go and make sure you have the proper licensing and permits with a quick visit to this site.

Washington Trails Association
www.wta.org

The association is dedicated to preserving and maintaining trails in the state and promoting hiking. There's great hiking information and trail news here.

Washington State Parks and Recreation Commission
www.parks.wa.gov

This site contains all you need to know about Washington's state parks, including the ability to make reservations. Purchase a Discover Pass, which is necessary to enter all state parks, here.

CULTURAL EVENTS

Washington Festivals and Events Association
www.wfea.org

Wondering what to do while you're on the Olympic Peninsula? Chances are there is a festival going on somewhere, especially in the summertime. Find news of everything from the Slug Festival to the Lavender Festival here.

Washington State Fairs
www.wastatefairs.com

Learn more about both small and big fairs on the peninsula (and across the rest of Washington).

Index

A

B

C

D

E

F

G

H

IJ

K

L

M

N

O

P

Q

R

S

T

UVWXYZ

List of Maps

Photo Credits

Title page © Mickey Thurman; page 6 © dreamstime.com; page 7 © dreamstime.com; page 8 (upper left) © Mickey Thurman, (upper right) © dreamstime.com, (bottom) © dreamstime.com; page 9 (top) © Mickey Thurman, (bottom left) © Mickey Thurman, (bottom right) © dreamstime.com; page 10 © Mickey Thurman; page 11 (top) © dreamstime.com, (bottom left) © Jeff Burlingame, (bottom right) © Mickey Thurman; page 12 © Mickey Thurman; page 15 © dreamstime.com; page 16 © dreamstime.com; page 17 © Jeff Burlingame; page 18 © dreamstime.com; page 20 © dreamstime.com; page 21 © dreamstime.com; page 22 © dreamstime.com; page 24 © Tim Gohrke/123rf.com; pages 25, 26 © dreamstime.com; pages 35, 41, 43, 48, 51, 61, 62 © Jeff Burlingame; page 70 © dreamstime.com; pages 71, 88, 89, 101, 111, 112 © Jeff Burlingame; pages 116, 117, 130 © dreamstime.com; pages 153, 155 © Mickey Thurman; page 173 © Brian Carlson; pages 120, 123, 130, 137, 147, 148, 149, 162 © Jeff Burlingame; page 177 © dreamstime.com; page 191 (top) © Jeff Burlingame, (bottom) © dreamstime.com

Acknowledgments

This edition of *Moon Olympic Peninsula* exists thanks in part to the assistance I received from many people. Those many praise-worthy souls include:

Aberdeen Museum of History, Darren Alessi, Pat Anderson, Kat Bennett, Bremerton-Area Chamber of Commerce, Ed Burke, Andrew Burlingame, Jim Burlingame, Tim Burlingame, Brian Carlson, Marjorie Clark, *The Daily World,* Allison Ferre, Forks Chamber of Commerce, Gig Harbor Chamber of Commerce, Grays Harbor Chamber of Commerce, HistoryLink.org, Kevin Hong, John Hughes, KXRO, Nikki Ioakimedes, Jefferson County Chamber of Commerce, Kitsap Peninsula Visitor and Convention Bureau, Erik Kupka, Jerry Lacey, Carrie Larson, John Larson, Michael McIntosh, *The (Montesano) Vidette,* Dave Morrison, Matt Nash, National Park Service, North Hood Canal Chamber of Commerce, Ocean Shores-North Beach Chamber of Commerce, *The Olympian,* Olympic Peninsula Tourism Commission, Kyle Pauley, Bill Pitts, Polson Museum, Port Angeles Chamber of Commerce, PTguide.com, Mike Rolston, Jill Sanford, Sequim-Dungeness Valley Chamber of Commerce, *The Sequim Gazette,* Shelton-Mason County Chamber of Commerce, *The (Tacoma) News Tribune,* Mickey Thurman, Washington Trails Association, Westport-Grayland Chamber of Commerce, Ben Wilcox, and Michael Worden.

Friends and family have played a large role in every book I've written, and this one is no exception. This one is for Lisa, Tierney, and Grayson, whose patience and presence help lift me to heights that might otherwise be impossible to reach.

MOON OLYMPIC PENINSULA
Avalon Travel
an imprint of Perseus Books
a Hachette Book Group company
1700 Fourth Street
Berkeley, CA 94710, USA
www.moon.com

Editor: Nikki Ioakimedes
Series Manager: Kathryn Ettinger
Copy Editor: Alissa Cyphers
Graphics Coordinator: Darren Alessi
Production Coordinator: Darren Alessi
Cover Design: Faceout Studios, Charles Brock
Moon Logo: Tim McGrath
Map Editor: Kat Bennett
Cartographer: Stephanie Poulain
Indexer: Rachel Kuhn

ISBN-13: 978-1-63121-006-8
ISSN: 2166-9171

Printing History
1st Edition — 2012
2nd Edition — May 2015
5 4 3 2

Front cover photo: Sea stacks at Ruby Beach © Bryan Mullennix / Alamy
Back cover photos: © Mark Rasmussen/123rf.com

Printed in Canada by Friesens